Third World Modernism

The first volume to map multiple positions on architectural modernism across the developing world, this book offers an international perspective on the practices and consequences of modernist architecture in the mid-twentieth century. Presenting fresh case studies from Asia, South America, Africa, and the Middle East, experts in this volume challenge canonical architectural historiography which identifies the West as the sole yardstick to measure the beginning and end, success and failure, of modernism. They show that modernism in Third World nations took trajectories radically different from those in developed societies during the same historical period. The intersections between modernist architecture, globalism, developmentalism, nationalism, and postcolonialism are explored. Chapters illustrate modernism's part in the transnational development of building technologies, the construction of national and cultural identity, and the geo-historical entanglements of nations.

Creating new openings for cross-cultural analysis of modernism, this provocative book has a key place in the historiography of modern architecture in non-Western societies.

Duanfang Lu is Senior Lecturer in the Faculty of Architecture, Design and Planning at the University of Sydney and author of *Remaking Chinese Urban Form: Modernity, Scarcity and Space, 1949–2005*.

For the New Third World

Third World Modernism

Architecture, development and identity

Edited by Duanfang Lu

Routledge
Taylor & Francis Group

LONDON AND NEW YORK

First published 2011
by Routledge, 2 Park Square, Milton Park, Abingdon, Oxon, OX14 4RN

Simultaneously published in the USA and Canada
by Routledge
711 Third Avenue, New York, NY 10017

Routledge is an imprint of the Taylor & Francis Group, an informa business

Typeset in 9pt Univers by Saxon Graphics Ltd, Derby

British Library Cataloguing in Publication Data
A catalogue record for this book is available from the British Library

Library of Congress Cataloging-in-Publication Data
Third world modernism : architecture, development and identity / edited by
Duanfang Lu.
p. cm.
Includes bibliographical references and index.
1. Modern movement (Architecture)–Developing countries. 2. Architecture and
society–Developing countries–History–20th century. 3. Architecture and
globalization–Developing countries–History–20th century. I. Lu, Duanfang.
NA1614.T48 2010
724'.6–dc22
2010015853

ISBN13: 978-0-415-56457-1 (hbk)
ISBN13: 978-0-415-56458-8 (pbk)
ISBN13: 978-0-203-84099-3 (ebk)

Contents

Acknowledgements   vii
IIllustration credits and sources   ix

1   Introduction: architecture, modernity and identity in the Third World   1
DUANFANG LU

Part I The will of the age   29

2   The Other Way Around: the modernist movement in Brazil   31
DANIELA SANDLER

3   Depoliticizing Group GAMMA: contesting modernism in Morocco   57
AZIZA CHAOUNI

4   Agrupación Espacio and the CIAM Peru Group: architecture
and the city in the Peruvian modern project   85
SHARIF S. KAHATT

Part II Building the nation   111

5   Campus Architecture as Nation Building: Israeli architect
Arieh Sharon's Obafemi Awolowo University Campus, Ile-Ife,
Nigeria   113
INBAL BEN-ASHER GITLER

6   Modernity and Revolution: the architecture of Ceylon's
twentieth-century exhibitions   141
ANOMA PIERIS

7   This is not an American House: good sense modernism
in 1950s Turkey   165
ELÂ KAÇEL

Part III Entangled modernities   187

8   Modernity Transfers: the MoMA and postcolonial India   189
FARHAN SIRAJUL KARIM

Contents

9 Building a Colonial Technoscientific Network: tropical architecture, building science and the politics of decolonization   211
JIAT-HWEE CHANG

10 Otto Koenigsberger and the Tropicalization of British Architectural Culture   236
VANDANA BAWEJA

11 Epilogue: Third World Modernism, or Just Modernism: towards a cosmopolitan reading of modernism   255
VIKRAMĀDITYA PRAKĀSH

Selected Bibliography   271

Contributors   277

Index   281

Acknowledgements

Some of the essays in this volume were first presented at the Society of Architectural Historians 61st Annual Meeting, held in Cincinnati, Ohio, 23–27 April 2008. The editor and contributors wish to express our sincere appreciation to conference participants who offered valuable comments and posed insightful questions. In particular, we would like to thank Professor Nezar AlSayyad, for being discussant of the session 'Third World Modernism' and for his unflagging support of our volume. Deep gratitude is extended to Professors Swati Chattopadhyay, Hilde Heynen, Anthony D. King, Jon Lang, Peter Scriver, and Richard Williams for their thoughtful comments. We are also indebted to Georgina Johnson-Cook, Pamela McLaughlin, Rob Brown, and Marie Lister for their sensitive work throughout the book preparation and publication process. The editor wishes to express appreciation for the support provided by a Discovery Project research grant from the Australian Research Council, the J. Paul Getty Fellowship, and a small grant from the Faculty of Architecture, Design and Planning, University of Sydney, which have all helped the production of this volume. Aspects of the issues discussed in the Introduction were presented in the Department of Architecture at the Chinese University of Hong Kong, the Department of Geography at Guangzhou University, the Institute of Postcolonial Studies at the University of Melbourne, the Graduate School of Design at Harvard University, and at the Second 'China Architectural Thought Forum' in Shenzhen. The editor wants to thank her hosts and her audiences for their rigourous engagement and insightful feedback. Many thanks go to Farhan Sirajul Karim and Cassi Plate for their valuable research assistance. Last but not least, Duanfang Lu would like to thank her family for their love, support, and patience.

Illustration credits and sources

The editor, contributors and publisher would like to thank all those who have granted permission to reproduce illustrations. We have made every effort to contact and acknowledge copyright holders, but if any errors have been made we would be happy to correct them at a later printing.

Cover: © Duanfang Lu

Chapter 1

1–3 © Duanfang Lu

Chapter 2

1–5 Source: Warchavchik Family Archive
6–7 © The Instituto Lina Bo e P. M. Bardi

Chapter 3

1 Top Source: Archive ETH Zurich
1 Bottom © Fonds Zevaco, FRAC Orléans
2   © Yannnick Beunard
3   Source: Archive ENA, Rabat.
4   Source: Personal archive of the architects, Rabat.
5   Source: Personal archive of Elie Azagury, now transferred to IFA, Paris
6   © Fonds Zevaco, FRAC Orléans
7   © gta/ETH, Zurich
8   © A+U
9–10 Source: Personal archive of Elie Azagury, now transferred to IFA, Paris
11   © Aziza Chaouni
12   Source: Personal archive of Elie Azagury, now transferred to IFA, Paris
13   © A+U
14   © Fonds FRAC Orléans

Chapter 4

1   Source: Sert Collection, Loeb Library, Harvard University Graduate School of Design
2   © *El Arquitecto Peruano.*
3   © Miró Quesada family
4a and 4b Source: Luis Sert Collection, Loeb Library, Harvard University Graduate School of Design
5   Source: *Oficina Nacional de Planeamiento Urbano* (ONPU) *Plan Piloto de Lima*, Lima: Empresa Gráfica T. Scheuch, 1949, p. 28
6   © *El Arquitecto Peruano*
7   Source: *Oficina Nacional de Planeamiento Urbano* (ONPU) *Plan Piloto de Lima*, Lima: Empresa Gráfica T. Scheuch, 1949, p. 30
8   Source: *Modern Architecture in Latin America since 1945*, Museum of Modern Art Exhibition Catalogue, New York, 1955, pp. 132–33
9   © Adolfo Córdova

Chapter 5

1–9 © Yael Aloni

Chapter 6

1–5 © Associated Newspapers Ceylon Ltd.
6   © Anoma Pieris
7   © Jack Kulasinghe, National Housing Development Authority

Chapter 7

1   Source: Vanlı, *Mimariden Konuşmak*, vol. 1 (2006), p. 211. Used with permission of the Şevki Vanlı Architecture Foundation.
2   © The Istanbul Metropolitan Branch of the Union of Turkish Chambers of Engineers and Architects
3   Source: *Dostluk*, no. 19 (28 August 1957), p. 6
4   Source: *Dostluk*, no. 18 (14 August 1957), p. 3
5   Source: *Bütün Dünya*, no. 94 (November 1955), p. 627
6   Source: *Arkitekt*, vol. 19, no. 3–4 (1950), p. 71
7–10 © The Istanbul Metropolitan Branch of the Union of Turkish Chambers of Engineers and Architects

Chapter 8

1   © Farhan Sirajul Karim
2   © The British Museum, London
3–6 © MoMA, NY
7   © National Library of India, Kolkata
8   © National Institute of Design, NID, Ahmedabad, India

Chapter 9

1   © George Atkinson
2–4 Source: *Colonial Building Notes*

Chapter 10

1   © Vandana Baweja
2–3 Source: Redrawn by Simon Barrow, based on an axonometric of the Kuwait
     Mat-Building published in Alison and Peter Smithson, *The Charged Void:
     Architecture* (New York: Monacelli Press, 2001)
4   Source: Redrawn by Simon Barrow, based on sun diagrams published in
     Tropical Advisory Service, "Climate analysis and design recommendations
     for Kuwait Old City" (London, prepared for Peter and Alison Smithson by
     Tropical Advisory Service, Department of Tropical Architecture,
     Architectural Association School of Architecture)
5   Source: Redrawn by Simon Barrow based on sun diagrams published in
     Lorenzo Wong, *Climate Register: Four Works by Alison and Peter Smithson*
     (London: Architectural Association, 1994), p. 47.

Chapter 11

1–2 © The Aditya Prakash Foundation, Chandigarh

Chapter 1

Introduction: architecture, modernity and identity in the Third World

Duanfang Lu

This book examines modernity's multiplicity by documenting cutting edge research on architectural modernism in the developing world during the middle decades of the twentieth century. Originating in interwar Europe, modernist architecture – as a way of building, a knowledge product, a style-of-life consumer item, and above all, a symbol of modernity – has traversed national boundaries throughout the world. Despite the extensive adoption of modernist architecture in developing countries, standard history books focus on its development in the West. Up until the last three decades, academic inquiry into the built environment in developing societies concentrated on traditional forms. With the exception of the work of a very small number of acclaimed non-Western architects such as Hasan Fathy and Charles Correa, little attention was devoted to modern architecture in the Third World, which was considered merely lesser forms of Western modernism. This orientation has been changed as canonical narratives which privilege Western modes of thinking and aesthetics are challenged, and orientalist perspectives on other cultures are debunked. Informed by turbulent theoretical debates throughout the humanities and social sciences, scholarship on the far-reaching variability of modernism has begun to grow, advancing our understanding of how modernist architecture was adopted, modified, interpreted, and contested in different parts of the world.[1] This discourse has focused on national building projects and their confrontation with and assimilation of modernism. Is it possible to transcend binary oppositions such as modern/traditional and core/periphery while still recognizing the ongoing making of global modernity? Can the history of modernist architecture be more responsive to the realities of other histories? How did architectural modernism develop with reference not only to Western epistemology, but also to the experiences and knowledge of other Third World countries? And how did the implications of modernist architecture continuously shift in the context of conflicting relations involving nationalistic concerns, global aspirations, and the problems of underdevelopment?

Third World Modernism aims to address these issues by connecting debates on modernism that have unfolded in different geographic regions in the mid-twentieth century, a historical period characterized by processes including independence, decolonization, nation building, architectural modernization, and the development of the Cold War. The book problematizes the global spread of modernist architecture against this broad socio-political context and highlights what is at stake in the study of the intertwined relationship between architecture, modernity, and identity in the developing world.

To think the modern is to think the present, which is necessarily caught in the ever-shifting social, political, and cultural cross-currents. For many decades, modernization was depicted in social sciences as a broad series of processes of industrialization, rationalization, urbanization, and social changes through which modern societies arose. This approach has been heavily criticized for its Eurocentric assumptions in recent years. It assumes, for example, that only Western society is truly modern and that all societies are heading towards the same destination. With the epistemological break triangulated by postmodern, poststructuralist, and postcolonial theories, the dominance of progressive histori-cism and its associated binaries (modern/traditional, self/other, center/periphery, etc.) is being challenged. Questions about modernity, understood as modes of experiencing and questioning the present, are being rethought.

This book is an attempt to contribute unique perspectives to the crit-ical rethinking of the modern by unraveling the complex meanings of "Third World modernism." The term "Third World" has been an important addition to the political vocabulary of the past century. First coined by the French demogra-pher Alfred Sauvy in 1952, the phrase gradually gained popularity as a classifica-tion describing the emerging arena of global politics associated with neither Western capitalism nor Soviet socialism in the early 1960s.[2] This arena included the developing nations of Africa, Asia, and Latin America which shared broad historical, economic, social, cultural, and ideological commonalities: a history of colonization, relatively low per capita incomes, culturally non-Western, and agri-culturally-based economies.[3] The meeting of Afro-Asian nations held in Bandung, Indonesia in 1955 marked a significant step in the institutionalization of the nona-ligned/Third World identity, which was consolidated through subsequent assem-blies (in Belgrade in 1961, Cairo in 1964, Lusaka in 1970, Algiers in 1973, Colombo in 1976, Havana in 1979, New Delhi in 1983, and Harare in 1986).[4] Third World nations were therefore also referred to as "nonaligned nations," although this was not entirely accurate. For example, despite being part of the Third World, Turkey and Pakistan were not part of the nonaligned membership due to their close ties to Western capitalism via the Central Treaty Organization (CENTO) and the North Atlantic Treaty Organization (NATO) respectively.[5]

Compared with other alternative phrases such as "developing coun-tries," "less developed countries," "non-industrialized countries," and "the South," the Third World is more than merely a socio-economic designation. It has come to represent a forceful ideology, a meaningful rallying point, a widely shared mentality, and a unique source of identity. The phrase has proven rhetorically, politically, and theoretically effective.[6] Despite the end of the Cold War, the term "Third World" remains viable in contemporary geopolitical vocabulary, as seen in leading scholarly journals such as *Third World Quarterly* and *Journal of Third World Studies*.

This book is concerned with issues related to the development of modernist architecture in developing societies from the end of the Second World War in 1945 to the late 1970s, a period which witnessed the steady growth of Third World solidarity. On the one hand, chapters in this volume demonstrate that there are multiple ways of being modern, which are not the less perfect, incomplete versions of an idealized full-blown modernity, but constituencies with their own trajectories, discourses, social institutions, and categories of reference. On the other hand, these studies show that as a result of social production under similar historical conditions, and representation of similar values and beliefs, modernist architecture in these societies shared some common characteristics and trajectories that were sharply different from those shared by developed societies during the same historical period. This book uses the concept of "Third World modernism" to describe, analyze, and theorize these distinctive meanings, practices, trajectories, transformations, and consequences of modernist architecture in developing countries in the mid-twentieth century. By doing so it aims to overcome the earlier hegemonic assumption which identified the West as the sole yardstick to measure the beginning and end, success and failure of modernism. It shows how canonical architectural historiography has universalized experiences with modernity that were actually peculiar to the Euro-American context.

Until now, most existing volumes have been monographs on the development of modernist architecture within a single nation or anthologies that focus on a single region.[7] *Third World Modernism* is the first edited volume that addresses the development of architectural modernism in countries across the Third World. It represents an opportunity to map multiple positions in related debates. The book highlights sites of encounter, connection, and negotiation. Many nation-based histories of modern architecture picture architectural histories as disconnected variations, each confined to an a priori state-defined space and following an internal logic. To quote Eric Wolf, this is a "model of the world as a global pool hall in which entities spin off each other like so many hard and rounded billiard balls."[8] In contrast, by mapping the concrete routes to and through modernity, the original scholarship of this volume points to the importance of multiple patterns of interlocking not only between non-Western and Western locales, but also among non-Western ones. Together the essays reveal the intrinsically paradoxical differences at the very heart of the modern, on the one hand, and the geo-historical entanglements of modernities from a global perspective, on the other.

In the following, I will discuss "Third World modernism" from four interconnected perspectives, namely, modernism as globalism, modernism as developmentalism, modernism as nationalism, and modernism as postcolonialism, which both sets up theoretical and historical frameworks for the book and introduces the chapters that follow. I will close the chapter with a discussion of the epistemological implications of this study. A significant implication has been that in order to reach a true dialogism, we need to recognize not only the histories of different modernities, but also the legitimacies of different bodies of architectural knowledge. It is my hope that the notion of "Third World modernism" will eventually come to represent the aspirations for a more sustainable built environment of humanity.

Modernism as globalism

The term "modern" originated from the fifth-century Latin term *modemus* which was then employed to distinguish the Christian present from the pagan past. From the fifteenth to the eighteenth century, three vital transitions – the discovery of the Americas, the Renaissance, and the Reformation – formed "the epochal threshold" to modern times in Europe.[9] While the processes of modernization began around the fifteenth century, the kinds of art, literature, architecture, and music we term "modernism" did not appear until the late nineteenth century. Marshall Berman characterizes modernity as a historical experience that seeks to ceaselessly transform the very conditions that produce it.[10] In the same vein, modernism has been a reaction to societal modernization, which is modern in its celebration of newness and the break from tradition, and anti-modern in its critique of modernization's betrayal of its own human promise.

In architectural discourse, the very idea of modernism is culturally and historically constructed into a heroic interwar modernism and a revisionist post-Second World War modernism, which are characterized by different manifestations of the modern in architecture. The modern movement in architecture originated from the avant-garde spirit shared by modernist painting, music, and literature. Compared with their literary and artistic counterparts, whose counter-modern gestures called the authority of Western rationality into question, early modern architects were more allied with societal and industrial modernization. Their manifestos and practices often affirmed the very beliefs and values of modernization being attacked by other streams of modernism: progress, technology, and rationality.[11] Walter Gropius in his description of the Bauhaus program, for example, proclaimed that "A breach has been made with the past, which allows us to envisage a new aspect of architecture corresponding to the technical civilization of the age we live in; the morphology of dead style has been destroyed; and we are returning to honesty of thought and feeling."[12]

Similar expressions can be found in the writings of the modern movement's other polemicists such as Le Corbusier and Sigfried Giedion, the manifestos of the Congrès Internationaux d'Architecture Moderne (CIAM), and subsequent canonical architectural histories.[13] In fact, most technical advancements required by modernist architecture took place before the advent of the twentieth century. The significance of the modern movement lies in developing a set of new design and aesthetic principles to correspond to technical conditions that were already in place, as well as forming a cohesive position on modernist architecture among avant gardes. Through a successful cultural politics of self-construction, modernism was associated with a set of positive attributes and gradually attained its ascendancy. By purifying traditional restrictions and decoration, reconceptualizing space-time, following the logic of function, and modulizing its components, modernist architecture was considered to embody modern modes of living, thinking and production based on rationality, efficiency, calculation, the obsession with novelty and abstraction, as well as the moral pretension of advancing social and political goals through design practices. Notably, modernism was acclaimed "International" and conceptualized as exemplifying the positive aspect of globalism: the interests of the entire world were placed above those of individual nations.[14] In the polemical picture of the modern movement, the new forms, spatial principles, and technologies of modernism were a matter of universal knowledge unrestrained by national boundaries and an expression of zeitgeist which held an epochal force that no society could escape.[15]

Modernism conceived as such, however, did not match the actual driving forces behind the development of modernist design at a dynamic formative moment of industrial capitalism. The practices of the Weimar Bauhaus, for example, reflected the initial idea of establishing the *Werkbund*: to improve the global competitiveness of national industry by integrating mass-production techniques and traditional crafts. There were also multiple contesting positions against the transnational claims of early modernists, as shown in the perceptions of the *Weissenhofsiedlung* at that time. First exhibited in the city of Stuttgart in the summer of 1927, the *Weissenhofsiedlung* was part of a series of exhibitions with the overall title of "Die Wohnung" (The Dwelling) directed by Mies van der Rohe, and is often considered the moment when modernist architecture first became institutionalized.[16] The Weissenhof architecture featured flat roofs, white walls, cantilevered balconies, roof gardens, sun terraces, and large verandas. As these characteristics were initially inspired by Mediterranean, middle-eastern, and north African vernacular buildings, the Weissenhof architecture was assaulted in racist terms by both traditionalists and proto-Nazi critics.[17] The *Siedlung* was nicknamed "Little Jerusalem" soon after its opening in 1927 and its style was frequently sneered at as "orientalist," "colonial," or "north African."[18] A satirical postcard with figures of Arabs and camels montaged onto the view of the Weissenhof estate was circulated throughout the 1930s. Conflicts among Western countries preceding the Second World War added additional layers of entanglements. French critics considered the promotion of architectural internationalism an attempt by Germany to impose the style upon western and central European nations. Within Germany, however, cosmopolitanism associated with the international qualities of architectural modernism was frequently used by Nazi propagandists to demean "anti-national" and "rootless" Jewish intellectuals.[19]

Despite the conflicting views at the early stage of its development, modernism nonetheless achieved its global reach in the subsequent decades. Standard history books fail to problematize this process, as if the worldwide spread of modernist architecture were natural and spontaneous. When the issue is discussed, it usually evokes notions of dissemination, progress, and enlightenment. This leaves many questions unanswered: Who initiated the dissemination and for what purpose? How did the meanings of modernism shift during the process? Why was modernism widely adopted regardless of existing regional building cultures? And what were its global cultural, social, environmental, and epistemological consequences?

A close examination of these questions reveals that the globalism embodied in modernism has much more complicated meanings beyond those constructed by the early modernists. Indeed, modernist architecture developed at a time when benevolent late colonialism was at its peak.[20] Although the common view considers classic form an arm of colonialism and modernism its antithesis, recent studies on colonial modernities show that modernist design and planning were not necessarily a denial of colonialism.[21] Instead, the colonies were often employed as laboratories of the newest design ideas, through which the metropolis imposed political and cultural influence upon the rest of the world. While previous models presupposed modernity (and with it modernism) to be the result of economic and technical advancements in Europe, these studies reveal Western expansion through colonization as an indivisible feature of modernity, and colonial modernities as an integral part of global modernity.

A number of chapters in this volume extend this argument by looking into the development of modernist architecture under both neocolonialism and Cold War cultural politics, exemplifying the other side of globalism embodied in modernist design practices: that is, viewing the world as an appropriate arena for one nation to project its influence. In Chapter 9 Jiat-Hwee Chang illustrates the production of tropical architecture as technoscientific knowledge in the context of complex socio-political relations between the British Empire and the postcolonial nations. According to Chang, there were attempts to replace the earlier modes of economic exploitation and political dominance with new discourses and institutions of welfare and development since the depression of the 1930s. Many new regional research stations in the colonies were established and modeled after the metropolitan model for this purpose. For instance, following the establishment of the Building Research Station in Watford in 1921, which carried out research on building materials and construction methods in order to provide efficient solutions to post-First World War housing shortages, it was proposed that the Colonial Housing Bureau be attached to it and model itself after it. Regional research establishments like this greatly facilitated not only the acceptance of modernist architecture for tropical building but also the continuation of British influence after the Second World War.

Meanwhile, with the establishment of two co-existing superpowers in the Cold War context, the connotations of modernist architecture went through radical changes. The socialist ideals of its European pioneers were replaced by a commitment to democracy, which was employed strategically to expose the defects of the liberal West's enemies. Under the new political aura, modernist architecture was Americanized and exported to different parts of the world.[22] Chapters 4, 7 and 8 provide fresh evidence of how modernist architecture was promoted via vehicles such as the postwar CIAM, the Ford Foundation, and the Museum of Modern Art (MoMA) in Peru, Turkey and India as part of the attempts to implement American globalism. In Latin America, Roosevelt's administration sponsored CIAM members to evangelize new democracies in Latin American countries with the idea of using modernist architecture and planning as a means of modernization during the mid-1940s. In Turkey, knowledge about the "International Style" and American domestic design was widely publicized in the wake of a series of mutual aid agreements between the USA and Turkey in spheres including economy, military, technical assistance, and culture in 1945, which reached its peak with the Marshall Plan. In India, the US policy to promote India as a democratic counterweight to China resulted in a number of influential exhibitions on modernist design organized by MoMA, in addition to financial aid totaling US$10 billion in 1954–64.

Although largely neglected by previous observers, some newly independent countries also exercised globalism through modernist design during the postwar era. In Chapter 5, Inbal Ben-Asher Gitler shows that the planning and design of the Obafemi Awolowo University Campus in Ile-Ife, Nigeria was an organized governmental initiative of Israel. In the context of its political and economic isolation brought about by Arab boycotts, Israel aimed to gain strength through its relations with Third World countries. Decolonization processes in Africa, in particular, were considered a historic opportunity for establishing diplomatic and economic ties. To achieve this objective, Israel initiated comprehensive technical assistance programs in various countries, of which architecture and construction were an integral part.

My own research on the development of building projects in Third World countries as part of China's foreign aid programs shows China as another important player in this.[23] Since the founding of the Third World coalition at Bandung in 1955, China has consistently identified itself with the Third World and has considered strengthening cooperation with other Third World nations its basic foreign policy. Extensive Chinese architectural exports began in 1956 as part of overseas aid programs within the Cold War context. In the decades that followed, Chinese architects built construction projects ranging from major national buildings to factories in Asia, Africa, and the Middle East. Many of these buildings adopted modernist style, among which the Bandaranaike Memorial International Conference Hall (BMICH) in Colombo, Sri Lanka, represents one of the most significant examples.[24] Designed by Dai Nianci, a prominent figure in the history of modern Chinese architecture, BMICH echoes both postwar tropical architecture and the iconography of Maoist utopianism (Figure 1; see also the

Figure 1
**Dai Nianci, the
Bandaranaike Memorial
International
Conference Hall,
Colombo, Sri Lanka,
1973. Photograph taken
by the author, 2010.**

book cover photo). Due to its striking aesthetic appeal, BMICH has become a symbol of national identity and a premier tourist attraction in Sri Lanka.

Notably, BMICH successfully hosted the Fifth Non-aligned Summit Conference in August 1976, which in turn helped Sri Lanka project its own global influence among Third World nations.[25] Many delegates who attended the conference were impressed with the architecture and facilities of BMICH. It was reported, for example, that Iraq, who had been provisionally selected to host the Seventh Non-aligned Summit Conference in 1982, wanted to construct a similar complex. The Iraq government sought Sri Lanka's assistance in this respect and planned to send a team of architects and engineers to study the plans. Several other countries such as Pakistan were also interested in constructing something similar, which marked BMICH as an interesting case in modernism's global dissemination.[26]

A quick overview reveals the complexity and contradictions involved in the worldwide diffusion of modernism. It suggests that the rise of modernist architecture as a global phenomenon should not be taken for granted. Instead, the global reach of modernism in the postwar era registered the rise of a new world order which marked new forms of control, new ways of collaboration, and new partnerships in international affairs. Global modernist design practices were performed by a wide range of players and tangled with multiple political purposes in the process. On the one hand, it must be more than coincidental that modernism achieved its worldwide hegemony when financial capitalism was on the rise. Affirmed by the 1944 Bretton Woods Agreements, the new financial system achieved circulation, control, and exploitation that did not require that much physical support of locales compared with that required by colonialism. Hence, the new system was abstract and independent of the specificities of place, of which the sterile and faceless modernist architecture served as the proper symbol.

On the other hand, modernism traveled in the name of knowledge transfer, overseas aid, and new forms of cooperation among newly independent countries. Successful modernist design proved effective in helping the nations that offered it to create expanded spaces in the global political arena, as well as bringing international recognition and faster-paced modernization to the host societies. Seen in this light, the postwar spread of modernism not only signaled new relations between Western and non-Western modernities, but also among Third World ones. Today, many studies on non-Western modernities continue to be preoccupied with the centre–periphery dichotomy, while neglecting other relations that used to be so prominent in the actual "postcolonial" vision during the 1950s and 1960s. The emphasis on both types of relations in the formation of Third World modernism, therefore, is methodologically significant, as it allows a theoretical break from the normative historiographical emphasis on the West/non-West confrontation in much of current postcolonial scholarship.

Furthermore, previous accounts highlighted the "immigrant boat" (émigré and refugee architects) as the main vehicle for modernism's dissemination. Instead, the studies of this volume show that the mediums through which modernist architecture spread were much more diverse and often highly institutionalized. Apart from moving about as a means of exercising globalism, modernist architecture also travelled to the Third World on the wings of developmentalism, to which we now turn.

Modernism as developmentalism

Dipesh Chakrabarty considers colonial historicism to be the colonizers' way of saying "not yet" to non-European peoples, who were forced to wait until they became "civilized enough to rule themselves."[27] After independence, despite the end of direct colonial rule, the modernist vision of a rationally progressing universal history persisted, which considered that all nations were heading for the same destination; some arrived earlier than others. With the acute self-awareness of the temporal lag turned into a nationalistic aspiration for development, an all-encompassing project of modernization was at the top of the national agenda of many Third World countries.[28] New infrastructure, housing, administrative and educational buildings were constructed to accommodate new functions, new organizations, and new citizens.

It is in this broad context that modernist architecture was intimately tied to state patronage and assumed a vital mission in Third World nation building.[29] Despite its claims to universality in time and space, interwar modernism was developed at a time when "ascetic objects" were necessitated by economic depression and postwar rebuilding.[30] Practically, design doctrines such as "form follows function" and "building = function × economics" articulated by early modernists served particularly well in the developing world where people and institutes constantly struggled with scarce resources and insufficient funds. For example, modernist architecture achieved a decisive victory in China as part of the "anti-waste" movement in 1955. Modernism was first introduced to China as early as the 1920s, but under Soviet influence revivalist architecture became dominant in the early 1950s.[31] 1955 saw a major reorientation when a resolution was made which denounced the tendency of impractical extravagances in construction. Nationalistic structures with big roofs and traditional ornamentation were condemned as wasteful under the new austerity policy. The modernist style, considered more economical and efficient, was established as the preferable style in development. The promise of modernist architecture in providing affordable and high-density housing also attracted many developmental states to integrate it into their policy interventions. In Singapore, for instance, instead of adopting the incremental approach to low income housing, the state espoused the large-scale development of modern high-rise apartment buildings, which proved effective in achieving comprehensive housing access in the land-scarce city-state.[32]

Symbolically, the precepts of modernism constructed by early modernists as innovative, liberating, universal, and rational were embraced by Third World societies. The formalistic features of modernist architecture, which appeared clean, open, dynamic, and neutral, presented enough distance from both native and imperialist buildings. As such, along with modern factories, bridges, dams, and power plants, the images of modernist architecture frequently appeared in official propaganda publications as representations of modernization. These visible symbols powerfully shaped the desire of the age, the standards against which things were judged, and the collective conscious of what a modern nation should look like.[33] In practice, they were often taken as abbreviated signs of order, efficiency, and development, which James Scott has typified as the logic of high modernism, with the city of Brasilia being one of the most striking architectural examples.[34]

Elsewhere I have argued that an important dimension of Third World modernism has been the utopianization of modernity.[35] If utopia is the "expression of the desire for a better way of being and living," industrial modernity was turned into this better way of being in Third World countries.[36] The numerous blueprints sparked by official utopianism in these countries often did not go beyond what had already happened or was happening in the developed world: abundance, industrialization, electricity, and automation.[37] It was precisely because modernism had not happened, but was yet to come, that the potential existed to employ the vision to "teach desire to … desire better."[38]

A number of recent studies have illustrated modernism's postwar ascendancy as salvation for underdevelopment as a result of the "education of desire" provided by America-led Cold War cultural politics. Annabel Wharton's study of Hilton International Hotels built in postwar Europe and the Middle East provides a proper example.[39] The luxury hotels that Hilton International constructed abroad in the 1950s and 1960s introduced a remarkable visual contrast to the local architectural forms of host cities such as Istanbul, Cairo, and Jerusalem. Often the highest and most sumptuous building in the town, the Hilton created a dramatic panorama for impoverished local populations and realized a powerful presence of the United States. Such effects were consciously made, as Conrad Hilton acknowledged, "to show the countries most exposed to Communism the other side of the coin – the fruits of the free world."[40]

Studies of modernist architecture as the imposition of a specific set of political and cultural values, forms, and knowledge upon developing nations to some extent echo recent post-development discourse in social sciences. Arturo Escobar, for example, argues that developmentalism constructs underdeveloped nations as subjects located in a preliminary stage of historical evolution and thus in need of improvement through development projects in order to be modern, industrialized, and capitalist nation-states. This is done "by creating abnormalities ('the poor,' 'the malnourished,' 'the illiterate,' 'pregnant women,' 'the landless') which it would then treat or reform."[41] As these subjects adopt policies influenced by international agencies, it is precisely the promise of development that provides the conditions for the center to realize its continued surveillance of peripheral nations and their citizens.

While existing research reveals power and hegemony involved in the diffusion of modernist forms, knowledge, and technology, it often implies a linear path and reduces the complexities surrounding local appropriations, (mis)interpretations, transformations, and resistances. The three chapters in Part I of this volume present a more complicated picture by examining the transplantation of modernist architecture as a two-way process in Brazil, Morocco, and Peru. Importantly, they demonstrate the localization of modernism as a process in which people worked actively to make themselves modern, instead of merely being made modern. They show that modernism entered the local scene much earlier than the launch of the Cold War, and played a powerful role in introducing societies into modernity. The domestication of modernist architecture involved dense local practices of translating, selecting, mixing, and reinventing. The chapters highlight two dilemmas in the course of pursuing modernism as developmentalism. First, modernist architecture in many developing nations arose at a time when societies lacked the typical prerequisites for modernism, such as industrialization and modern construction technologies. The second problem was to find the balance between the specificities of the local context and the homogenizing effects of modernist design.

In "The Other Way Around: The Modernist Movement in Brazil", Daniela Sandler offers an account of Brazilian modernism not as an outcome of modernity, but as its harbinger. Canonical narratives consider industrialization as prerequisite for modern construction, modernity as the cultural context for modern forms, and urbanization as the setting for modern typologies. Sandler argues that these criteria would exclude much of the twentieth-century output of Latin American countries. Her analysis concentrates on the ambivalences and contradictories surrounding two important markers of Brazilian modernism: Gregori Warchavchik's own house on Rua Santa Cruz in São Paulo (1927), known as Modernist House (Casa Modernista), and Lina Bo Bardi's Museum of Art of

São Paulo, known for its acronym, MASP (1958–68). Sandler argues that the usual transplanted perspective of Warchavchik and Bo Bardi was neither inauthentic nor inappropriate. The adjustments the designers of the two projects made in the specific context of Brazil might at times seem to veer away from the canon or to result in "failures." Yet they were nonetheless quintessentially modernist, because the adaptations they made were precisely part of the dynamic and constantly dislocated quality of modernism itself.

In "Depoliticizing Group GAMMA," Aziza Chaouni observes a disjuncture in the existing studies of the modernist movement in Morocco between CIAM's ideas and practices before independence and local reinterpretations of modernism's precepts after independence. Her chapter concentrates instead on the continuity in the development of modernist architecture in Morocco by looking into the work of a group of young Moroccan and French architects from the 1950s to the early 1970s. Group Gamma, a Moroccan CIAM branch, was established in 1953, which promulgated a modernist architecture in line with Corbusian precepts, yet aspiring to be more in touch with the specificities of the local context, climate, and human habits. Group Gamma formed its architectural ideas under French rule, and put them into practice in its numerous public commissions for the Moroccan state after independence. Group Gamma's contested modernism was not merely a product of national identity assertion or of a will to rupture with the colonial past, Chaouni argues, but rather a result of a local legacy of contest initiated by architectural experimentations.

In "Agrupación Espacio and the CIAM Peru Group," Sharif Kahatt investigates transfer and transformation that occurred in modernist architecture from the European avant-garde, American modernism, to the creation of a hybrid architectural culture in Latin America. He shows that on the one hand, there were many European and American initiatives to spread modern design in Latin America. On the other hand, there was great interest from local architects who made a great effort to adopt, transform, and deploy imported forms and techniques. Led by Luis Miró Quesada, the Lima-based intellectual movement Agrupación Espacio played an important role in this. Kahatt examines the relationship between Agrupación Espacio and postwar CIAM by comparing the theories and practices the two adopted in their search for the modern city. Although canonical Latin American architectural historiography assumes that Espacio was CIAM's "franchise" in Lima, Kahatt's findings demonstrate that the relationship between these two groups was far more complex. The Peruvian Modern Project led by Espacio turned out to be a product of cultural hybridization rather than a direct borrowing of Western forms.

Modernism as nationalism

The concept of nationalism is a modern invention, associated with processes of modernization such as urbanization, the development of industrial capitalism, and the push for popular sovereignty that came with the French Revolution and the

American Revolution in the late eighteenth century. Europe was radically recon-
structed according to the concept after the First World War and the breakup of
the Habsburg and Ottoman empires. The European ideologies of self-determination anticipated the nationalist movements in Africa and Asia, where most countries gained political independence following the Second World War. As many
have observed, the nationalism that drove the independence movement was not
the same as the post-independence one.[42] The national unity formed against an
alien force before independence was replaced with the need to cultivate and
consolidate national identity in face of multiple contending groups from within.
Carefully manipulated built forms played a significant role in promoting a corresponding identity in terms of national culture.[43]

It is rather ironic that modernist architecture, disseminated in the
name of "International," was employed in many Third World countries – Turkey,
Brazil, Morocco, Ghana, India, Pakistan, Bangladesh, Indonesia, Singapore,
among others – to represent nationhood, which was generally conceptualized as
being rooted in remote antiquity and grounded in cultural uniqueness. A careful
dissection reveals that the mechanisms behind this are multi-layered. First, in the
context of Third World developmentalism, modernity became the nation's new
identity: something that informed the nation's new sense of self and directed a
people's imagination.[44] What follows is that modernism, the symbol of modernity, became a preferred means to project national identity and bring international
recognition. Grandiose modernist buildings served as visible representations of a
developing nation's capacity to equal the developed nation on its own terms.
Second, stylistic differentiation served as an important strategy in the art of identity making. Despite multiple intersections between modernism and colonialism,
the architectural culture of the time managed to establish sufficient distance
between modernism and the system of architectural representation under colonialism. While architectural classicism was considered authoritative and culturally
specific, modernism was welcomed in young nations as a new technology free
of the ties of the past and suitable for widespread adoption. Third, it was essential for the postcolonial state to impose a national homogeneity upon a multitude
of groups with divergent interests and cultural claims. Very often, the choice of
symbols of a specific ethnic group to communicate a unifying national identity
aggravated ethnic cleavages. In contrast, the use of modernism, which appeared
neutral and universal, could help to reduce social, cultural, political, and religious
tensions.

A reading of the making of Chandigarh in India illustrates multiple
issues involved in modernism as nationalism in a specific Third World context.
The building of Chandigarh, the new capital of Punjab, took place against the
background in which the state was partitioned and lost its capital to Pakistan;
many people lost their lives during this process due to religious violence. In
Chapter 11 of this volume, Vikramāditya Prakāsh argues that apart from symbolizing both modernization and a new beginning, the adoption of modernism for
the design of Chandigarh demonstrated the determination of the Nehruvian

regime to wrap the Indian constitution with an explicitly secular code. Being a modernist rather than a "Sikh" or "Hindu" city, Chandigarh served as a visible negation of former colonizers' historicist reading of the colonial subjects as religious subjects who were not yet ready to be modern citizens. Here, the constructed non-identitarian quality of modernism was strategically motivated to create a national identity that was modern, secular, and unfettered by colonial historicism. The rejection of New Delhi as the prerequisite of the architectural style of Chandigarh can be understood as the newly independent nation-state's rejection of Eurocentrism. Chandigarh's modern architecture, Prakash suggests, should be viewed as the adoption of a non-Western, or non-Eurocentric, modernism.

Despite the alleged objectives, the making of Chandigarh, however, was not without its own problems. The grand scale of Chandigarh in many ways echoed that of New Delhi. Despite stylistic differences, both featured large-scale administrative buildings and oversized public spaces, which served the purposes of a search for legitimacy and a demonstration of state power. As Mark Crison observes, compared with the monumental symmetry of New Delhi, the plan of Chandigarh sought to tease off the central axis, "as if the spatial symbolism of democratic power in relation to executive power was being reconfigured rather than reconceived."[45] Like Brasilia, no design attention was paid to the place of unskilled manual workers in the city. As a result, squatters' settlements grew after the completion of the project.[46] The making of Chandigarh hence exemplified a pitfall of modernism as nationalism shared by many post-independent cities: the construction of a national identity through the modern façade concealed the pressing problems of underdevelopment.

There were other tensions surrounding modernism as nationalism; the uneasy relationship between tradition and modernity remains the most striking one. Under colonialism, tradition was mobilized by some nationalists to form a collective denial of colonial modernity, while for others the relation between tradition and modernity did not have to be oppositional – indeed the non-dialogic relation between the two might well be part of colonizers' strategies of differentiation and separation.[47] After independence, tradition assumed a new role in cultivating national cultures through a process of what Eric Hobsbawm and Terence Ranger have described as "the invention of tradition": modern nations generally appeared so natural as to require no justification, but in fact they were recent constructs resting on novel practices of manipulating historical consciousness.[48] As such, there were attempts to develop a national architecture based on the mixing of modernism and historic precedents even in countries where modernism had become dominant, which were not always successful.[49] As Lawrence Vale points out, the cultural richness negated by modernism was sometimes resurrected in cartoon form, reducing architecture to "a three-dimensional, government sanctioned billboard advertising selected aspects of indigenous culture."[50] Still others sought to restore tradition via a discourse of authenticity. National museums were exemplary institutions in such exercises, whose displays meant to transcend the young nation's divisions and its recent colonial past so as to present a common past and incite aspirations to nationhood.[51] According to Ananya Roy, the two moments – the consolidation of modernism through the taming of tradition, and the revival of tradition on the ashes of the modern – are "both part of the same grand narrative of geopolitical order and discursive legitimacy."[52] They both assume a rigidly dualistic narrative that marks the traditional off from the modern, which was inherited from colonial historicism and remains a primary dilemma of Third World modernism even today.

The use of modernism in designing major national buildings such as museums and parliament buildings has been addressed by many studies. The three chapters in Part II of this volume explore the role of modernist architecture in search of national identity by looking at three other important building types (the university campus, the exhibition complex, and the residential building). Educational architecture represented a significant segment of post-independent nation building in Africa. Gitler's chapter investigates the design and construction of Obafemi Awolowo University (OAU) campus in Ile-Ife, one of the most important national commissions that followed Nigeria's independence. Designed by Israeli architect Arieh Sharon in collaboration with his son, and often cited as a master-piece of the Modern style in African architecture, the complex displayed an inter-pretation of national style that contested both mandatory and colonial rule. The strategy was to express a specific ethnic identity, the Yoruba, one of Nigeria's largest ethnic groups, through a formalistic approach. To be sure, the search for a cultural language combining modernism with African visual heritage was not unique to Sharon and Sharon during this period. Developed from the discourse of Africanism and negritude, this approach to Modernism has been an important part of cultural production in Africa since the 1950s. Sharon and Sharon's architecture, however, integrated locality in an unambiguous manner, which was rarely seen in large-scale civic commissions at the time.

Post-independence exhibitions in Colombo can be viewed as micro-environments for the playing out of Asia's cold war political alliances, and reflect a marked departure from the colonial tradition of international expositions. In her chapter "Modernity and Revolution: The Architecture of Ceylon's Twentieth-Century Exhibitions," Anoma Pieris looks at Ceylon/Sri Lanka as a significant microcosm of the broader processes that were shaping the Third World. In the early 1950s, adopting anti-colonial nationalism, Ceylon moved from postwar domi-nation by a neo-colonial Commonwealth to socialist republicanism. In the years that followed, Ceylon attempted to maintain its independence through non-align-ment despite competing foreign interventions upon her. Using the Colombo Plan exhibition of 1952, Ceylon 65, and the *Gam Udawa* (Village Re-awakening) exhibi-tions as important registers of national culture and its revolutionary socio-political transformation, the chapter maps the social production of twentieth-century exhi-bitions in Ceylon. Pieris situates modernism and its humanist ideals within the wider socio-political framework which highlighted the emergence of the Third World as a category. The exhibitions she described span several aesthetic moments in the self-fashioning of the nation-state, providing insights into a specific nationalistic vision that was later terminated by liberalization. The subsequent depoliticization and commodification of aesthetic trends, she argues, signaled the social relevance of that earlier modernity practiced and produced at the margins.

In "This is Not an American House: Good Sense Modernism in 1950s Turkey," Elâ Kaçel questions historical narratives of postwar modernism that take for granted the "Americanization of modernism" in Third World countries without contextualizing the International Style within local discourses of architecture. Drawing upon Antonio Gramsci's distinction between common sense and good sense, Kaçel suggests that modernism is concomitant with real processes of modernization through which ideologies are turned into common sense, that is, things that are uncritical, passive, and unconscious. In Turkey, the so-called "International Style" was propagated under the postwar sponsorship of the United States as modern culture in the 1950s. The term "Hiltonculuk" was soon coined by the architect and critic Şevki Vanlı to describe a fad among prominent Turkish architects who uncritically modeled their buildings after the Istanbul Hilton Hotel (1952–5). Built at the peak of "Hiltonculuk," the vacation house that architect Maruf Önal designed for his family in Bayramoğlu, however, did not fit under the categories either of a formulaic Americanism or of a "perfect mediocrity." Through a detailed analysis of Önal's house, Vanlı's critique, and the context in which they were situated, Kaçel illustrates how "ordinary" architects employed the relational knowledge networks into which they were embedded to critique popular clichés of postwar modernism and endowed their own architectural practice with a new sense of identity.

Modernism as postcolonialism

Independence did not mark the sudden disappearance of colonial influence. Instead, the steady progression of decolonialization gradually turned the formerly polarized relation between the metropolis and colonies into a more complicated and ambiguous relationship in various arenas. Despite the residual effects of colonialism, there were more spaces for connectivity, reciprocity, and entanglement in the name of development assistance, commercial exchange, knowledge and technology transfer, overseas aid, partnership, and collaboration. How did modernism intersect with this new postcolonial condition?

Following James Clifford's seminal pairing of "roots and routes," which conceptualizes the borders between fixity and mobility as porous and subject to crossings from both sides,[53] I suggest that we need to look at crisscross paths, flows, and networks that connect multiple platforms as important arenas for the diffusion and development of modernist architecture in the postcolonial context. Despite a flourishing vocabulary of mobility and hybridity in the past two decades,[54] global links, flows, entanglements, and networks are still treated as marginalized categories filling in the interstices between bounded territorial units. National or local architectural histories are presented as co-existing but disconnected variations, which has presented difficulties for studies of issues such as the transnational development of design discourses. Much of postcolonial scholarship is still preoccupied with a dichotomy that "defines the colonized as always engaged in conscious work against the core."[55] Part III of this volume attempts to go beyond both nation-based historiography and the clear-cut core–periphery model to view connection, dispersion, entanglement, and mobility as an important dimension of Third World modernism.

Certainly, the continuing presence of global unevenness means that the positions of different parties in these transactions were not necessarily equal.[56] As a result, heterogeneous and peculiar moments and results were generated. The development of modern tropical architecture exemplifies some of such postcolonial moments in the history of Third World modernism. In colonial discourse the term "Tropics" was often used to refer to "colonies," as if the latter could be defined as a homogenous climatic zone.[57] Developed by Otto Koenisgberger, Maxwell Fry, Jane Drew, Fello Atkinson and others in the postwar era, modern tropical architecture is regarded as an adaptation of modernist design principles for a distinctive (hot and humid) climatic condition by incorporating passive solar design and ventilation systems, and vernacular building elements such as verandas, louvered windows, and perforated walls. The Architectural Association School of Architecture (AA) in London initiated a diploma in tropical architecture in 1954, and the University of Melbourne established a similar program in 1962. The institutionalization of tropical architecture allowed former colonial powers to maintain their influence in former colonies, on the one hand, and helped train the early generation of Third World architects, on the other.[58] In recent decades, with the booming of the tourist industry, neo-tropical architecture has been developed in various parts of the developing world to create exotic and picturesque resort hotels for Western tourists. This new landscape, with locals as labour and Westerners as consumers, tends to reproduce social and class relations under colonialism.[59]

Despite its rich cultural meanings, tropical architecture is still considered a neutral and technical development in much of architectural discourse. Chapters 9 and 10 re-examine the early evolution of tropical architecture as a social phenomenon. Jiat-Hwee Chang's chapter investigates the under-studied technoscientific dimensions of the circulation and transformation of modernism. There has been little critical scholarship on modernism in relation to the institutionalization of building science in the mid-twentieth century, and the attendant establishment of research stations, changes in architectural education, and the technicalization of architectural knowledge and practice. Chang's chapter fills the gap by examining the work of the Tropical Building Section of the Building Research Station in Britain and a network of similar research stations working on tropical building problems in the British Empire/Commonwealth during the mid-twentieth century. Drawing on the interdisciplinary scholarship in postcolonial science studies and post-development studies, he reveals the production of technoscientific knowledge on tropical architecture by these building research stations as a Foucauldian power-knowledge regime, which was inextricably bound up with the politics of decolonization. Chang argues that the technoscientific knowledge, as produced and articulated in the name of welfare and modernization, should be considered as a new form of expertise that served to ensure Britain's ongoing politico-economic relevance in the tropics after formal decolonization.

Vandana Baweja's chapter challenges the binary categories such as center/periphery embedded in the recent histories of tropical architecture. She starts with the career trajectory of Otto Koenigsberger (1908–99), who is best known for his contribution to climatic responsive design. Baweja then contrasts Koenigsberger's practices with those of Peter and Alison Smithson, who focused on the temporality of the climate and its relationship with architecture at the level of the building form. The chapter ends with a discussion of the shifting discourse of tropical architecture as sustainable design. While canonical architectural histories treat tropical architecture as a commodity exported from the metropolis to the tropics, Baweja's chapter tells a different story. In the process of imposing architectural knowledge to the tropical Third World, Baweja argues, architects unwittingly developed a body of knowledge that later constituted the intellectual foundation for the discourse of tropical architecture at the AA and was eventually subsumed into the contemporary discourse of sustainable architecture.

In the chapter "Modernity Transfers: The MoMA and Postcolonial India," Farhan Sirajul Karim observes that India's post-independence practice of domesticity experienced a multi-directional turn. Albeit celebrating a model of affluence, India was experiencing a resurgence that explicitly challenged the indulgence of domesticity and the exuberance of material fetish, a portion of the history of domesticity that had long been veiled by the dominant discursive practice of Western modernity. The ambivalence and tension that emerged from the exchanging of modernity between India and the West are studied through two exhibitions that were organized by MoMA during the 1950s: one about India mounted in New York and titled "Textile and Ornamental Arts of India" and the other about the West, mounted in India and titled "Design Today in Europe and America." On the one hand, the promotion of modernity of affluence by America sought to demonstrate a fantastic view of future domesticity before an Indian audience. On the other hand, India sought to promote itself as a model of a non-industrial material world. Based on rich first-hand archival material, Karim shows that in a bid to forge a true hybrid of ascetic modernity, Pierre Jeanneret sought to reconcile these two streams by synthesizing the modernist trope of machine-made, luxurious consumer goods with the asceticism of a Gandhian material culture.

Finally, Vikramāditya Prakāsh's Epilogue reflects upon the necessity of creating a new framework for understanding modernism as a global construct, in parallel with the discussion of "cosmopolitan modernism" prevalent in art history currently. He calls for the move towards a horizon where "the asymmetries in the postcolonial reading of modernism can be productively drawn into dialogue with the more disciplinary reading of modernism as the negotiation between the universal and the particular."

Spaces of hope[60]

During a visit to the United States in 1943, Chinese anthropologist Fei Xiaotong noted the differences between China, where contemporary life was engulfed in the thick layers of the accumulated past, and America, where people were future-oriented but nonetheless dominated by an alienating order.[61] Ghosts, in Fei's vision, represented the presence of the specter of the past that continuously haunted the present and made up the very core of being Chinese: "Life in its creativity … melds past, present, and future into one inextinguishable, multilayered scene, a three-dimensional body. This is what ghosts are."[62] In contrast, living in brightly lit American rooms, Fei wrote, "gives you a false sense of confidence that this is all of the world, that there is no more reality than what appears clearly and brightly before your eyes."[63]

This volume sets out to complicate a picture of Third World modernism in the mid-twentieth century oversimplified by the smooth transfers assumed by the official history of modern architecture. Despite the "false sense of confidence" in the universality, rationality, and homogeneity of the modern given by dominant discourses, the chapters of this volume reveal in modernism the constant wrestling with "ghosts" of all sorts that have been there from the very beginning and will not go away. They show that, wrestling with the differences in historical, social, cultural, political, and economic conditions, modernism took heterogeneous trajectories in Third World nations. They also show that these trajectories were radically different from those of developed nations during the same historical period.

With the rise of consumption-orientated society and the development of the welfare state amid postwar prosperity, the field of architecture in the West appeared to be coming apart in the mid-twentieth century. Practitioners pursued their idiosyncratic interests in the face of uncertainty over modernity, generating a diverse body of work which Sarah Goldhagen and Réjean Legault have aptly described as "anxious modernisms."[64] While practitioners of interwar modernism were obsessed with the utopian goals of transforming society through revolutionary architecture, postwar architects adapted their design vocabularies to the new social and cultural conditions of commercial society.[65] In contrast, during the same period of time, Third World architects focused on the explorations of modernism as a means of development, nation building, and identity making. The spread of modernist architecture in developing nations was characterized by a global diffusion of modernist design knowledge and construction techniques, continuing Western expansionist practices, new forms of collaboration and solidarity, quests for national and cultural identity, large-scale developmental projects, and above all, spaces of hope.

Today, to quote Max Horkheimer and Theodor Adorno, the wholly "modernized" earth "radiates under the sign of disaster triumphant."[66] Like never before, modern architecture has reached every corner of the planet. Designers are mass produced based on more or less similar curriculums. Jet travel and new information technology allow architects to design projects at distance with ease.[67] "Starchitects" are driven to produce the same theatrical effect everywhere instead of attending to the unique differences of each site. A new level of abstraction is achieved as people, places, and local knowledges are effectively bypassed by globalized processes of architectural production. Even in poorer urban areas and remote rural regions, people choose to build modern style buildings in concrete instead of adopting more sustainable local forms and materials (Figures 2, 3). As a result, indigenous building knowledges and technologies have been disappearing rapidly in many places. The spread of modern architecture (and the lifestyles associated with it), not unlike the spread of chemical pesticides, has produced destructive ecological effects and reduced cultural diversity. It is reported that buildings now account for forty percent of total energy consumption in developed countries. There is an urgent need to correct the tendency of spatial homogenization, which has become fiercer under the spread of a globalized consumer culture in our time.

It is against this context that I would like to sketch out the beginnings of a new framework for the study of Third World modernism based on a radical transformative imagining of epistemological diversity in architectural production. As recent postcolonial scholarship has made clear, no chapter in Western modernity is complete unless it includes the history of the epistemological violence that European colonial power did to other peoples. During the course of constructing the contemporaneity of other cultures as the primordial prehistory of the dominant self, the West dwarfed other knowledges as irrational narratives that should be exorcised for lack of epistemological validity.[68] With this calculated refusal, the way was paved for the spread of the sovereignty of Western knowledge throughout the world, which has enduring consequences long after the end of colonialism. On the one hand, other regional intellectual traditions, "once unbroken and alive," are treated as purely matters of historical research devoid of any theoretical lineage.[69] On the other hand, the very regionality of Western thought is masqueraded as uncontestable universalism, whose cognitive formula assumes a central role even in places where realities are completely out of sync with happenings in the metropolis.[70] One of the violent effects of the denial of other knowledges has been the establishment of a false historical dichotomy – "Western knowledge" *vis-à-vis* "native experience" – in social sciences (most notably in anthropology and area studies), which assumes any epistemic category that makes sense of the latter as belonging to the former. This cognitive inclination is still well with us despite epistemological sophistication brought about by recent theoretical constructs.[71]

The global sovereignty of architectural modernism and the suppression of other architectural knowledges have had destructive consequences for

Figure 2
**Modern urban housing
in Hanoi, Vietnam.
Photograph taken by
the author, 2006.**

Figure 3
**Local rammed earth
buildings have been
increasingly replaced by
concrete and brick ones
in Kanshi, China.
Photograph taken by
the author, 2005.**

the built environment across the world. The past five decades witnessed waves
of debates that sought to address the ubiquitous problem of placelessness, with
the idea of critical regionalism developed by Kenneth Frampton and others being
one of the most influential academic propositions since the 1980s.[72] Systematic
assessments of critical regionalism have been made elsewhere.[73] My polemic

here is to use critical regionalism as an example to highlight a fundamental failure of contemporary architectural discourse in responding to the reality of other knowledges. In the words of Frampton, "[t]he fundamental strategy of Critical Regionalism is to mediate the impact of universal civilization with elements derived *indirectly* from the peculiarities of a particular place [emphasis as in the original]."[74] To achieve this, Frampton suggests taking inspiration from local specifications such as the light condition, topography, climate, place-form, and so on, with the tectonic and tactile dimensions stressed. John Utzon's Bagsvaerd Church is cited as an example "whose complex meaning stems directly from a revealed conjunction between, on the one hand, the *rationality* of normative technique and, on the other, the *arationality* of idiosyncratic form [emphasis as in the original]."[75]

Frampton's prescriptions are certainly helpful in moving beyond postmodernism's nihilistic play of signs for consumption and to pursue a more sincere and sensitive architecture. My concern has been that the operation of critical regionalism preempts the possibilities of local architectural knowledges, as if the latter do not exist at all. While Frampton is highly critical of the *tabula rasa* tendency of modernist design, the local is treated here as an epistemological "*tabula rasa*", which can at best provide some "arational" idiosyncrasies for metropolitan architectural virtuosity. The drama of critical regionalism can only be played out with reference to "universal modernism," which is presumed to be the only genuine knowledge emanating from rationality. This scenario, however, is utterly ironic when we consider that the majority of people on Earth still live in varied types of sophisticated "regional architecture" designed and constructed by local builders who do not have access to "normative" modernist building knowledge and techniques. For them, so-called "universal modernism" is merely another regional reality.

Yet in critical regionalism as articulated by Frampton, the inherited regional culture is posited as a necessary object for destruction, rather than living knowledge with the same epistemological significance as "universal civilization" – read here as Western "scientific, technical, and political rationality." As such, one must seek an alien knowledge to defamiliarize with and destruct the regional culture in order to sustain a critique of universal civilization. Here, critical regionalism falls well within the jurisdiction of Eurocentric epistemology: other cultures are construed as unregenerate irrationality waiting to be expelled, although part of them may be dissected and then reassembled only to revitalize the fading spirit of Western rationality. By eschewing the possibilities of other knowledges altogether and projecting modernism's anxiety with its inner crisis onto other locales, critical regionalism's cultivation of regional cultures turns out to be another operation to sustain modernism's schizophrenic obsession with itself.

Could the rich regional building traditions not merely be raw material for metropolitan maneuvers but living knowledges with their own epistemological claims in architectural production? Is it possible to launch a critique of modernism that acknowledges the contemporaneity of multiple epistemic spaces? And could different knowledges be contested and updated not just with reference to Western thoughts and forms but with historical reference to one another? My study on the aftermath of the people's commune movement in China (1958–60) points to such possibilities.[76] During the commune movement, concurrent with sweeping institutional changes, architects boldly experimented with modernist design in rural China, but their proposals rarely progressed from paper. The failure of the commune plan problematized the issue of modernist architecture. As the country was short of steel and concrete, and little state funding was available for rural construction, designers recognized the importance of combining both modern and traditional methods. There arose a new need for collective self-understanding and other knowledges besides those of the West. Hence, 1963 saw a sudden expansion of knowledge of traditional built forms in different parts of the country. Surveys of vernacular architecture were conducted and published, and efforts were taken to integrate local building conventions with modern design. Meanwhile, the influential *Architectural Journal* (*Jianzhu xuebao*) started to provide extensive coverage of architecture in Third World countries. The 1963 issues covered architecture in Indonesia, Cambodia, Burma, Cuba, North Korea, Vietnam, and Albania, while the 1964 issues added Egypt, Mexico, Ghana, Guinea, and Syria to the list. Unlike typical Western representations, Chinese authors focused on modern developments in architecture rather than the traditional forms of these nations. They paid particular attention to how designers adapted buildings to local social, geographical, climatic, and cultural conditions. In a 1963 report on Cuban architecture, for instance, innovative roof systems for industrial structures and well planned residential districts in Havana were extolled.[77]

Through these discursive parameters, the architectural practices of other developing countries were linked with those of China, creating a world of synchronic temporality and shared spatiality. As these coeval knowledges fuelled new imaginings of modern Chinese architecture, the early 1960s saw a flourish of design projects with a strong local flavor. The new orientation destabilized the previous discursive framing of "Western modernist architecture," which became a subject of intellectual contention. This conceptual twist was reflected by Wu Huanjia, who commented on the "ten greatest buildings in the 1960s" selected by the American journal *The Architectural Forum*.[78] Wu found the work of "master architects" (including Le Corbusier, Louis Kahn, and Eero Saarinen, among others) "chaotic," "ugly," and "sick." Saarinen's expressionist TWA Flight Centre, for example, was denounced for the lavish abuse of technology for purely visual concerns.

These comments were certainly made under specific historical and political circumstances, but they help to illustrate the matter of fact that there is an "exterior" to an allegedly "universal modernism," where it may be challenged or even deemed irrelevant. It is from this discursive space that we can start to confront the regionality and finitude of modernism on the basis of other experiences. From the above example, we see that the crisis of modernist architecture in China in the early 1960s differed greatly from its crisis in the West during the same period. Chinese architects were forced to face the historically constituted condition of scarcity after the failure of commune design; it was from this vantage point that they posited modernism among other knowledges and developed a new vision of Chinese architecture. The rich regional building traditions revealed through this example are not "ghosts" of the past to be disenchanted, but knowledges that continue to build upon the present.

My position here is both similar and dissimilar to that of Dipesh Chakrabarty in his book *Provincializing Europe*.[79] Non-European peoples were considered not yet ready to rule themselves under colonialism.[80] Chakrabarty argues that the contemporary historicist framework commits the same error by considering the persisting world of peasants, which involves "gods, spirits, and supernatural agents as actors alongside humans," an anachronism in Indian political modernity.[81] He sets out to dismantle the linear notion of time by reconceptualizing the present as "constantly fragmentary" with diverse ways of being-in-the-world. Like Chakrabarty, I stress the contemporaneity and synchronicity of multiple life worlds. Yet unlike Chakrabarty, who focuses on reinstituting a coevalness of irrationalities such as "gods, spirits, and other supernatural beings" with political modernity in India, I seek to build on the coevalness of different rationalities and knowledges. Chakrabarty is correct in his claim that it is better to see reason as "one among many ways of being in the world," but his designation of the native life world as a phenomenological immediacy fraught with blind faith and superstition tends to repeat the false historical dichotomy between an inherited domain comprised of native religions and customs, and a colonized domain comprised of Western political economy and science. Yet in reality, even Western modernity has never been completely disenchanted – a powerful Christian religion, for example, is always coeval with capitalist modernity in countries such as the United States.

My contention is that a large part of native life worlds, like the Western ones, are constituted by rationalities and knowledges developed and accumulated over time, despite the divine or super-human presences in them. The rich and sophisticated regional building traditions across the world are the testimony. Yet our modern architectural discourse and educational system have effectively delegitimized these other knowledges. With the very regionality of modern Western forms disguised as authentic universalism, modernist design is defined as the only "valid" knowledge taught in design studios everywhere. Other regional building traditions are either ignored or reduced to material for stylistic borrowings or historical research, devoid of any potential as resources for thinking about the present. As long as Western-centric epistemological assumptions remain dominant and other knowledges are considered residual, we are still very much in the shadow of Sir Banister Fletcher's "Tree of Architecture."[82]

I argue that the recognition of other modernities has to be posited at the level of epistemology in order to imagine an open globality based not on asymmetry and dominance but on connectivity and dialogue on an equal basis. It is important to recognize not only the histories of different modernities, but also the *legitimacies of different knowledges*. Unless other modernities are recognized as legitimate spaces of knowledge production, the march toward social homogeneity and environmental destruction will remain unchecked. It is time to enfranchise other spatial rationalities and architectural knowledges to create a more sustainable, just, and culturally and ecologically rich world. And it is time to open our architectural education to a multi-logical program that encourages mutual persuasions amongst different understandings of dwelling and building.

Notes

1   See, for example, James Holston, *The Modernist City: An Anthropological Critique of Brasília* (Chicago: University of Chicago Press, 1989); Jon Lang, Madhavi Desai, and Miki Desai, *Architecture and Independence: The Search for Identity – India 1880 to 1980* (Delhi: Oxford University Press, 1997); Edward R. Burian (ed.), *Modernity and the Architecture of Mexico* (Austin: University of Texas Press, 1997); Valerie Fraser, *Building the New World: Studies in the Modern Architecture of Latin America, 1930–1960* (New York: Verso, 2000); Sibel Bozdogan, *Modernism and Nation Building: Turkish Architectural Culture in the Early Republic* (Seattle: University of Washington Press, 2001); Zou Denong *Zhongguo xiandai jianzhu shi* [Modern Chinese Architectural History] (Tianjin: Tianjin kexue jishu chubanshe, 2001); Vikramāditya Prakāsh, *Chandigarh's Le Corbusier: The Struggle for Modernity in Postcolonial India* (Seattle: University of Washington Press, 2002); Peter G. Rowe and Seng Kuan, *Architectural Encounters with Essence and Form in Modern China* (Cambridge, Massachusetts: MIT Press, 2002); Mark Crinson, *Modern Architecture and the End of Empire* (London: Ashgate, 2003); Elisabetta Andreoli and Adrian Forty (eds), *Brazil's Modern Architecture* (London: Phaidon, 2004); Duanfang Lu, *Remaking Chinese Urban Form: Modernity, Scarcity and Space, 1949–2005* (London: Routledge, 2006); Sandy Isenstadt and Kishwar Rizvi (eds), *Modern Architecture and the Middle East: Architecture and Politics in the Twentieth Century* (*Seattle:* University of Washington Press, 2008); Richard J. Williams, *Brazil: Modern Architectures in History* (London: Reaktion Books, 2009); Zhu Jianfei, *Architecture of Modern China: A Historical Critique* (London: Routledge, 2009).

2   Alfred Sauvy coined the expression ("tiers monde" in French) in 1952 by analogy with the "third estate," the commoners of France, as opposed to priests and nobles. The term was used at the 1955 Bandung conference of Afro-Asian countries. For a lucid analysis of the emergence of Third Worldism, see Gerard Chaliand, *Revolution in the Third World: Myths and Prospects* (New York: Viking, 1977).

3   Elbaki Hermassi, *The Third World Reassessed* (Berkeley, California: University of California Press, 1980).

4   Allen H. Merriam, "What Does 'Third World' Mean?" in Jim Norwine and Alfonso Gonzalez, *The Third World: States of Mind and Being* (Winchester, Massachusetts: Unwin Hyman, Inc., 1988), pp. 15–22.

5   *Ibid.*

6   *Ibid.*

7   One of the significant exceptions has been Mark Crinson's *Modern Architecture and the End of Empire* (London: Ashgate, 2003), which covers several geographical areas to present a broad picture of architecture's relation to the end of imperialism.

8   Eric R. Wolf, *Europe and the People without History*, 2nd ed. (Berkeley, California: University of California Press, 1997 [1982]).

9   Jurgen Habermas, "Modernity versus Postmodernity," *New German Critique* 22 (1981), pp. 3–14.

10   Marshall Berman, *All that is Solid Melts into Air: The Experience of Modernity* (New York: Simon and Schuster, 1982).

11   Hilde Heynen, *Architecture and Modernity: A Critique* (Cambridge, Massachusetts: MIT Press, 1999); Ulrich Conrads, *Programs and Manifestoes on 20th-Century Architecture*, tr. Michael Bullock (Cambridge, Massachusetts: MIT Press, 1970).

12   Walter Gropius, *The New Architecture and the Bauhaus* (Cambridge, Massachusetts: MIT Press, 1965), p. 19.

13   Le Corbusier, *Towards a New Architecture*, tr. Frederick Etchells (London: John Rodker, 1927); Henry-Russell Hitchcock and Philip Johnson, *The International Style* (New York: Norton, 1932); Siegfried Gidion, *Space, Time and Architecture: The Growth of a New Tradition* (Cambridge, Massachusetts: Harvard University Press, 1941); Nikolaus Pevsner, *The Sources of Modern Architecture and Design* (New York: Praeger, 1968); Leonardo Benevolo, *History of Modern Architecture* (Cambridge, Massachusetts: MIT Press, 1971).

14   Hitchcock and Johnson, *The International Style*.

15   Conrads, *Programs and Manifestoes on 20th-Century Architecture*.

16   Karin Kirsch, *The Weissenhofsiedlung: Experimental Housing Built for the Deutscher Werkbund, Stuttgart, 1927* (New York: Rizzoli, 1989).

17   Paul Overy, "White Walls, White Skins: Cosmopolitanism and Colonialism in Inter-war Modernist Architecture," in Kobena Mercer (ed.), *Cosmopolitan Modernisms* (London: Institute of International Visual Arts, 2005), pp. 50–67.

18   *Ibid.*

19   *Ibid.*, p. 56.

20   Crinson, *Modern Architecture and the End of Empire*.

21   Anthony D. King, *Urbanism, Colonialism, and the World-Economy: Cultural and Spatial Foundations of the World Urban System* (London: Routledge, 1990); Gwendolyn Wright, *The Politics of Design in French Colonial Urbanism* (Chicago: University of Chicago Press, 1991); Nezar AlSayyad (ed.), *Forms of Dominance: On the Architecture and Urbanism of the Colonial Enterprise* (Aldershot: Avebury, 1992); Zeynep Çelik, *Displaying the Orient: Architecture of Islam at Nineteenth-Century World's Fairs* (Berkeley, California: University of California Press, 1992); Zeynep Çelik, *Urban Forms and Colonial Confrontations: Algiers under French Rule*, Berkeley, California: University of California Press, 1997); Swati Chattopadhyay, *Representing Calcutta: Modernity, Nationalism, and the Colonial Uncanny* (London: Routledge, 2005); Mia Fuller, *Moderns Abroad: Architecture, Cities and Italian Imperialism* (New York: Routledge, 2007); Peter Scriver and Vikramāditya Prakāsh, *Colonial Modernities: Building, Dwelling and Architecture in British India and Ceylon* (London: Routledge, 2007).

22   Jeffery W. Cody, *Exporting American Architecture, 1870–2000* (London: Routledge, 2003).

23   Duanfang Lu, "Exporting Chinese Modernism: Reading the Bandaranaike Memorial International Conference Hall, Colombo, Sri Lanka," paper presented at the Chinese Studies of Australian Association Biennial Conference at the University of Sydney, 7–9 July 2009 (Sydney, Australia); Duanfang Lu, *Unsettled Modernism* [*Weiding de xiandaizhuyi*] (published in both English and Chinese) (Beijing: China Architecture & Building Press, forthcoming).

24   *Ibid.*

25   *Ibid.*

26   *Ibid.*

27   Dipesh Chakrabarty, *Provincializing Europe: Postcolonial Thought and Historical Difference* (Princeton: Princeton University Press, 2000), p. 8.

28   Duanfang Lu, "Third World Modernism: Modernity, Utopia and the People's Commune in China," *Journal of Architectural Education*, 60, 3 (2007), pp. 40–8.

29   Bozdogan, *Modernism and Nation Building*.

30   Paul Betts, *The Authority of Everyday Objects: A Cultural History of West German Industrial Design* (Berkeley, California: University of California Press, 2004).

31   Lu, *Remaking Chinese Urban Form*, Chapter 1.

32   Belinda Yuen, "Romancing the high rise," *Cities* 22, 1 (2005), pp. 3-13.

33   Bozdogan, *Modernism and Nation Building*.

34   James C. Scott, *Seeing Like a State: How Certain Schemes to Improve the Human Condition Have Failed* (New Haven: Yale University Press, 1998).

35   Lu, "Third World Modernism."

36   R. Levitas, *The Concept of Utopia* (London: Philip Allan, 1990), p. 8.

37   Bozdogan, *Modernism and Nation Building*.

38   E. P. Thompson, *William Morris: Romantic to Revolutionary* (Merlin Press: London, 1977), p. 791.

39   Cody, *Exporting American Architecture*; Annabel Jane Wharton, *Building the Cold War: Hilton International Hotels and Modern Architecture* (Chicago: University of Chicago, 2001); Jane C. Loeffler, *The Architecture of Diplomacy: Building America's Embassies* (New York: Princeton Architectural Press, 1998).

40   Wharton, *Building the Cold War*.

41   Arturo Escobar, "Imagining a Post-Development Era? Critical Thought, Development and Social Movements," *Social Text*, 31–2 (1992), p. 25.

42   Lawrence J. Vale, *Architecture, Power, and National Identity* (New Haven: Yale University Press, 1992).

43   *Ibid.*

44   Lu, *Remaking Chinese Urban Form*, pp. 6–7.

45   Crinson, *Modern Architecture and the End of Empire*, p. 13.

46   *Ibid.*, p. 14.

47   AlSayyad, *Forms of Dominance*; Nezar AlSayyad (ed.), *End of Tradition?* (New York: Routledge, 2004).

48   Eric Hobsbawm and Terence Ranger (eds), *The Invention of Tradition* (Cambridge: Cambridge University Press, 1993).

49   Duanfang Lu, "Architecture and Global Imaginations in China', *Journal of Architecture* 12, 2 (2007), pp. 123-45. Crinson, *Modern Architecture and the End of Empire*, Chapter 7.

50   Vale, *Architecture, Power, and National Identity*, p. 54.

51   Benedict Anderson, *Imagined Communities: Reflections on the Origin and Spread of Nationalism*, revised edition (London: Verso, 2006), Chapter 10.

52   Ananya Roy, "Nostalgias of the Modern," in AlSayyad, *End of Tradition?*, pp. 63–86.

53   James Clifford, *Routes: Travel and Translation in the Late Twentieth Century* (Cambridge, Massachusetts: Harvard University Press, 1997).

54   Homi Bhabha, *The Location of Culture* (London: Routledge, 1994); Duanfang Lu, "The Changing Landscape of Hybridity: A Reading of Ethnic Identity and Urban Form in Late-Twentieth-Century Vancouver," *Traditional Dwellings and Settlements Review*, 11, 2 (2000), pp. 19–28; Nezar AlSayyad, *Hybrid Urbanism: On the Identity Discourse and the Built Environment* (Westport, CO: Praeger, 2001); Stephen Cairns (ed.) *Drifting: Architecture and Migrancy* (London: Routledge, 2004).

55   Jane M. Jacobs, *Edge of Empire: Postcolonialism and the City* (London: Routledge, 1996), p. 15.

56   Arif Dirlik, *Global Modernity: Modernity in the Age of Global Capitalism* (Boulder: Paradigm Publishers, 2007).

57   Crinson, *Modern Architecture and the End of Empire*, Chapter 6.

58   Lai Chee Kien, "Tropical Tropes: The Architectural Politics of Building in Hot and Humid Climates," unpublished paper presented at the 8th IASTE International Conference, Hong Kong, 12-15 December 2002; cited in Anoma Pieris, "Is Sustainability Sustainable? Interrogating the Tropical Paradigm in Asian Architecture," in Joo-Hwa Bay and Boon Lay Ong (eds.) *Tropical Sustainable Architecture: Social and Environmental Dimensions* (Oxford: Architectural Press, 2006), pp. 267-86.

59   Anoma Pieris, "Is Sustainability Sustainable? Interrogating the Tropical Paradigm in Asian Architecture," p. 279.

60   The argument of this section is further articulated in my forthcoming chapter "Entangled Modernities in Architecture" in Greg Crysler, Stephen Cairns and Hilde Heynen (eds.), *Architectural Theory Handbook* (London: Sage).

61   R. David Arkush and Leo O. Lee (eds and tr.), *Land without Ghosts: Chinese Impressions of America from the Mid-Nineteenth Century to the Present* (Berkeley, California: University of California Press, 1989), pp. 174–81.

62   *Ibid.*, p. 178.

63   *Ibid.*, p. 181.

64   Sarah Williams Goldhagen and Réjean Legault (eds), *Anxious Modernisms: Experimentation in Postwar Architectural Culture* (Montréal: Canadian Centre for Architecture, 2000).

65   *Ibid.*, p. 11.

66   Max Horkheimer and Theodor W. Adorno, *Dialectic of Enlightenment: Philosophical Fragments*, ed. Gunzelin Schmid Noerr; trans. Edmund Jephcott (Stanford, California: Stanford University Press, 2002 [1947]).

67   Donald McNeil, *The Global Architect: Firms, Fame and Urban Form* (New York: Routledge, 2009).

68   Edward W. Said, *Orientalism* (London: Routledge, 1978).

69   Chakrabarty, *Provincializing Europe*, p. 5.

70   Rajagopalan Radhakrishnan, "Postmodernism and the Rest of the World," in Fawzia Afzal-Khan and Kalpana Seshadri-Crooks (eds), *The Pre-Occupation of Postcolonial Studies* (Durham, North Carolina: Duke University Press, 2000), pp. 37–70.

71   Jennifer Robinson, *Ordinary Cities: Between Modernity and Development* (New York: Routledge, 2005).

72   Alexander Tzonis and Liane Lefaivre, "The Grid and the Pathway," *Architecture in Greece* 15 (1981), pp. 164–78; William J. Curtis, *Modern Architecture Since 1900* (Englewood Cliffs, New Jersey: Prentice-Hall, 1982); Kenneth Frampton, "Prospects for a Critical Regionalism," *Perspecta* 20 (1983), pp. 147–62; Kenneth Frampton, *Modern Architecture: A Critical History*, 3rd edn (London: Thames and Hudson, 1992 [1980]); Kenneth Frampton, "Towards a Critical Regionalism: Six Points for an Architecture of Resistance," in Hal Foster (ed.), *The Anti-Aesthetic: Essays on Postmodern Culture* (New York: The New Press, 1998 [1983]), pp. 17–34; Alexander Tzonis, Liane Lefaivre and Bruno Stagno (eds) *Tropical Architecture: Critical Regionalism in the Age of Globalization* (Chichester: C. Fonds, 2001).

73   Alan Colquhoun, "The Concept of Regionalism," in Gülsüm Baydar Nal-bantoglu and Wong Chong Thai (eds), *Postcolonial Space(s)* (New York: Princeton Architectural Press, 1997), pp. 13–23; Keith L. Eggener, "Placing Resistance: a Critique of Critical Regionalism," *Journal of Architectural Education* 55, 4 (2002), pp. 228–37; Gevork Hartoonian, "Critical Regionalism Reloaded," *Fabrications* 16, 2(2006), pp. 123–9.

74   Frampton, "Towards a Critical Regionalism," p. 23.

75   *Ibid.*, p. 25.

76   Lu, "Third World Modernism."

77   Liu Yunhe, "Guba jianzhu" [Cuban Architecture], *Jianzhu xuebao* [Architectural Journal] 9 (1963), pp. 20–7.

78   Wu Huanjia, "Ping xifang shizuo jianzhu" [A Review of Ten Buildings in the West], *Jianzhu xuebao* [Architectural Journal] 6 (1964), pp. 29–33.

79   Chakrabarty, *Provincializing Europe*.

80   *Ibid.*, p. 8.

81   *Ibid.*, p. 11.

82   The "evolutionary tree" in Sir Banister Fletcher's famous frontispiece to *A History of Architecture on the Comparative Method* (London: B. T. Batsford, 1897) depicts the evolution of Western architecture as dynamic and historical while considering the architecture of other cultures non-historical and having no impact upon the "History of Architecture".

Part I

The will of the age

Chapter 2

The Other Way Around: the modernist movement in Brazil

Daniela Sandler

The study of Brazilian modernism often conjures up a litany repeated by historians and critics. Modernist ideas were allegedly an import from Europe, "out of place" with relation to Brazil's sociopolitical and material realities.[1] These ideas lacked some crucial or essential precondition, producing a paradoxical "modernism without modernity."[2] Brazilian modernism was out of time, lopsided, proposing forms and designs "well ahead of economic and technological realities."[3] It supposedly put the cart before the horse, introducing concepts and proposals that anticipated rather than expressed modernity and modernization.[4] The implication is that modernism in Brazil was derivative, imitative, and subordinate to European modernism, and as such was doubly inauthentic: it neither expressed "genuine" Brazilian experiences, nor did it live up to the "original" European models.

These contradictions are inextricable from issues of dependency, colonialism, and power relations between center (Europe and, later, North America) and periphery (in this case, Brazil and Latin America). The tensions outlined in the paragraph above are constitutive of the Brazilian experience, and not only in architecture; they are as pervasive as they are irreducible. It is not a matter of demonstrating whether Brazilian modernism was original or subsidiary, modern enough or still lacking, but rather of sustaining these tensions as the analytical fulcrum to understanding modernist architecture in Brazil. This "tense" understanding of modernism, riddled with contradictions, might reverberate not only with other peripheral (or third-world) examples, but also with modernism at the center – if, as Gwendolyn Wright notes, we understand modernism as having come "into being in a world framed by colonialism, where visions for improvement and innovation overlapped with and often caused brutal destruction."[5] Modernism involved from the start an international traffic of ideas in many forms: imposition, transplant, adaptation, exchange; this means that foreignness, alienation, and dislocation are intrinsic to the modernist movement.

I will tease out these issues by analyzing two markers of Brazilian modernism. At the beginning of the movement is Gregori Warchavchik's own house on Rua Santa Cruz in São Paulo (1927), later known as Modernist House (Casa Modernista). This building has been described variously as the inaugural work of Brazilian modernism, and as a not-quite-there-yet staging of transplanted ideas. At the other end is Lina Bo Bardi's Museum of Art of São Paulo, known by its acronym, MASP (1958–68). The MASP can also be seen in opposite ways – as an expression of Brazil's mid-century modernist bravado, and as a critical departure from it. These two works are not intended to encompass all the nuances of Brazilian modernism, but to foreground the issues relevant to my discussion: the relationship between margins and center, and the critical or constructive possibilities of modernism. The Modernist House on Rua Santa Cruz presents an *ambiguous* modernism, whose adaptations and compromises inadvertently produce a critical perspective on the movement's basic principles. Four decades later, the MASP provides an intentional critique, but a critique realized from within the tenets and conditions of modernism: an *ambivalent* building that both deploys and rejects modernist principles.[6]

The distinction between modernity and modernization is central to my argument. That these two words are often conflated is no accident, but rather, as Nicola Miller argues, a result of both Eurocentrism and technocentrism.[7] Miller's distinction between modernity and modernization is motivated by the unique conditions of Latin America. She describes modernization as:

> ... historical processes that can roughly be dated to the late eighteenth century and located in (parts of) Europe, namely capital formation and the emergence of capitalist relations of production; industrialization and urbanization; the privileging of empirical science ... state bureaucratization ... and the advent of mass politics.[8]

If modernization refers to specific processes, modernity is an emancipatory project, a vision for socio-political and cultural organization. It is a concept rooted in philosophical explorations,[9] but also embedded in political movements and, more diffusely, in social constructs and expectations. Modernity is harder to locate than modernization. It is, following Miller, "a state that is always achievable, but always already deferred,"[10] a perpetually receding horizon of social progress, development, and emancipation. But modernity is also realized in and by social exchanges. It is not only a receding horizon but also, at the same time, a socio-cultural reality that exists in relationships and mindsets, in the *present*.

This has implications for the discussion of architectural modernism as an agent of both modernity and modernization. Modernity as a project for material and economic development and socio-political emancipation is not necessarily tied up with the patterns of industrial capitalism and rational bureaucracy prevalent in Europe and North America. Miller proposes a "distinctively Latin American modernity" as imagined by the continent's intellectuals, artists, and politicians.

The Latin American project for modernity is less encumbered by binary oppositions between past and present, and it tempers technocracy and rationalism with "spiritual quest, solidarity, hospitality."[11] Brazilian modernism can be seen as uniquely connected to its context, since architects did not break with the past but looked to it as a source – for Richard Williams, Brazilian modernists even prefigure Kenneth Frampton's critical regionalism, "a modern architecture sensitive to place and context, tough, pragmatic and local."[12]

These distinctions help recast the conflicts that pervade Brazilian modernist architecture in different terms. Modernization was and has been incomplete, uneven, and in many ways deficient in Brazil when compared to Europe or North America. But this incipient modernization did not preclude the development of a modern consciousness, of modernity as a project and as a mindset. The role of modernism is magnified in this understanding of modernity, as artistic and architectural concepts and designs provide a path of their own to socio-cultural and material transformations. Brazilian modernism – despite being heavily and often directly influenced by European and later North American sources – can be understood as a proactive set of initiatives that were often aware of the gaps between material realities and social goals, and which sought to magnify the role of art, design, and intellectual life in the construction of a modern (if not always fully modernized) society.

Ambiguous modernism: the Modernist House

Ukrainian-born émigré Gregori Warchavchik is often, if not unanimously, credited with pioneering architectural modernism in Brazil by building what is considered the first modernist house in the country – the house on Rua Santa Cruz – and publishing the earliest texts on modernist architecture in Brazil, starting in 1925.[13] For all the recognition of Warchavchik's contribution, his work occupies a delicate position in accounts of Brazilian architecture. Warchavchik was downplayed in publications about Brazilian modernism, including the *Brazil Builds* book and exhibition.[14] His role was de-emphasized or criticized by Brazilian architects and historians such as Lucio Costa and Carlos Lemos.[15] Warchavchik's work was so underestimated that a later slew of scholars, from Geraldo Ferraz in 1965 to José Lira in 2007, felt compelled to correct the injustice by demonstrating the value of his production and analyzing the omissions and biases of historians and critics.[16]

The criticism leveled at Warchavchik is twofold. On the one hand, Warchavchik is accused of not being modernist enough, of putting forth a stage-set version of modernism more preoccupied with form and style than with the "substance" of materials, technologies, and volume.[17] His modernism is seen as inauthentic, a watered-down version when compared with the "authentic seeds" planted by the "creative genius" of Le Corbusier in his 1937 visit to the country.[18] On the other hand, Warchavchik is chided for not being Brazilian enough, for lacking a connection with the "national genius" that expressed itself in Oscar Niemeyer and produced the "unique visage" of Brazilian architecture.[19]

His starkly geometric, bare-surfaced white houses too greatly resembled European modernism to make an impression on authors such as Philip Goodwin and Henrique Mindlin, who looked to distinguish Brazil's contributions in the earliest surveys of Brazilian modernism.[20]

Warchavchik arrived in Brazil in 1923.[21] After studying architecture in Odessa, he worked in Italy for Marcello Piacentini, one of the most influential architects in the Fascist regime. Warchavchik studied the novel developments in technique and design in Europe, but under Piacentini he did not practice an unbridled modernism. His move to Brazil unfolded new possibilities: rapid urban growth created unprecedented demand for building, and the professional milieu was less established, offering more freedom to young architects. It is easy to imagine, as Ferraz does, the newly arrived Warchavchik as a kind of fresh emissary of modernism, "bringing his contribution to the new world."[22]

In a way Warchavchik might have arrived too early. Modernist architecture in Brazil lagged behind arts and literature. In the 1910s and 1920s, writers and artists experimented with novel techniques and subject matter, drawing from European avant-gardes and from a search for national identity.[23] These artists coalesced in collaborative groups, putting forth publications, exhibitions, and events. Despite inner conflicts and dissension, artists and writers displayed a self-awareness of content and purpose, joined in a multifarious *Movimento Modernista* (modernist movement). Through intellectual debates and interactions with the political and economic élites that patronized them, the *modernistas* were forced to hone their positions, justify their aesthetic decisions, and clarify their artistic and social mission. This provided a convergence of efforts and principles, however provisional, that in the 1910s and early 1920s was still lacking in architectural circles.[24] In the early twentieth century, the most significant attempt to break with architectural tradition was a relatively circumscribed Neo-Colonial movement, which revisited Portuguese colonial architecture as a source instead of Beaux-Arts principles.[25]

Warchavchik intended his buildings and texts to bring about social and spatial change, to go beyond themselves and carry out a "modernist mission." Despite his self-consciousness, his first initiatives were isolated both from a wider architectural movement (which did not exist at the time) and from the literary and artistic movement, which by then had considerable impact. Although Warchavchik established relationships and collaborations with modernist artists and intellectuals,[26] he was never a central figure in the *Movimento Modernista*. This isolation might partly explain the less bombastic quality of Warchavchik's individual contributions not only with relation to the artistic and literary output of the 1920s, but also in comparison with the later, louder architectural movement that gathered around Lucio Costa in the 1930s in Rio de Janeiro.[27]

When Warchavchik conceived his own house on Rua Santa Cruz, he defined his professional ideals as the search for a "rational" and "logic" architecture, which did not succumb to formalism or style, but expressed the tenets of its own time. These tenets were associated with industrialization, telecommunications, and the "constructive material of our era," reinforced concrete.[28] Warchavchik subscribed not only to principles of European modernism culled from Gropius, Le Corbusier and Mies van der Rohe, but also to principles of European modernization. In doing so he set himself up for an inevitable clash with the less modernized conditions of production in Brazil, but a clash in many ways subtle and for this reason all the more ambiguous. The contradictions some critics perceive in Warchavchik's architecture pervaded material, social, and cultural structures in Brazil. Warchavchik's work did not create these contradictions, but made them tangible, and in doing so, however inadvertently, provided us with a magnifying lens onto particular conflicts of a broader historical context. These conflicts were part and parcel of processes of modernization and visions of modernity in a country marked by a colonial past and by ongoing relationships of economic and political dependency on Europe and North America.

Most of Brazil remained underdeveloped by European standards: rural, technologically backward, and dominated by conservative political and cultural values. But Warchavchik settled in São Paulo, which was by then a rapidly growing city, experiencing industrialization, financial growth, and demographic explosion.[29] If São Paulo could not compare to New York, London, or Berlin at the time, it nonetheless changed at ever-rising speed, and presented distinctive signs of modern cosmopolitanism: high-rise buildings, traffic, crowds, factories, telegraph lines, lively commerce, electric lights, nightlife, immigration. Warchavchik arrived at the rise of the modernization tide. In hindsight it is easy to point out that the tide did not quite sweep the whole country, but at the time it might have appeared simply as *nascent* as opposed to *insufficient*. And Warchavchik was not alone in his perspective. His vision of a machine-age architecture was in synch with the sensibilities of the local avant-garde. The writers and artists of the *Movimento Modernista* focused insistently on the kaleidoscopic experience of modernization as representative of their place and time: looming skyscrapers, honking automobiles, and throngs of strangers of different classes, ethnicities, and cultural backgrounds.[30]

Nonetheless, the proposal for modernism articulated in Warchavchik's texts, starting with the inaugural manifesto "Acerca da Arquitetura Moderna" (On Modern Architecture), published in 1925, appears to historian Renato Fiore as an import from Europe, with little concern for local realities.[31] Fiore implies a gap between Europe and Brazil, with both modernism and modernity defined by European standards and thus always already inadequate in the Brazilian context. José Lira suggests a more nuanced reading. Lira notes that Warchavchik spent his first years in Brazil working for a large-scale developing company; this was his first direct contact with Taylorized systems of construction. Lira argues that this experience informed Warchavchik's conception of a mechanized modernism – indeed, his hope for a widespread modernist architecture of the industrial age – more than European paradigms. At the beginning of the century Warchavchik and many other intellectuals, artists, politicians, and entrepreneurs in Brazil saw themselves at the forefront of a sea-change that seemed promising and potentially boundless. Warchavchik did not develop his modernist theory and practice in a vacuum, "without modernity," but *in dialogue* with a nascent modernization, which his work could help carry out.

But in the promisingly modern city of São Paulo, as Warchavchik found out when he started to build his house on Rua Santa Cruz (Figure 1), it was much cheaper and easier to procure traditional materials and techniques.[32] He put it simply: "In São Paulo ... concrete is expensive and bricks are cheap."[33] The local labor force was familiar with masonry, wood, and ceramic tiles, and most elements were custom-made on site. Warchavchik could not build a reinforced-concrete structure, but had to use load-bearing masonry walls. He could not find a wide range of industrial products such as handles, frames, mullions, and other fixtures; the few products he found featured traditional designs. Although in his writing he called for an architecture of the industrial age, for his modernist house he had to commission custom-built components. Far from the clean assembly process promised by standardization, Warchavchik had to perform the role of master builder, supervising the local workers and teaching them how to build more efficiently.[34]

Warchavchik's adaptations were not immediately perceived as shortcomings. The house made the news in São Paulo, and stood out for its strikingly unadorned, abstract composition as an example of forward-thinking architecture that would pave the way for the future city.[35] Soon, however, reinforced concrete became more easily available – Warchavchik himself used it in subsequent buildings. In the 1930s and 1940s, the material was employed with increasing exuberance by Brazilian architects, from the massive pilotis of the Ministry of Health and Education to the sinuous shells and canopies of the Pampulha complex.

Figure 1
Gregori Warchavchik, House on Rua Santa Cruz, 1927. Courtesy of Warchavchik Family Archive.

Compared with these later developments, it was easy for critics such as Carlos Lemos to read Warchavchik's technical adaptations as fatal flaws: "Warchavchik's first house is not quite a specimen of Modern architecture. The house on Rua Santa Cruz was made of traditional brick masonry, its extremely ordinary wooden floors nailed to wood beams, its roofing made of vulgar ceramic tiles ...".[36]

Lemos's verdict is symptomatic of Warchavchik's contested space in narratives of Brazilian Modernism. Warchavchik was not modern enough because of the "incongruity between aesthetics and constructive technique."[37] Lemos was invested in creating a structurally sound narrative for Brazilian modernism, which meant, among other things, asserting parity with Europe. In this light, Warchavchik's effort seemed at best a proto-modernism that simply prefigured, but did not quite prepare the ground for, the supposedly true modernism of the Ministry of Health and Education, the Pampulha complex, and Brasília.[38] For Lemos, the use of traditional materials irrevocably *compromised* the building's modernist aspirations.

Warchavchik was aware of the discrepancy between his modernist principles and their built results. He explained this by pointing out that concrete in Europe and the United States became popular in part for economic reasons: "In France, Germany and the United States, bricks and ceramic tiles are expensive, while concrete is attractively priced. Thus the aesthetic-economic theories of Le Corbusier and Gropius are justified."[39] If modernist principles called for logic, economy, rationalism, and pragmatism, it seemed only logical to "employ materials that abound in the region where one builds."[40] As I mentioned earlier, Warchavchik had first defined concrete as the quintessential modern substance. Now, however, he questioned its necessity and inevitability. What made concrete, already used by the Romans, essentially modern? Why could not other materials, such as wood and ceramic bricks, undergo radical developments and be seen as modern too? With his disclaimer, Warchavchik laid bare the arbitrariness of concrete as a sign of modernism.

Critics were also bothered because Warchavchik's architecture seemed uncomfortably, although not obviously, formalist. His spare, straight lines were not blatantly personal. But Warchavchik's refusal to express conventional materials through conventional forms drew attention to the clean, minimalist lines of modernism as a formal choice. Warchavchik defended his design because simple cubic forms "produce work that, in its lines at least, in its conception, corresponds to the present time."[41] We can understand "lines" and "conception" here largely as "form." This preoccupation with aesthetics struck critics such as Lemos as a departure from supposedly true ideals of modernism such as technique, economy, or social causes. But modernist architecture never did away with formal concerns, even if it often attempted to legitimize them with reference to function, technique, or volume.

The emphasis on form is related to the programmatic character of Warchavchik's architecture. His designs had a didactic, demonstrative intent – each building a speech act in his larger architectural discourse. Warchavchik took advantage of the public interface of architecture, the many forms of propagation of design principles: news stories in daily papers, programmatic texts, and the display of buildings in the cityscape. In this connection between architecture and media he can be seen as entirely modern, in tune with new forms of production and circulation of ideas, just as his contemporaries in Europe – for instance, Le Corbusier.[42] Warchavchik's next building, the house on Rua Itápolis (1930), soon nicknamed Casa Modernista (Modernist House),[43] was conceived as an exhibition house to showcase the new architecture in integration with art and design – it was set up with modernist artworks and furniture, surrounded by modernist landscaping, and the bookshelves were filled with works by modernist writers.

The house on Rua Itápolis was a clear declarative gesture to propagate modernist principles. So was Warchavchik's house on Rua Santa Cruz, which conveyed his vision for a new architecture through *forms* rather than constructive techniques or materials.[44] Warchavchik's emphasis on the modernism of his building was a rhetorical strategy comparable to the literature of the *Movimento Modernista*. Writers and artists were forceful and hyperbolic, depicting a much more modern São Paulo than the one we might glean from historical records. This was an expression of the visionary and transformative mission of modernism, aimed at bringing about new social relations, cultural values, and material realities – modernism as the *harbinger* of modernity.

The house on Rua Santa Cruz is ambiguous in other ways. The building looks different depending on the side. The more public side, facing Rua Santa Cruz, is strikingly simple: a symmetrical, stepped white cubic façade punched by metal-framed windows, with no cornice, moldings, or ornaments. On the ground floor, large windows wrap around the corners. This was possibly the first instance of corner windows in Brazil;[45] their transparency, airiness, and structural daring were quite novel. The gardens were landscaped by Warchavchik's wife, Mina, who departed from the French tradition prevalent at the time and set a free-form and exuberant arrangement of native plants. She included cacti which, placed against the white backdrop of the house, appeared sculptural and abstract. The more private side of the house, however, is closer to the domestic architecture of São Paulo, and to colonial Brazilian architecture in general, "the vernacular architecture of the *casa grande*"[46] (Figure 2). It has a sloping roof covered with ceramic tiles, hidden and invisible on the front. The porch with slender columns is also a common feature of Brazilian homes. Coupled with the sprawling garden that spreads on all sides of the very large plot, the private side of the house is reminiscent of farmhouses, evoking an atavistic, pre-modern rural setting.

The plan is also similar to the layout of traditional Brazilian houses (Figures 3 and 4). Restricted by the masonry walls, the plan is a sequence of boxy rooms with clearly divided functions. On the ground floor, the main entrance leads to a conventional vestibule, and separate rooms fan out for the office, living room, and dining room. There is no free plan, no seamless flow of spaces in either plan or section. A stairway in the central hallway leads to the upper floor, where the bedrooms are located. Functional divisions were all conventional, as

Figure 2
**Gregori Warchavchik,
House on Rua Santa
Cruz, 1927. Courtesy of
Warchavchik Family
Archive.**

Figure 3
**Gregori Warchavchik,
House on Rua Santa
Cruz, 1927, ground
floor. Courtesy of
Warchavchik Family
Archive.
St = Studio
En = Entrance
J = Dining room
L = Living room
T = Terrace
De = Storage
C = Kitchen
Cp = Pantry**

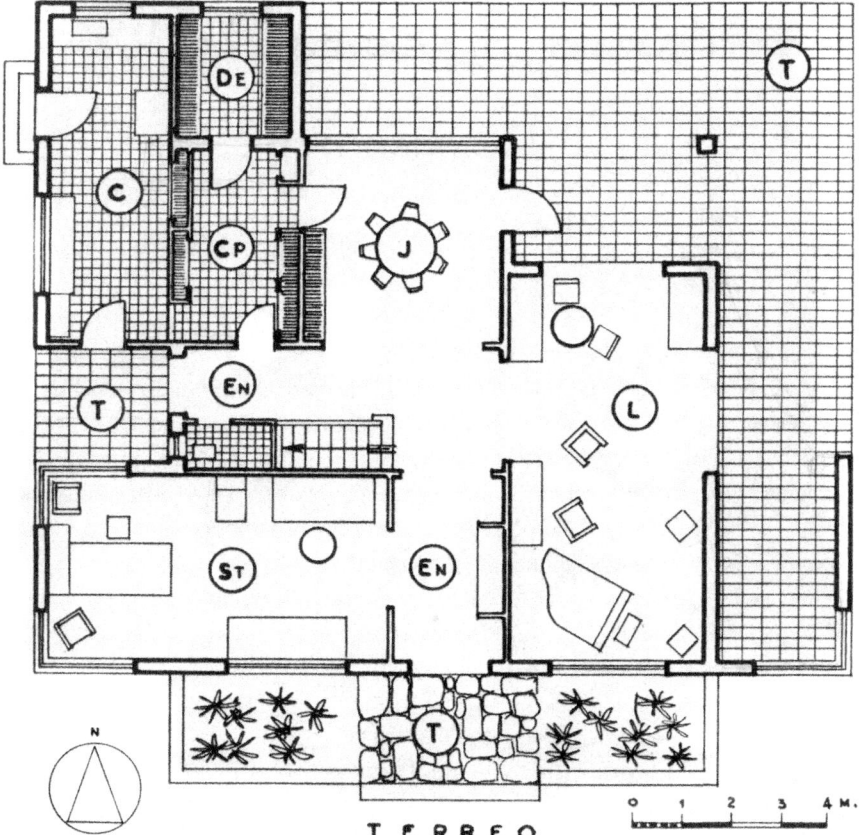

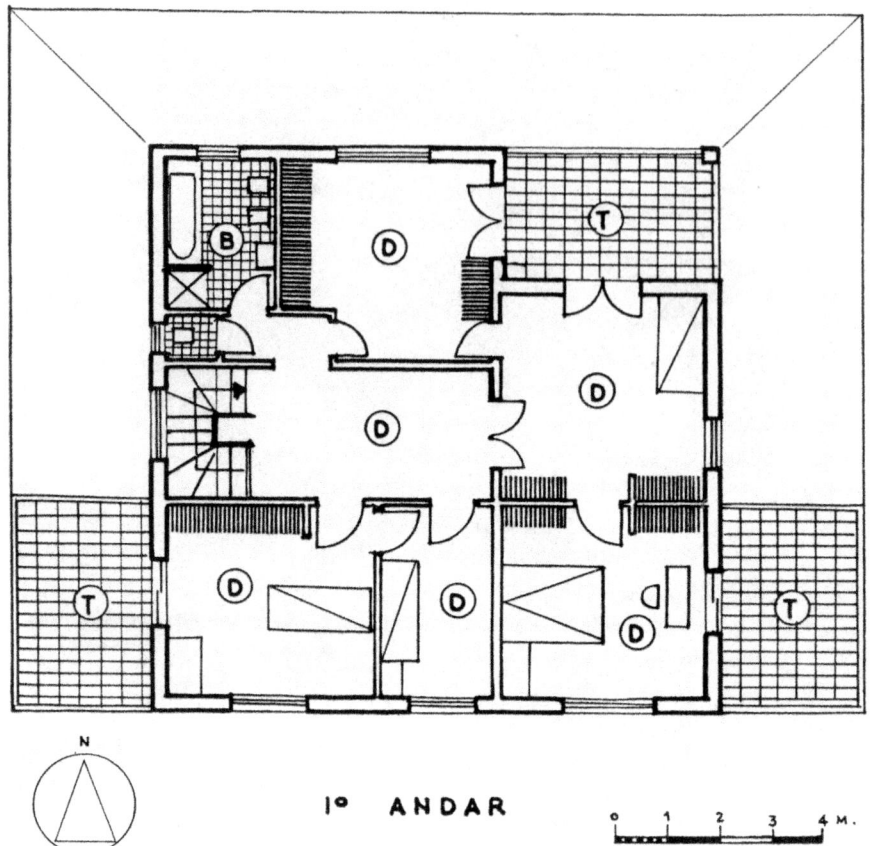

I° ANDAR

was the separation and hierarchy between public and private uses (living and sleeping), with service areas (kitchen, pantry) set apart and pushed to the back. Lemos characterized the plan, pejoratively, as "absolutely normal and traditional."[47] If the blueprints appear so, the experiential effect of Warchavchik's clear, simple arrangement is visually and spatially integrated, thanks to the diffuse light filtered by the windows and porch, the wide circulation spaces, and the generous openings and doorways between rooms, in addition to clean-lined furnishings and details (Figure 5). The overall character is airier and sparser than traditional houses. Inside and out, the house combines modernist and traditional elements, Brazilian and international influences.

The evocation of Brazilian spaces did not go unnoticed by visitors, including Le Corbusier – who noted the adaptation of modern principles to Brazil's tropical landscape – and Brazilian educator Anísio Teixeira, who remarked: "Warchavchik is Russian [sic], yet never have I had a stronger impression of the Brazilian house ... than when I visited his home."[48]

Soon, however, the house did not look Brazilian enough. The 1930s saw the development of the so-called Escola Carioca (Rio School), a prolific group of young architects led by Lucio Costa, and including Oscar Niemeyer, Affonso

Figure 5
**Gregori Warchavchik,
House on Rua Santa
Cruz, 1927, view from
main hall, ground floor.
Courtesy of
Warchavchik Family
Archive.**

Figure 5
**Gregori Warchavchik,
House on Rua Santa
Cruz, 1927, view from
main hall, ground floor.
Courtesy of
Warchavchik Family
Archive.**

Eduardo Reidy, and the Roberto brothers. Their production was blatantly modern: they made ample use of reinforced concrete in large, daring structures, from high-rises to airport buildings; they used the free plan, pilotis, glazing, free façades, and blended inside and outside in flowing and integrated spaces. But they were also overtly Brazilian. They used local stones for cladding; adapted colonial elements such as the *muxarabi* (brought by the Portuguese, in turn influenced by Moorish architecture) into pre-cast concrete grilles, pergolas, and *brise-soleil*; and incorporated Brazilian imagery in colorful murals and mosaics by modernist artists. Buildings such as the Ministry of Health and Education, the Pampulha Complex, and the Brazilian Pavilion in the 1939 New York World's Fair displayed a curvilinear, gestural aesthetics of sweeping curves, imaginative structural supports, and organic compositions.

These buildings drew attention to what appeared as a uniquely Brazilian language, and were privileged as the country's prime expression of modernism in contemporary publications and subsequent histories of architecture. Warchavchik's subtle mix of modernist and traditional elements paled in comparison. As Carlos Martins puts it, the critical reception of Warchavchik's work was "marked by the difficulty of placing him within the narrative thread that prioritizes the Brazilian character of modern architecture developed in the key instances of the Ministry [of Health and Education] and of Pampulha."[49]

The successive and often contradictory perceptions of the house on Rua Santa Cruz outlined above suggest not only a change in context and perspective on the part of critics – how the house appeared in the late 1920s, when it was first built, as opposed to the late 1940s and 1950s, when the first surveys on Brazilian architecture were published – but also a kind of conceptual lability that resides in the house itself. Such a slippery object does not lend itself well to clear-cut pronouncements about what is Brazilian and what is modernist. But the house is not an odd building out. Its contradictions were present in Brazilian society in general, and in the modernist endeavor that attempted to develop and overhaul the country. The heroic period of Brazilian modernism – from the late 1930s to the inauguration of Brasília in 1960 – merely kept these contradictions latent, repressed under the smoothed-out surfaces of concrete shells and high-rises.

Developmentalism

Warchavchik's house on Rua Santa Cruz is in many ways a limited example – an architect's house, a bourgeois residence. But the challenges faced by the architect and the ambiguities of the house raise questions relevant to larger socio-economic realities: the country's incipient modernization, the search for appropriate solutions to the Brazilian context, and the definition of what a Brazilian modernity should look like (and how it could be achieved). In the 1920s and early 1930s Brazil was under the rule of an oligarchy of landowners. The country grappled with severe social, cultural, and material disparities stemming from colonialism and slavery, and its development was hampered by dependency on foreign capital and industries. Growing discontent with the old, corrupt Republic culminated in a political revolution and the creation of the Estado Novo (New State), a centralized, authoritarian regime that promoted state-led industrialization and a modern bureaucracy.[50]

The top-down modernization of the country encompassed the creation of new social, cultural, and political programs, and the investment in physical infrastructure. One of the first and most visible architectural commissions of the new government was the Ministry of Health and Education. This reinforced-concrete Cartesian slab demonstrated the potential and power of Brazil through its monumental scale, construction materials, and innovative spaces. There were no glaring contradictions, just a slick fusion of Corbusian Modernism and local adaptations such as murals and gardens. The Ministry is often brandished as proof of the originality and inventiveness of Brazilian modernism, with its mix of local and universal, ornament and structure, organic curves and rational lines.[51] This building was a proud affirmation not only of modernist ideals, but also of their success.

For the next two decades the same mindset persisted despite political changes, upheaval, and the reverberations of World War II. The politics of developmentalism – intensive industrialization promoted by the government with the goal of developing social and economic structures in a short time – reached its peak with the presidency of Juscelino Kubitschek, whose motto was "Fifty years in five."[52] Kubitschek continued to use modernist architecture to build the modern country, not only by creating infrastructure and an industrial base, but also by projecting a confident national image through the buildings and urban spaces of the new capital, Brasília. Government policies promoted modernization according to European and, increasingly, North American standards of industrialization, technology, and finance.

Developmentalism boosted the country's economy, but development was uneven. On a national scale, modernization and economic growth were concentrated in larger cities in the south and southeast, such as Rio de Janeiro and São Paulo, while large swaths of the country remained bereft of resources. The pattern of uneven development was repeated within the large urban centers, with small pockets of wealth coexisting with poor areas. The inadequacy of modernization standards imported from global centers of capitalism was revealed in urban, economic, and labor practices that deepened social disparities. As Pedro Arantes notes, Brazilian "capitalism, based on severe social inequality, low wages, and the productive combination of backwardness and modernization, did not rely on the same logic of incorporation" of low-income classes into the consumer market as Europe and North America. Developmentalist policies "excluded a large contingent of workers from the benefits of modernization."[53]

This was clear in the construction of Brasília, as Arantes argues: "The construction of an entirely new capital city in the uninhabited interior of the country, undertaken on an unprecedented scale, starkly illustrated the enormous contrast between modernist design and outdated and unsafe methods of production."[54]

The city's futuristic layout embodied a promise of modernity that turned out, in many ways, to be an empty symbol. The shortcomings of an inadequate modernization were visible for all to see, as a kind of return of the repressed, in the unplanned satellite cities of Brasília. Similarly, in large cities such as São Paulo and Rio, which had become poles of massive migration and employment opportunities, the inadequacies of modernization became visible in the form of growing *favelas*, slums, and homelessness.

Instead of the emancipated, developed, just society promised by visions of modernity, the incomplete modernization of Brazil relied on labor exploitation and the economic and political exclusion of large sectors of society. The attempt at modernizing Brazil through developmentalism, with which modernism was complicit, did not engender functional environments and emancipated social realities. Utopian visions such as Brasília, or the Pedregulho Residential Complex in Rio – an ambitious representative of the Carioca School, which provided a novel housing design with a civilizing mission – began to crack under the pressure of Brazil's mounting social problems.[55] Modernism had its share of the burden: "The masses were excluded not only from citizenship rights, but also from design."[56]

Ambivalent modernism: the Museum of Art

Lina Bo Bardi began practicing architecture in Brazil shortly before these social contradictions erupted and turned the tide of optimistic modernization. Bo Bardi arrived in Brazil in 1946. Like Warchavchik, she was an immigrant – born in Italy, she had also worked as a designer and draughtsman in the Fascist era, when she was close to the Rationalists. Unlike Warchavchik, she spent the war in Italy. Her arrival in Brazil was thus mediated by two factors: one, the different stage of modernization in the country (nascent and promising in the 1920s, established and increasingly problematic in the mid-century); two, the first-hand experience of war and its aftermath. While Warchavchik's adaptations to local reality created ambiguities that inadvertently function as points of criticism, Bo Bardi's architecture became explicitly and intentionally critical, revealing the contradictions of modernization and modernism.

Bo Bardi's work has garnered plenty of attention in Brazil and abroad, but almost as a parallel and unique development, a cult following of sorts, leading Esther da Costa Meyer to lament that "Despite the extraordinary oeuvre she has left behind, Bo Bardi has not gained the recognition she deserves in surveys on Brazilian architecture, with their perennial focus on Oscar Niemeyer, Lúcio Costa, and Affonso Eduardo Reidy."[57]

Bo Bardi's work is too quirky and whimsical to fit into the canon of Brazilian modernism; although her influence and prominence in the country are quite strong, her trajectory remains singular. If Warchavchik is an uneasy starting point for an account of Brazilian modernism, Bo Bardi is a suitably uneasy ending. As a woman and an immigrant, Bo Bardi did not enjoy immediate professional integration, even if she and her husband, curator Pietro Maria Bardi, were soon socially integrated into the country's economic and cultural élites. In her first years in Brazil Bo Bardi designed jewelry, clothes, and furniture; her first building was her own house, known as the Casa de Vidro (Glass House), built in 1951.

The new MASP building was Bo Bardi's next architectural commission after the Glass House. Pietro Bardi was the director of the MASP, and Lina had designed the interior of the museum's temporary headquarters in downtown São Paulo in 1947. In 1957 the rapidly growing institution commissioned new headquarters on Avenida Paulista, a southward axis of urban and economic growth. A canyon of tall modernist slabs was rising along the avenue: banks and financial institutions, corporate headquarters and office buildings, apartments and movie theaters.[58] The site for the MASP was a prime spot at the center of what became São Paulo's financial hub. The Avenida Paulista was a showcase of the modernist cityscape, and of postwar ideals of financial and corporate modernization. The MASP could be seen as the avenue's cultural validation. Backed by Brazilian businessman Assis Chateaubriand, Pietro Bardi assembled a world-class collection of works; the museum was proof of the successful and civilizing mission of Brazil's modernization. In many ways Bo Bardi's architectural design reaffirmed this through the use of modernist language, materials, and technology (Figure 6). In other ways, though, the design challenged both its architectural principles, and the social and cultural values behind its program.

Even before the unveiling of the building, all attention was focused on its groundbreaking structure. The galleries were contained in a glass-and-concrete box 26 feet above ground, hanging from two parallel beams, each supported by

only two pillars more than 230 feet apart. Chief engineer José Carlos de Figueiredo Ferraz, a central figure in Brazilian modernism, defined the task of designing the structure as no less than "utopian," a defiance of "classical concepts of safety and stability."[59] In a lecture in 1993, the engineer recalled how Bo Bardi herself stood in apprehension and awe when the scaffolding was removed and the structure was left standing by itself.[60]

Figueiredo Ferraz used a method for pre-stressed reinforced concrete that he had developed a few years earlier. He showcased the new technique on the building site, with the presence of São Paulo's mayor, at a photo op that celebrated the structural prowess (Figure 7). The public celebration of the technological achievement fitted in with the narrative of a heroic Brazilian modernism at the height of developmentalism − by that time Brasília was a monumental construction site. In this context, it may be easier to understand why the reception of the museum focused so starkly on its structure. It is also helpful to consider that the generation of architects practicing in the 1940s and 1950s had been strongly oriented towards engineering (many architectural schools in Brazil were originally created as departments in engineering or polytechnic schools).[61] Even Niemeyer's curvy designs were as much obsessed with the properties of poured concrete as they were with organic forms.

The MASP structure, however, was not purely or mainly an exercise in technical daring. The structural solution had to do with site restrictions, and with Bo Bardi's pursuit of a free and open public space, as I explain below. The building restrictions were related to the setting. The site is located in the middle of the

Avenida Paulista, at the point where the ridge where the avenue is built is intercepted by a valley. Since it overlooks the open valley, the site affords a vast, spectacular view of the city towards downtown. A building law required the preservation of this view – quite a feat considering the limited area of the site and the program of the museum.[62] Bo Bardi's solution was to divide the program in two massive, distinct volumes, burying the lower floors into the sloping ground and suspending the upper galleries over the avenue, leaving a cavernous gap in between (Figure 6). This gap is in effect a covered plaza open on all sides, unobstructed by structural elements, fully integrating the avenue with a belvedere overlooking the valley. The museum galleries hover over this space, supported only by four large piers. But the museum's architectural contributions go far beyond the structure, and in these contributions Bo Bardi starts to break away not only from functionalist and rationalist rigidity, but also from the social, cultural, and labor relations implied by the museum. Bo Bardi's critical "interventions" include an innovative display system for two-dimensional works; the integration of the museum's interior with the surrounding city; the public and open character of the covered plaza; and the use of color and texture.

The museum's main galleries were conceived as free, open spaces fully encased by glass. Artworks were to be arranged freely in space, unencumbered by walls or by any sequence of smaller spatial divisions. Two-dimensional works such as paintings and prints were sandwiched between two panes of glass set in a block of concrete. Bo Bardi conceived the displays as "crystal easels" that would present a painting closest to its conditions of production, "because a painting is born in the air, on an easel."[63] She clarified her intention as a democratizing, demystifying gesture: "my intention was to destroy the aura around a museum, to present the artwork as labor, as the vision of a labor within the reach of all."[64] Evoking the production of art as labor would bring each artwork closer to the viewer as a historically produced object, as opposed to a relic. It would display the creation of art as an accessible and potentially democratic process, as the emphasis on labor could make art comparable (if not equal) to other processes of form-making, from construction to popular crafts.[65]

The free-standing displays were arranged on the gallery floor so that visitors could walk around them and move freely in all directions; there was no prescribed path from artwork to artwork. Bo Bardi broke with hierarchical or sequential exhibition strategies. Visitors should build their own path, and each visit or itinerary could create new and unexpected connections. The information on each artwork was displayed on the back of the glass encasing, so that the first encounter with the works would be unmediated by explanations or categories. The displays also enhanced the perception and use of the space, as the body was "forced" to make decisions about where and how to move instead of following a linear path. The overall effect of the display system in the galleries, the rectangles of glass sticking out of their concrete bases, echoed the materials and volumetric relationships of the cityscape outside. The city was indeed fully visible through the glazed façades of the galleries – both the view over downtown and the long perspective of the Avenida Paulista. Renato Anelli notes the democratizing, even iconoclastic effect of joining the gallery space with the city around it, creating a "transparent museum." Anelli calls the integration of gallery space and urban space a "miscegenation of images," which "goes against all the established rules of museum display." He continues:

> The transparency of the glazed façades and of the painting displays establish a continuity between artwork and everyday life, which bury any auratic pretensions and, according to the architect, take away "from the museum its church airs," which exclude humble folk.[66]

The impulse to open up the museum, to break the divisions between "high art" and "popular culture," was also present in the conception of the covered plaza. In Portuguese the space is commonly referred to as *vão livre do MASP* – the free span of MASP. This nomenclature is used popularly, as when people set up a meeting point, in news stories, and official materials (in the announcement of events, for instance).[67] The name is telling, as it refers to the empty or void quality of the space, more so than a functional or programmatic reference to a plaza or square (the official name is Trianon Terrace). Bo Bardi devised the *vão livre* as a flexible place for popular gatherings, concerts, markets, playgrounds, even a circus – in 1972, the popular Piolin Circus set up tent at the *vão livre* to celebrate the 50th anniversary of the Modern Art Week of 1922.[68] The *vão livre* expressed a plural view of culture, making room both for popular manifestations and traditional works of art, for a circus to be mounted under Raphael and Renoir. Bo Bardi was less interested in the constant praise for "the world's largest free-span with permanent loads and a flat ceiling" than in achieving what she called an "architecture of freedom." In her words:

> When the North American musician and poet John Cage came to São Paulo, driving along Paulista Avenue, he told the driver to stop in front of the MASP, got out of the car, and, walking from one side to the other of the belvedere, with his arms up in the air, he exclaimed: "This is the architecture of freedom!" I was used to receiving compliments for the "largest free-span in the world ..." and I thought that this great artist's assessment perhaps communicated what I wanted to express when I designed the MASP: the museum was a "nothing," a search for freedom, the elimination of obstacles, the capacity to be free in face of things.[69]

Bo Bardi's stress on freedom must be understood with relation to the political context of Brazil at the time of the museum's construction, which went from 1958 to 1968. When the project began, Brazil was under the presidency of Kubitschek. His term ended in 1961, and he was succeeded by an increasingly unstable but still democratic government until 1964, when a military coup instituted authoritarian rule in Brazil. The military dictatorship curtailed civil liberties, imposed censorship on artistic and cultural manifestations, and quenched any perceived or real dissent with terror and violence. As Zeuler Lima and Vera Pallamin argue, Bo Bardi "referred to this space as the space of freedom in reaction to the increasing censorship imposed by the military regime at that time."[70]

While she attempted to subvert political oppression with her unbounded public space, Bo Bardi ended up changing one important feature of the original design out of fear of political persecution. Early sketches for the museum, in 1958, called for the beams and pillars to be painted in "firetruck red." The idea was dropped and the building was left gray and unpainted until 1990, when it was finally painted red at Bo Bardi's request. According to architect Marcelo Ferraz, who worked closely with Bo Bardi in the 1980s, she later explained that she had dropped the idea for so long because she feared that the military dictatorship might interpret the red color as some sort of allusion to Communism. It was, after all, the Cold War era. Brazil's extreme-right dictatorship, aligned with and supported by the United States, saw Communism and left-wing politics as menacing; censorship and repression were particularly virulent towards perceived communists or sympathizers. Bo Bardi feared that the perceived association with Communism by the dictatorship could jeopardize the whole endeavor and even put her at risk.[71]

Bo Bardi herself was a liberal, but it is unlikely that she used the red color as a political symbol. Rather, her incorporation of color was related to the playful and whimsical quality of her architectural designs. She had already toyed with the idea before, in 1951, in her studies for the Museum of Art of São Vicente (not built). The São Vicente museum would also have been a glass box suspended by a red exoskeleton of columns and beams, built on a beach in the city of São Vicente. It was, like the MASP, an unusual take on a museum: a transparent, free-flowing space floating over the sand right next to the sea. The art inside would have merged with the natural landscape outside, and the museum would have been a seamless continuation of the beach, accessible via a long open stairway. Most urban beaches in Brazil are quintessential public spaces, used by different social classes for recreation and socialization; the museum would thus fulfill Bo Bardi's democratic goals and bring together art and leisure, high and low.[72]

Both in the São Vicente museum and in the MASP, the use of a primary color to highlight the structure was a bold gesture – the color was not confined to details, murals, or interiors, but rather was displayed prominently on the structure, the most technical and supposedly "rational" part of the building. The red structure signaled a move away from pure rationalism. The red was a subjective choice, more related to artistic creativity than to functional concerns. It was a painterly element, unabashedly vibrant, in contrast with the severe gray or neutral white of most contemporary buildings. The color contaminated the architectural object with non-architectural associations: painting, flatness, ornamentation; it drew attention to surface rather than volume. The shiny layer of paint that coated the modernist object also evoked associations with clothing and make-up appended to the body of the building. The red pillars and beams of the MASP broke the modernist rigidity of an otherwise severe concrete building.

Bo Bardi also went to great lengths to keep the irregular marks of the wooden formwork, not for aesthetic effect but as the imprint of construction labor. The building should not be a sleek product of the machine age, but rather reveal the human effort involved in its production. This social conscience was related not only to construction workers, but to craft in general. Bo Bardi made the case for sourcing design theory and practice in popular crafts, folk art, and recycled mass-produced objects – an aesthetics of roughness and improvisation, or "rudeness," as she put it.[73] The aesthetics of roughness was informed by her observation and experience in Brazil – in particular the years she spent in the northeast region, which was much less urban, industrialized, and modernized than São Paulo. There she explored popular culture, crafts, and historical architecture, and was impressed by the resourcefulness and creativity with which people made or recycled objects – an anonymous, popular, everyday design. When she returned to São Paulo and designed the MASP, her architecture was rougher and more concerned with social inclusion and democratization than before. As Da Costa Meyer argues, this was not a full-on rejection of modernism, but a complex interweaving of influences and impulses:

> It would be naïve … to see Bo Bardi's new direction as prompted exclusively by her experience in the Northeast. If she looked to the vernacular, she did so from a cosmopolitan perspective. MASP shows how attentive she was to contemporary trends in art and architecture;

the growing importance of concrete, bold use of color, and reliance on "poor" materials were not unrelated to experiments overseas. But Bo Bardi had gained enormously in self-confidence in the intervening years and did not need input from others to shape her vision. She was no longer content to design a European building on Brazilian soil.[74]

The ambivalent modernism of the MASP attempts to engender a more inclusive social environment in which art and design enable personal and social development and emancipation. The MASP contains the project of an alternative modernity attuned to Brazilian realities without fully turning its back on the international developments and influences that shaped modernism. It is possible to interpret the building in terms of the tensions mentioned at the outset of this text – tensions between center and periphery; industrialization and craft; the pursuit of modern concerns such as technology and "high art" on the one hand, and the struggle to develop basic social conditions such as economic and political justice on the other. The MASP does not solve these tensions; rather, it is structured around them, it exists at their intersection. And by making these tensions visible, the MASP provides subsidies for a critical and productive perspective.

Conclusion

The idea of a unique Latin American modernity should not be interpreted as a separate or alternative path. The many iterations of modernism across time and space are in dialogue with each other. Latin American modernism was not simply influenced by European or North American currents, but was generated by the tensions, exchanges, and adaptations between different geographical locations and cultural realities. The spread of modernism in Latin America is itself a function of the universalist and international tendencies of the movement. It must not have escaped the reader that both Bo Bardi and Warchavchik were immigrants. In this they were not unusual, and can be aligned with a host of notorious émigrés who helped spread modernism from Europe to other parts of the world. Nor were they exceptional in Brazil, where immigration from Italy and Eastern Europe was intense in the late 1800s and early 1900s. Their status as foreigners is not circumstantial; rather, it is connected to the development of modernism more broadly.

Raymond Williams notes in "The Metropolis and the Emergence of Modernism" that the modern metropolis was a novel and unstable environment marked by "strangeness and distance, indeed ... alienation." This strangeness can be understood from the perspective of newly arrived migrants and immigrants, and also from the perspective of local inhabitants confronted with a rapidly changing and diverse realm. Williams connects the intrinsic foreignness of the metropolis to the emergence of artistic and literary modernism:

> Liberated or breaking from their national or provincial cultures, placed in quite new relations to those other native languages or native visual

traditions, encountering … a novel and dynamic common environment from which many of the older forms were obviously distant, the artists and writers and thinkers of this phase found the only community available to them: a community of the medium; of their own practices.[75]

This assertion provides the framework for Williams to explain tenets of modernism such as the tendency towards abstraction and universalism, the connection to an emerging visual culture, the focus on the medium, the break with the past, the view of traditional language as "arbitrary," and the preoccupation with novelty and originality.[76] Modernism emerged precisely because of the international character of modern metropolises, and because of the web of foreign exchanges that passed through these sites.

Bo Bardi and Warchavchik responded to the complexity of Brazilian society from their viewpoint as cosmopolitan foreigners. They had experienced not only the progressive optimism of modernity, but also its destructive manifestations: political revolutions, World War I, anti-Semitism, Fascism, World War II. Their immigration to Brazil, while marked by the positive outlook of starting anew in a peaceful and welcoming country, was also prompted by necessity and survival, by the violence (or threat thereof) of modern Europe.[77] Their foreign perspective, therefore, might have afforded them a more critical or nuanced take on modernism and modernity than their Brazilian counterparts could have at the time. And as foreigners, they also approached the Brazilian context from a different standpoint, possibly less anxious about asserting parity with Europe or demonstrating signs of "genuine" Brazilianness. They might have been more open, for example, to recognizing where and how adaptations were necessary, taking into account local realities such as labor, available materials, economy, basic social needs, and cultural formation.

Questions of labor, for instance – manual labor, exploitation, social disparities, workers' rights, housing, and craft – appear in the work of Warchavchik as adaptation (custom-building), and in the work of Bo Bardi as critical reflection (the aesthetics of roughness, the tension between high and low). That these issues are generally and continuously relevant for Brazilian and Latin American architecture is evidenced by the practical and theoretical explorations of architects who, in the second half of the twentieth century, searched to redefine technology in terms of local materials and workforce (for instance, Eladio Dieste in Uruguay); who explored self-construction to address housing demands and urban problems (for example, Carlos Gonzalez Lobo in Mexico); or who attempted to revolutionize the building site as a way towards more just social relations (such as Sérgio Ferro, Rodrigo Lefèvre and Flavio Império in Brazil).[78] The changing context of the twenty-first century, with the benefit of hindsight, also transforms the meaning of earlier contributions. Warchavchik's house on Santa Cruz Rua, with its sourcing of available materials adequate to local conditions, was perceived as a compromise in the mid-twentieth century, whereas today it could be interpreted as an example of responsible sustainability.

The foreign, transplanted perspective of Warchavchik and Bo Bardi was neither inauthentic nor inappropriate; it was quintessentially modernist. The adaptations they made – adaptations of modernism to the local context, and adaptations of local elements to modernist principles – were part of the dynamic and constantly dislocated quality of modernism itself, even if these adjustments seemed to veer away from the canon or to result in "failures" or incongruities. Their production adumbrates possible paths towards a "distinctively Latin American modernity," as Nicola Miller put it, where both the definition of modernity and the tenets of modernism have to be rethought and qualified according to local realities.

Acknowledgements

I wish to thank architect Carlos Warchavchik and the Instituto Lina Bo and P. M. Bardi for the reproduction rights of the images used in this chapter.

Notes

1   Renato Ortiz, *A Moderna Tradição Brasileira* [The modern Brazilian tradition], São Paulo: Brasiliense, 1988, pp. 32–7.

2   Ramón Gutiérrez, "Arquitectura latinoamericana: Haciendo camino al andar" [Latin American architecture: The road is made by walking] in R. Gutiérrez (ed.), *Arquitectura latinoamericana en el siglo XX* [Latin American architecture in the twentieth century], Barcelona: Lunwerg Editores, 1998, pp. 20, 21, 24.

3   Mauro Guillén, "Modernism without Modernity: The Rise of Modernist Architecture in Mexico, Brazil, and Argentina, 1890–1940," 2004, *Latin American Research Review*, vol. 39, no. 2, p. 7.

4   See Randal Johnson's critical analysis of these views, especially his discussion of Renato Ortiz and Florestan Fernandes, in "Brazilian Modernism: An Idea Out of Place?" in A. L. Geist and J. B. Monléon (eds), *Modernism and Its Margins: Reinscribing Cultural Modernity from Spain and Latin America*, New York, London: Garland, 1999, pp. 188–9.

5   Gwendolyn Wright, "Building Global Modernisms," 2002, *Grey Room* 7, Spring, p. 125.

6   Brian McLaren proposes the idea of "ambivalent modernism" in his study on modernism and the Fascist Italian rule of Libya. McLaren identifies a tension between modernism and the preservation of local culture in the Italian colonial efforts with relation to tourism. Although the implications and meanings are very different from those in the MASP, the idea of ambivalence and opposing impulses within modernism seems especially resonant with colonial and post-colonial contexts. See McLaren, *Architecture and Tourism in Italian Colonial Libya: An Ambivalent Modernism*, Seattle, WA: University of Washington Press, 2006.

7   Nicola Miller, *Reinventing Latin America: Intellectuals Imagine the Future, 1900–1930*, New York: Palgrave Macmillan, 2008, p. 3.

8   Ibid., p. 4.

9   Jürgen Habermas, *The Philosophical Discourse of Modernity: Twelve Lectures*, Cambridge, Mass.: MIT Press, 1987, and *The Structural Transformation of the Public Sphere: An Inquiry into a Category of Bourgeois Society*, Cambridge, Mass.: MIT Press, 1989.

10   Miller, op. cit., p. 4.

11   Ibid., pp. 9, 18.

12   Richard Williams, *Brazil*, London: Reaktion, 2009, p. 40. For Frampton's discussion of critical regionalism see Kenneth Frampton, *Modern Architecture: A Critical History*, London: Thames and Hudson, 1992.

13   Carlos Martins, "Gregori Warchavchik: Combates pelo Futuro" [Gregori Warchavchik: Struggles for the future], in Carlos Martins (ed.), *Arquitetura do século XX e outros escritos* [Twentieth-century architecture and other writings], São Paulo: Cosac Naify, 2006, pp. 12–21.

14   Philip Goodwin, *Brazil Builds: Architecture New and Old*, New York: The Museum of Modern Art, 1943.

15   Martins, op. cit., pp. 13, 19.

16   Ibid.; Geraldo Ferraz, *Warchavchik e a Introdução da Nova Arquitetura no Brasil: 1925 a 1940* [Warchavchik and the introduction of the new architecture in Brazil], São Paulo: Museu de Arte de São Paulo, 1965; José Lira, "Ruptura e Construção: Gregori Warchavchik, 1917–1927" [Rupture and construction: Gregori Warchavchik, 1917–1927], in *Novos Estudos* [New studies], no. 78, July 2007, pp. 145–67; Agnaldo Farias, *Arquitetura Eclipsada: Notas sobre Arquitetura e História, a Propósito da Obra de Gregori Warchavchik, Introdutor da Arquitetura Moderna no Brasil* [Eclipsed architecture: Notes on architecture and history, with respect to Gregori Warchavchik's work], M.A. thesis, 1990.

17   Carlos Lemos, "Arquitetura Contemporânea" [Contemporary architecture], in Walter Zanini, *História Geral da Arte no Brasil* [A history of art in Brazil], Rio de Janeiro: Instituto Walter Moreira Salles, pp. 825–66.

18   Lúcio Costa, "Carta Depoimento" [Testimonial letter], in *Lúcio Costa: Registro de uma Vivência* [Lúcio Costa: Recorded experience], São Paulo: Empresa das Artes, 1995.

19   Ibid.

20   Goodwin, *Brazil Builds*; Henrique Mindlin, *Modern Architecture in Brazil*, Rio de Janeiro: Colibris, 1956.

21   Ferraz, op. cit., p. 20.

22   In the original: "o moço europeu que vinha trazer a sua contribuição ao novo mundo." In Ferraz, op. cit., p. 21. Ferraz uses the word "moço," which means "lad," perhaps connoting the energy of a young professional confident in his mission and in the new ideas of his time.

23   On the Brazilian modernist movement in arts and literature see among others: Aracy Amaral, *Artes Plásticas na Semana de 22: Subsídios para uma História da Renovação das Artes no Brasil* [Visual arts in the Week of 22: Subsidies for a history of the renovation of Brazilian art], São Paulo: Perspectiva, 1976; Jorge Schwartz, *Vanguarda e Cosmopolitismo na Década de 20: Oliverio Girondo e Oswald de Andrade* [Avant-garde and cosmopolitanism in the 1920s: Oliverio Girondo and Oswald de Andrade], São Paulo: Perspectiva, 1983; Jorge Schwartz, *Vanguardas Latino-Americanas: Polêmicas, Manifestos e Textos Críticos* [Latin American avant-gardes: Polemics, manifestoes, and critical texts], São Paulo: USP/Iluminuras, 1995; Maria Eugênia Boaventura, *22 por 22: a Semana de Arte Moderna vista pelos seus contemporâneos* [22 by 22: The Modern Art Week seen from its time], São Paulo: EDUSP, 2001; Mário da Silva Brito, *História do modernismo brasileiro: antecedentes da Semana de Arte Moderna* [History of Brazilian modernism: precedents for the Modern Art Week], Rio de Janeiro: Editora Civilização Brasileira, 1964.

24   Ferraz, op. cit., p. 21.

25   Joana Mello, *Ricardo Severo: Da Arqueologia Portuguesa à Arquitetura Brasileira* [Ricardo Severo: From Portuguese archaeology to Brazilian architecture], São Paulo: Annablume, 2007.

26   This happens when he gets the chance to publish in modernist publications, such as an interview entitled "Arquitetura Brasileira" [Brazilian architecture], in *Terra Roxa e Outras Terras* [Purple soil and other lands], 17 September 1926; and also when modernist writers recognize and address him in their texts – for example, Oswald de Andrade, "A Casa Modernista, o Pior Crítico do Mundo e Outras Considerações" [The modernist house: The worst critic in the world and other thoughts], originally published in *Diário da Noite* [Evening news] (São Paulo), July 1930; reprinted in *Arte em Revista* [Art in review] no. 4, 1980, p. 10; Mario de Andrade, "Exposição duma casa modernista" [Exhibition of a modernist house], originally published in *Diário Nacional* [National news] (São Paulo), April 5 1930; reprinted in *Arte em Revista* [Art in review] no. 4, 1980, pp. 7–8. Mario de Andrade and Oswald de Andrade were arguably the two main writers and spearheads

of Brazilian modernism in literature, arts, and culture. For discussions of their views on modernist architecture in general and on Warchavchik in particular, see Guilherme Wisnik, "Plástica e Anonimato: Modernidade e Tradição em Lucio Costa e Mário de Andrade" [Plastic and anonymity: Modernity and tradition in Lucio Costa and Mário de Andrade], in *Novos Estudos* [New studies], no. 79, 2007, pp. 169–93; and José Lira, "Localismo Crítico e Cosmopolitismo Arquitetônico" [Critical localism and architectonic cosmopolitanism], 1999, online, available: http://www. docomomo.org.br/seminario%203%20pdfs/subtema_A1F/Jose_tavares_lira.pdf (accessed 1 February 2010).

27 Martins, op. cit., p. 13.

28 Gregori Warchavchik, "Acerca da Arquitetura Moderna" [On Modern Architecture], in Martins, *Arquitetura do século XX*, pp. 34–6.

29 On São Paulo see Nicolau Sevcenko, *Orfeu extático na metrópole: São Paulo, sociedade e cultura nos frementes anos 20* [Extatic Orpheus in the metropolis: São Paulo, society and culture in the frantic 1920s], São Paulo: Companhia das Letras, 1992; Margareth da Silva Pereira, "Time of the Capitals: Rio de Janeiro and São Paulo: Words, Actors, and Plans," in Arturo Almandoz (ed.) *Planning Latin America's Capital Cities 1850–1950,* London: Routledge, 2002, pp. 75–108; Charles Perrone, "Performing São Paulo: Vanguard Representations of a Brazilian Cosmopolis," *Latin American Music Review,* vol. 23, no. 1, 2002, pp. 60–78.

30 Claude Lévi-Strauss depicts this emphasis on a rising modernization as a kind of cultural fixation with the new. For him, cities such as São Paulo, "with a very short evolutionary cycle," are "perpetually young, yet never healthy." Lévi-Strauss implies a pathological failure; he offers another approach to the contradictions of modernization in Brazil. In Lévi-Strauss, *Tristes Tropiques,* New York: Penguin, 1992, pp. 95–105. For examples of Modernist representations of São Paulo see works by Mario de Andrade, especially *Paulicea Desvairada* [Insane Paulicea], São Paulo: Casa Mayenca, 1922; *Contos novos* [New short stories], São Paulo: Livraria Martins Editora, 1947; *Amar, verbo intransitivo* [Love, intransitive verb, published in English as *Fraulein*], São Paulo: Livraria Martins Editora, 1944; and *Macunaima, o herói sem nenhum caráter* [Macunaíma, the hero without character, published in English as *Macunaíma*], Rio de Janeiro: Jose Olympio, 1937; and by Oswald de Andrade, such as *Serafim Ponte Grande*, Rio de Janeiro: Ariel Editora, 1933; the trilogy *Os condenados* [The damned], Porto Alegre: Livraria do Globo, 1941–1983; and *Memorias sentimentais de João Miramar* [Sentimental memoirs of João Miramar], São Paulo: Independencia, 1924.

31 Renato Fiore, "Warchavchik e o Manifesto de 1925" [Warchavchik and the 1925 Manifesto], *ArqTexto,* v. 2, 2002, p. 81.

32 My comments and images refer to the earlier design of the house, which Warchavchik altered in 1934.

33 Warchavchik, "Arquitetura do século XX," p. 67.

34 Ferraz, op. cit., p. 28.

35 See Ferraz, op. cit., p. 26, for excerpts and images from the original newspaper stories.

36 Carlos Lemos, "Os Três Pretensos Abridores de uma Porta Difícil" [The three supposed groundbreakers of a difficult path], in *Warchavchik, Pilon, Rino Levi: Três Momentos da Arquitetura Paulista* [Warchavchik, Pilon, Rino Levi: Three Moments of Architecture in São Paulo], ex. cat., São Paulo: Funarte, Museu Lasar Segall, 1983, p. 5.

37 Martins also notes that Lemos could not accept "the justifications offered by Warchavchik regarding local labor and technical difficulties; [Lemos] sees a purely formalist manifestation." In the original, "as justificativas de Warchavchik quanto às dificuldades técnicas e de mão-de-obra locais, vê aí uma clara manifestação formalista." Martins, op. cit., p. 19.

38 For accounts in English of these three works, along with other examples of Brazilian modernist architecture, see Valerie Fraser, *Building the New World: Studies in the Modern Architecture of Latin America,* London: Verso, 2000; Elisabetta Andreoli and Adrian Forty (eds), *Brazil's Modern Architecture,* London, New York: Phaidon, 2004; Zilah Quezado Deckker, *Brazil Built: The*

Architecture of the Modern Movement in Brazil, London, New York: Spon, 2001; and Lauro Cavalcanti, *When Brazil was Modern: Guide to Architecture, 1928–1960*, Princeton: Princeton University Press, 2003. Portuguese-language surveys include Hugo Segawa, *Arquiteturas no Brasil, 1900–1990* [Architectures in Brazil, 1900–1990], São Paulo: EDUSP, 1999, and Yves Bruand, *Arquitetura contemporânea no Brasil* [Contemporary architecture in Brazil], São Paulo: Perspectiva, 1981, among others.

39   Warchavchik, "Arquitetura do século XX," p. 67.

40   Ibid.

41   Ibid.

42   Beatriz Colomina, *Privacy and Publicity: Modern Architecture as Mass Media*, Cambridge, Mass.: MIT Press, 1994.

43   Both the house on Rua Santa Cruz and on Rua Itápolis are known as Casa Modernista. The House on Rua Itápolis received the moniker when it was opened to the public in 1930, because of its explicit association with the *Movimento Modernista*. The House on Rua Santa Cruz only began to be called Casa Modernista later.

44   As Valerie Fraser puts it, "propagandistic subterfuge." Fraser, *Building the New World*, p. 166.

45   Jacqueline Barnitz, *Twentieth-Century Art of Latin America*, Austin: University of Texas Press, 2001, p. 167.

46   Williams, *Brazil*, p. 34.

47   Lemos, op. cit., p. 5.

48   Le Corbusier's statements were published in the paper *Diário da Noite* [Evening news], November 30 1929; Teixeira was interviewed by the newspaper *A Tarde* [Afternoon news], October 1929. Both cited in Ferraz, op. cit., p. 27.

49   Martins, op. cit., p. 15.

50   Lucia Lippi Oliveira et al., *Estado novo: ideologia e poder* [*Estado novo*: Ideology and power], Rio de Janeiro: Zahar, 1982; José Augusto Ribeiro, *A era Vargas* [The Vargas era], Rio de Janeiro: Casa Jorge, 2001.

51   Valerie Fraser, "Cannibalizing Le Corbusier: The MES Gardens of Roberto Burle Marx," *Journal of the Society of Architectural Historians* 59, no. 2, 2000, pp. 180–193.

52   Juscelino Kubitschek, *Meu caminho para Brasília: [memórias]* [My road to Brasília: memoirs], Rio de Janeiro: Bloch, 1974–1978; Ronaldo Costa Couto, *Brasília Kubitschek de Oliveira* [Brasília Kubitschek de Oliveira], Rio de Janeiro: Record, 2001, p. 256; José William Vesentini, *A Capital da geopolítica* [The capital of geopolitics], São Paulo: Ática, 1986, p. 101.

53   Pedro Fiori Arantes, *Arquitetura nova: Sérgio Ferro, Flávio Império e Rodrigo Lefèvre, de Artigas aos mutirões* [New architecture: Sérgio Ferro, Flávio Império and Rodrigo Lefèvre, from Artigas to self-building], São Paulo: Editora 34, 2002, p. 35.

54   Pedro Fiori Arantes, "Reinventing the Building Site," in Andreoli and Forty (eds), *Brazil's Modern Architecture*, p. 174.

55   The Pedregulho complex was created to provide "not only housing, but also services and facilities to contribute to reeducate the habits and customs" of low-income civil servants. Many of these services, such as automated laundry rooms, failed for failing to recognize the cultural and economic realities of the inhabitants. See Lauro Cavalcanti, *Quando o Brasil era moderno: Guia de arquitetura 1928–1960* [When Brazil was modern: architecture guide, 1928–1960], Rio de Janeiro: Aeroplano, 2001, pp. 32, 35–6.

56   Arantes, *Arquitetura nova*, p. 36.

57   Esther da Costa Meyer, "After the Flood: Lina Bo Bardi's Glass House," in *Harvard Design Magazine*, no. 16, Winter/Spring 2002, online, available: http://www.gsd.harvard.edu/research/publications/hdm/back/16decosta_meyer.html (accessed 1 February 2010).

58   Marta Bogéa, *Two-Way Street: The Paulista Avenue, Flux and Counter-Flux of Modernity*, San Diego: San Diego State University Press, 1995.

59   Lecture, 1991, Museum of Art of São Paulo, promoted as part of the exhibition "50 years of the History of Brazilian Engineering." Cited in "José Carlos de Figueiredo Ferraz, 1971–1973," online, available: http://www.figueiredoferraz.com.br/empresa/midia/prefeitojosecarlosfigueiredoferraz.pdf (accessed 1 February 2010).

60   Round-table on the work of Lina Bo Bardi, 1993, Museum of Art of São Paulo, author's own notes.

61   Guillén, "Modernism without Modernity," 25.

62   Zeuler Lima and Vera Maria Pallamin, "Reinventing the Void: São Paulo's Museum of Art and Public Life along Avenida Paulista," in Clara Irazábal (ed.), *Ordinary Places, Extraordinary Events: Citizenship, Democracy and Public Space in Latin America*, New York: Routledge, 2008, p. 59.

63   Lina Bo Bardi, "Explicações sobre o Museu de Arte" [Explanations about the Museum of Art], in *O Estado de São Paulo*, April 5 1970, quoted in Renato Anelli, "O Museu de Arte de São Paulo, o Museu Transparente e a Dessacralização da Arte" [The Museum of Art of São Paulo, the transparent museum, and the desacralization of art], in *Arquitextos* 112, September 2009, online, available: http://www.vitruvius.com.br/arquitextos/arq112/arq112_01.asp (accessed 1 February 2010).

64   Ibid.

65   The original layout was changed in 1998 by architect Julio Neves, who presided over the institution from 1994 to 2008. Neves removed the crystal easels, blocked the glazed façade, and divided the galleries into a sequence of smaller, boxy rooms with walls on which to hang artworks. While discussing this case is outside the scope of this essay, it is worth noting that the changes to the MASP provide a further example of ongoing conflicts over visions of modernity and modernization. For instance, Neves invoked "world-class" museum standards when planning the changes. For a more detailed discussion, see Olivia de Oliveira, *Lina Bo Bardi: Obra construída* [Lina Bo Bardi: Built work], Barcelona: Editorial Gustavo Gili, 2002, pp. 11–19.

66   Anelli, "O Museu de Arte de São Paulo."

67   The space is also known as "vão do Masp." See Lima and Pallamin, op. cit., p. 60.

68   Lima and Pallamin, op. cit., p. 75.

69   *MASP: A cor da paixão pela arte* [MASP: The color of the passion for art], pamphlet, Suvinil/Glasurit/BASF, 1990.

70   Lima and Pallamin, op. cit., p. 60.

71   Personal email interview with architect Marcelo Ferraz, February 2005.

72   *Lina Bo Bardi*, São Paulo: Instituto Lina Bo e P. M. Bardi, 1996, pp. 90–3.

73   Lina Bo Bardi, *Tempos de grossura: o design no impasse*, São Paulo: Instituto Lina Bo e P. M. Bardi, 1994. The title can be translated as "Times of Rudeness: Design at an Impasse," or also "Times of Roughness."

74   Da Costa Meyer, op. cit.

75   Raymond Williams, *The Politics of Modernism*, London: Verso, 1989, p. 45.

76   Williams, op. cit., pp. 45–6.

77   According to José Lira, Warchavchik's position in Italy was increasingly complicated by his status as a Ukrainian Jew – a double liability under the Fascist government. See Lira, "Ruptura e Construção," pp. 152–3. Some scholars speculate that Lina Bo and Pietro Maria Bardi left war-torn Italy at least partly because of Pietro's former ties to the Fascist government. See Da Costa Meyer, op. cit.

78   Stanford Anderson, *Eladio Dieste: Innovation in Structural Art*, New York: Princeton Architectural Press, 2004; Eladio Dieste, *Eladio Dieste: La estructura cerámica* [Eladio Dieste: The ceramic structure], Bogotá: Escala, 1987; Arantes, *Arquitetura nova*; Sérgio Ferro, *Arquitetura e trabalho livre* [Architecture and free labor], São Paulo: Cosac Naify, 2006; Carlos González Lobo, *Vivienda y ciudad posibles* [Possible dwelling, possible city], Santa Fé de Bogotá, Colombia: Escala; México City: UNAM, 1999.

Chapter 3

Depoliticizing Group GAMMA: contesting modernism in Morocco

Aziza Chaouni

The study of Modernism in Morocco continues to employ a bifurcated paradigm that is overdetermined by political history. As a result, the modernist movement is fractured by the axis of 1956 into two disparate phenomena: the first, embedded in the colonial political discourse rooted on the legitimizing concept of "civilizing mission,"[1] the second expressing the modernizing aspirations of the newly independent Moroccan state. Such stress on political events leads to a misleading periodization, which implies a discursive as well as a formal disjuncture. Ultimately, possibilities of architectural continuity, legacy, and fertilization are veiled (Figure 1).

The rare instances in recent scholarship on Moroccan Modernism that acknowledge continuity are not free from distortion either. There, the relation of the post-independence architectural production to that of the colonial era is reduced to a mere elaboration; more specifically in the case of social housing it is described as "improving without introducing any radical changes."[2] This opposite distortion homogenizes history and denies agency to the actors and institutions whose praxis responded to the ruptures of 1956.

Nuance is crucial to the specific context of Morocco, where not only did the political reality encourage the retention of foreign professionals after independence but also architectural production from the 1950s to the 1970s was in a sense, were monopolized by the young Moroccan and French architects who composed the "Groupe d'Architectes Modernes Marocains."[3] GAMMA's members produced most of Morocco's post independence public commissions. They promulgated a modern architecture investigating topics such as context, climate, and human habits, thus reverberating the internal criticisms developed within CIAM after the Second World War, and later amplified by Team 10. In sum, GAMMA was the buffer that mediated between the political and discursive shifts of the mid-twentieth century and set the character of the Moroccan modernist movement.

Figure 1
TOP – Jean Hentsch and Andre Studer in Sidi Othman, 1955. Courtesy of Archive ETH Zurich. BOTTOM – Jean-François Zevaco, Housing for teachers in Quartzazate, 1963. Courtesy of Fonds Zevaco, FRAC Orléans.

An examination of the forces that have shaped the discourse and architectural and urban production of GAMMA can offer a privileged lens through which to view and gauge the modern movement in Morocco. The official disbanding of GAMMA in 1959 and that of CIAM that followed have prevented scholars from tracing the continuities and cross fertilization that occurred across the Moroccan proclamation of independence in 1956, especially considering that GAMMA's members continued to meet informally and were ultimately reunited for several years for the reconstruction of Agadir, which was swept away by a deadly earthquake in 1959 (Figure 2). An analysis of this exceptional period, still largely under-studied by scholars despite the contemporary publications such as *Architecture d'Aujourd'hui* and the six issues of *Architecture + Urbanism* published between 1964 and 1968 by Group Gamma, reveals the continuity of

Figure 2
**Agadir in the aftermath
of the earthquake, 1959.
Courtesy of Yannnick
Beunard.**

Figure 2
**Agadir in the aftermath
of the earthquake, 1959.
Courtesy of Yannnick
Beunard.**

GAMMA's early, pre-independence concerns *housing for the largest number*. GAMMA undertook through formal investigations and engagement with the cultural, social and geographic context to further these concerns. Developments within GAMMA allowed the genesis of a post-colonial Modernism in Morocco, rather than a blatant historical revivalist movement, symptomatic of many young nation states.

This chapter will outline the establishment and development of GAMMA as an institution pre and post independence, and establish the continuity in the modernist movement in Morocco through the investigation of the genesis and development of one of the central themes in Group Gamma's discourse: *housing for the largest number* (or social housing), whose rigorous research and application was instigated by Ecochard, the very creator of GAMMA. Attention to continuity in this paper, however, will not come at the price of ignoring various appropriations and negotiations of this central theme after Morocco's independence.

The genesis of Group Gamma[4]

After the Second World War, when CIAM resumed its activities, it had to face new geopolitical conditions, where non-Western contexts, including the colonies, emerged as readily industrializing and expanding economic centers with specific emerging urban problems. Within the French colonial territories, CIAM groups were successively formed in Algeria by Pierre Andre Emmery and Jean de Maisonnseult (1947), in Tunisia by Bernard Zehrfuss (1947), and in Morocco by Michel Ecochard (1951).[5] Actually, these CIAM chapters were among the Junior groups that emerged under the influence and encouragement of the old guard wishing to rejuvenate CIAM. This transition, which is often wrongly depicted as an abrupt generational breach,[6] was explicitly planned by Siegfried Gideon and Walter Gropius, and its roots can be retraced to the 8th congress in Hoddesdon in July 1951, where two new council members were elected from the young generation (Candilis and Howell) and the delegate of the Junior groups was named (Norber Schultz).[7] At that meeting, Ecochard, representing CIAM Morocco, which was not yet called GAMMA, presented to the panel "core of a new town," the project for the transformation of a squatter settlement into a satellite city of 40,000 inhabitants located near the twin cities of Rabat-Salé (Figure 3).[8] This project was characterized

Figure 3
Youssoufia quarter masterplan project. Courtesy of the architecture archive at l'Archive ENA, Rabat.

by the provision of a new gridded infrastructure of streets and utility lines, the building of one-story courtyard houses placed on an 8 × 8 matrix, and a heavy reliance on analysis of traditional Moroccan types of dwelling.[9]

Ecochard, who was the director of the Town Planning Department of the French Protectorate in Morocco from 1946 to 1952, has been instrumental in initiating and shaping an organized CIAM group in Morocco. First contacted by Gideon in December 1947, two years after their meeting in New York, Ecochard accepted his invitation to make a contribution to the next CIAM 7 in Bergamo.[10] He then a simple member and took part in the plenary session chaired by Le Corbusier on the "Application of the Athens Charter" along with George Candilis, who was then was the project architect for the *Unité d'Habitation* in Marseilles.[11] The Moroccan group was considered to be in a "formative stage," a category that was created at the Bridgewater Congress to encompass the Algerian and Tunisian groups. Several letters sent by Ecochard from 1947 to 1951, urging Moroccan architects to form a CIAM Maroc group, demonstrate his dedication and reiterate the support of CIAM members for such an enterprise.[12] He failed at first to get the attention of the scattered Moroccan architectural scene, whose different allegiances mirrored the split in Metropolitan France: between the followers of Lods, Le Corbusier's and the group "La Cité."[13]

However, the lectures of the prominent CIAM members Lods and Bodiansky in 1949 in Casablanca, coupled with the visit of Lods in 1951, and the arrival of George Candilis that same year, precipitated the formation of a ten person group.[14] Candilis was then a young member of the CIAM council, who came to direct the ATBAT Afrique[15] office in Morocco. And finally, it is only at the end of the CIAM 8 congress in Hoddesdon, after Ecochard's rite of passage presentation, that GAMMA was officially accepted as a legitimate sub-group of CIAM.[16] During the congress, GAMMA was asked to be part of Commission II of the Sitguna preparatory meeting. Commission II's goal was to determine the method of presentation to be used for the CIAM 9 congress which would focus on "habitat,"[17] since the grid developed by Corbusier had been criticized for being too rigid and not suited to twentieth century city problematics.

Thus, starting from September 1951, GAMMA, presided over by Ecochard, started to meet once a month, alternatively in Rabat and Casablanca, in its members' houses or offices.[18] As a result, a group of GAMMA members composed of Ecochard, Candilis, Azagury, Mas, and Tastemain shared a car and made a memorable trip through Europe to the CIAM 9 preparatory meeting in Sigtuna, Sweden in 1952. GAMMA member Elie Azagury stresses that the discussions at Sitguna were instrumental in crystallizing new systems of values for GAMMA, such as favoring environment over autonomy, change through time over static conditions, place over placelessness, and a wholesome approach to the city over the Athens Charter's four function of living zoning.[19] The theoretical changes that emerged at Sigtuna would materialize in projects presented by GAMMA and other younger groups a year later at the CIAM 9 meeting in Aix-en-Provence.

The combination of Ecochard and Candilis with vibrant local architects who left Morocco before 1939 for their education and returned after the war (like the late Elie Azagury and Jean-François Zevaco) created a very fertile environment for the formulation and development of GAMMA's ideas. Aside from this intellectual milieu and CIAM's newly introduced concepts, their interests were influenced by the country's economic condition, wavering between economic prosperity and rapid pauperization of its urban fringes; a condition which on the one hand spurred the re-consideration of the non specific CIAM precepts, and on the other, provided the financial means to implement those new approaches. Hence, the generation of housing solutions for *the largest number*, the breach with the universalizing Athens Charter, and the tackling of social issues and cultural specificities were at the core of those early GAMMA efforts. Their materialization necessitated the invention of and experimentation with new research and representation methodologies as well as adapted formal vocabularies. Those socially inclined approaches, mainly developed by Ecochard and the ATBAT, ran against the conservative views of the colonial administration which ignored native problematics. Their ideas and implemented projects crystallized a solid platform for both post independence experimentations and a certain depoliticized form of urban planning.

The influence of Ecochard and his "habitat pour le plus grand nombre"

The ground-breaking character of the urban planning and architecture produced by GAMMA did not start with the formation of the group nor with CIAM's mounting longing for a less universalizing architecture in the 1950s, but rather was largely indebted to Ecochard's thoughts that developed in Morocco as early as 1946. Indeed, Ecochard introduced a work methodology deeply rooted in the local specificities of Morocco that rested on two key concepts. The first was the knowledge of the social and physical characteristics of the local context, which should rely on sociological and building surveys as well as on cartographic and statistical analyses in order to shed light on the population dwelling habits. The second was his consideration of history and evolution. Ecochard materialized these ideas by introducing the neighborhood unit. The unit was conceived as a self contained and self-sufficient urban entity, composed of basic amenities (including educational, health and leisure facilities) and a grid of 8 m × 8 m housing units. Additionally, the traditional Moroccan cities' pedestrian network typology of *cul-de-sac* access, used to protect the household's privacy, was applied to the neighborhood unit.

Aside from his new methodology, Ecochard advanced an approach to urbanism that departed from the pre-war colonial era, where native Moroccans were either confined to their medinas or resigned to live in squalid shantytowns. The massive rural exodus that resulted from the rapid growth of the industrial sector was simply ignored by the protectorate power, which shifted the responsibility to industrialists. In reality, only few of them provided housing quarters for workers. These remained insignificant relative to the gargantuan demand.[20] The Moroccan urban population had swelled by 232% from 1930 to 1946.[21] Ecochard immediately recognized as crucial the problematic of *habitat for the largest number*, which he saw as a matter both of "technology and of conscience for France."[22] The signature by Bodiansky of a UN Social and Economic charter for housing for the largest number in 1952 further legitimized Ecochard's concerns among the Moroccan political sphere and CIAM.[23]

The impact of Ecochard's ideas and methods among GAMMA's members was potent. First, his authority is most visible in the composition of the group, which comprised in 1952 of 15 members whose expertise included architecture, planning, sociology, and geography.[24] Second, Ecochard's reform of the administrative system of the Urbanism Department heavily depended on hired designers for projects in order to stimulate collaboration with the private sector. As such, this organizational model effectively disseminated Ecochard's ideas among the architectural community while generating a platform where GAMMA's members could deploy the experimentations necessary to address the challenges raised by the Moroccan shantytowns, for which there were yet no clearly formulated answers.[25] For instance, the re-housing of the shantytown in Casablanca called Carrières Centrales (1951–1955) involved several of GAMMA's members, such as Bodiansky, Candilis, and Woods. Finally, as the minutes of GAMMA's meetings suggest, Ecochard's preferred theme, *habitat for the largest number*, was prevalent in the majority of their discussions.[26] It appeared in debates on social housing and low cost construction techniques as well as in discussions of completed or ongoing housing projects and projected publications and exhibitions.[27] Also, from a seminar in Geneva regarding emergency housing that he attended in November 1952, Ecochard brought back a translated report to GAMMA's members, and encouraged them to review it and be prepared to discuss it in their next meeting. This report advocated a cross-disciplinary method where the government, the planning authorities, and the users are equally involved in the design process, paralleling Ecochard's own approach.[28]

Despite his supremacy in GAMMA, Ecochard's authority started to be challenged during the preparation of the CIAM 9 congress, where his apologetic support of the Athens Charter and its strict urban zoning and CIAM's rigid presentation grids,[29] which he viewed as "an instrument of the first order",[30] stirred some opposition. The criticism, led by Chemineau and Candilis, was about the need for a new definition of "*habitat*," which for them, needed to go beyond the dwelling unit as "a living machine" and to deal more directly with existing dwelling habits. They also argued for presentation grids that would be more adapted to highlighting their multidisciplinary approach to planning and architecture. Their criticism echoes other voices appearing after the Second World War amid CIAM, especially those from the Dutch group MARS which, since the CIAM Bridgewater meeting in 1947, had been raising similar questions regarding changes in methodologies. Furthermore, backed by the native

Moroccan member Elie Azagury, Candilis started to plead for dense vertical housing for the Muslims, who simply wanted, according to him, "low rent public housing like everyone else,"[31] rather than the one-story courtyard unit proposed by Ecochard. After numerous heated discussions, Ecochard conceded the adaptation of the CIAM presentation grid to best address the specific context of Morocco's shantytowns and his Department's "in situ" research methods. In fact, the final grid presented by GAMMA at Aix-en-Provence broke from the traditional CIAM grid organization by displaying images of shantytowns, vernacular Moroccan dwellings, and analytical data resulting from fieldwork as well as housing projects that embraced their local contexts (Figure 3). These negotiations demonstrate that GAMMA was neither unilaterally influenced by a singular voice nor the direct transliteration of CIAM's debates, which themselves were the outlet for groups with multifarious agendas. Instead, GAMMA was a vibrant platform where contextual realities, internally developed ideas, and debates emerging from CIAM's meetings brought about an original approach.

One cannot deny the impact of Ecochard's housing projects, which are celebrated by both past and present scholars coining them as socially inclined. In fact, Ecochard defied the power in place in Morocco as he ran against the general political consensus that ignored providing accommodation for the indigenous population, leaving that provision to the private sector, which could by no means face the demand. However, such a focus can easily obscure Ecochard's use of urbanism: architecture remained subservient to the colonial rule, which was actually flexible enough to allow for certain adjustments. More precisely, Ecochard's housing for the greatest number can be viewed as control and segregationist mechanisms, an argument which was expressed by Layla Dawson and Marion Von Osten, and regarding the French rule at large in Morocco by Wright, Abu Lughod and Rabinow.

Ecochard's housing for Moroccans was located on the city's outskirts, separated by a "sanitary zone" free of construction, a configuration that facilitated surveillance and riot management. Moreover, specific housing typologies were designed for each ethnic group: the Muslims, the Jews, and the Europeans, along an evolving spectrum of civilization. The delineation of these ethnic groups' characteristics and needs, despite being backed by rigorous field research, was strongly tinted by a colonial agenda and fell into generalizing racial clichés and over simplifications. For instance, Europeans were assigned the most modern facilities in the form of mid and high rise buildings similar to those produced at that time in Europe; for Jews there was mid-rise housing comprising an average amount of openness; and finally Muslims were confined to introverted units with an enclosed courtyard, a multipurpose room, a faucet and a Turkish toilet. The archaic form of the dwellings assigned to Moroccans, even though upgraded through the addition of proper sanitization and a rational grid layout, was still the paradigm in most of Echochard's low cost housing. Using a constraining budget as justification, it was totally insensitive to the large size of Moroccan families, condemning them to live in crowded conditions.

The assumption of most projects that shantytown inhabitants came from the countryside and wanted a fully introverted house was erroneous, as most shantytown inhabitants were in fact second or third generation city dwellers. Moreover, the uncritical embracing of introversion for Muslim dwelling reiterates a common cliché regarding privacy and the seclusion of women which, in the context of modernizing Casablanca, should have been more precisely assessed.[32] A most disturbing illustration are Ecochard's famous diagrams that were part of the CIAM 9 Moroccan presentation and in which Muslims are shown as needing to evolve from shantytown, to patio houses, to mid-rise housing blocks. Architecture plays a role where it modernizes habits through the provision of convenience. Yet, architecture falls short of ever bringing the same level of "civilization" that Europeans have; their dwellings are fully supported by functionalist theory, whereas the locals' housing is substantiated solely by their ethnicity and climate.[33] By implying that Moroccans were not ready for civilization, albeit in the near future, Ecochard remained intimately in line with the *Civilizing Mission* of French rule, which justified occupation by debasing colonized populations as inferiors in need of assistance. The projection in the future of eventual access to high rise unveils the paradox inherent in the *Civilizing Mission* rhetoric: once the Moroccans reached modernity, would the Mission be judged accomplished? And how then would colonialism's exploitative praxis be justified?

Interestingly, despite being the only colonial CIAM group to have a native member, namely Elie Azagury, GAMMA, to a certain degree, remained apolitical until Morocco's independence, as it never questioned the colonial power in place, and only criticized its neglect of locals' problems. This apolitical inclination extends to CIAM at large, since no congress ever tackled the issue of colonialism. This complete silence is startling, especially in the 1950s context where anti-colonial movements were numerous, the most notable example being the surrealists, who had famously challenged the colonial exhibition as early as 1936.[34] More strikingly, Morocco had seen the birth of liberation movement actions as well riots in 1952 that were violently repressed, facts that never surfaced in GAMMA's discussions. Nevertheless, Azagury remembered that while several of GAMMA's members were fervent opponents of the colonial rule, they kept their opinions private as the group included conservative architects and planners working for the government, such as Focheron.

Even when Ecochard was dismissed from his job in December 1952, and the Candilis ethos prevailed, this detachment *vis-à-vis* the political question lingered alongside the *habitat for the largest number* theme.

GAMMA and Candilis, ATBAT Afrique

Candilis' arrival in Morocco as head of ATBAT Afrique in 1951 was an essential component in the launching of GAMMA.[35] In fact, Candilis had already been active in CIAM since 1933.[36] While in Morocco, he engaged several of Ecochard's precepts regarding *habitat for the largest number*, which were in line with his own interest in linking architecture to a social, human project.[37] This interest was long-lasting, as he relentlessly revisited it in his practice (Candilis-Josic-Woods) after he left Morocco in 1955.[38] Within GAMMA, Candilis represented one of the critical voices, advocating new architectural and urban models that answered specific postwar contexts. In a way, he found in Ecochard's Morocco, which launched several social housing projects, a propitious terrain and pre-established tools to investigate those models, inventing in the process a formal vocabulary that amalgamated cultural and geographic conditions with the Athens Charter's hygiene concerns. The commissions his office received in the Carrières Centrales from Ecochard resulted in much photographed and published housing buildings and can be perceived, along with Ecochard's 8 × 8 grid, as the earliest embodiment of GAMMA's dogma.

In the same vein as Ecochard, Candilis wished to produce a "progressive and humanist architecture," fully adapted to local conditions and constraints.[39]

Candilis followed Ecochard's methodology that started with an in-depth site analysis. In the Semiramis and Nid d'Abeilles, he turned towards previously unconsidered local architectural typologies. This choice emerged from the attention he paid to the origin of shantytown dwellers at the Carrières Centrales: the Atlas Mountains and the south, where villages are composed of high, earth built dwellings, the Kasbahs. For the first time in Moroccan colonial architectural production, the medina was superseded by another referent, and the rural earth vernacular became the departing point for the understanding of the Moroccans' living patterns and the generation of a formal vocabulary. The cover of *Architecture d'Aujourd'hui*'s issue dedicated to Morocco in 1951 displays a Kasbah juxtaposed to the tallest high rise building in Casablanca.

After Candilis, other GAMMA members took the Kasbahs as a formal and programmatic inspiration. For instance Studer, in his pyramidal housing scheme for Sidi Othman (1954, unbuilt) and after independence, Faraoui and Demazière in three hotels located in the south of Morocco (1971, 1972 and 1974), also derived their volumetric distribution and geometry from the Kasbah (Figure 4).

In order to justify the transfer of Moroccan housing from horizontal to vertical schemes, Candilis seems to have overextended the Kasbah as a referent, projecting a biased reading onto this building type. In fact, he called the Kasbah a *cité verticale*, whereas this vernacular building usually houses one extended family rather than neighbors, and in many cases it is not assembled in clusters. Also, Candilis ignores the fact that 70% of the inhabitants came from the Atlas Mountains, whereas the rammed-earth Kasbas are specific to sub-Saharan Moroccan regions. This underlies the fact that Candilis emphasised aesthetics over his actual analysis of the building type. Thus, as in Ecochard's case, Candilis displays a clear orientalist tone in his re-appropriations, which remained unquestioned at the time, veiled by the beautiful formal outcome.[40]

The patio, which in Ecochard's housing schemes was central to answering the need for "cultural appropriateness," was also crucial for Candilis. Its resolution in the Nid d'Abeille is original, since Candilis adapted the courtyard home typology to the vertical datum. He disposed patios staggered on the southern façade, leaving the circulation on the northern façade. Studer from ATBAT worked on the same theme and produced a stunning interplay of voids and solids in a 30 degree, staggered, hanging patio scheme. In the projects mentioned above, the rapid change of the patio into an enclosed room, becoming either a living room or bedroom,[41] further demonstrates the erroneous a priori that ATBAT and Studer applied to their concept of habitat. The small apartments with patios are miniaturized caricatures of the locals' rural homes. Ironically, in order to adjust, dwellers had to adapt their units, which were meant to be already *adapted housing* fitted to their new urban living conditions!

However, these missteps are not what most influenced GAMMA during the Candilis years that stretched from 1953 to 1955. Rather, it was the sudden possibility of a formal liberation embedded within those projects, especially in the constraining typology of social housing. In some respects, regardless of their failure, those projects are the concrete embodiment of the integration of a local typology with the functional rationales of circulation, ventilation, and lighting. These endeavors, if unprecedented in their typological execution, were not new. In fact, since 1949, Moroccan born GAMMA members Jean-François Zevaco and Elie Azagury had been attempting to integrate climatic conditions into their architecture by incorporating *brise-soleil* in the vocabulary of their buildings (Figure 5). From those ATBAT projects, the plastic quality of the facade, which capitalizes on the strong shadows in Morocco as a design element, furthered by the separation of planes from roofs and structures, would be retrieved later in projects by GAMMA after independence. It is particularly apparent in Zevaco's housing blocks in Agadir and in Ouarzazate (Figure 6). Thus, paradoxically, what constituted the essence of his legacy in Morocco is what Candilis claimed to abhor the most: formalism. He used to set himself against Le Corbusier's "magnificent play of forms in light."[42]

Figure 5
Villa by Elie Azagury, in Casablanca, Morocco. Courtesy of personal archive of Elie Azagury, now transferred to IFA, Paris.

Figure 6
Affordable housing, Jean-François Zevaco. Marrakech, Morocco. Courtesy of Fonds Zevaco, FRAC, Orléans.

At the CIAM Congress in Aix-en-Provence, the photogenic Carrières Centrales projects presented by Candilis undeniably placed Morocco on the world architectural scene, launching a stream of publications dedicated to Morocco,[43] and most importantly gained critical acclaim from the Smithsons, who viewed the housing blocks as the embodiment of the "new universal" and the best building after the Unité d'Habitation.[44] However, it also revealed a divisive crisis within GAMMA whose outcome would linger after independence. In fact, Ecochard's forced departure from Morocco in December 1952, decried by all GAMMA's members, left Candilis to present the CIAM 9 grids prepared by Ecochard's Service of Urbanism team, led by Pierre Mas.[45] According to a letter from Ecochard to André Bloc, Candilis hijacked the presentation to buttress his own projects in the Carrières Centrales, presenting the Service of Urbanism research and projects on shantytown re-housing as a backdrop for his own work. The wrath of Ecochard was increased by the fact that Candilis and Woods used some documents produced by his Service of Urbanism in the December 1953 Issue of *Architecture d'Aujourd'hui* without quoting him or the service (Figure 7). All GAMMA members sided with Ecochard, and displayed their support by naming him the honorary president of GAMMA.[46] This break not only echoes the latent crisis between the older CIAM generation and the emerging Team 10 members, but anticipates GAMMA's post-independence allegiance. This allegiance should be viewed more as a personal than an ideological one, since even though Candilis appeared as a vociferous critic of the old Modernist guard, he was on many occasions highly apologetic its contribution, claiming that there were "no other than better rules than the Athens Charter's."

The transition after independence

In the same vein as Ecochard and Candilis, GAMMA's discussions[47] after Morocco's independence were imprinted with an ambivalence worthy of consideration. At first glance, their discourse remained referential to the Athens Charter. A result of Echochard's persisting influence and Le Corbusier's authoritative figure, this embracing of CIAM's prewar ideas should be considered closely. In fact, there seems to be a disjunction between the topics discussed among GAMMA's members after independence, as illustrated by their fascination with the Athens Charter and the Cité Radieuse,[48] and their architectural production and publication which displayed concerns both with contextual specificity, functionalist methods and new voices in Modernism, especially in Brazil and in Japan. As a result, post-independence GAMMA produced a coherent body of work, affected as much by outside voices as by pre-independence legacy.

The nuanced continuity of GAMMA's ideas between pre and post independence eras has been undermined by the focus of present scholars on the pre-colonial area, and its influence upon the European architectural arena, as well as by the assumption that the post-colonial period simply applied pre-established colonial principles. There is no doubt, as we have seen earlier, that ideological

Figure 7

"The Moroccan Habitat, or Habitat for the Greatest Number," grid panel from CIAM 9 by GAMMA group, 1953. Courtesy of gta/ETH, Zurich.

and institutional frameworks in architecture and urban planning disciplines persisted beyond Morocco's independence. Their continuity was as much the product of the physical presence and activity of key figures as of institutional unity, and the persistence of GAMMA as an intellectual platform, despite its "official" dismantling. Yet the continuity of these frameworks has also been the enabler of innovations and adaptations, informed by Morocco's new political and social contexts. In fact, there were rampant shantytowns to deal with as well as under-urbanized territories from the previously Spanish colonies in need of urban plans. But most importantly, the principal user group of projects shifted from the "colonial objects" – second-class exploited individuals with few rights – to free "subjects,"[49] citizens in a burgeoning new nation in which, they were assured, "they would benefit from the evolution of the modern world and from the advantages of a democratic regime free from all racial discrimination and inspired by the universal Declaration of Human Rights."[50] In this context, Modernism's language came to represent, beyond an organizational model, a symbol for progress that was synonymous with a modern, industrialized way of living and working.

Continuity of GAMMA as an institution

The smooth, conflict free transition between the pre- and post-colonial periods of GAMMA enabled a certain continuity of ideological frameworks. After Candilis's departure in April 1954, Chemineau was appointed as GAMMA's primary delegate and was in charge of preparing for the CIAM 10 Congress to take place in Dubrovnik. Chemineau and Tastemain, a French architect who also trained under Ecochard's Service of Urbanism between 1948 and 1949, attended the preparatory meeting for the congress that took place in Paris in June 1955 at UNESCO's headquarters.[51] Afterwards, they prepared two grids documenting recent social housing projects undertaken in Morocco, but none of which were finally presented.[52] Six months after Morocco acquired independence, the GAMMA delegation present in Dubrovnik in August 1956 comprised the architects Chemineau, Riou and Azagury, who attended the panel "Town Planning as part of the Habitat." After Morocco's independence, some French members of the group such as Jaubert and Chemineau left for France, after representing GAMMA at the La Sarraz CIAM meeting in 1957. After that date, Elie Azagury took charge of GAMMA's leadership. Azagury's engagement *vis-à-vis* CIAM is corroborated by the continuing exchanges he had with José Louis Sert, Ernesto Rogers, Paul Nelson, Richard Neutra, and Ralph Erskine. GAMMA's meetings mostly took place informally in his office and his house. Discussions centered on technical construction issues, the impressive projects coming out of Brazil, and for the first time on the possibility of creating an architecture department at the Ecole des Beaux Arts in Casablanca, a school that had been the bastion of conservative colonial orientalism.[53]

After Azagury's attendance at CIAM 11 in Otterlo in 1959, the group ceased to officially exist, but it remained intellectually active, keeping monthly meetings.[54] These meetings are described by its members as informal discussions and site visits among friends.[55] In 1960, the Agadir earthquake and the subsequent unique national reconstruction effort enabled the GAMMA veterans, along with a new generation of Moroccan born architects recently educated in France, such as Faraoui, Demazière, Ben Embarek, and Amzallag, to coalesce and work collectively on an entire city. Backed up by an efficient administrative apparatus,

architecture + urbanisme

Figure 8
Cover of the fifth issue of the magazine *A+U*.

the commission for the reconstruction, and progressive and young leaders – Faraoui (head of the Service of Urbanism from 1959 to 1961) and then Mourad Ben Embarek (head of the Service of Urbanism after 1961) – the reconstruction gave birth to a very specific aesthetic that resulted as much from the experimental vein inherited from pre-independence GAMMA, as from the technical requirement of earthquake regulations. Ben Embarek started publishing the first post-independence architecture magazine in 1964, *A+U*, which is today the main source of information regarding the late discourses and projects of GAMMA (Figure 8).[56] From analysis of its themes and articles, one of *A+U*'s main concerns appears to intersect with pre-independence GAMMA's theme of *habitat for the greatest number*. Each issue tackles one of the following issues dear to Ecochard: demographic growth, the study of vernacular architecture and dwelling habits, as well as urban, geographical and sociological emerging patterns. Issue 7 of *A+U* was entirely dedicated to *housing for the largest number* and stemmed from a conference organized by the Union Internationale des Architectes.[57]

Another crucial reason for the continuity of approaches in GAMMA and by extension in Morocco's architectural discourse and production is that, unlike in other newly independent countries, many French professionals including architects, planners, landscape architects, and engineers remained in Morocco. In a letter renouncing the French license he acquired in Marseilles during the pre-independence turmoil, Jean-François Zevaco explained his change of mind due to his deep attachment to Morocco, the country where he was born and that still held many of his ongoing projects.[58]

Beyond the enduring presence of key architects, continuity in Moroccan modernism was the result of the persistence of administrative bodies such as the Service of Urbanism (now called CHU),[59] which was part of the Public Works Ministry, and of professional organizations such as the Order of Architects, the *Union Internationale des Architectes*, and the *Association des Architects*. An example of this continuity is best seen in the Service of Urbanism, until the late 1970s, developed strategies initiated under Ecochard, including an extensive land bank, and masterplans for both urban and rural centers, as well as some housing projects following the 8 × 8 grid.

Development of GAMMA's anthropological approach

One of the main ideological legacies of pre-independence GAMMA is the work methodology Ecochard developed for his social housing projects, that took clues from local self-built environments as models for understanding the intricacies of social and cultural patterns. The continuity of Ecochard's methodology is not surprising, since Pierre Mas, Ecochard's right hand, played a central role in the CHU until the late 1960s.

A good illustration is the analysis for the project of the urbanization of the shantytown of Borj Al Omar located in the city of Meknes. The analysis was based on a detailed survey comprised of questionnaires set to outline the population's composition, origins, and income, and of drawings of the dwellings with a focus on construction techniques and usage patterns. Statistics and a photographic essay summarized the findings.[60] Though very much reminiscent of the analysis of the population of shantytowns led by the Ecochard team, this analysis included detailed drawings of each room typology, similar to the drawings done of the Mahieddine shantytown that the Algerian CIAM presented in CIAM 9. Moreover, the fundamental shift in methodology did not rest on the actual tools and techniques applied in the site research but rather in the transfer of those findings onto the design of the planning and architecture of the project. While the conclusions of Ecochard and Candilis were limited by their acceptance of the colonial rhetoric of paternalism and subordination, post independence GAMMA members made a more rigorous and genuine transfer of their findings. The voices of Moroccans, as represented in the concluding analysis data, became central to the design process.

For instance, after independence, GAMMA members gave full consideration to Moroccans' wishes to have high-rise dwellings with larger interior spaces and their rejection of the courtyard, which was judged too retrograde by some. A good example of this shift is the first high-rise building with no courtyards designed for Moroccans, executed by Gaston Jaubert, a GAMMA member, in collaboration with Pierre Coldefy in 1957. It is composed of a long, sinuous five-story bar (262 units) and four shorter three-story bars (48 units each), without courtyards. The ensemble followed one of Ecochard's tenets: limiting the investment on common infrastructure and instead focusing on the quality of public open spaces and the building itself. The façades are articulated with alternating panels creating L-shaped patterned windows, a rhythm and surface play that is reminiscent of Candilis's formal aesthetic. The organization of the interior spaces is the most representative of innovation in approach: services are flanked along the circulation corridor in order to produce large living spaces that benefit from the most exposure to sun and ventilation. Finally, the kitchen is sometimes open to the living area to attenuate its constrained size, and the bathrooms, always relegated to secondary importance in post-independence schemes, gain here generous proportions and a modern toilet seat.

Another notable result of this methodological shift is the expansion of the Ecochard paradigmatic models for shantytown upgrades (the *trame sanitaire*, the one-story 8 × 8 courtyard unit, and the mid-rise building with units with patios). Based on the low income level data gathered in their surveys, as well as the capacity of dwellers to self construct, the CHU proposed a new model where empty plots, serviced with basic infrastructure, would be rented at very low prices to shantytown dwellers, who would build on them themselves thanks to a micro-credit loan and following prototype plans. This model was an updated version of Ecochard's grid called TSA (or *trame sanitaire ameliorée*). Those plans were mostly developed by GAMMA members after independence, and some were tested first in experimental housing projects such as Derb Jdid in Casablanca by Azagury (1958) and another one in Marrakech by Zevaco (1959). Then, in 1962, the plans were compiled in a book, made available to solvable shantytown dwellers and private developers (Figure 9).[61] Using these plans, the CHU developed 9000 social housing units throughout seven Moroccan cities. With the hope of alleviating its deficiencies in housing stock, the Moroccan state further promoted self-construction by creating CERF in 1959, a research center focusing on low cost auto-construction techniques.[62] However, the application of innovations introduced by the center's director engineer Alain Masson and

Figure 9
Unit Basil for the Derb Jdid project, Elie Azagury. Courtesy of personal archive of Elie Azagury, now transferred to IFA, Paris.

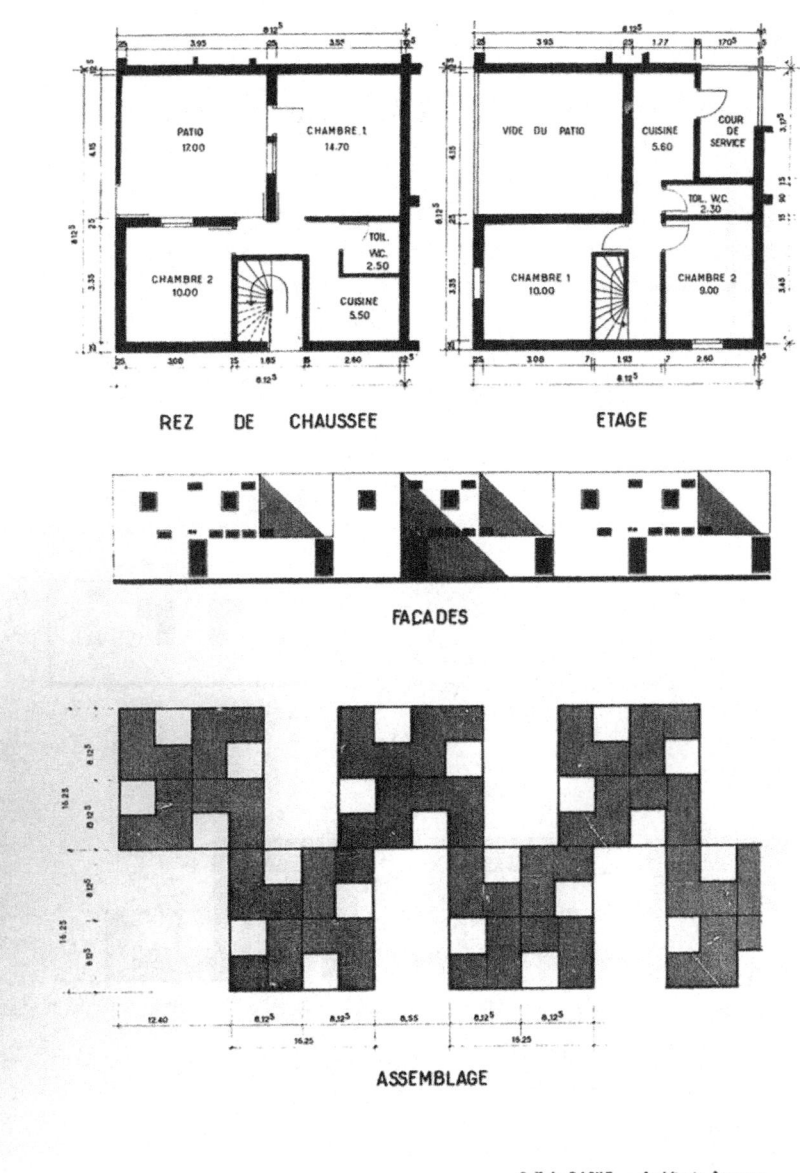

REZ DE CHAUSSEE   ETAGE

FAÇADES

ASSEMBLAGE

Cellule BASILE — Architecte Azagury

collaborator Jean Hensens, an architect who took part in the discussions of post independence GAMMA and wrote articles for the magazine *A+U*, remained unfortunately limited to one experimental project in Ouarzazate (1969).

Another post-independence innovative social housing approach that addressed the actual condition of shantytown dwellers, that is, their rapidly increasing family members, is Evolving Housing (*Habitat évolutif*); a concept which Candilis advocated in the Carrières Centrales project without fully resolving it. Evolving Housing proposed single or double family units that could be enlarged by the owner when his budget allowed him to do so. In contrast, for Ecochard the concept of Evolving Housing meant housing that evolves according the user's civilization level.

The best example of such "evolving housing," also labeled by GAMMA as "active urbanism",[63] are the units developed by Elie Azagury in his Derb Jdid project (Figure 10) in 1958, the first large scale shantytown urbanization scheme to be launched after Morocco's independence. Set on a masterplan designed initially by Ecochard, Azagury's project proposed different housing typologies: single and two family dwellings conceived as two-storied structures as well as more conventional three-story collective housing blocks. On the level of the clustering, these units employed carefully placed setbacks that could allow for potential expansion, mainly in the form of the covering of the outdoor areas, without endangering the sanitization requirements of the cluster. Accordingly, Azagury's two-story units were organized in Swastikas (Basil Type), in an undulating figure (Arsene Type) or in shifted U-figures (Maxime Type). Thus Azagury, alongside other GAMMA architects who developed other double dwelling variations in Derb Jdid, integrated for the first time into the low budget,

Figure 10
Derb Jdid project, Elie Azagury. Courtesy of personal archive of Elie Azagury, now transferred to IFA, Paris.

domestic unit the notions of evolution and growth, beating Candilis to the punch. In fact, even though Candilis claimed that his Nid d'Abeille building was designed to allow for modes of appropriations, he was never explicit about how. The unforeseen covering of the building's hanging patios resulted in the units becoming dark and unventilated (Figure 11). Interestingly, in Azagury's project all units have today expanded as was predicted, but their growth through self construction had mitigating results, as neither heights nor additions were strictly controlled.

At last, this bottom-up approach reached its paroxysm in one of the social housing projects developed in Agadir in the New Talborjd district by Armand Amzallag and completed in 1965 (Figure 12).[64] The project grew from intensive community meetings and interviews seeking to define the needs of future users. The final design resulted in double family dwellings, organized in a 10 m × 10 m

grid, each with two-story units grouped in clusters of eight. The involvement of the users from the early stages of design spurred a strong feeling of ownership, resulting in little transformation of the architecture.

Development of GAMMA's vernacular interest

At the heart of Ecochard's anthropological field research approach lies the study of vernacular architecture, a theme that will remain a leitmotif in GAMMA's post independence discourse, albeit in a different form. Ecochard's team not only looked at shantytown habitat but also at rural vernacular architecture, ignoring the urban vernacular in Morrocco: the medinas. The medinas were perceived as the arena of the colonial 1920s and 1930s period that adopted a historicist style (called Arabisance) that GAMMA rejected all together. The fascination for the shantytown and the southern rammed-earth Kasbahs by colonial GAMMA was driven by the search for cultural specificity, mainly to understand the pattern of usage of space, as opposed to using the social/physical specificity advocated by the Smithsons or the historical specificity advocated by the Italian CIAM group.[65] On the contrary, post-independence GAMMA was interested in the vernacular not only because of the urgency to preserve and protect it, but most importantly for learning from its forms, its adaptation to climate and its construction methods. In the first issue of *A+U*, the editorial board urges the "modernist architect to research [vernacular architecture] since it will form a fertile base for his/her work, since its volumes, plans and materials can be viewed as modern."[66] Thus, with its latent capacities to inform modern praxis, vernacular architecture acquires with post-independence GAMMA an expanded role: not only are its cultural specificities studied, but also its architectonic, environmental and social specificities. By defining a new epistemology for design and a new openness to the past as a source of knowledge, GAMMA's new approach to vernacular architecture echoes suggestions already raised during CIAM 9 by Van Heyk, who thought that architects could learn the quality of "vital harmony" from the balanced life of primitive civilizations.[67] He considered these cultures to be models for integrated, culturally based, environmentally responsive habitats. Van Heyk later elaborated on these ideas in the magazine *Forum*, whose issue number 1 was discussed between Zevaco and Azagury in the early 1960s. In this issue, which displayed Mexican rammed-earth villages similar to Morocco's vernacular desert architecture, Van Heyk, along with a group of young Dutch architects, stressed the importance of social and historical analysis for developing a new urban and architectural language, which gave rise in their discourse to clustering systems as guiding principles. Their approach is very much in line with the hotels developed by GAMMA member Faraoui and Demazière in the early 1970s. Before Van Heyk's group, interest in the vernacular can be traced in other instances throughout the 1950s, such as in the exhibitions "Mostra di Architettura Spontanea" by Gian Carlo Di Carlo (1951) and "Architecture without architects" by Bernard Rudowsky at the MoMA (1956).

Figure 13
Agadir affordable housing project. Courtesy of *A+U* magazine

Within Morocco, GAMMA's interest in the vernacular was further incited by the artist Belkahia, the lively new director of the Beaux Arts School in Casablanca, where some GAMMA members taught design courses. Belkahia took charge of the school in 1962, with the agenda to move Moroccan arts away from the domineering orientalist aesthetic, which strangely persisted despite decolonization. To do so, he promoted the introduction of local crafts and materials into modern art practices.[68] After independence, GAMMA followed a similar route. A good instance of use of traditional material in an innovative manner is the Evolving Housing project developed by the CHU in Agadir in 1961 (Figure 13). The project's planning was not innovative per se since a normative 8×8 grid Ecochard grid was used due to the urgency of providing housing after the 1959 earthquake. But its construction method was novel: traditional rammed-earth construction was mixed with modern materials and construction techniques complying with seismic norms. Rammed-earth construction's low cost, thermal capacity and ease of construction were incentives for its usage. Each unit comprised a concrete flowing, and walls constructed of bricks made from a mix of rammed earth and cement, using a press developed by the United Nations. Units were fitted with a pre-fabricated, lightweight, self-supporting roofing system made out of cement and asbestos.

Another example of the integration of traditional crafts into GAMMA's housing projects is the New Talborj in Gaadir by Amzallag. Despite the limited budget, the units of this social housing project demonstrate very fine detailing: the carved, painted doors, and the window bars were produced by local wood craftsmen.

Finally, in addition to materials, the transfer of vernacular architecture in GAMMA's housing projects was also processed conceptually. On the urban level, vernacular models, especially the medinas, re-emerged as sources of inspiration for generating a humane urban landscape for housing quarters. For example, in the masterplan for the social housing project designed by husband and wife team Henri Tatemain and Elaine Castelnau and located in Agadir, the diversity of building typologies and the generous spacing between units created a heterogeneous public landscape that contrasted with Ecochard's monotonous repetitive mats. On the architectural level, specific components of traditional dwellings were analyzed and subtly reinterpreted. The most elemental of these is the courtyard.

After independence, the courtyard was sometimes done away with, but in other cases it was kept. In the latter case, the patio was however re-conceptualized as an architectonic and social component, such as in the row houses developed by Zevaco in Agadir in 1965 (Figure 14). The limited budget of the project required an organization of two blocks: one with six type A (three bedrooms) and four type B (four bedrooms), and the other with seven type B and three Type A. These constraints inevitably led to two orientations for the two typologies, and one was always detrimental. To alleviate this difficulty Zevaco investigated how the patio could be reinterpreted to allow for a double exposure of each room, leading to its explosion into six outdoor spaces: an entrance patio, two privately oriented patios, a living room patio, a kitchen terrace and a service courtyard.[69] This multiplicity of courtyards, each with a specific function, extending the interior programs into the outdoors, has proven very successful as it weaves nature in with the domestic realm, clearly separating service patios from the leisure oriented ones. Thus, unlike previous GAMMA work such as Candilis's Carrières Centrales dwellings, the patios acquire here a spatial complexity which leads to formal innovations where architecture is constantly interwoven with nature. Rather than a space reduced to its reductive post-colonial interpretation, the patio gained all its hidden potential: one that answers the population's changing needs where the patio is not limited to services only, but extends to leisure and relaxation purposes. As such, the courtyard was freed from its rural

Figure 14
Villas by Jean-François Zevaco, Agadir, Morocco. Courtesy of Fonds FRAC Orléans

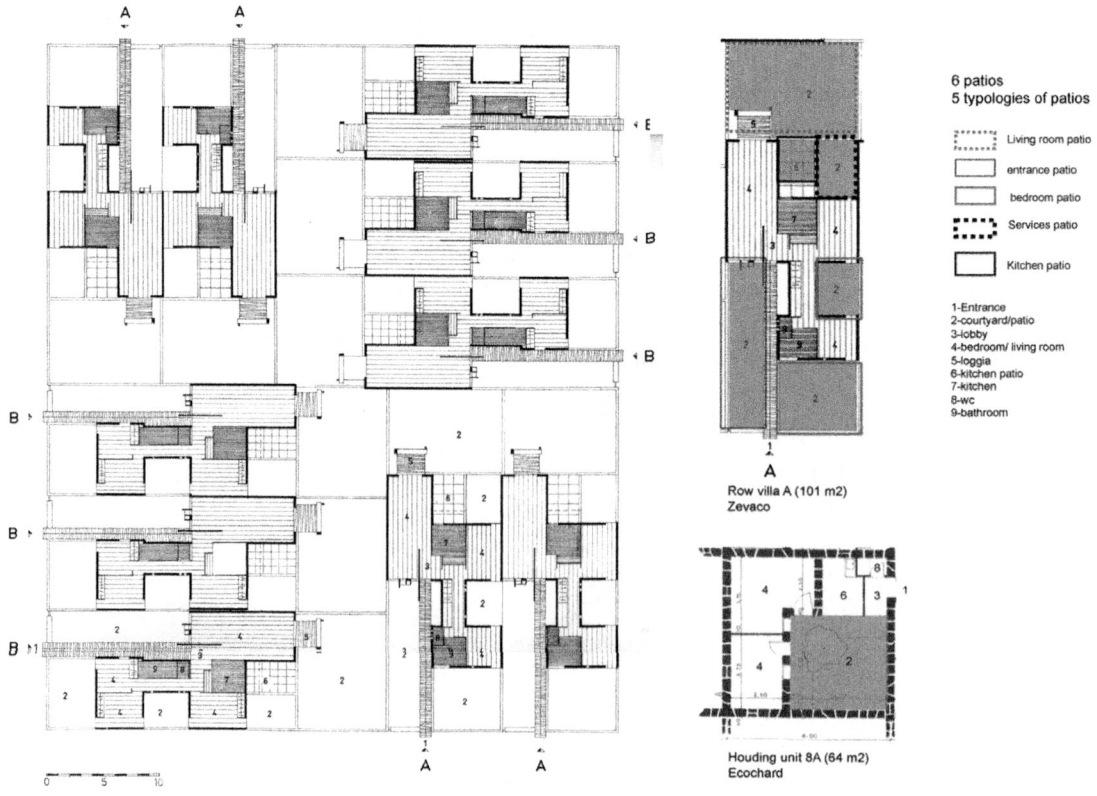

6 patios
5 typologies of patios

- Living room patio
- entrance patio
- bedroom patio
- Services patio
- Kitchen patio

1-Entrance
2-courtyard/patio
3-lobby
4-bedroom/ living room
5-loggia
6-kitchen patio
7-kitchen
8-wc
9-bathroom

A
Row villa A (101 m2)
Zevaco

Houding unit 8A (64 m2)
Ecochard

house referent, which limited it to services only. It was expanded to other Moroccan referents such as the Arabo-Andalousian courtyard, whose lush vegetation invites reflection and peacefulness.

Conclusion

Group GAMMA's analysis from its inception in 1951 to the two decades following Morocco's independence, while focusing on their favoured theme of housing for the largest number, have shown us that Modernism as a systemic language and theoretical platform had been used for different political agendas: ordering and controlling during the colonial era, and advancing progress in independent Morocco. Its flexibility to accommodate conflicting political contexts allowed for a continuity of work methodologies and ideas. This legacy was not accepted passively, but developed in different directions, was circulated and was renegotiated, shaped as much by the new Moroccan social context as by the concepts developed in the West by both postwar and prewar CIAM groups, exhibitions, and publications. This synthesis of seemingly contradictory ideas underscores the mythical character of the schism between old and young CIAM groups, postwar and prewar modernism; a simplification which scholars such as Jean Lucien Bonillo, Claude Massu and Daniel Pinseau believe veils legacies, transformative processes, and voices like Alvar Aalto, José Luis Sert, and Ernesto Rogers who forecast Team 10's criticisms.[70]

The refinements and changes that post-independence GAMMA proposed in social housing projects were highly innovative and brought Ecochard's and Candilis's ideas to a new level of resolution, a fact that has rarely been acknowledged. For instance, GAMMA's evolving housing schemes, responses to climate and cultural habits, and anthropological design approach, which were theorized by early GAMMA members but whose materialization remained problematic on many levels, were given imaginative solutions in the post-independence period. Their pioneering edge lay in their actual integration of Moroccan voices within the design process as well as social, environmental, urban and architectural specificities, themes that were taken beyond the social housing typology. Thus, post independence GAMMA generated a new facet of Modernism that we conceptualize along the lines of Sarah Goldhagen as a multifarious and plural discourse, rather than a mainstream western core with "other" or "situated" offspring.

The singularity and cohesiveness of the architectural discourse and production generated by GAMMA after independence begs for the reconsideration of the primacy given to 1950s Morocco as a "laboratory" for European modernism.[71] Instead, the period should be as much acknowledged as the catalyst for the development of Moroccan post-colonial modernism. However, the peculiarity of the modernism developed in the aftermath of independence quickly gave way at the end of the 1960s to a brutalist aesthetic, leaving many investigations incomplete and burgeoning themes unexplored.

Acknowledgements

Research for this chapter was supported by a Graham Foundation Grant. I would like to thank GAMMA members who generously answered all my questions, in particular the late Elie Azagury. I am also indebted to DuanFang Lu, Director Marie-Ange Brayer of the FRAC Center, the School of Architecture of Rabat, Daniel Weiss and Professor Laurent Stalder from ETH Zurich.

Notes

1   The civilizing mission, or "mission civilisatrice," was raised as an official doctrine of the French Third Republic to justify and legitimize the conquest of indigenous populations. It mainly rested on the fundamentals of French cultural superiority and the perfectibility of human beings. For a critical reading of the term please refer to: Alice Conkin, *A Mission to Civilize: The Republican Idea of Empire in France and West Africa, 1895–1930*. Stanford: Stanford University Press, 2000.

2   Monique Eleb, "An alternative to Functionalist Universalism, Ecochard, Candilis, and ATBAT-Afrique," in *Anxious Modernism*. Cambridge: MIT Press, 2000, p. 69.

3   GAMMA stands for Groupe d'Architectes Modernes Marocains (Moroccan Modern Architects Group). Gamma was founded on July 1951 at the 8th *Congrès International des Architectes Modernes* (CIAM) in Hoddesdon. GAMMA members, whose number fluctuated throughout the years due to returns to France and departures due to political conflicts, attended all congress meetings until the last one in Otterlo in 1959. CIAM congresses and meetings attended by at least one GAMMA member: CIAM 8 (1951), CIAM Meeting Sigtuna (1952), CIAM 9 (1953), Paris CIAM council meeting (1954), CIAM 10 (1956), La Sarraz reorganization committee meeting (1957) and CIAM 59 (1959). Eric Mumford *The CIAM Discourse on Urbanism, 1928–1960*. Cambridge: MIT Press, 2000.

4   I am indebted to Jean-Louis Cohen's article "The Moroccan Group and the Theme of Habitat" which traces GAMMA's early developments. My article brings new additions thanks to the review of archives of architects and GAMMA members Jean-François Zevaco, Henri Tastemain and Elie Azagury as well as files from the Ministère de l'Habitat in Rabat and personal interviews of surviving GAMMA members, who are all in their late 80s today. This research was enabled by a Graham Foundation grant received in 2007.

5   For a detailed history of CIAM's groups, please refer to Mumford. op. cit.

6   Regarding the generational changes in CIAM see Annie Pedret, *CIAM and the emergence of Team 10 thinking: 1949–1953*. Unpublished dissertation. Cambridge: MIT, 2009.

7   Schultz's Team magazine – "a magazine for young architects and artists" – was the first manifestation of involvement of the young generation in CIAM. Team magazine stirred a lot of debates about the future direction of CIAM as it would plan a controversial Junior CIAM congress alongside the Aix-en- Provence one. At the end, their contention was peacefully absorbed into the 9th Congress. See Joe Bosman, "Team Ten out of CIAM," in *Team Ten: 1953–1981 in Search of a Utopia of the Present*. Rotterdam: NAi, 2005.

8   This project for a city of 40,000 presented in Hoddesdon has been identified by Jean Louis Cohen as the District Yacoub Al Mansour located in Rabat. However, from the drawings of this district shown in Ecochard's article in *Architecture d'Aujourd'hui* no. 60 the district is described as being one for 25,000 inhabitants and its aerial photo does not match the plan presented at CIAM 9, and which is published in *Ciam 9: The Heart of the City*.

9   Mumford, op. cit., p. 211.

10   Jean-Louis Cohen, "The Moroccan Group and the Theme of Habitat", in *Rassegna,* 1992, no. 52, December, pp. 58–67.

11   Mumford, op. cit., p.192.

12   Cohen, op. cit., pp. 58–67.

13   Personal interview with Elie Azagury, October 2007.

14   Cohen, op. cit., p. 59.

15   ATBAT (Atelier des Batisseurs) is a multidisciplinary organization of architects, engineers, technicians, site managers, and administrators based in Paris and active from 1947 to 1966. It was created under the leadership of Vladimir Bodiansky on the initiative of Le Corbusier, originally to handle the construction of the Unité d'Habitation in Marseilles.

16   The history of this group is hard to retrace because of the lack of archival materials. For this paper, I used the personal archives of Jean-François Zevaco in the Ecole Nationale d'Architecture in Rabat and the FRAC in Orléans, the personal archive of Henri Tastemain in Rabat, and the Ministry of Habitat and the gta-Zurich archives.

17   Pedret op. cit.

18   Michel Ecochard, "Habitation pour le plus grand nombre. Position du problème par rapport a l'habitat normal" (CIAM 42-JT-10-137/140.)

19   The Athens Charter promulgates the planning of the city into four zones each dedicated to a specific activity: recreation, living, working, and transportation.

20   Before 1939, Edmond Brion built two workers' housing quarters: the Laforge quarters and the Compagnie Sucrière Marocaine quarters, and these were interestingly visionary; they offered evolutive housing. See: J-L. Cohen and Monique Eleb, *Colonial Myths and Architectural Ventures*. NY: the Monacelli Press, 2002.

21   Michel Ecochard, *Casablanca, roman d'une ville*. Paris: Ed. de Paris, 1955, p. 38.

22   Ibid., p. 45.

23   1952 Report of ECOSOC to the General Assembly, A/2430. NY: Dag Hammarskjöld Librar, 1952.

24   Mumford, op. cit., p. 92.

25   "Problèmes d'Urbanisme au Maroc," *Architecture d'Aujourd'hui*, no. 35, Mai 1951.

26   The GAMMA meeting summaries were assembled from Henri Tastemain's and Jean-François Zevaco's personal archives and span a period between 1949 and 1955.

27   Minutes of Gamma meetings, J-F. Zevaco archives, ENA Rabat.

28   Recommendations à l'Administration de l'Assistance Technique des Nations Unis établie à Génève, November 25th and 26th 1952. Zevaco Archives, ENA.

29   The CIAM grid which was introduced by Le Corbusier at the Bergamo Congress in 1949 in order to present projects. The grid is composed of 21 cm × 33 cm panels indexed along the horizontal axis by the themes of context, built volume, ethic and aesthetic, economic and social influences, and finance and legislation; and along the vertical axis by the functions of living defined by the Athens Charter: work, dwelling, leisure and transportation.

30   Pedret, op. cit.

31   Interview with Candilis, *Ingénieurs et architectes suisses*, p. 492. As quoted in: Eleb, op. cit., p. 73.

32   For detail on Casablanca's native population's rapidly changing habits please refer to Adam, André, *Casablanca, essai sur la transformation de la société marocaine au contact de l'Occident*. Editions du Centre National de la Recherche Scientifique, Paris, 1968.

33   Monique Eleb mentions this psychophrenic behavior but does not directly criticize it nor condemn it.

34   Zeynep Ceylik, "The ordinary and the third world at CIAM IX," in *Team Ten: 1953–1981, in Search of a Utopia of the Present*. Rotterdam: NAi, 2005.

35   Zevaco archives, ENA, Rabat. In his personal notes dated 1954, Zevaco remarks that Candilis's persona was a binding glue for the architecture community in Morocco. Personal interviews with Elie Azagury in 2006 and 2007 support this claim.

36   Pedret, op. cit.

37   Tom Avermaete, *Another Modern, The Postwar Architecture and Urbanism of Candilis-Josic-Woods*, Rotterdam, NAi, 2005.

38   Toulouse Le Mirail is a good example.

39   George Candilis et al., *Candilis-Josic-Woods, a decade of architecture and urbanism*. Stuttgart: Karl Kramer Verlag, 1968, p. 8.

40 Alison and Peter Smithson, "Collective housing in Morocco," *Architectural Design*, January 1955, p. 2.

41 André Adam notes that the transformation of this housing was almost immediate. Op. cit., p. 111.

42 G. Candilis et al., op. cit., p. 9.

43 "Maroc," *Architecture d'Aujourd'hui*, no. 35, Mai 1951. "Maroc (II)," *L'Architecture française*, no. 131–132, April 1953.

44 Alison and Peter Smithson, op. cit.

45 Present in Aix-en-Provence: Tastemain and his wife E. Castelnau plus Azagury, Bodiansky, Kennedy, Piot, Woods, Godefroy, Ecochard, Beraud.

46 Summary of March 1954 GAMMA meeting, Zevaco's archive in the Ecole Nationale d'Architecture, Rabat.

47 As noted from the minutes of various meetings among GAMMA peers found in Zevaco's archives in ENA, Rabat, and also from personal interviews with Mourad Ben Embarek and Elie Azagury in 2006–2007.

48 GAMMA Minutes, 1953–1958, Fonds Jean-François Zevaco. Centre FRAC, Orléans, France (the archive has not been fully sorted, so documents do not have numbers yet.)

49 Layla Dawson, "Colonizing zeal," *Architectural Review*, February 2009.

50 Mohammed V. speech of December 7th 1955 in *Sa Majesté V, Ministère de l'information et du tourisme*, Rabat, Tome 1:1955–1957..

51 Pedret, op. cit., p. 353.

52 Cohen, pp. 62.

53 This department never materialized, even though members of GAMMA such as Zevaco taught a few general design courses there. The first architecture school in Morocco would only open in 1981 in Rabat. Regarding the relationship between French rule and the Ecole des Beaux Arts of Casablanca, please refer to Irbouh, Hamid, *Art in the service of colonialism: French art education in Morocco, 1912–1956*. NY: Tauris Academic Studies, 2005.

54 Zevaco archives, ENA, Rabat.

55 From a personal interview with Elie Azagury in 2007.

56 Thierry Nadau, "La Réconstruction d'Agadir" in *Architectures Françaises d'Outre Mer*. Liège: Margada, 1992, pp. 146–175.

57 The conference took place from April 28th to May 5th 1968 in Agadir.

58 Zevaco archive at ARCHILAB, Orléans.

59 The Service of Urbanism was renamed CHU (Circumscription of Urbanism and Habitat) but kept the administrative structure established by Ecochard.

60 Mont Marin M, "Urbanisation du bidonville de Borj Al Omar," *Bulletin Economique et Social*.

61 Claude Vignaud, *Nouvelles cités d'habitat économique au Maroc: 1960–1962*. Rabat: Ministère des Travaux Publics, Circumscription de l'Urbanisme et de l'Habitat, 1962.

62 Nadau, Thierry, op. cit., p. 152.

63 Pierre Mas, "Architecture, urbanisme et développement" in *A+U* no. 1, 1964, p. 6.

64 Nadau, op. cit., p. 158.

65 Pedret, op. cit., p. 140.

66 *A+U* Editorial board, "L'Architecture populaire régionale en péril," *A+U* no. 5, 1967, p. 17.

67 Pedret, op. cit., p. 144.

68 Irbouh, op. cit., pp. 238–239.

69 Fonds Jean-François Zevaco. Centre FRAC, Orléans, France.

70 Jean-Lucien Bonillo, Claude Massu, Daniel Pinson (eds), *La Modernité critique. Autour du CIAM 9 d'Aix-en-Provence*, Imbernon, 2006.

71 The definition of "laboratory" was first developed by Monique Eleb and Jean-Louis Cohen, and was further investigated in the exhibition "The Desert of Modernity" organized in 2008 in Berlin. The exhibition traveled in 2009 to Casablanca. Both the exhibition and Eleb and Cohen mainly focused on the relationship between pre-colonial GAMMA production and their post-colonial European impact.

Chapter 4

Agrupación Espacio and the CIAM Peru Group: architecture and the city in the Peruvian modern project

Sharif S. Kahatt

There is an assumption that Latin American architecture lives within the paradox of modernism without modernity. This assumption is based on the fact that this geo-cultural region has not achieved "modernity" in standard terms of industrialization and capitalism. Nevertheless, modernization has penetrated the cultural landscape and produced a particular state of development. This could be understood as a mixture of pre-Columbian and Spanish-colonial cultural patterns with the clash of the American Anglo-Saxon modernization of the twentieth century. In this particular secular hybridization, in which modernism coexists with cultural traditions and rooted customs, Latin American modernity can be defined essentially as a "multiplied outcome of overlapping cultures." As identified by Garcia Canclini, "modernity in this region is a hybrid culture based on the negotiation of modern and traditional practices and unique to each country."[1]

It is within this context of cultural overlap and transformation at the mid-twentieth century that the Peruvian "Modern Project" emerged and consolidated as a national project in the country and endured for several decades. It should be understood as a national political and cultural project, in which the government, nation, and state worked together on new strategies for the progress of the country. The buildings and urban spaces produced in the Peruvian Modern Project reflect its essence, the hybridization of contemporary culture charged with the richness and complexity of dealing with different cultural patterns. Hybridization is a never-ending process of cultural negotiation, and therefore it should not be assumed as a problem of syncretism. As Felipe

Hernandez has pointed out, hybridization is a concept that engages broader political, social, and cultural processes and reveals "coexistence for a permanent struggle for survival."[2]

Furthermore, intellectual movements such as the Lima-based Agrupación Espacio were working towards the modernization and transformation of the cultural and architectural landscape. Espacio gathered architects, such as Luis Dorich, Adolfo Córdova, Santiago Agurto, Eduardo Neira, Carlos Williams, and others, under the leadership of Luis Miró Quesada; Espacio emerged to clash with the architectural establishment, aiming to produce a modern urban culture that would give form to modern efforts.[3] Ultimately, the members of Espacio working independently and for different national offices would theorize, project and build the most relevant urban model for the Peruvian Modern Project *unidades vecinales*. Later on, with the same goals, they also worked on the improvements of *barriadas*, the most popular form of urbanization in Lima since the 1960s and the biggest urban phenomenon in third world cities.

Following the guiding principles of its manifesto towards the production of "a contemporary architecture of the new era", Espacio worked towards modern cultural expressions and brought together architects with a wider array of artistic constituencies that included poets, painters, musicians, and, later, sociologists and engineers. Coincidentally, during the 1940s the American government sponsored *Congress International d'Architecture Moderne* (CIAM)[4]-related architects in traveling to Latin America to persuade new democracies to deploy modern architecture and urban planning as a means of modernization. Modern architects, including Espacio and CIAM groups, believed that architecture, urban planning, and the arts were catalysts for a socio-cultural revolution.

From lectures by Richard Neutra, Paul Lester Wiener and José Luis Sert in Lima in the mid-1940s to Dubrovnik's CIAM crisis and the dissolution of Espacio in the late 1950s, most cities experienced simultaneously the dramatic process of "modernization" and unplanned growth which led people to distrust urban experts. In order to understand the Peruvian scene as a specific case study of this process within Latin America, it is pertinent to address the parallels between postwar CIAM and Agrupación Espacio, a peripheral group that adopted, transformed, and developed its ideas in search of the modern functional city. In the canonical Latin American architectural historiography there is a simplistic assumption that Espacio was CIAM's "franchise" in Lima. However, the relationship between these two groups was far more complex and to date has not been thoroughly researched.[5] Furthermore, the work of Espacio, which triggered new cultural expressions in Peru through its cultural activism, has hardly been studied in its full dimension.

Therefore, this chapter concentrates on the architectural and urban ideas that these groups shared in their searches for the modern city. It also looks at the ideological appropriation and transformation that occurred in Peruvian architecture; that is to say, the ideological hybridization in Peru's modern culture, juxtaposing European avant-garde and American modernism onto local architectural landscape. Finally, this chapter also reconsiders the group's achievements and architectural production within its cultural project.

The challenge of the Peruvian Modern Project

As has been explained in different publications, the US government was interested in establishing good relations with its Latin American neighbors following the Nazi threat in Europe in the late 1930s and early 1940s. "The Good Neighbor Policy" had the aim of strengthening relationships among the "Americas". According to Bryce Woods's book, Franklin D. Roosevelt's administration claimed responsibility for the protection of the lives and property of its citizens and the advancement of democracy in Latin America while providing support for the military defense of the region as well as technical, economic and cultural influence.[6] Therefore, as Irwin Gellman's book points out, cultural and military contacts became major diplomatic considerations, and multilateral cooperation reached levels unseen in earlier times.[7]

During the war years, Peru's economic and political context was not strong, and it was exacerbated by the earthquake of 1940 and confirmed the same year by the national census. Therefore, Manuel Prado's administration (1939–45) initiated the country's modernization process, passing industrial laws and creating special initiatives.[8] Following the American model, Prado's administration also launched national corporations to encourage investment in different regions and decentralize development through national infrastructure projects. Three major state enterprises were established between 1942 and 1943, based on Roosevelt's Tennessee Valley Authority (TVA) idea.[9] *Corporación Peruana del Amazonas* (CPA) was dedicated to industrializing the oil, rubber and latex business originating from the Peruvian Amazon; *Corporación Peruana de Aeropuertos y Aviación Comercial* (CORPAC) was in charge of aviation communications development; and *Corporación Peruana del Santa* (CPS) was devoted to developing the northern region of the Peruvian coast with the requested support of American engineers from the TVA mission.[10]

In May of 1942, President Prado paid an official visit to President Franklin D. Roosevelt, becoming the first Latin American president officially received by the American government. The deference is not surprising, since Peru was among the countries targeted in the "good neighbor" plans, follower of the American development guidelines, and was part of the Inter-American Conference sponsored by the Roosevelt administration.[11]

Subsequent to Prado's mandate, the new government of José Luis Bustamante y Rivero (1945–48) announced a shift in the economic guidelines by confronting the influence of the American government. However, in practical terms, it did not stop any of the new policies or major state initiatives. In fact, CPS – the *Peruvian TVA* that included the redevelopment plan for the city and port of Chimbote – was kept as one of the main instruments to develop the northern region. The Chimbote project (Figure 1) – along with the Peruvian

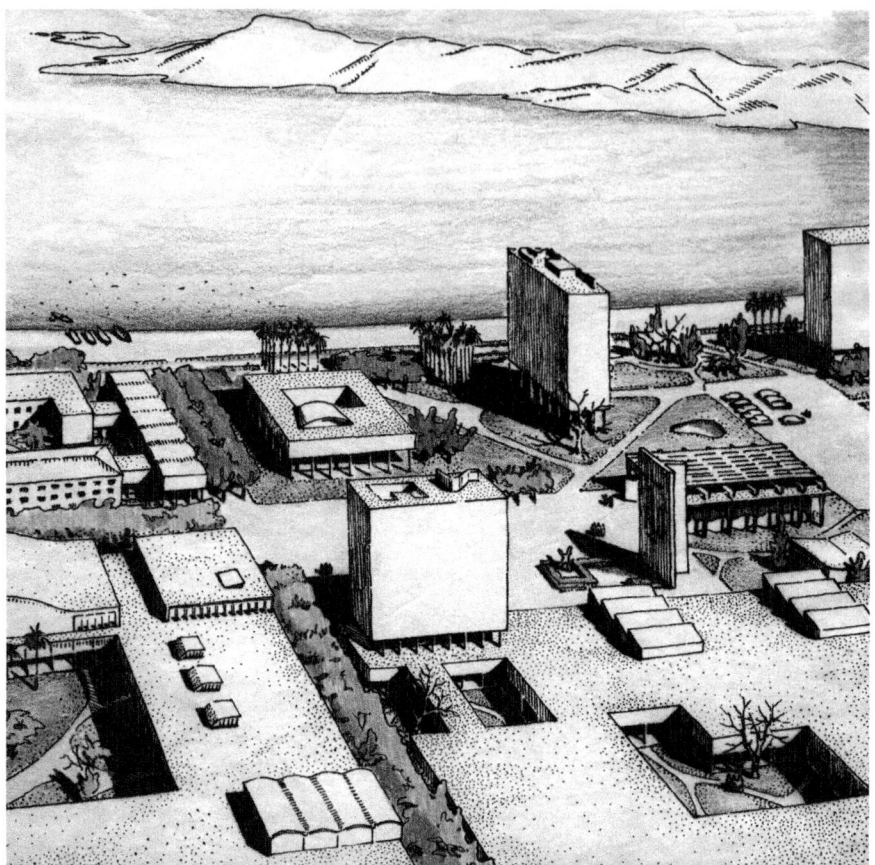

Figure 1
José Luis Sert and Paul Lester Wiener (Town Planning Associates), *Chimbote Plan*, downtown area, 1946–1948 for *Corporación Peruana del Santa*, Peru. Courtesy of Josep Lluis Sert Collection, Loeb Library, Harvard University Graduate School of Design.

corporations – was an example of extraordinary effort by a Latin American country to adopt and adapt the American development model to its context. In the new government, appropriation and transformation of American modernization was already taking place in the same way in which the new *Urbanistic Legislation* was established by young Lima's deputy Fernando Belaúnde.

The election in 1945 of the American-educated architect-planner Fernando Belaúnde as a deputy for Lima – for the government's party – had an important effect on architecture and urban planning in the Peruvian political agenda. Due to his position and network, the Belaúnde campaign's *Lima Housing Plan*, for which he designed and provided the legal and financial framework, became an official capital city project sooner rather than later. With the support of *Instituto de Urbanismo* founding members, he developed *Plan de Vivienda* (Lima's Housing Plan), a mass housing project based on the idea of seven *unidades vecinales*, the Peruvian neighborhood units.[12] Along with this effort, by the beginning of 1947, Belaúnde had "four laws" in place for his plans and the "four city functions." The so-called "Horizontal Property Law" provided the basis for the capitalistic and fast development of high-rise buildings with share ownership; the law for the establishment of the *Oficina Nacional de Planeamiento*

Urbano (ONPU) was dedicated to planning the expansion and renewal of cities; the law for the founding of *Corporación Nacional de la Vivienda* (CNV) covered the design, construction, and management of workforce housing nationwide; and the law for the "Popular Recreational Program" addressed the need for providing recreation facilities for the working class. *Centro Vacacional Huampaní* near Lima (Figure 2) was the most notable project developed under this law and considered by Belaúnde as "testimony to the renewed and progressive spirit and an essential part of Lima's social architecture movement."[13]

In this fashion, CIAM's four functions of "living, working, recreation, and circulation" were covered and helped transform Belaúnde's plans and ideas into buildings and works of infrastructure that would radically transform Peruvian urban landscapes. Hence, under the direction and incentive of the government and with the engagement of the private sector, Belaúnde and soon after Agrupación Espacio were expecting "to grasp the mirage of the functional city", so to speak, in the midst of the consolidation of the Peruvian Modern Project.

Figure 2
**Santiago Agurto
(Corporación Nacional
de la Vivienda),** *Centro
Vacacional de
Huampaní,* **Lima
1949–1955 (as published
in** *El Arquitecto Peruano*
**N210–11, January–
February, 1955).
Courtesy of** *El
Arquitecto Peruano.*

CIAM's evangelization and the Peruvian pioneers of modern architecture

Simultaneously, the Harry Truman administration (1945–53) continued tightening bonds with the "Americas" and sponsored several cultural activities in these southern countries in association with previous efforts such as MoMA's exhibitions dedicated to Latin American Arts and Architecture and Design.[14] As explained by J. F. Liernur in the "The South American Way", the *"Brazilian miracle"* was not only an architecture boom for this country during the 1930s and 1940s but also a cultural construct of the US government in the former Portuguese colony mainly during the war years.[15] Along the same lines, the State Department also sponsored architects and planners to lecture and to promote the infrastructural and architectural work done in the United States as a model of progress.[16] The lectures had the goal of reaching influential people to convince them of the fundamental role of democracy in the modernization process of their countries. And in spite of the great interest of Latin American governments in inviting and listening to these modern architects, these lectures can be seen as an American attempt at persuasion regarding the pragmatic process of modernization and the techniques and imagery of modern architecture and urban planning.[17]

On 2 June 1944, in response to Neutra's request, Paul L. Wiener sent a memo to José Luis Sert, Walter Gropius and Sigfried Giedion referring to the need to work towards the general acceptance and recognition of CIAM principles. This memo, as well as subsequent correspondence from Wiener, mentioned that it was necessary to prepare a list of American and foreign officials to be convinced of CIAM's intentions.[18] Then he wrote to Fernando Belaúnde – among other Latin American contacts – to get easy access to the Peruvian political elite and get invited to deliver lectures on modern architecture and planning. Belaúnde, a young architect trained in the USA, founder of the *Instituto de Urbanismo* in Lima and director of *El Arquitecto Peruano* journal,[19] professor of urban planning, and future President of Peru (1963–68 and 1980–85), was then a just-elected deputy for Lima with a mass-housing-oriented platform. Therefore, Belaúnde saw this as an opportunity to get unanimous support for his plans and quickly managed to extend an official invitation to Wiener – signed by the Ministry of Education – to lecture in Lima and other Peruvian cities.[20]

Hosted by Belaúnde, Luis Dorich, Carlos Morales Macchiavello, and Luis Ortiz de Zevallos, founding members of *Instituto de Urbanismo* in Lima, Wiener addressed the subjects of regional planning, new town planning, block rehabilitation and neighborhood unit development, as well as creativity in modern architecture and planning. Wiener's lectures were reported by Belaúnde's journal and described as having great impact in Lima professional circles.[21] In this manner, *El Arquitecto Peruano* (EAP) became a major channel for the dissemination of modern architecture and the most important advocate for implementation of new planning techniques. In fact, Belaúnde acting in his multiple roles recommended subjects for Weiner to address.[22] Wiener's acquaintance with these topics allowed him to offer his professional services as a "town planner" to the Peruvian government. As expected by Belaúnde, right after his visit *Corporación Peruana del Santa* offered the Chimbote Project (1946–48) to Wiener and Sert, partners at Town Planning Associates (TPA), to redesign this northern port city and transform it into a development magnet.[23]

Following CIAM's plan of influence, Richard Neutra, President of the temporary CIAM, was the next to travel to Latin America to lecture on modern architecture as well as urban planning in August of 1945.[24] As Eric Mumford has explained, during the war years the "transplanted CIAM" adopted the name of *CIAM Chapter for Relief and Postwar Planning*, aiming to be treated like any other American professional association, but they could not get that official support. Ultimately, the group was only a temporary CIAM, formed mainly by European émigrés who did not want to lose contact with CIAM while residing in the USA.[25] However; the trip was also sponsored by the US State Department which had local officials waiting for Neutra in all countries of destination, including Peru.

In his conference in Lima, *Metropolitan Future of a City with a Great Historical Heritage*, Neutra lectured on modern architecture and infrastructure projects as products of democracy and also emphasized the potential of this capital city to develop modern buildings in a meaningful city center.[26] Shortly after, in his "travel report from Latin America", Neutra informed the CIAM secretary Sigfried Giedion that:

> CIAM is well-known in Latin America. Many Latin American architects assisted in CIAM gatherings... Delegations of this Chapter will be organized in the coming weeks in Chile, Peru, Venezuela and Mexico. These countries are interested in building techniques in the United States and especially in the development of new systems of prefabrication applied to low-cost housing.[27]

In reference to CIAM group in Peru, he referred to an initiative to start a modern architecture group in Lima that was organized in Lima by Dorich and Carlos Morales. The group, *Frente de Arquitectura Moderna* (FAM), later adopted that name following Wiener's and Neutra's suggestion to create a local CIAM group.[28] Although FAM members were working individually on modern projects for the city of Lima, the attempt to establish a CIAM-Peru group was not successful.

In September 1945, EAP reported that Neutra's lecture was a great contribution to the modernization and progress of architecture.[29] The journal also commented on his assessment of Lima's Housing Plan based on *unidades vecinales* as a great idea. In the same article, the EAP journal also emphasized the *unidad vecinal* idea as the perfect means for humanizing the city because of its human scale and the provision of all material and spiritual needs for everyday life. With his Lima *Plan de Vivienda* of 1945 in mind for advancing his political career, Belaúnde saw in the prefabrication industry and the neighborhood unit concept the solutions for Lima's two biggest problems: the ineffective construction industry (costly and slow) and the great housing deficit (increased by the lack of mass housing plans). Indeed, Neutra's and Wiener's advocacy for neighborhood unit plans and prefab housing was evident since it was the core of the prewar CIAM discourse within its functional city model. Thus, Wiener and Neutra lectures caught the attention of Peruvian architects and city officials just as Belaúnde and the European architects had expected.

The year of 1945 was crucial for the process of introducing and consolidating modern architecture in Lima, and the EAP journal gave good indications of this transformation. Although it continued publishing some neo-colonial-style houses and eclectic buildings, the journal increasingly displayed the work of modern architects from Brazil and the United States, as did the American magazines that arrived regularly at the library of the recently created Department of Architecture (1943) at the *Escuela Nacional de Ingeniería* (ENI).[30] By then, EAP had also published, in November of 1943, the "principles of modern planning" as shown by José Luis Sert in *Can Our Cities Survive?* (1942),[31] but without reference to the book. Hence, young architects and students of architecture were getting acquainted with the "new architecture" which encouraged them to explore new trends and to go beyond their technical and beaux-arts education. Also in 1945, Luis Miró Quesada published *Espacio en el Tiempo. La arquitectura moderna como fenómeno cultural*. It was the first book about modern architecture in Lima, and the first articulate claim for modern culture as well as an attack on revivals and historicist styles in the culture of Peruvian architecture.[32]

Miró Quesada's *Espacio en el Tiempo* is the founding text of modern architecture, urban planning, and arts in Peru, and it constitutes a plea for the "true expression of the new times." Miró Quesada's text lays claim to a new architecture in the modern world as a part of human evolution. Interested in all the "modern masters", Miró Quesada merged all avant-garde architectural ideologies into one broad feeling of the "modern times", which should have produced an architecture that "is the materialization of the most sublime of all arts by the demonstration of space in time."[33] According to Miró Quesada, in close connection with Le Corbusier's ideas, the times of man's new spirit should also be represented by "our architecture and today's arts, which capture and symbolize the new feeling of humanity in the cosmos."[34] In order to be able to perceive the new art of architecture, one should be aware of the new unity of "space-time" as well as the new era, based on a new sensibility and a new spirit, an obvious reference to Giedion's *Space, Time and Architecture*.[35]

The need for light, clean air, and minimum living space and social responsibility, and the rejection of all kinds of historicist styles in modern buildings were also part of his interpretive discourse. Taking images and ideas presented by pioneering books that advocated modern principles, Miró Quesada's syncretism towards the so-called modern movement hybridized with Peruvian traditions allowed him to build a theory that exposed the values of modern architecture's faith in building techniques, along with local building patterns, as well as new forms and spaces interpreted with the geometric abstraction of pre-Columbian cultures. Shortly after, in 1947–48, several premises would be materialized in the projection and construction of *Casa Huiracocha*, his own house in Lima (Figure 3); and later on in the 1950s *Unidad Vecinal de Matute* would consolidate this hybridized architectural language in the modern project.

Therefore, not only was the book a turning point in students' beaux-arts education, but it also provided access to a Peruvian view of early European avant-garde and American modernism. It emphasized the spatial and formal quality of European architecture as much as its social role, along with the bold and simple structures of modern construction. The text also highlights technical advancements in building techniques in the USA along with the organic approach of Wright's oeuvre. As a result, within the context of a Spanish-colonial city with heavy pre-Columbian imagery and *Espacio en el Tiempo*'s mixture of it with European poetics and social values and American pragmatism, young Peruvian architects started to visualize new building forms to manifest the national Modern Project. As A. Ballent has pointed out, "the key issues of Latin American architecture in the post-war period for the international critic seem to combine formal synthesis of modern languages and a nuance of primitive sensibility."[36] Indeed, this hybridization reveals the appropriation and transformation of western modern cultures with Peruvian cultural traditions, emphasizing the vitality of a modern cultural project in the process of becoming.

Espacio en el Tiempo was received with little enthusiasm by the old generation of architects, but with great excitement by the architecture students at ENI. Furthermore, in short time, *Espacio en el Tiempo* became in the student's hands a modern primer that in many ways triggered the emergence of Agrupación Espacio.[37]

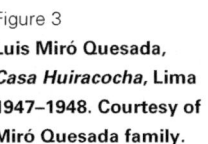

Figure 3
**Luis Miró Quesada,
Casa Huiracocha, Lima
1947–1948. Courtesy of
Miró Quesada family.**

Agrupación Espacio and the search for the modern city

In 1946, after a progressive acquaintance with modern architectural culture, a group of students led by Adolfo Córdova at ENI demanded changes in educational methods, particularly after learning from the works of many modern architects and the enlightened discourses of *Vers une Architecture* and *Espacio en el Tiempo*. The group asked for more "design" studios as opposed to drawing classes and new professors interested in the production of *contemporary* architecture.[38] As a result of the students' request, a new and young faculty entered the school to teach new courses *a la Bauhaus*,[39] including Luis Miró Quesada (Analysis of Architectural Function), Fernando Belaúnde (The National Housing Problem), and Enrique Seoane (Design Studio) and *bauhausler* (former Gropius student) Paul Linder (Arts Philosophy), among others, whom the students would later join as assistants and eventually faculty members. Shortly after, the core of this group of students organized themselves as *Agrupación Espacio* under the leadership of young professor Luis Miró Quesada. Since the first gatherings in 1947, the group had worked for the establishment of modern architecture in Peru and for the recognition of modern cultural expressions. On May 15 1947, *Expresión de Principios de la Agrupación Espacio* was published by the newspaper *El Comercio*, also appearing later in June in the journal *El Arquitecto Peruano*.[40]

This "manifesto" was the result of the group's need to express frustration with the cultural stagnation of society. It denounced the existing gap between their Peruvian cultural sphere and the "modern world."[41] It also evidenced self-determination as opposed to the traditional way of looking at architecture, arts and the city, and made a claim to reversing the situation.[42] Like many avant-garde groups, Espacio opened its manifesto declaring that "man is a product of his time" and the "times have changed into a modern era." The manifesto identified architecture as a key factor in human evolution and a sign of man's progress. Espacio stated that the origins of contemporary man were already in the past, and, as an example of the new man in these times, one could look at the work of architects such as Le Corbusier, Gropius, Mies, Niemeyer, Neutra, Wright, and others. For Espacio, as for Le Corbusier and Miró Quesada, architecture had to provide basic living conditions, such as housing and green areas. They proposed modern architecture and planning techniques as the means to those ends.[43]

Agrupacion Espacio fought for the establishment of modern architecture and urban planning, as well as for all other expressions of modern culture. Their "enemies" (as with many avant-garde groups) were the architectural revival styles, and particularly the government's pseudo official neo-colonial style. As declared by the group in a letter to Le Corbusier that same year of 1947, Espacio's mission was "to fight official academicism in the Peruvian context and to create a new path to the contemporary world."[44] Following the release of the manifesto, Espacio organized a series of lectures and public events to spread their ideas in the city. Music, theater, painting, literature, architecture and urban planning were the main topics chosen for these events.[45] With these actions, the young group was also attempting to make the public aware of new trends in architecture and urban planning and their social responsibility towards the city.

In addition to that, the group launched *Colabora la Agrupación Espacio,* a weekly newspaper article designed to approach the public in a very simple way and attract them to the new architecture while bringing to their attention the need for city planning. With the same goals, the group started *Espacio* magazine in 1949.[46] While showing modern buildings and explaining how they were fulfilling the new needs of the times, it advocated the creation of new parks and public spaces as well as greater social responsibility towards the city. In this way, Espacio worked from its beginnings with the aim of bringing new ideas of modern architecture, urban planning and arts into the academic, professional, and public spheres.

Espacio – as well as Belaúnde – believed in architecture and urbanism as instruments for improving cities, and therefore the young group had Belaúnde's crucial support to take leading positions in academia and government offices dedicated to the design and planning of urban environments. In this way Belaúnde and Espacio's cultural activism introduced to the broader audience the principles of modern architecture and urban planning in Peru. However, it is important to point out that even though the young group had a great influence in the development of Peruvian cities through the design of master plans, collective housing, public buildings and commercial buildings, it was not until the 1950s that single family houses (the most popular housing typology for the middle class in Lima) gave up historicist and revival styles to adopt a modern language in the new neighborhoods.

Since the late 1940s, modern principles in urban planning had been applied nationwide through *Oficina Nacional de Planeamiento Urbano* (ONPU) and *Corporación Nacional de Vivienda* (CNV) plans, such as city zoning schemes, transportation plans, and mass housing developments, as well as commercial and civic centers. Led by Espacio members Luis Dorich and Santiago Agurto respectively, these organizations were the most decisive agencies in the physical development and transformation of Peruvian cities, particularly Lima. In most cases, ONPU and CNV coordinated the location of new highways, mass housing and industrial areas. Among ONPU city plans, the one that stands out is Lima's *Plan Piloto* (1947–49). Designed by a team led by Luis Dorich at ONPU – with the collaboration of Sert and Wiener and the advice of Ernesto N. Rogers[47] – the *Plan Piloto de Lima* was essentially based on the creation of a *sector central* (Lima's civic center and business area), *unidades vecinales* (neighborhood units, called *Unidades de Barrio*), the designation of land use (city functions such as dwelling, work, industry and green areas), and the construction of a new highway system that connected the capital with other Peruvian cities (circulation).[48]

Sert and Wiener produced sketches, drawings, models, and plans with new circulation patterns, and new block arrangements for Lima's central area, with inner parking lots and plazas. In the *sector central*, they proposed many sketches and drawings of new building typologies of "contrasting heights", looking for the integration of modern building into the colonial grid while creating public civic spaces (Figures 4a and 4b).[49] Lima's new civic center presented in ONPU's *Plan Piloto* deployed the "towers and podium" idea (contrasting heights), but the *sector central* area disregarded that typology and was primarily composed of towers and inner courtyards within the colonial grid (Figure 5).

Besides the well-published ONPU's civic center and business area, *unidades vecinales* were probably the most distinctive component of *Plan Piloto de Lima*, and certainly the most important product of the Peruvian encounter with modern architecture and urbanism. The *unidades vecinales* – as defined in the Lima Housing Plan – are autonomous neighborhoods that generate their own urbanity, since they allocate nearly 1000 families (more than 5000 people) with a civic center that included all city services such as schools, churches, shopping centers, clubs, parks, and plazas, other collective spaces within a pedestrian-scale precinct which is never crossed by vehicular traffic.[50] They had the aim to provide not only housing facilities, but the sense of community in the modern city.

Unidades vecinales were proposed in Lima as a solution for the housing crisis that affected thousands of people living in slums and blighted areas. Combining new models of urbanization such as Garden City, Siedlung, neighborhood units and *existenz-minimum* for mass housing, the ideas were adopted, adapted, and transformed from their original context in the American and European cities into Peruvian conditions. *Unidades vecinales* were the core of Lima's 1945 Housing Plan which planned to rebuild ruined city blocks after relocating the population into these new neighborhood units. This scheme, largely influenced by Gropius's ideas,[51] aimed to build seven neighborhoods for

Figure 4a and b
José Luis Sert and Paul Lester Wiener (Town Planning Associates), Civic Center studies, 1947–1949, *Plan Piloto de Lima, in collaboration with Oficina Nacional de Planeamiento Urbano*. Courtesy of Josep Luis Sert Collection, Loeb Library, Harvard University Graduate School of Design.

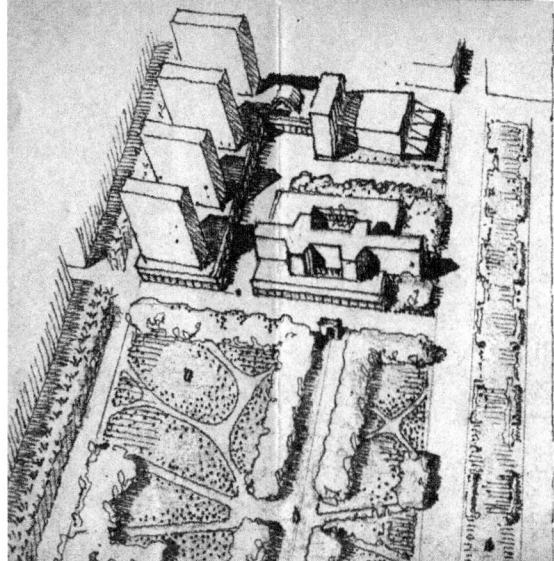
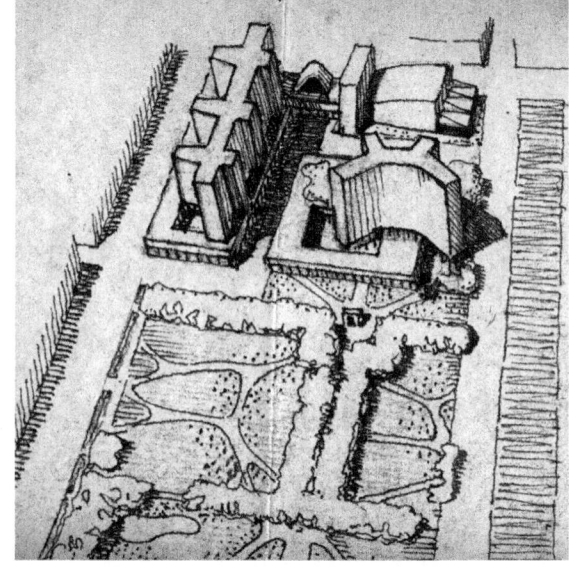

Figure 5
"El Sector Central,"
Plan Piloto de Lima
(1947–1949), Luis Dorich
(Director). Source:
Oficina Nacional de
Planeamiento Urbano
(ONPU) Plan Piloto de
Lima, Lima: Empresa
Gráfica T. Scheuch,
1949, p. 28.

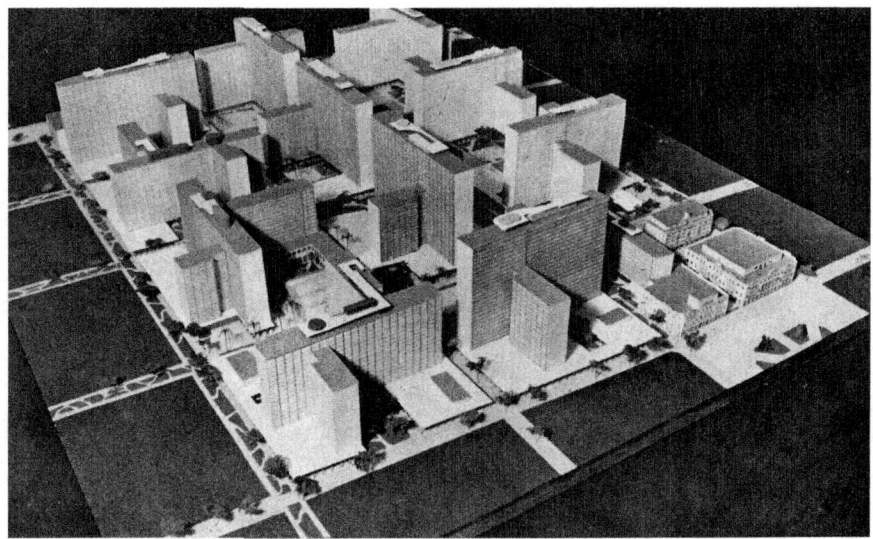

more than 35,000 people, and hence expand the city within a planned organization, assuring sound conditions for all these citizens. *Unidad Vecinal N° 3* was the first to be built, and therefore has become a landmark in the architectural and urban landscape of Lima and Latin American cities (Figure 6). This collective housing project also contributes to our understanding of a vast phenomenon that has had several incarnations in Lima and other important cities of America, Europe, Africa and Asia mainly during the postwar period.

For Dorich and Belaúnde, neighborhood units, civic centers and the four functions were the basis for Lima's plan – based on postwar-CIAM ideas – and were therefore easily celebrated by Sert and Wiener and Rogers (Figure 7). Espacio members, TPA partners and Belaúnde saw Lima's *Plan Piloto* as the remedy for improving the chaotic city center and as a tool for regulating the expanding boundaries of the capital city, whereas the Chimbote Plan was seen as the model for urban renewal of emerging Peruvian industrial cities. After about two years of work between Lima and New York, Wiener and Sert's Peruvian projects were almost ready in 1949, and CIAM VII Bergamo was therefore the first congress where they were presented.[52]

Nevertheless, TPA Peruvian projects – as with many other Latin American plans – were not successfully implemented. On the one hand, the Chimbote Plan was put on hold in 1949 by the new military regime of General Manuel Odría (1948–50 and 1950–56) and eventually canceled.[53] On the other hand, after extended negotiations with the congress, Lima's plan was approved in 1949 but never successfully implemented. According to W. Ludeña, it was greatly restricted by the political lobbies and evidently not useful as an urban development guideline.[54] Due to these developments, by the end of 1950 both the Lima and Chimbote efforts were beyond recovery. Conflicts between institutional plans and private interests did not allow the implementation of any of

Figure 6
"Una gran realización Peruana, la Unidad Vecinal No 3," *Unidad Vecinal N° 3,* Lima 1945–1949, Fernando Belaúnde (consultant); Luis Dorich, Carlos Morales Macchiavelo, Alfredo Dammert, Eugenio Montagne, Juan Benítez, Manuel Valega, as published in *El Arquitecto Peruano,* N146, Septiembre 1949. Courtesy of *El Arquitecto Peruano.*

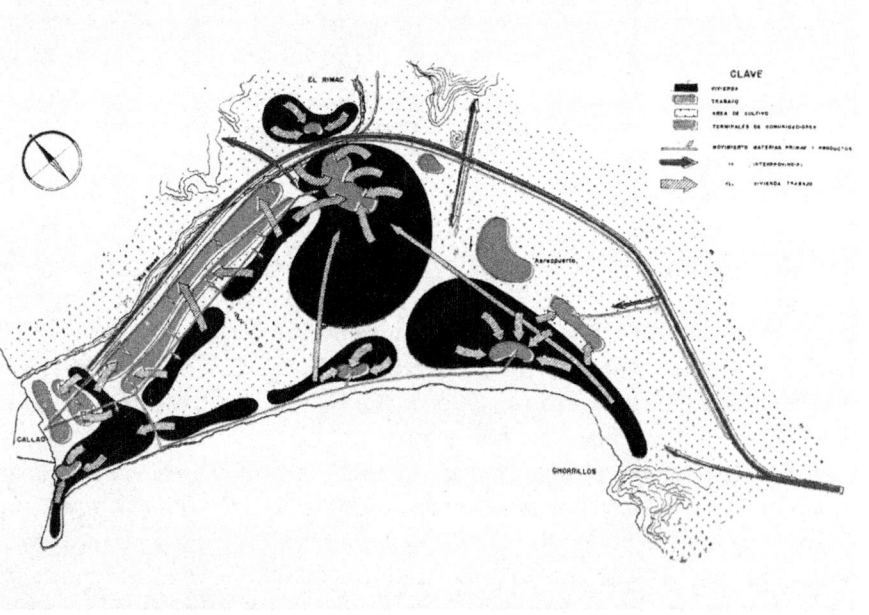

Figure 7
"Dinámica propuesta," *Plan Piloto de Lima* (1947–1949), Luis Dorich (Director). Source: *Oficina Nacional de Planeamiento Urbano* (ONPU) *Plan Piloto de Lima,* Lima: Empresa Gráfica T. Scheuch, 1949, p. 30.

these plans. Suddenly, the two most interesting plans for the growth and redevelopment of Peruvian cities lay stagnant.

Nevertheless, and in spite of all these problems, CIAM ideas generated positive responses in Peru and Latin America, mainly due to prewar congressional efforts and the projects of its leading figures, such as Le Corbusier and Walter

Gropius. As a consequence, young groups of architects in Cuba, Colombia, Peru and other Latin American countries became interested in absorbing, interpreting and expanding CIAM ideals into their own contexts, aspiring to become part of the congress. In the case of Lima, after establishing close contact with Sert, Rogers, and Le Corbusier, Agrupación Espacio attempted to turn its gathering into an official "national group" and become the "CIAM-Peru group."[55]

Espacio and the challenge of the CIAM-Peru Group

After two years of work, Espacio felt that its bonds with CIAM (with Sert and Wiener in particular) were strong enough to justify officially joining the congress As stated in a letter from Dorich to Sert on January 29 1949, Agrupación Espacio was interested in joining CIAM. Dorich wrote: "During the last meeting of Agrupación Espacio, all members showed interest in belonging collectively to CIAM."[56] Sert answered with positive comments, sending Espacio the "statutes" of the congress. Apparently, it was the best moment for Espacio to become part of the congress. Since his initial visit to Lima in 1947, Sert had worked actively in establishing closer contacts with the CIAM Latin American groups. Those contacts were made not only to further the success and influence of CIAM's ideas regarding modern architecture in the third world, but also to introduce Sert himself as a prominent expert in the field of urbanization, which was associated with modernization and progress and would ultimately lead to new commissions.

Because of his popularity within CIAM and the government support he enjoyed in Peru, Sert even thought of organizing a CIAM in Lima. Before departing to work on the Chimbote and Lima plans, Sert wrote to Giedion, giving him an update on the CIAM VI organization and proposing Lima as the next congress city:

> I am leaving the day after tomorrow for Lima. […] From Lima I hope to be able to work for CIAM by organizing a local group there and establishing closer contact with all Latin American delegates. I also believe it would be possible for us to do some work for the next congress with a young group in Lima. We have facilities because we will work with the government offices down there.[57]

It is important to mention that Sert had become president of CIAM at that Bridgewater meeting in June 1947, and since then his role among the Europeans, Americans, and Latin Americans had become even more vital to the success of the congress. He was aware that new modern architecture groups were emerging in Latin America under the auspices of "the modern masters" and he therefore established close contact with national group leaders, such as Luis Dorich and the Espacio group in Peru, Oscar Niemeyer in Brazil, Jorge Gaitán in Colombia, Luis Bonet – a fellow Catalonian who was working in Uruguay and Argentina – and Jorge Ferrari Hardoy, a Le Corbusier pupil working in Argentina, among other modern architects from Chile, Venezuela, and Cuba. Peru had no official group in the congress yet; therefore, Sert invited Dorich, Belaúnde, and even Hector Velarde to attend the meetings several times, always acting as individuals.[58] Espacio members Mario Bianco and Eduardo Neira wrote Giedion on April 11 1949, explaining the circumstances and confirming their wish to join the CIAM congress by creating the CIAM-Peru group.[59] But the bureaucratization of CIAM caused problems for the Peruvian group's incorporation.

In the summer of 1949, CIAM VII was held in Bergamo to discuss new topics such as the "Charter of Athens in Practice" and the "Synthesis of the Arts", among others. The Italian congress was organized by E. Rogers and included only two Latin American representatives, with no Peruvian participation. Shortly before the meeting, noting the imminent absence of Latin Americans in the next Bergamo congress and still working in Lima, Sert wrote to Gropius to insist on the idea of holding a congress in Latin America. With master plans in Colombia and Peru and aiming to get work in Venezuela and Chile, Sert considered holding CIAM VIII in Lima, among other Latin American cities:

> I have been considering the possibility of suggesting a location for this congress somewhere on the American continent. What do you think about it? There are quite a few young groups in South America, as you know, and the universities and schools of architecture are easier to reorganize there than in European countries... Cuba, Bogotá or Lima would be possible meeting places, and I am sure we would get a very lively congress although many people from Europe would not be able to attend.[60]

Certainly, it would have been an important step to reinforce CIAM ideas with local architects and government officials, and indeed, it would have allowed him to establish solid relations with country officials and achieve his ultimate goal: to get built work. But again the European groups pushed to get CIAM back to Europe and the congress was finally held in Hoddesdon, England. At the CIAM VIII congress, the Colombian group was the only participant from Latin America, and the Peruvian group only figured in a later publication as a "group in formation," for which Luis Dorich was referenced as the contact person.[61] That was Espacio's last attempt to create an official CIAM-Peru group, and its first and last appearance in a CIAM publication.

There is no clear evidence yet of an official answer from CIAM to Agrupación Espacio's request, but while there were many problems in preparing the VII and VIII congresses, it seems likely that Giedion never wrote back with a formal refusal. In a letter from Giedion to Sert, Espacio's intention was mentioned, but it can be inferred that no one wanted to deal with more issues regarding American or Latin American groups.[62] Giedion could not stand the South American way of not being punctual and clear with their commitments, while Sert detested the fact that the "poor European countries" were paying their fees and the Americans were not.[63] Without question, there was a clear lack of interest by most American members in CIAM statutes and bureaucratic organization, while European national groups were trying to relocate CIAM management back to Europe. Shortly after, as the slim threads that linked CIAM and the Peruvian group slowly dissolved, young CIAM members aimed to displace the older generation – which, according to them, was directing CIAM from the Harvard University Graduate School of Design, in reference to Gropius, Sert and Giedion – and return to the idea of a small-group discussion format to avoid large audiences and bureaucracies.

In the early 1950s, differences between the urban approaches to the city espoused by the European CIAM groups and the Latin American factions started to increase, diminishing interest in both CIAM and Espacio respectively. While Dorich and Miró Quesada (Agrupación Espacio) and others at the *Instituto de Urbanismo* in Lima were still lecturing on the "functional city" model, Le Corbusier, Sert and CIAM members were working to overcome the lack of a symbolic dimension (new monumentality) in the modern city while the Smithsons and the emerging Team 10 were influenced by existentialism (urban structuring). Moreover, with the new panorama of modern architecture, in the context of the Pan-American Congress of Architecture, Espacio and other Latin American groups disregarded Eurocentric CIAM and focused on the regional congresses. This interest was shared along with common problems and goals in the new South American metropolises. The paradox in this situation is that the Latin American architects grew up with an inferiority complex towards CIAM's leaders, although their performance – as recognized by Giedion himself in 1956 – was highly superior to the Europeans' and of great relevance for the development of the discipline worldwide.[64]

The end of Espacio and the end of CIAM

CIAM IX, the last genuine CIAM gathering, was held in 1953 in Aix-en-Provence with no Latin American presence. The symbolic dimension of the closing party on the *Unité d'Habitation* roof seems now a perfect farewell for all those idealistic architects. Soon after, when Sert and Gropius visited Lima in January 1954, Espacio and CIAM were neither as active nor in as close contact as in previous years. Yet the modern masters were invited by Belaúnde – Chair of the Architecture Department at ENI – with the collaboration of Professor Paul Linder, a *bauhausler* German émigré and former student of Gropius. The aim of the trip to Lima was to lecture the students on architecture, urban planning and the architect's social duties in modern cities.

That same year of 1954, during the preparation for the CIAM X congress, the "interval groups" were divided and the new generation advocated structural changes that would transform CIAM and its urban approach. The same young members who were pulling CIAM back to Europe and criticizing the old generation, emerged from CIAM as Team 10. They felt they needed to redirect the congress and readdress the understanding and design of the city based on social and phenomenological structures in opposition to the functional model. When this last congress was held in Dubrovnik in 1956, Le Corbusier's absence was a clear sign that the core group was already thinking of withdrawal from and/ or dissolution of the congress.[65] Simultaneously with this crisis, Espacio was dealing with similar concerns: the impasse within the group and the impossibility of modern architecture reaching its goals. After years of having "won" the battle for modern architecture in Peru and having produced dozens of city plans, mass housing projects, and minimal dwelling prototypes, Espacio still could not find an effective solution to urban problems, the housing crisis and citizens' needs. Although Espacio members had contributed to the search for housing deficit solutions with several clever, locally rooted mass housing projects such as *Unidad Vecinal N° 3, Unidad Vecinal de Matute* (Figure 8) and many others, they were still looking for more direct and efficient ways to provide essential strategies to solve the persistent housing crisis.

    In 1955, when MoMA exhibited *Unidad Vecinal Matute* by Santiago Agurto at CNV as Peruvian modern architecture within the *Modern Latin American Architecture since 1945* show,[66] Agrupación Espacio had left behind the "modern standard" approach (*unidades vecinales*). They were already exploring new urban architectural processes in the informal city. Espacio members such as Adolfo Córdova, Eduardo Neira, and Santiago Agurto, together with other Peruvian architects, were experimenting with new strategies to overcome lack of housing and adequate urbanization conditions for the great numbers of people living on Lima's outskirts. Their work was focused on the improvement of Lima's emerging *barriadas*, which were becoming the newest and largest neighborhoods in the

Figure 8

Santiago Agurto, Architect (*Corporación Nacional de la Vivienda*), Unidad Vecinal de Matute, Lima 1950–1953. Source: *Modern Architecture in Latin America since 1945*, Museum of Modern Art Exhibition Catalogue, New York, 1955, pp. 132–133.

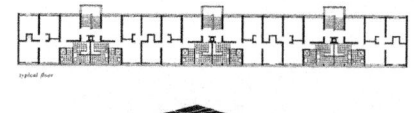

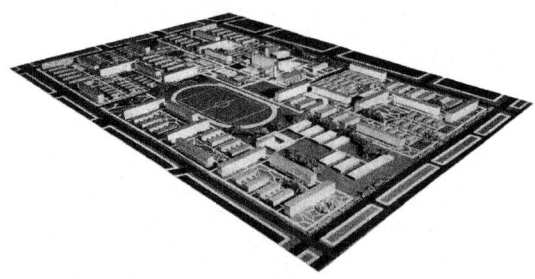

city. They not only transformed the conception of *barriadas* (shanty towns) from an "urban cancer" – described by the EAP journal in the 1940s – to an "urbanization model". Researching vernacular methods of *auto-construction* (self-help) and community structuring (clusters of lots), Peruvian architects since the mid-1950s were trying to integrate the emerging shanty towns into the city to meet people's basic needs. In this way – some years before the arrival of John Turner in Peru and the internationalization of squatting theories in the 1960s – "site and services" and "self-help" strategies emerged within the work of Espacio, CNV, and the recommendations of *Comisión de la Reforma Agraria y de la Vivienda* (CRAV, 1956–58).[67] It is in this way that Peruvian architects since the mid-1950s started to work on shanty towns as a new approach to improve Lima's popular living standards.[68]

Coincidentally, that same year of the MoMA show, some Espacio members organized a trip to Huarochiri, a small town near Lima. Led by sociologist José Matos Mar, the expedition brought together architects, engineers, sociologists, and other professionals, working as a group to explore how architecture could help to improve people's living standards. Still encouraged by some of their modern principles and the group's early philosophy, Espacio members from different fields worked intensively to improve the living conditions of this poor town. By addressing the problems of Lima's outskirts in this way, they thought they could propose new solutions to the housing shortage on a larger scale. As H. Heynen has pointed out in the impasse of modern architects that sought to solve the workers' housing in the 1930s, it can be said that Agrupación Espacio understood that "architecture inevitably has to deal with the tension that exists between modernity and dwelling" and therefore, reached the limits of the architectural discipline.[69]

Espacio realized not only that architecture could not change society – nor solve poor living conditions by design – but also that the group had divided ideologies regarding the role of architecture and the architect in society. In the broadest discussions, Espacio was calling for an unconditional commitment towards correcting social imbalances while confronting the limits of the discipline. While some of the members had already decided not to participate in the Haurochiri project and continued to work within the discipline's traditional limits, the bulk of the group joined a political project attempting to achieve deep social changes. The *Movimiento Social Progresista* political group was a response to Espacio's impasse, and in many ways it triggered the dissolution of the group.[70]

As distressing as it should have been for the CIAM core group to recognize the end of the congress, it was disappointing for Espacio to realize that modern architecture, the functional city and the interrelationship of the arts could not be accomplished most of the time and that when it was possible, architecture would not be enough to solve the urban problems of modern life.[71] Nevertheless, it did not stop the architects from continuing to produce architectural projects of great quality nor from exploring the formal, spatial, structural, and cultural limits of Peruvian hybridization in modern architectural culture, as in the work of

Figure 9
Adolfo Córdova, Carlos Williams (Córdova-Williams Arquitectos), *Air Force Housing Complex,* **Chiclayo, 1955. Courtesy of Adolfo Córdova.**

Cordova-Williams during the following decades, particularly at the FAP Housing Complex in Chiclayo, 1959 (Figure 9).

During the next two decades, the Peruvian Modern Project continued in various forms, especially with the return of Manuel Prado to the government (1956–62) and finally with the government of Architect Fernando Belaúnde (1963–68). The Modern Project was carried out during these two administrations with the collaboration of many people in the political and technical realms who had started the project years back in the 1940s, including some former Agrupación Espacio members in charge of national planning offices and architecture departments and some governmental positions. Thus the project went on – assuming different incarnations – until the 1970s, when a military regime took power (1968–80), initiating the mirage of the "Peruvian Revolution". Within that context, the "Charter of Machu Picchu" (1977) was released and signed in Lima by many former Espacio members and CIAM-related architects.[72] In this "manifesto" Santiago Agurto and Luis Miró Quesada, Fernando Belaúnde, José Luis Sert, and Oscar Niemeyer among others, recognized that the city "should not follow a functionalist approach, but a contextual and multifunctional one," as well as "integrate informal city agglomerations (*barriadas*) within the city structure", among other ideas, reinforcing the instability of architecture and the city, which in many ways represents the end of the search for the functional city.[73]

Modern architecture for a Modern Project

As has been explained in this chapter, the Peruvian Modern Project emerged in the mid-1940s as a product of cultural hybridization. This hybridization phenomenon was a consequence of the overlap and transformation of local cultural patterns and Anglo-Saxon modernization strategies. Therefore, it can be said that there is no "colonization" process in light of the introduction and development of modern urban culture. Traditional historiography and cultural studies in architecture have focused only on European and American initiatives to spread their modernization techniques on the Latin American continent, without paying attention to the great interest, expectations and efforts by those countries to adopt, transform, and deploy these modern tactics. Indeed, there was a simultaneous reaching out in both directions, one diffusing the ideology, the other absorbing and hybridizing it.

In this sense, the encounter was twofold: on one side, while the Peruvian government and state apparatuses were seeking modernity concentrated in American development techniques, the American administration was also trying to influence the Peruvian political scene and induce the southern country to use their methods of modernization. On the other side, while young Peruvian architects were getting acquainted with modern architecture and CIAM ideas and were adopting, adapting and transforming them into their own context, CIAM émigrés in the USA – with the support of the State Department – started to visit Latin American countries to persuade country officials and architects to use modern architecture and planning as the means of modernization.

These twin modernization phenomena shaped two important architectural and cultural products that would give form and character to the Peruvian Modern Project. On the one hand, versatile architect Belaúnde coordinated a team to developed the most important Peruvian contribution to the post-war architecture culture in Latin America, the *unidad vecinal* concept. On the other hand, hybridizing interwar European social values, poetry of modern spaces and American pragmatism with the pre-Columbian formal abstraction and imagery, Agrupación Espacio emerged to clash with the conservative cultural establishment and give form to the modern project. The group achieved a cultural and architectural transformation to the new era – as occurred in many Latin American capital cities – particularly in the design of *unidades vecinales*; urban architecture projects that embodied the Peruvian Modern Project as its best.

Despite attempts by Espacio and colleagues at *Corporación Nacional de Vivienda* and *Oficina Nacional de Planeamiento Urbano* to become congress members and Sert's enthusiastic proposal of Lima as a possible meeting place, an official CIAM Peru group was never established in Lima and no Peruvian architect participated in or attended the congress meetings. Soon after, the simultaneous crises of CIAM and Espacio dealt with similar facts and concerns: the impossibility of architecture accomplishing real social change, which forced an important part of the Peruvian group to attempt social transformation through the political sphere. Links between CIAM and Espacio slowly dissolved as these core groups broke up. But besides the specific circumstances of each one, the main reasons for the dissolution of Espacio and CIAM are analogous: both groups broke up after recognizing the end of the search for a planned city and accepting the uncertainty of growth and the unpredictable transformation of architecture and cities.

But beyond the impasse, modern architecture in Peru and the Peruvian Modern Project continued developing new forms and looking for new strategies to improve the quality of life in the metropolis for many years. Therefore, the recognition of the unending housing crisis provoked in Espacio members the re-examination of Lima's *barriadas*, recognizing their potential as a mass housing urbanization model. Cordova, Neira, and other members were instrumental in the reversal of shanty-town assessment, from a problem to a solution. Later on, the new project of the "military and revolutionary government" installed new paradigms that led to the demise of the Peruvian Modern Project and distrust of architecture and urbanism as tools for social transformation.

Nowadays, Espacio remains in the history of Peru as the seminal group that embraced modern architecture as a principle and worked towards its introduction, transformation and development within the local culture of Peru. Furthermore, the group's role in modern Peruvian culture is immeasurable, as remarkable as its buildings. Its thinking changed the urban development of the country and went beyond Peruvian borders through their work as educators of outstanding architects in Lima and many other world cities. For now, the projects, works, and actions of Agrupación Espacio occupy a central place in Peruvian architecture, but they are still waiting for the recognition they deserve in the historiography of modern architecture.

Acknowledgements

Special thanks to Mary Daniels and Ines Zalduendo, JLS SC & CIAM SC; Bruce Tabb, PLWC; Simon Elliott, RNA-UCLA; Isabelle Godineau, FLC; Daniel Weiss, ETHZ-CIAM; Miguel Cruchaga, EAP; Miró Quesada family; Santiago Agurto; Adolfo Córdova.

All translations from Spanish are the author's.

JLS SC: Josep Luis Sert Collection, Special Collections, Loeb Library, Harvard University Graduate School of Design; CIAM SC: CIAM Collection, Special Collections, Loeb Library, Harvard University Graduate School of Design; ETHZ-CIAM: CIAM Archive, Institute of History and Theory, Department of Architecture, ETH Zurich; PLWC: Paul Lester Wiener Collection, University of Oregon Library; WGAHL: Walter Gropius Archive, Houghton Library, Harvard University; RNA-UCLA, Richard Neutra Archive, Department of Special Collections, University Research Library, University of California Los Angeles; FLC, Fondation Le Corbusier.

Notes

1 Néstor García Canclini, *Culturas híbridas. Estrategias para entrar y salir de la modernidad*, Buenos Aires: Paidós, 2001.

2 See Felipe Hernandez, "On the notion of architectural hybridization in Latin America," in *The Journal of Architecture*, vol. 7, no. 1, London: New York, Routledge, 2002, pp. 77–86.

3   "Expresión de Principios de Agrupación Espacio" was first published on May 15 1947 in *Diario El Comercio* in Lima. In June of the same year the same document was published in the journal *El Arquitecto Peruano*. After this public announcement, the group organized several conferences over the space of a month where they explained the modern expression of architecture and arts to the general public. *Agrupación Espacio* members were mainly architects. Under the leadership of Luis Miró Quesada, the group was made up of architects and planners, such as Paul Linder, Mario Bianco, Adolfo Córdoba, Luis Dorich, Carlos Williams, Eduardo Neira Alva, Javier Cayo, Santiago Agurto, Carlos Cueto F., Luis Vera, and Samuel Pérez Barreto, among others. The manifesto had a group of "adherents" consisting of poets, painters and musicians. Later, the group included sociologists and engineers.

4   *Congrès International d'Architecture Moderne* – CIAM is used in this chapter as the name of the group of leaders as well as that of the official congress.

5   There are few publications on the subject. Wiley Ludena, "Urbanismo moderno en el Perú: El aporte de la Agrupación Espacio. Aproximaciones', *Urbes1*, 2003 is one of the most relevant publications on this subject, but it hardly addresses Espacio and CIAM relationship.

6   Bryce Wood, *The Making of the Good Neighbor Policy*, New York: Columbia University Press, 1961, p. 7.

7   Irwin F. Gellman, *Good Neighbor Diplomacy. United States Policies in Latin America, 1933–1945*, Baltimore: The Johns Hopkins University Press, 1979, p. 2.

8   See Thorp and Bertram, *Peru, 1890–1977: Growth and Policy in an Open Economy*, New York: Columbia University Press, 1978, p. 186.

9   "Mensaje del presidente del Perú, Doctor Manuel Prado y Ugarteche, ante el congreso nacional, el 28 de julio de 1943'; Museo del Congreso de la Republica del Perú, Mensajes Presidenciales.

10   See Tennessee Valley Authority, *TVA as a Symbol of Resource Development in Many Countries*, Knoxville Tennessee: TVA Technical Library, January 1952.

11   See Alberto Adrianzén, "Continuidades y rupturas en el pensamiento político," in Alberto Adrianzén (ed.), *Pensamiento Político Peruano 1930–1968*, Lima: DESCO, 1990.

12   "El plan de vivienda del Gobierno Peruano," in *El Arquitecto Peruano*, September 1945. Within the intellectual framework of *Instituto de Urbanismo* (1944), Belaúnde, Luis Ortíz de Zevallos, Carlos Morales M., and Luis Dorich planned Lima's Housing Plan as well as the *Urbanistic Legislation*.

13   See "La Corporación Nacional de la Vivienda cumple un honroso encargo social,' *El Arquitecto Peruano*, January–February, 1955, N210–11.

14   Museum of Modern Art in New York (MoMA) exhibitions during the 1940s included *Twenty Centuries of Mexican Art* (1940), *Organic Design*, an exhibition of the results of a competition of industrial design only for American countries (1942), and *Brazil Builds* (1943), among other initiatives.

15   See Jorge F. Liernur, "The South American Way. El 'milagro Brasileño,' los Estados Unidos, y la segunda Guerra mundial (1939–1945)," in *BLOCK N4 Brazil*, Buenos Aires: UTDT, 1999, and "Vanguardistas vs. Expertos," in *BLOCK N6 Tercer Mundo*, UTDT, 2004.

16   In a letter from the Coordinator of Inter-American Affairs to Paul L. Wiener in 1945: "This will confirm our understanding that you will make a lecture tour of approximately three months' duration of certain other American Republics including Peru, Brazil...," PLWC, Correspondence, Box 14.

17   The Wiener tour included Colombia, Bolivia, Peru, and Brazil. Letter from Wiener to the Coordinator of Inter-American Affairs, PLWC, Box 12.

18   Paul Wiener, CIAM Memo, June 2, 1944, CIAM SC C4; and letter from Wiener to Gropius, July 25, 1944, PLWC, Box 12.

19   *El Arquitecto Peruano* was founded in 1937 by Fernando Belaúnde and directed by him until 1963, when elected President of Peru. The last issue of the journal was published in 1977. See Eduardo Zapata, *El Joven Belaúnde*, Lima: Editorial Minerva, 1995.

20   Wiener had previously established contact with Manuel B. Llosa (Paris Exhibition 1937), a figure in the political and academic circles of Peruvian society. Llosa referred Wiener to Belaúnde and also recommended that the Minister invite Wiener officially. PLWC, Incoming Correspondence, Box 7.

21   See "El pensamiento creador en la arquitectura y el urbanismo. Extractos de las conferencias de Paul Lester Wiener," *El Arquitecto Peruano*, April 1945, N93.

22   Correspondence between Belaúnde and Wiener started in December of 1944 and continued over years. Arrangement of details for the conferences in Peru was done at the beginning of 1945 in several letters. PLWC, Box 12.

23   The correspondence between the client's representative David Dasso (President, CPS), Belaúnde (Deputy of Lima), Luis Dorich (Director, ONPU), and Sert and Wiener (TPA partners) had started back in September of 1945 when Peruvian officials wrote to confirm their interest and express great expectations for the project.

24   "I shall have conferences in Lima, Buenos Aires, Montevideo, Sao Paolo and Rio and shall report to you later…," Letter from Neutra to Giedion, September 29 1945, CIAM SC C4; see also Richard Neutra, "Observations on Latin America,, *Pencil Points*, May 1946, N5, pp. 67–72.

25   The CIAM Chapter was the core of CIAM architects that were exiled in the USA due to the war. Included were Gropius, Mies, Neutra, Breuer, Sert, Weisman, and a few Americans who soon after withdrew from the groups such as Wallace Harrison and Lonberg Holm. See "Transplanting CIAM 1,2" and "CIAM Chapter for Relief and Postwar Planning," in Eric Mumford, *The CIAM Discourses on Urban Planning 1928–1960*, Cambridge, London: MIT Press, 2000.

26   "Declaración de Ingenieros, Lima, 3 de Octubre 1945," RNA-UCLA, Box 178, File 4.

27   CIAM Chapter for Relief and Postwar Planning, c.1946. ETHZ-CIAM Archive, 42-JLS-6-96/97.

28   "Your visit had quite a stimulating effect in the architectural field as well as among city planners. On June 1, I had a meeting together with Morales Machivaello and five other young architects. We have formed a society called Frente de Arquitectura Moderna (F.A.M.)…," Dorich letter to Wiener, June 6 1945, PLWC, Box 14.

29   See "La Visita de Richard L. Neutra," *El Arquitecto Peruano*, September 1945, N98.

30   See AA.VV, *Historia de la Universidad Nacional de Ingeniería 1876–1955, Tomo I, II, III*, Lima: Universidad Nacional de Ingeniería, 1999.

31   See "Algunos Principios de Urbanismo," *El Arquitecto Peruano*, November 1943, N76.

32   Luis Miró Quesada, *Espacio en el Tiempo. La Arquitectura como fenómeno cultural*, Lima: Impresiones Gráficas, 1945.

33   Ibid., p. 12.

34   Ibid.

35   Besides these canonical books, it is also easy to recognize the influence of two others that are no less important: Le Corbusier's *La Charte d'Athens* and Hitchcock-Johnson's *The International Style*.

36   Anahí Ballent, *El Diálogo de los Antípodas: El CIAM y América Latina*, Buenos Aires: FADU, UBA, 1995, p. 34.

37   Interview with Adolfo Córdova, February 2004.

38   Ibid.

39   After Gropius's visit to Lima in 1953, Miró Quesada wrote to him expressing appreciation for his work, particularly Bauhaus ideas. Letter from Luis Miró Quesada to Walter Gropius, 16 April 1954. HLWGA.

40   The origins of the group Espacio can be found in a public letter by Córdova and Williams sent to a newspaper claiming "for an original architecture product of the times, with a logical expression of the materials and the feeling of the people themselves." *Diario el Sol*, Cuzco, December 23 1946.

41   Interview with Adolfo Córdova, February 2004.

42   "Expresión de Principios de la Agrupación Espacio,' *El Arquitecto Peruano*, June 1947, N119.

43   Ibid.

44 "Maestro: [...] Nuestra intención es informarlo del estado actual de la arquitectura en el Perú y del establecimiento en Lima de la 'Agrupación Espacio' destinada a luchar contra el academismo entronizado en nuestro medio y dispuesta a forjar un sendero de contemporaneidad entre nosotros." Carta a Le Corbusier de la Agrupación Espacio (Córdova, Williams y Pérez-Barreto), Lima 3 de Julio 1947, addressed to the French Embassy in Colombia. FLC, FDL-D1-19-361-B-LC.

45 "50 Aniversario, Agrupación Espacio," in Revista 1/2 de Construcción, 1997.

46 The section in the newspaper was called Colabora la Agrupación Espacio (1947–1949). The first number of Espacio – the official voice of the group – was released in May of 1949. The last issue appeared in December 1951 as a double edition of N9–10.

47 After many communications between Belaúnde, Dorich, and Wiener which began in 1945, Sert and Wiener finally received and signed the contract for the Chimbote project in August of 1947. Working in Lima for Chimbote, Wiener and Sert, with an occasional visit of Ernesto N. Rogers, participated in the development of the master plan for Lima; PLWC, Peru Box.

48 Lima's Plan Piloto had been promoted by EAP since the 1940s. As part of the government party, Belaúnde coordinated the efforts toward developing the master plan for Lima at ONPU directed by Dorich.

49 "In working out the tridimensional plan, two contrasted heights have been considered...' See Wiener and Sert with the ONPU, A Pilot Plan for the City of Lima, Peru, Revised Copy, June 24 1950, p. 14; PLWC, Box 12, Outgoing Correspondence.

50 See Oficina Nacional de Planeamiento y Urbanismo, Plan Piloto de Lima, Lima: Empresa Gráfica T. Scheuch, 1949, p. 30.

51 Belaúnde's definition of "unidad vecinal" started in EAP in 1944 under the "Barrio-Unidad" concept, in a direct translation of the English term "neighborhood unit" using Gropius's work at Harvard Unversity studios published as "A Program for City Reconstruction" in Architectural Forum, July 1943, N79. In 1945 Belaúnde's appropriation and transformation of Clarence Perry's and Walter Gropius's ideas was introduced in Peru as "unidad vecinal" in the Housing Plan of 1945. Gropius's influence is acknowledged by Belaúnde, and the way the implementation of their ideas was planned in Lima is notorious.

52 The Lima and Chimbote Plans were well presented and documented in the exhibition and soon became prominent examples of culturally rooted modern architecture. See J. Tyrwhitt, E. N. Rogers, J. L. Sert (eds), The Heart of the City. Towards the Humanization of Urban Life, London: Lund Humphries, 1952.

53 After replacing the Chief Executive Officer of the Corporación Peruana del Santa, the new "client" denied part of the payment established by the contract, arguing that he had not hired TPA and did not want to hear more about the project. Furthermore, the new military regime resolved to legalize the squatter settlements in the area and cancel the project in its entirety.

54 See Wiley Ludena, "Urbanismo moderno en el Peru: El aporte de la Agrupación Espacio. Aproximaciones," in Urbes1, 2003.

55 Espacio member Roberto Wakeham worked in Le Corbusier's office in 1948–49, at Unité d'Habitation, which motivated Carlos Williams, Adolfo Córdova, and Samuel Perez Barreto to invite Le Corbusier while he was working with Sert and Wiener in Colombia; FLC, D1-19/356-378.

56 Dorich letter to Sert and Wiener, Lima, 29 Enero 1949; PLWC, Incoming Correspondence, Peru Folder. Later on, the final letter to the official members of the CIAM-Peru group was sent by Luis Dorich to Sigfried Giedion on January 3 1950, and includes many more architects than the "official" Espacio group. The prospective members were: Santiago Agurto Calvo, Augusto Álvarez Calderón, Mario Bianco, Juan F. Benítez, Enrique Biber P., Adolfo Córdova, Javier Cayo, Luis Dorich, Mario Gilardi, Ernesto Gatelumendi, Jorge Garrido Lecca, Paul Linder, Gerardo Lecca, Luis Miró Quesada G., Oscar Vargas Méndez, Ricardo Malachowski B., Louis Maurer, Raul Morey, Eduardo Neira Alva, Jorge de los Rios, Teodoro Scheuch, Hilde Scheuch, Alberto

Seminario T., José Sakr, Renato Suito, Fernando Sánchez-Griñan, Gabriel Tizón F., Luis Vásquez, Ramón Venegas, Luis Vera, and Carlos Williams.

57   Sert letter to Giedion, December 16 1947; SC CIAM C004.

58   Velarde was invited to the *Artes Plástiques* and Belaúnde to the *Urbanisme* commission; PLWC, Outgoing Correspondence, Box 12.

59   Due to the lack of US currency under the military regime, Espacio could not disburse funds, the very first requirement of membership. Finding themselves in the midst of these odd circumstances, some Espacio members talked to Sert and Rogers in Lima, but they recommended that the young Peruvians write to CIAM secretary Giedion. ETHZ-CIAM, 42-SG-33-241.

60   Sert letter to Gropius, June 21 1949; SC CIAM C006.

61   In the CIAM 8 Conference Report at the ETHZ-CIAM, Dorich figures as contact person with his personal address. In *The Heart of the City* (1952), Dorich appears as contact person at the Oficina Nacional de Planeamiento Urbano (ONPU).

62   Giedion letter to Sert, May 6 1949; SC CIAM C006.

63   Sert letter to Giedion, May 4 1949, SC CIAM C006.

64   See Sigfried Giedion, "Introduction," in Henrique E. Mindlin, *Modern Architecture in Brazil*, New York: Reinhold Pub., 1956.

65   See Eric Mumford, *The Emergence of Urban Design in the Breakup of CIAM*, Harvard Design Magazine. Spring–Summer 2006; Dirk van Huevel and Max Risselada (eds.), *TEAM 10 1953– 1981*, Rotterdam: NAi, 2005.

66   Henry R. Hitchcock, *Latin American Architecture since 1945*, New York: MoMA, 1955.

67   According to the CRAV housing report, directed by Cordova, the government should provide support for *barriadas* improvement, since it is a solution to the Peruvian housing crisis. See *Comisión de Reforma Agraria y de Vivienda* (CRAV), *Informe sobre la vivienda en el Perú*. Lima: CRAV, 1958. This study was also supported by the work of another Espacio member, sociologist Jose Matos Mar, *Las barriadas de Lima 1957*.

68   The early approach and seminal work of "site and services" strategy in the shanty towns of Lima would be the basis for the PREVI Experimental Housing Project (1968–1975) in Lima. PREVI Housing was the last attempt to adapt and transform the neighborhood units concept along with new ideas of standardization, mass production, and self-help to local conditions in Lima.

69   See Hilde Heyen, Architecture *and Modernity. A critique*, MIT Press, Cambridge MA, 1999.

70   Soon after the trip, Espacio ceased to exist without a date or a clear event. One faction decided to enter into politics, founding *Movimiento Social Progresista* to accomplish "real social change." The other felt that the role of architects was to stay within traditional boundaries and keep working for a better society from within the architectural discipline. See Luis Miró Quesada, "Entrevista, El grupo Espacio y la Arquitectura Nacional," *Cuadernos Urbanos* (CENCA), Marzo 1987, N19, p. 25.

71   In 1940, Lima registered approximately 645,000 citizens. In 1957 Lima had nearly 1,500,000 inhabitants and 56 *barriadas* with approximately 120,000 inhabitants; by 1972, Lima had almost 3,303,000 inhabitants, of which 805,000 people lived in *barriadas*.

72   Santiago Agurto Calvo, Fernando Belaúnde, Luis Miró Quesada Garland, Carlos Morales Machiavello (Peru); Bruno Zevi (Italy); et al. *Adherentes*, José Luis Sert, Charles Eames, Buckminster Fuller, Gordon Bunshaft, Jerzy Zoltan, Paul Roudolph, Bruce Graham (USA); Kenzo Tange, Kunio Mayekawa (Japan); Oscar Niemeyer (Brazil); among others.

73   See *La Carta de Machu-Picchu*, Lima. Cuzco: Congreso de la UIA, December 1977.

Part II

Building the nation

Figure 1

Arieh Sharon and Eldar Sharon, Obafemi Awolowo University campus: view of the main piazza, Ile-Ife, Nigeria, 1962–1976. Arieh Sharon archive, courtesy of Ms Yael Aloni.

Chapter 5

Campus Architecture as Nation Building: Israeli architect Arieh Sharon's Obafemi Awolowo University Campus, Ile-Ife, Nigeria

Inbal Ben-Asher Gitler

> What I do see is a new voice coming out of Africa, speaking of African experience in a world-wide language.
>
> – Chinua Achebe[1]

Introduction

The campus of Obafemi Awolowo University (OAU), Ile-Ife, Nigeria, the first phase of which was built in the years 1962–76, presents one of the most interesting examples of modernist architecture in Africa (Figure 1). As a case study of a large-scale national commission that acquired specific regional significance as well, the OAU campus provides important perspectives when discussing the assimilation of the modernist style in post-colonial Africa. Its design is intriguing also due to the fact that it was built by Israeli architect Arieh Sharon (1900–84), aided by his son, Eldar Sharon (1933–94). Arieh Sharon, one of the most important figures in the history of Israeli architecture, was a graduate of the Bauhaus school in Dessau, and became a leading exponent of the International Style in Israel/Palestine from the mid-1930s onwards.

While the OAU campus has been frequently cited as a masterpiece of the Modern style in African architecture in both popular and scholarly accounts, its development and interpretation in the frameworks of Modernism have not been addressed. This paper discusses the campus's architecture, analyzing how architecture was exported to newly-independent Nigeria, a Third World country beginning to define itself as a nation. It investigates the context of Modernism and its assimilation, addressing the roles of Yoruba identity and of Israeli architects in creating this campus.

Post-colonial Nigeria and the founding of OAU

Nigeria was historically established as a colonial entity by the British in West Africa in 1914. The colony, an artificial entity, the largest in West Africa, had a heterogeneous ethnic composition. The three major ethnic groups were the Hausa-Fulani in the north, the Yoruba in the west and the Igbo in the east.[2] The tumultuous post-colonial politics in Nigeria were characterized by dichotomies of consolidating a united nation while at the same time preserving and acknowledging ethnic diversity.[3]

Within two years of Nigeria's independence in 1960, four new universities in different regions of the country were opened, thus greatly expanding possibilities for higher education, which during the colonial era had comprised one British-sponsored institution: the University of Ibadan.[4]

Nigerian discourse of the late 1950s and early 1960s emphasized education as a crucial aspect of creating a modern state, and the fostering of an educational philosophy that highlighted local culture expressed an anti-colonial statement.[5] Stephan Awokoya, first Minister of Education in the Yoruba-dominated Western Region, accurately anticipated the need to integrate African Studies with Western ones, which would become a major aspect of the new Nigerian universities' curricula.[6] In addition to cultural heritage as an element usurping colonialism, Nigerian nationalists stressed the promotion of vocational studies in any area that would foster scientific, industrial and economic progress and self-reliance, such as science and engineering.[7] Writing in 1965, Nnamdi Azikiwe, among the founders and first chancellor of the University of Nigeria, Nsukka (between 1961 and 1966), and later first president of the Federation of Nigeria, emphasized the necessity of providing "amenities of modern life" to the people of each member-state of the Federation. Among these he listed, as an example, free education and libraries and, in his capacity as university chancellor, implied higher education as well.[8] Azikiwe's perspective was a pan-Nigerian one, where regional institutions would foster national unity.

Thus, during the first steps of independence, Nigeria's ethnic diversity prescribed the formation of new universities as an act promoting regional and ethnic agendas as well as national ones.[9] New university campuses were therefore one of the clearest and most prominent landmarks of the new state, and were an important aspect of a paced development towards a modern country with modern institutions. Encompassing the aspirations of a nation, and institutionalizing the path towards knowledge, they expressed the cultural act of nation building, for which Modernist architecture was the idiom of choice, defining progress, and symbolizing Nigeria's entrance into the modern world.[10]

In accordance with regional aspirations, the founding of OAU was a product of Yoruba cultural self-definition. It was Sanya Onabamiro who, prior to formal reception of independence, promoted the consecration of a university for the Western Region. This was viewed as extremely important, since an increasing number of applicants from Yorubaland were being denied education at the now two available institutions – Ibadan and Nsukka – due to student overflow.[11] Onabamiro chaired a planning committee that proposed an institution that would include faculties of African Studies and fine arts, which would foster cultural heritage with a Yoruba focus.[12] As Awokoya had earlier hoped, Yoruba art, music and drama were now to be integrated with "coming into the world heritage of knowledge."[13]

The establishment of Obafemi Awolowo University, then called "Ife University," was approved by government on March 23 1961, and Chief Jeramiah Obafemi Awolowo, one of Nigeria's most prestigious politicians and an education activist, was nominated chair of the future institution's Planning Committee. That the committee upheld the concept that the future university needed to be established upon the experiences and examples of leading institutions from around the world, was clearly evident in the formation of a delegation, dispatched to tour Brazil, Mexico, the USA, and Israel. Krieger dates this trip to mid-1961, and this is apparently the delegation of which the campus architect, Arieh Sharon, was also a member, as his account of the trip's objectives, route and timeframe is similar.[14] It is significant that the trip included Third World universities in South America, which would have supplied the Ife University Committee with possible solutions to the challenges of establishing universities in developing countries.[15] No less important is the fact that Sharon joined them at this preliminary stage, indicating the importance attributed by the committee to the architectural and physical aspect of the new university. Ife University began operations in 1962 and moved to its permanent campus, which is the focus of this discussion, in 1967.

The OAU campus and Israeli technical assistance programs to Africa

Commissioning Sharon to plan the OAU campus was one of the first steps in promoting relations between Nigeria and Israel. As a new state since 1948, Israel constantly reassessed its international status, and perceived the accelerated decolonization process in Africa, during the 1950s and 1960s, as a historic opportunity for establishing diplomatic and economic ties.[16] The importance of these contacts was magnified by Israel's political and economic isolation, brought about by Arab boycotts and hostile diplomacy. Israel hoped to gain strength through its relations with Third World countries in general, and those of the African continent in particular, and perceived African states as a potential mediator for future attempts in promoting Arab–Israeli dialogue.[17]

Israel saw itself as a progressive, modern nation, and was eager to export science and technology as a basis for diplomatic ties. A comprehensive technical assistance program, of which architecture and construction were an integral part, was devised to this end.[18] Israeli aid to developing countries was an organized government initiative, and it was the government who established contacts between Israeli institutions and commercial companies, and their foreign counterparts.

For African nations, receiving assistance from Israel was particularly appropriate since it had no part in the colonial legacy. Moreover, Israel too rejected the British mandate and was liberated from it. This shared experience was underscored, for example, by Michael Iheonukara Okpara, Premier of Nigeria's Eastern Region (between 1959 and 1966), who described Israel and Nigeria as having attained independence after "a long fight against imperialism."[19] In addition, African leaders saw Israel's progressiveness as a model for the potential technological and scientific growth of small and isolated countries, geographically located off the charts of "First World" success stories.[20] As President Jomo Kenyatta of Kenya proclaimed in 1967, Israelis "have shown what a small country can do for itself through hard work and faith in its destiny. The good example of Israel has been a useful lesson which other developing countries are trying to follow."[21] The economic gains that Israel expected to achieve were obviously important as well, yet these were tempered by these shared resemblances that were further accentuated by similarity of climatic conditions, adding another incentive for assistance or cooperation.[22]

An additional important aspect was Israel's socialism. Socialist ideology was reflected in an economy of an integrative nature, with a developed cooperative sector sustained by industry and cooperative settlements such as the kibbutz and the moshav. Israel is a democracy, and during its first three decades it was led by the socialist Labor Party with a coalition upholding a similar ideology. Israel's success in achieving a socialist regime while remaining unaligned with the Soviet Union appealed to African nations, many of which espoused socialism and strove to implement it in their own countries.[23] Israeli socialist leaders anticipated its potential as a role model in these aspects when nurturing initial ties with representatives of new nations during international labor and socialist movement meetings. Pre-independence relations with Nigeria commenced through these venues as well.[24]

Israeli socialist institutions, such as the powerful Federation of Trade Unions (*Histadrut*), played an important role in propagating Israel's technical assistance programs. Solel Boneh, the construction company involved in building the OAU campus, was a prominent example. In 1960 the *Histadrut* also established the *Afro-Asian Institute*, which underwrote the initiative of bringing Asian and African trainees to Israel to study technology, engineering, medicine, agriculture and so forth. At the program's peak, thousands of students participated in it annually.[25]

Comprising a significant aspect of Israeli foreign policy, technical aid programs were early on also condemned as masking imperialist and neo-colonialist intervention, a view promoted largely in the framework of diplomatic battles between Israel and its Arab neighbors.[26] By the end of the 1960s and during the early 1970s, the impetus of technical aid programs to Africa declined.[27] The programs were officially discontinued following the October 1973 war, with the gradual severing of diplomatic ties with all the nations of Black Africa, Nigeria included.[28] As discussed below, many projects, including construction of the OAU campus, were continued on an informal level.

The initiatives of various African governments where Israeli architects and engineers were involved, comprised mostly national projects such as infrastructure for tourism, roads, and water supply, as well as planning and construction of civic architecture such as parliament buildings, universities, and health facilities.[29] Sharon received his commission for the planning of the OAU not directly from the Israeli government, but from the above-mentioned Solel Boneh construction company.[30] One of the largest of its kind in Israel, it presided over projects in Nigeria, Ghana, Sierra Leone, and Ivory Coast, as well as projects in Asia. Establishing a technical aid program with a public company belonging to Israel's Federation of Trade Unions exemplified the endorsement of socialist ideals. The nature of cooperation and aid was such that Solel Boneh would establish a partnership with a local company, and following a five-year apprenticeship the company would become an independent entity belonging to the country being assisted. With the proliferation of projects, Solel Boneh established a sub-division which would address solely planning and design, so as to separate these from construction. This sub-division operated as a separate company, called A.M.I. (in Hebrew, the initials of *adrichalim*, *mehandesim*, *yo'atzim*, that is, architects, engineers, consultants).[31] Thus, managerial and technical knowledge was transferred in a way that enabled future projects to be carried out independently by the developing countries, releasing them from constant dependency upon foreign technological aid.[32]

The partnership approach was paramount to the new African nations as a policy for preventing neo-colonialism. Weary of expatriate firms taking control of their developing markets, joint partnerships, designated by contract to be transferred to national or private local ownership, were a method of ensuring and encouraging local entrepreneurship. In addition, the forming of partnerships, realized by Solel Boneh in all of its African projects, stemmed from socialist cooperative ideals, and should be seen within broader educational contexts, whereby Israel supplied its African counterparts with not only technical knowledge, but also philosophies of trade unionism, agricultural cooperatives and many other aspects of socialist governance.[33] The construction company thus saw itself as taking part in a mission to assist in creating a "new society" in the up-and-coming decolonized nations.[34] It is remarkable that while these noble motives certainly hark back to the older tropes of the "civilizing mission" of colonialism (only this time in the guise of socialism), the joint venture was perceived as a remedy for Western intervention, rather than its continuation. As mentioned above, it indeed received neo-colonialist criticism, but at the height of cooperation with Israel this criticism was dismissed in the interest of strengthening diplomatic ties. The partnerships were thus perceived as abiding by the highest moral standards, as the nature of cooperation expressed complete trust in the developing countries' abilities to meet the goals of running their own companies in a relatively short time. It was non-exploitative, and promised relatively little profit to the expatriate companies involved, a fact of which both the Israeli and African governments were aware. As far as construction and planning were concerned, the transfer of knowledge comprised the export of technical equipment and personnel as well as the services of Israeli experts, such as Sharon, who worked in cooperation with their Nigerian counterparts. In addition, courses in Israel were held for African trainees: for example, Israel's Productivity Institute conducted a "Foreman Training Course" in building and construction.[35] Arieh Sharon succinctly hailed this cooperation in his opening speech presented at the consecration of the OAU campus's Assembly Hall, describing architecture and construction as presenting "nowadays a sophisticated and engineering problem of building technology, science and organization... Such a complex enterprise can only succeed, if everybody is ready to contribute from his knowledge, experience, goodwill and personal devotion to the work."[36]

For the project of planning the OAU campus, A.M.I. contracted Sharon and entered into partnership with Nigerian architect A. A. Egbor, whose office was in Lagos.[37] For the purpose of this cooperation a joint company, named EGBORAMI, was established, with the Sharon office as the head planning team.[38] It would appear that the role of the Egboramy company was in engineering and coordination of construction, but further research is needed to more accurately establish Egbor's part in the planning process. This cooperation lasted well into the 1980s.[39] Together with the Egborami Company, Sharon and Sharon drew up master plans for several other major commissions in Nigeria, although these were never completed.[40] This may be due at least in part to the severing of diplomatic ties with Israel by Nigeria in 1973 (formal relations were re-established in 1992).[41] However, as with other African countries, commercial relations were not only maintained but continued to grow despite this, and Solel Boneh continued its construction projects.[42] The OAU campus was brought to completion, and although the other projects were not built, an enduring cooperation was sustained, indicating that the knowledge and technology imported certainly had long-term significance.[43]

As far as the actual execution of the OAU project was concerned, cooperation extended beyond a business relationship to a planning process that included an ongoing discourse between architects and patrons. Sharon first met with local Obas (Yoruba town/tribal leaders), councilors and government officials; the preliminary tour of campuses abroad was participated in by the professors of the future university, the ministers of Culture and Labor, and by the leaders of the opposition, indicating the prime national importance of the project.[44] Once the project was under way, the architects consistently proceeded "in close cooperation with the vice-chancellor, the professors, the university council and the university's resident engineers and architect. Nothing was built before careful research was done and the problems involved jointly analyzed."[45] Members of the community participated in the making of the campus: Sharon emphasized the community's respect for the environment, and the joint effort to preserve as much of the natural vegetation while clearing the bush for construction. Harold Rubin, Sharon's project supervisor, describes the construction of the university campus as having a profound influence upon the town, and recalls how the residents of Ife pitched in when extra manpower was needed for the project, at times turning the building project into a celebration.[46] As they are based on the architects' perspective of the project, these testimonies need to be critically assessed, since they possibly reflect a romanticized view of those employed for the project, while in reality this enlistment of the local community could have had an exploitative nature. While the architects' views need to be read with this in mind, their testimonies can be seen as indicating an expression of the community's sense of ownership and identification with the project. Cooperation with community, university and state leaders was certainly reflected in the integration of local, especially Yoruba, art and architectural traditions into the campus's design, as I will show in the discussion that follows.

Commissioning Sharon

In selecting Arieh Sharon as the architect of the OAU project, the university's Planning Committee declared Modernism as the chosen architectural style for the campus. Sharon had the opportunity of giving his Nigerian patrons an unmediated impression of his work during their visit to Israel, and according to his own testimony they received his built projects with enthusiasm.[47]

Sharon immigrated to Palestine in 1920 from Austria-Hungary and lived on a kibbutz, working first as a beekeeper and then as a planner and constructor of simple farm buildings and dwellings. He began his education at the Bauhaus school in Dessau in 1926 and graduated in 1929. He then took charge of the Berlin office of his Bauhaus mentor, Hannes Meyer, and worked there until 1931.[48] With his education and experience, Sharon was among a small but prestigious group of Jewish architects who studied in Europe and upon arriving (or returning) to Palestine in the 1930s, championed the International Style, and became extremely influential in consequent architectural development in Palestine/Israel.[49] Modernist architecture became synonymous with the Jewish *yeshuv*, that is, settlement, in Palestine. Constantly following the latest trends in Europe and the United States, Modernism continued to thrive with the declaration of the State of Israel in 1948. Constituting the stylistic expression of the new state, it was perceived as an important formal and functional tool for paving Israel's way into the community of modern, Western nations, and represented rejuvenation and progress.[50]

After 1948, Sharon played a major role in planning grand programs for new scientific and public health facilities in Israel, whose execution provided him with valuable experience when planning for the Ife campus. Sharon not only created many buildings in the framework of Israel's paced development, but was also in charge of the National Master Plan that outlined the county's entire infrastructure, new towns and settlements.[51] In this capacity, he also represented the United Nations in 1954 as an expert on regional planning and housing at a seminar in New Delhi, and in the same year served as an advisor on regional planning in Burma.[52] Soon after embarking on the Nigeria project, Sharon received the Israel Prize in the field of architecture, for his design of the Soroka Medical Center in the city of Beer-Sheba (1962).[53] The Nigerian patrons thus chose an architect who had previously been appointed as an expert by the United Nations to advise on planning in Third World countries, and had received national recognition in his own country that was endorsed by rewarding him with the most prestigious prize in Israel. His socialist ideologies were probably appreciated as well, complementing the general approach of the Israeli technical aid programs discussed above.

In 1964 Sharon's son, Eldar, joined his practice. Eldar Sharon came to work with his father following a partnership with Zvi Hecker (1931–) and Alfred Neumann (1900–68). The latter was the two younger architects' mentor at the Technion Institute of Technology in Haifa, Israel, and introduced them to a structuralist approach in architecture. As Bruno Zevi commented in his foreword to Arieh Sharon's book, Eldar was not "a passive follower of his father...," and brought with him the experience of "several years of independent and original achievements."[54] The planning of the OAU campus was already under way when Eldar joined the office, yet his distinct approach had a significant impact upon the later structures built. Another important addition to the team at that time was Harold Rubin, whom Sharon appointed as head of the OAU campus project. Rubin was a native of South Africa who was hired by Sharon soon after immigrating to Israel. The planning team thus brought forth Sharon's guidance, Eldar's structuralist approaches as well as Rubin's unmediated knowledge of southern Africa.

The general plan of the campus

In the 1961 report submitted to the Nigerian government, Sharon recommended the town of Ile-Ife as the site for the new university. Ile-Ife is considered the "cradle of Yoruba culture,"[55] having been founded by Odúduwà, the mythic ancestor of the crowned Yoruba kings.[56] The city's spiritual importance appears to have been the decisive motive for its selection, even though Sharon stressed climatic and geographical considerations as well.

The OAU campus was developed by Sharon and Sharon during the course of about 20 years, the most recent master plan having been published in 1981. The campus includes the various faculties, residences for faculty and students, convenience shops, and some additional buildings such as the vice-chancellor's house. This paper focuses upon the main core, where most of the initial campus buildings were built, and accordingly deals with its development until the mid-1970s.

The campus's main core (Figure 2) is almost square in plan. It has a main piazza, located slightly left of a central axis, with pedestrian walkways leading from it to the other areas of the campus. Bordering the main piazza are the assembly hall, the library, and the secretariat. From its northeast corner, four buildings comprising the Humanities Faculty create an additional axis. Behind the library four more faculty buildings are located: Education, Social Sciences, Law, and Administration. Three of these are arranged symmetrically along the main core's northwest border, with the fourth located between them and the Humanities' axis. Intimate connecting squares are thus created between the various faculties. This was termed by Sharon a "loose grid design," and aptly describes the seemingly freeform and abstract arrangement of structures. He described his approach as "simple and organic," and explained it as follows: "the central rectangle, located on a slightly undulated slope against the background of the beautiful rocky hill – is a purely pedestrian area [and]… presents a closely knit complex of faculty buildings, gardens, patios li[n]ked by pergolas, ramps and terraces.'[57]

Figure 2
Arieh Sharon and Eldar Sharon, Obafemi Awolowo University campus: plan of the campus's main core, 1974. Arieh Sharon archive, courtesy of Ms Yael Aloni.
Legend: 1: Assembly Hall; 2: Secretariat; 3: Library; 4: Humanities; 5: Institute of Education; 6: Social Sciences; 7: Law; 8: Institute of Administration.

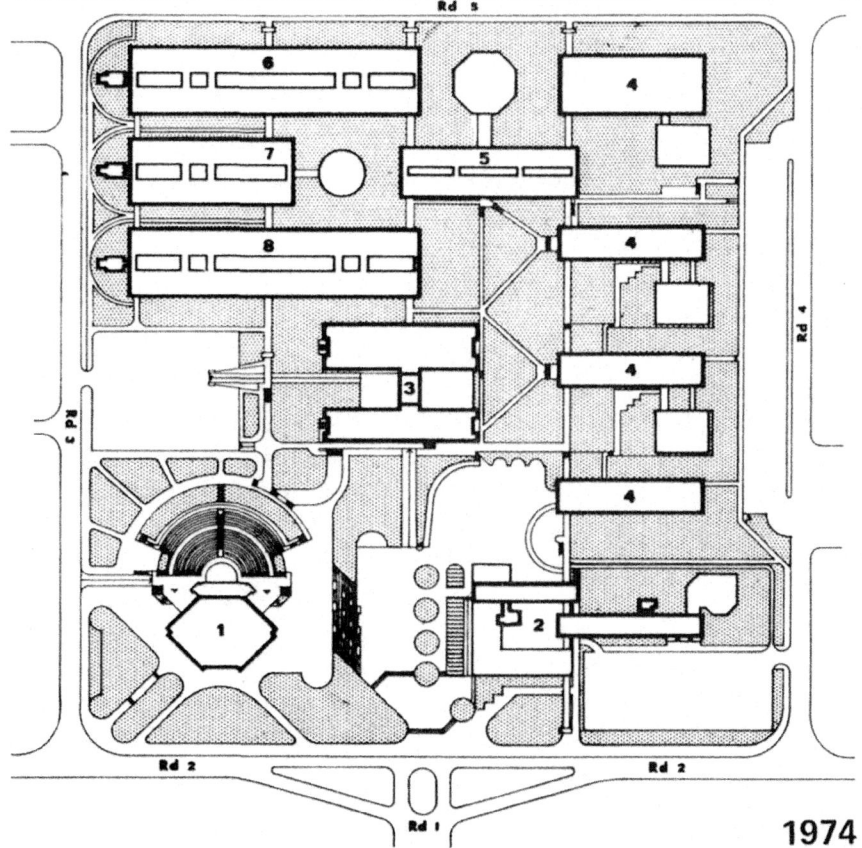

1974

Figure 3
**Arieh Sharon and
Benjamin Idelson,
Soroka Medical Center,
Beer-Sheva, Israel,
begun 1955. Arieh
Sharon archive,
courtesy of Ms Yael
Aloni.**

Of Sharon's projects, his hospitals and campuses built in Israel during the 1950s, planned with his associate at the time, Benjamin Idelson, deserve particular attention as precursors of the Ife project. The Soroka Health Center in Beer-Sheva (1955) (Figure 3) was his largest and most important commission during that time. It anticipated OAU in its "loose grid" layout. Long, flat-roofed pergolas with slim columns, similar in style to those of the OAU campus, connected the medical center buildings, shielding pedestrians from the desert sun and defining smaller courtyards.

The significance of courtyards as a connecting element between buildings can also be perceived in Sharon and Idelson's plans within the new campuses of the Technion Institute of Technology in Haifa and the Hebrew University in Jerusalem. The central core planned for the new Institute of Technology campus (1956) comprised, as in Ife, an auditorium, secretariat, and library. Inviting connecting courtyards were created within the three buildings, which here too were arranged in a freeform way. The student dormitories of the Hebrew University (1952) comprised a larger group of buildings arranged according to similar principles, albeit with greater emphasis upon a central courtyard.

Sharon wrote that on the campus-touring trip of 1961 the delegation, including himself, visited Harvard and MIT, where they saw the most recent works by "Le Corbu[sier], Gropius, Aalto and Sert...."[58] Of these, the scheme which can be seen to have had the deepest influence upon Sharon is his former master, Walter Gropius's, Harvard Graduate Center (1950).[59] Its eight buildings were freely arranged within their lot, and interconnected by long pergolas. Sharon must surely have been familiar with this project even before visiting Harvard, as it seems to have inspired the earlier Soroka Hospital and campuses in Israel as well.

Researchers of African architecture and landscape design who have briefly discussed the OAU campus, view its layout as not only deriving from contemporary modernist campus design, but also from the traditional Yoruba Palace.[60] The traditional palace, seat of the Yoruba monarch or *Oba*, is called *àfin*.

In the traditional evolution of the Yoruba town, including Ife, the àfin was located in the center of the city and surrounded by a thick wall. The palace usually had one huge porticoed gate, and the one in Ife was famous for its immense size.[61] The palace had open-air grounds or bushland where shrines and burial grounds were located. Its built area was made up of a series of interconnected courtyards surrounded by verandas, with rooms opening to them.[62]

As discussed in the next section of this paper, Yoruba art as a source of inspiration was clearly mentioned by Sharon. He did not, however, mention Yoruba palaces specifically as a source for the campus's layout, yet wrote that "[r]eviewing trends abroad of other universities, we agreed with the professors that, in view of the local conditions and *customs* [my emphasis]... the layout of the campus... should be as compact as possible."[63] The modest scale of Sharon's campuses in Israel was appreciated by the Nigerian delegation, indicating that the compact size of the main core, whose size is about 240 × 240 meters, was inspired by both Sharon's earlier work and the àfin.[64] Adopting a variant of the loose grid scheme was, moreover, akin to the succession of courtyards of the traditional àfin. In addition, the imposing campus entrance gate and sculptural secretariat gate (Figure 9) connote, in their monumentality, the importance of the gate in both Yoruba palatial architecture and shrines.[65] Thus, the choice of layout for the campus's main core closely followed modernist schemes, yet addressed local traditions of planning and architecture.

The interpretation of Modernism

The Humanities buildings (Figure 4), completed in 1962, were the first group to be designed. Sharon planned them as "reversed pyramids."[66] Environmental considerations were a major concern for Sharon, and the buildings' shape was intended for coping with the glaring heat and monsoon rains. Their four floors were cantilevered and thus each provided shade and protection to the one below. Deep recessed terraces created sharp contrasts of light and shade that bestowed a sculptural horizontal emphasis upon the pyramidal gradation. In each building, a semi-circular stairwell of exposed concrete created a vertical accent which interrupted the overall horizontal effect, and which received a conical appearance through contrasts of light and shade.

Sharon emphasized that the "reversed pyramids" were a new approach for addressing climatic concerns, as they involved the use of mass and shape for protection *and* ventilation, rather than planning the building and then adding "louvers and precast ornamental elements."[67] He mentions these devices as having been used in Nigeria by British architects, most likely referring to Maxwell Fry and Jane Drew's University of Ibadan (begun 1948). After the Second World War, Fry and Drew led the application of modernist architecture in the British Gold Coast (Ghana) and in Nigeria, as they advocated tailoring the international style to local climatic conditions.[68] In the context of campus architecture, it is important to note that one of the initial instances of

Figure 4
Arieh Sharon, Obafemi Awolowo University campus: the Faculty of Humanities Buildings, 1962. Arieh Sharon archive, courtesy of Ms Yael Aloni.

implementation of the modernist style to British West Africa in the heyday of the colonial era, was for improvement of the "natives'" education. The British hoped that by establishing a primary school system as well as universities, pioneered by Ibadan, they would ward off the growth of the independence movements.[69] Thus, modernist architecture was associated early on with education. However, in building one of the first post-colonial universities, the patrons of OAU obviously did not wish to emulate colonial modernism. The University of Ibadan, as a British-sponsored institution, was associated with internationalism and a general nationalist agenda rather with acknowledging internal Nigerian diversity of ethnic identities.[70] Just as the founders of OAU rejected the Ibadan model in its academics, promoting instead programs that would aid in the development of the region and foster Yoruba culture, so they rejected its architecture, which visualized the character of the senior institution.

The "tropical architecture' version of modernism implemented at Ibadan preceded OAU in its highly environmental approach. Its design brought climate considerations center-stage, and Fry and Drew adapted modernism to the tropical climate by situating the buildings in a way that accounted for insulation and wind directions. This was done, as Sharon observed, mostly by a different treatment of walls and windows.[71] Sharon's solution for diverging from colonial modernism lay in the pyramidal structures, which articulated the mass of the building rather than its shell.

Sharon was no stranger to the louvers and precasts from which he steered away in the planning of the Humanities buildings. He had made ample use of them in the Technion Institute of Technology and the Hebrew University, where recessed windows, deep terraces and vertical brises-soleil were used to cope with Israel's hot summers. While he did not abandon these completely, his construction at OAU certainly signaled the beginning of a new style and a shift from his earlier work in Israel. This change reflected Sharon's reaction to international late modernism and his adoption of new trends. The arrival of Eldar Sharon, who belonged to the new generation of modernist architects, strengthened this stylistic shift, and abstract elements and polygonal forms became dominant in the ensuing campus buildings.

A gradation of plains forming a less accentuated pyramid was also structured in the OAU campus library (1966) (Figure 5). In this building, each set of strip windows that run across the front and rear façades was shaded by a massive cement cantilever, and there were no terraces. The library can perhaps be seen as an intermediary stage in the campus's architecture: its emphasis is horizontal, and the gradated cantilevers are plastered. Its main entrance is not centrally located but shifted towards the west, and a long wide ramp leads up to it and accentuates it. The entrance interrupts the strong horizontality of the cantilevers in both shape and material. A rectangle of exposed concrete seems to fold over from the roof, contrasting with the white cantilevers. It is pierced by a very large, expressive circle that denotes a recessed entrance. Functionally, this abstract element shades the entryway, yet it certainly goes beyond the rationality of early modernism into the elaborate shapes that characterized the late phase of the style. Its sheer size and integration as a geometrical element emphasize the entrance, indicating the different function of this part of the building, where mobility is concentrated, as the staircase and hallways to the rest of the building are located there.

At the OAU library, not only the entrance but also the rectangular building's narrow sides were left with an exposed concrete shell, indicating an accentuated use of this material. It was used on the central part of the building, which seems to cut through its axis, an effect achieved by making it slightly longer and higher. The higher roof has rounded corners and its adjacent walls have concave crowns, so that an undulating, sculptural effect is achieved. The concrete was not simply poured into wooden molds, but into corrugated tin, creating a wavy texture for the finished building. This technique was implemented in the Assembly Hall (the Odúduwà Hall) as well. The corrugated texture of the

Figure 5
Arieh Sharon and Eldar Sharon, Obafemi Awolowo University campus: the Library Building, 1966. Arieh Sharon archive, courtesy of Ms Yael Aloni.

concrete imitated that of the famous bronze figures excavated in Ife and displayed in its museum, whose bodies were incised, creating a similar wavy effect. In the autobiographical survey of his work, Sharon mentioned the "special architectural interest [of] the Ife Museum, exhibiting world-famous bronze heads."[72] A photo of one such figure was presented opposite a close-up of the assembly hall's concrete texture, referencing this source of inspiration.[73]

Sharon used the corrugated texture for exposed concrete in Israel as well during this period, for example in the Agricultural Cooperatives Headquarters in Tel Aviv (1966), where an almost identical pattern was implemented.[74] Thus, an effect used in Israel as an expression of contemporary modernism, was supplied with an interpretation relating it to local art when applied in Nigeria. Locating modernism in the context of a Third World nation implied situating it within a local cultural referent. Such a connection between the texture of the concrete and the Ife bronzes is extremely abstract, and raises a question of agency: while the architect testified to the role of the sculptures in choosing this exterior treatment, it is far from certain that this connotation was made by the campus's population. Sharon obviously did not intend to reiterate a clear and legible cultural icon; rather, it guided him when making choices pertaining to which elements of modernism would be most appropriate for the Ife buildings. The implementation of the modernist style was, in this specific aspect, more a process of choice and reduction than one of appropriation.

The building for the Institute of Education (Figure 6), completed in 1970, has a clear reverse-triangle form. While Sharon called it, too, an "inverted pyramid,"[75] this is actually a sequence of double triangle structures with inverted vertices. This building is made principally of exposed concrete. The structure's diagonal trusses create two covered passages along the length of the building. The widening of the triangles' sides towards the top endows the passage with an airy, open feeling. As with the terraces of the Humanities buildings, these open

Figure 6
Arieh Sharon and Eldar Sharon, Obafemi Awolowo University campus: the Institute of Education, 1970. Arieh Sharon archive, courtesy of Ms Yael Aloni.

corridors are protected from rain yet remained open and ventilated, an approach that also differed greatly from colonial modernism.

Representing the earlier phase of the campus construction, the Humanities, Library and Education buildings retained a horizontality that was perhaps a legacy of the international style of the 1930s and 1940s, yet introduced the pyramidal gradation combined with vertical elements that contrasted with it, emphasized by exposed concrete. The type of gradation used in these buildings was later implemented by Sharon and Sharon in the building for the Bank of Israel, Jerusalem (1978), and is reminiscent of Le Corbusier's La Tourette Convent near Lyon, France (1957–60).

The Library and Humanities buildings were visually connected not only by the similarity of these characteristics and their proportions, but also by a long pergola constructed as a single-sided arcade of semi-circles (Figure 5, to the right of the Library building). This stark geometry of arched openings in a deep wall was very different from the slender pergolas that connected the Humanities buildings to each other. Similarities to the Agricultural Cooperatives Headquarters in Tel Aviv can again be perceived, in the horizontal strips countered by vertical emphasis, and in the use of the semi-circular arch, which in the Tel Aviv building separated its pedestrian access from the street. Sharon and Sharon thus exported to the Ife campus structural and stylistic elements used by them in Israel, yet adapted them to both climate and culture.

I would now like to turn to the assembly hall, named the Odúduwà Hall, after the mythic ancestor of the crowned Yoruba kings (Figure 7). The building was intended for theater and dance performances, as well as graduation ceremonies.[76] Begun in 1970 and completed in 1976, the assembly hall differed from the earlier buildings. It is located on the southwestern corner of the main

Figure 7
Arieh Sharon and Eldar Sharon, Obafemi Awolowo University campus: the Odúduwà Hall (the Assembly Hall), completed 1976. Arieh Sharon archive, courtesy of Ms Yael Aloni.

campus core. The wide stairs leading to it from the main piazza create an enclosing boundary for the latter. The building is a hexagonal mass echoed by a trapezoid, which connects an auditorium, planned to seat 1400, with an open-air amphitheater planned for 3500 spectators (Figure 8). A tall, impressive stage tower, whose exterior provides a vertical focal point for the campus core, connects the two performance areas. A concrete "tent"[77] surmounts the interior auditorium, forming a series of triangles in the taller part of the roof. The seating of both theaters is curvilinear, and the stages of both the interior and exterior performance spaces continue their shape and are semi-circular thrust stages, planned as such specifically to accommodate Nigerian theater, which traditionally comprises mostly thrust-stage performances.[78] The interconnected stages allow for flexibility and can be used simultaneously, and are an exception to the notion of fixed theater spaces.[79] This flexibility is particularly appropriate for Yoruba performance, which is rich and versatile.[80]

The foyer is located under the auditorium, and its staircases are aligned with the building's trapezoid geometry. It was left completely open to the outside. Harold Rubin explained that the tropical climate allowed this, and giving up what would have been a massive amount of fenestration enabled the architects to

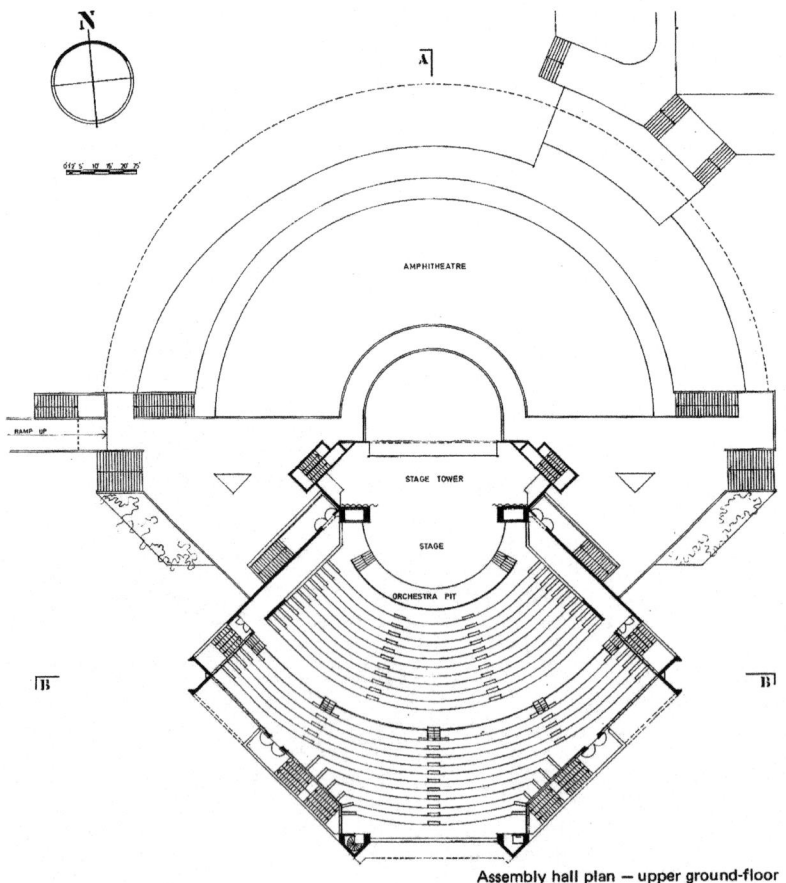

Assembly hall plan — upper ground-floor

Figure 8
Arieh Sharon and Eldar Sharon, Obafemi Awolowo University campus: the Odúduwà Hall (the Assembly Hall), plan of upper ground floor. Arieh Sharon archive, courtesy of Ms Yael Aloni.

remain within budget.[81] Tall walls frame the foyer's concrete stairs and galleries, each pierced by huge circles and semi-circles. These echo the Library's entrance and adjacent pergola, while giving lightness to the assembly hall's concrete mass. The stage tower's corners are shaped as semi-trapezoids, reflecting the shape of the building and culminating in beveled angles and accentuated eaves troughs.

The concrete façades of Odùduwà Hall were painted with white abstract and geometric forms, transforming the gray, windowless exteriors into striking monumental murals. Similar to the library building, the assembly hall's exterior walls are corrugated, so that the painted areas are endowed with a wavy effect. The eastern side of the building, which is the one that faces the piazza, is adorned with wing-like shapes and S-shaped strips which seem to frame a central motif of an abstract circle intersected by a strip reminiscent of a spear (Figure 7). The opposite side of the building has similar sinuous decorations. The exterior wall of the amphitheater stage is painted with a symmetrical shape where the contrast between gray and white creates two triangles intersected by arches that frame a thinner, white circle, located in the center of the wall. The spectator's eye completes the forms so that a larger double-circle is set at the center, again echoing the building's circular openings.

These abstract murals recall Yoruba wall paintings. The incredibly rich abstract vocabulary of Yoruba art includes dense geometric patterns, manifested not only in sculpture and wall painting, but also in textiles, festival costumes and ritual objects, forming a fundamental aspect of local visual culture.[82] In his library, Arieh Sharon had a small 1969 booklet by Chief M. A. Fabunmi called *Ife Shrines*.[83] Among the many images published in this book is one of the Oluorogbo Shrine, which has dark walls painted in light shades, featuring patterns of circles, triangles and sinuous lines. Wall paintings of this kind were, in all likelihood, a source of inspiration for the murals. Arieh Sharon's collection of Nigerian art is also testimony to his deep appreciation of it, and could have been a source of inspiration. He collected Yoruba and other African sculptures during his trips, as well as contemporary Nigerian art, notably paintings on wood and paper by Twins Seven Seven (1941–).[84] The works by Twins Seven Seven owned by Sharon integrated indigenous motifs, and those on paper were executed in black and white. Although the works are not dated, making it difficult to establish their direct influence on the planning of the assembly hall, they indicate Sharon's awareness of modern Nigerian art. Thus, the circle-and-triangles pattern applied to the stage façade, as well as the abstract shapes of the piazza-facing one, translate Yoruba abstract forms and repetitive pattern into a modern idiom. Here, again, the architects implemented a thoroughly modernist device of integrating immense geometric or abstract forms as an artistic element that underscored various aspects of the architecture. This device may be compared, for example, to Louis Kahn's use of large triangular and circular openings that create an abstract pattern on the massive walls of the National Assembly in Dacca, Bangladesh, built between 1962 and 1974. Another comparison may be suggested to the murals and mosaics decorating the exterior walls of the UNAM

(Universidad Autónoma de México) campus buildings in Mexico City, which Sharon saw during the Nigerian delegation's tour of university campuses. Juan O'Gorman's Library Building (1953) presented the most extreme aspect of this approach, as it is completely covered in paintings relating to Aztec heritage, reiterating this art.[85] Sharon wrote that the UNAM campus buildings left a deep impression on him and explained: 'I was able to exploit these impressions by proposing sculptural Yoruba elements in the Ife university buildings.'[86] Mexico, at the time also a developing country, thus served as a model for how modern architecture could be assimilated, yet could also express culture, place, and identity. In the OAU assembly hall, this totalizing approach to the painted façades was thus adopted, accenting the scale and geometry of the building and inscribing Yoruba art within the campus's architecture.

The architects' appropriation of traditional indigenous art follows suit with Western adoption of the abstract qualities of African art since the beginning of the twentieth century, in that it addressed the formal qualities of this art, and not contents or subject.[87] African art in general, and Yoruba art in particular, invoke a complex interplay between visual and verbal arts, and are interconnected to both daily life and religious rituals. Thus, when discussing the connection between art and the built environment, visual art is created in the context of home, town, or shrine, but is not dissociated from verbal annunciation in the form of texts, praise-poetry (oriki),[88] or aesthetic philosophy.[89] These are concepts that are difficult to describe and explain when relying on Western terminologies and theory, and attempts to explain them to Western audiences were only emerging in the early 1970s.[90] Thus it is unlikely that the architects, with all their appreciation of Yoruba art, were aware of these depths of meaning and of the full constructs of Yoruba visual culture. The reduction of Yoruba formal vocabulary and its translation into clear geometric planes, that seem to "float" on the wall in the Odúduwà Hall murals, clearly indicates the purely formal adaptation discussed above. Moreover, a university campus, as a new institution in the independent country, removed local art from its usual contexts. Its appearance in a novel architectural building type created an entirely new discursive space, where local art no longer directly related to the cultural spaces and realities implicitly attached to it. The Odúduwà Hall was not the only building where art or murals were incorporated: For example, the inner open corridors of the Institute of Education displayed white on gray, albeit smaller, murals; the narrow side of the secretariat building was incised with a repetitive sinuous motif that spanned its entire height.

Sculptural elements were also an important aspect of the visual inspiration derived from African art. The entry gate to the secretariat, whose significance has already been discussed here, was designed by Harold Rubin, and is reminiscent of a standing figure, with its head turned towards the sky (Figure 9). Rubin vividly explained his inspiration from African sculpture's abstract qualities:

> As a native of South Africa [I was aware] of the sculptures which are mostly figurative but are executed in very abstract forms. The

[sculptures] rely on the human form but they abstract it. I made the gate with a turned-up head, and it's almost figurative. The head and legs create the gate.[91]

Perhaps the most telling example of defining the cultural space of the Yoruba within the campus, is the concrete replica of Ife's famous *Opa Oranmiyan* (staff of Oranmiyan, also called the Ife Staff), an ancient 18-foot (5.18 meter) tall granite monolith which commemorates Odúduwà's son (Figure 5, to the right of the Library entrance ramp).[92] Facing the campus's main piazza, the replica was

Figure 9
Harold Rubin, sculpture for the entrance gate leading to the Secretariat (from the direction of the Faculty of the Humanities buildings), c. 1968. Arieh Sharon archive, courtesy of Ms Yael Aloni.

framed by a tall half-cylindrical obelisk of corrugated-textured concrete, referring again to the texture of the Ife bronze sculptures. It was located in front of the Library and visually functioned as a vertical accent to its horizontal mass. The importance of the staff stems from its representation of Oranmiyan, who was Odùduwà's heir as the king of Ife. Replicating it on campus thus commemorated the importance of Ife as origin of all the Yoruba kings, and its status as an ancient spiritual center.[93] The staff was perhaps intended to provide a link between the past spiritual centrality of Ife and the potential of the new learning center, the university, to promote spirituality as well, having been established with the idea of nurturing Yoruba culture. In addition, it alludes to Yoruba knowledge as a pinnacle of African culture and secures its place *vis-à-vis* Western disciplines.[94]

How can this translation of Yoruba art be interpreted in the setting of modernist architecture? I would like to suggest that this new discursive space opens up several interpretations. According to Yoruba artistic traditions, each work of art must invoke *ase*, creative power, allotted to it by its context and function.[95] Suggesting a new location for the *Opa Oranmiyan*, as an example, could be perceived as a rupture with tradition.[96] The abstract forms, recognizable as borrowings from local sources in their modern architectural guise, could be critically read as devoid of meanings, or worse, as an offensive attempt to assimilate them. On the other hand, the meaning of a work of art could change when presented in the new context of the university, a Western institution introduced to the region. As the university was the enterprise of the new independent country, and was applauded as crucial and important for the development of the region, and subsequently of the nation, new meaning could be invested in its architecture and the art represented through it.

Chika Okeke-Agulu, in his discussion of the work of Nigerian artist Uche Okeke (1933–) and artist/architect Demas Nwoko (1935–) during the 1960s, explains their integration of indigenous art into their modern Western painting style, as a "conscious attempt to create art that is both modern and Nigerian."[97] The two artists differed in their approaches, as Okeke drew inspiration from his Igbo roots, placing emphasis on ethnic diversity, while Nwoko turned towards a pan-Nigerian approach, integrating sources from various artistic traditions in the country.[98] Okeke-Ogulu sees their post-independence work as reflecting "the profound impact of decolonization politics on cultural production and modernist artistic practices" and views the "fashioning [of] a modernism in Nigeria at the time … [as] … a political gesture."[99] He emphasizes that the integration of indigenous art in the process of creating modernism was a *formal* process, meant to integrate color, line and shape.

Relating these expressions of modernism to the OAU campus architecture affords further insight as to its interpretations: As we have seen, the campus layout has been related to Yoruba palaces, Sharon clearly referred to the integration of Yoruba elements in the buildings, and a replica of the famed Ife staff was placed in the central piazza. All of these assimilations indicate a conscious reification of Yoruba ethnic identity, promoted by the project's patrons.

Thus it would seem that in the discourse of nationalism and ethnicity, historically crucial to Nigeria's political evolvement, the architecture of the OAU campus tended towards expressing a specific ethnic identity. Although built by foreign architects, when seen in relation to contemporary Nigerian art, the architecture of the campus reveals a similar trend of a commitment to indigenous art through a formalistic approach. The context was no longer traditional, and the search for a Nigerian modernism endowed it with new meaning. However, as the establishment of OAU was a national project, the reification of Yoruba art should also be seen in the wider framework of ethnic identity as constructing Nigerian nationalism, which is inherently characterized by cultural diversity.[100] The abstraction of Yoruba art, which detached it from its original cultural domain, facilitated this interpretation, as it interfered with direct, specific association.

This comparison of art and architecture becomes even more relevant when considering Nwoko's architecture which was contemporary with the OAU campus, such as the Dominican Monastery (1966–70) and the New Culture Design Centre, both in Ibadan.[101] Nwoko appropriated traditional indigenous elements in his buildings as well, a tendency also shared by, for example, Allan Vaughan-Richards (1925–89)[102] and Design Group Nigeria.[103] Thus, the search for a cultural language that would combine modern architecture with Nigerian visual heritage was not unique to Sharon and Sharon during this period. As discussed by Le Roux, this approach to Modernism developed from the discourse of Africanism and negritude, which were an important part of cultural production in Africa from the 1950s onwards. Coupled with a renewed emphasis upon place and materiality in Western and non-Western postwar modernisms, these frameworks encouraged a new search for syntheses between modernist and local traditions.[104] However, Sharon and Sharon's architecture defined a heightened discourse between modernism and its assimilation of a culture, especially when compared to the work of other expatriate architects. It integrated and displayed locality in a clear-cut and unambiguous manner, in an engagement previously rarely seen in such large-scale civic commissions. It challenged contemporary references to local African traditions within imported, modernist idioms which, despite claims of their integration by architects and their critics/historians, were comparatively subtle or resided largely in the realm of declared intentions.[105]

Conclusion

In his imperfect English, Sharon concluded his speech for the celebration of the opening of the Odúduwà Hall with the following paragraph:

> The great builder and bric[k]layer Wi[n]ston Churchill said once: Man is building his house, but later on, his house is building the man. And I believe that our architectural work is only a modest basis, and the teachers, students and university's people may develop this architectural basis into a human, social and cultural university entity.[106]

The slight irony of quoting Churchill aside, Sharon's words reiterate the importance attached to developing higher education in post-independence Nigeria. His perception of architecture as capable of molding society reverberates through Churchill's quote. His emphasis on the "modest" role of architecture, upon which the essence of the university is built, establishes it as a crucial aspect capable of giving a physical expression to the character of OAU. This physical expression was achieved through importation of modern architecture to post-colonial Nigeria which entailed an assimilation process that localized, yet sought to differentiate this architecture from earlier, colonial "tropical" modernism. In the planning of the OAU campus, Sharon and Sharon devised this by exploiting volume for environmental sustainability, and by expressively employing the plasticity of exposed concrete. In addition, modernist aesthetics were hybridized so as to express Yoruba art and culture through materiality and form. Abstraction of Yoruba art enabled a multiple reading of the campus architecture, simultaneously endowing it with both local and national significance.

The campus's architecture was also an embodiment of the emerging nation's progress: the implementation of modernist planning principles, materials, and stylistic vocabulary when establishing an institution for the advancement of knowledge, was perceived as a tool for achieving both technical and visual modernity. Through close and institutionalized cooperation between the Nigerian planning and construction team and the Israeli architects and Solel Boneh, the making of the OAU campus was projected to have a lasting technological impact, introducing new construction methods to the country.

The architecture of the OAU campus presents spatial and visual formulations that challenge current post-colonial issues of power, knowledge and alterity. Israel was not an ex-colonizer of Nigeria – on the contrary, it was an ex-mandate territory and itself a new nation, and its historical situation within First or Third world countries is complex.[107] The construction of modernist architecture in Nigeria through an Israeli conduit underscored its relevance, while American and European models, more closely or immediately associated with foreign power and colonialism, were mediated through it and thus made acceptable. However, Israel's exportation of architecture and building technologies can be seen as embodying knowledge as a commodity, and Israel's economic and, in this case, diplomatic profit were an important incentive for this cooperation. While this carries characteristics of post-colonial Western intervention, introduced to Africa under the more attractive concepts of "aid" and "assistance," it certainly does not fit into formulae of the persistence of European power, or American predominance.[108]

The cultural production of modern architecture in independent Nigeria entailed the translation of Yoruba alterity to a modern idiom, and its treatment as a cultural Other subjugated to Western architecture. This presumably suggests the usual framings of Self and Other in post-colonial discourse.[109] However, in constructing the campus, the architects fully collaborated with their Yoruba patrons. Thus, this was an architecture chosen and affected by its clients and users, and was by no means imposed upon them.

The process described here entails an ambivalence of agency, and reveals a complex relationship between architecture, politics and culture. Case studies such as this validate reassessments of post-colonial theories made, for example, by McClintock, in which she points to the problematic "tendency to view the globe within generic abstractions voided of political nuance."[110] The construction of the OAU campus and its built environment denote multiple expressions of Modernism as well as its intricate routs. An example of Modernism's disparate adaptations, the campus's architecture expressed the process of developing educational programs based upon Western models in post-colonial Nigeria. As such, it exposes precisely the need to review theory within specific historical/political circumstances. Directly related to its site and circumstances of coming into being, the architecture of OAU manipulated relations between art and architecture. Consequently, it exhibited both an Israeli and international Modernism merged with the Nigerian search for a contemporary style that would incorporate the visuality of one of its indigenous cultures, in defining national identity.

Acknowledgements

This research was first presented at the 61st Annual Meeting of the Society of Architectural Historians, Cincinnati, OH, 2008. I wish to thank Yael Aloni for generously opening her father's invaluable archive to me, and Edina Meyer-Maril, Ayala Levin, David Rifkind, Adedoyin Teriba, Hilde Heinen, Lily Kassner and Duanfang Lu for their help and insightful comments.

Notes

1   Chinua Achebe, "The African Writer and the English language," in Patrick Williams and Laura Chrisman, *Colonial Discourse and Post-Colonial Theory: A reader*, New York: Columbia University Press, 1994, p. 433.

2   Each of these ethnic groups had, and still has, a dominant religion: The Hausa-Fulani are predominantly Moslem, while the Igbo and Yoruba are Christian and pagan. It should be noted that this division into three ethnic groups or tribes is not wholly adequate, and is a relatively recent historical compartmentalization. The Yoruba themselves, while possessing the same language, are culturally and socially diverse. See: David D. Laitin, *Hegemony and Culture: Politics and Religious Change among the Yoruba*, Chicago and London: University of Chicago Press, 1986; Margaret Thompson Drewal, *Yoruba Ritual: Performers, Play, Agency*, Bloomington and Indianapolis: University of Indiana Press, 1992, p. 12.

3   For Nigeria's decolonization process see Ali A. Mazrui and Michael Tidy, *Nationalism and New States in Africa from about 1935 to the present*, Nairobi, Ibadan, London and Portsmouth NH: Heinemann, 1984, pp. 92–5.

4   Vincent Chukwuemeka Ike, *University Development in Africa*, Ibadan: Oxford University Press, 1976, p. 12.

5   Milton Krieger, "Education and development in Western Nigeria: the legacy of S. O. Awokoya, 1952–1985," *The International Journal of African Historical Studies*, vol. 20, no. 4, 1987, pp. 652–3.

6   Ibid., p. 654.

7   Ibid., p. 653.

8   Nnamdi Aziwike, "Essentials for Nigerian survival," *Foreign Affairs (pre-1986)*, no. 43, p. 458.

9   J. F. Ade Ajayi, "Higher education in Nigeria," *African Affairs*, vol. 74, no. 297, 1975, p. 421. Much has been written about the complexity of nationalism vs. ethnic diversity in Nigeria. See for example Ibeanu and Okechukwu, "Ethnicity and transition to democracy in Nigeria: explaining the passing of authoritarian rule in a multi-ethnic society', *African Journal of Political Science*, vol. 5, no. 2, 2000, pp. 45–65.

10   Hannah Le Roux, "Modern architecture in post-colonial Ghana and Nigeria," *Architectural History*, vol. 47, 2004, pp. 369, 381. For a discussion of architecture and nation building as a cultural act see Daniel A. Abramson, "History: the long eighteenth century," *Journal of the Society of Architectural Historians*, vol. 64, no. 4, p. 420.

11   Krieger, "Education and development in western Nigeria," pp. 644–8, 653–4.

12   Ibid., pp. 659–60; Arieh Sharon, *Kibbutz+Bauhaus: an architect's way in a new land*, Stuttgart: Kark Krämer, and Israel: Massada, 1976, p. 126.

13   Quoted in Krieger, op. cit., p. 652.

14   Ibid., pp. 658–9; Sharon, op. cit., pp. 126–7.

15   From the two South American locales chosen, Brazil was probably selected due to the long tradition of strong ties between the Yoruba and their kin who were deported as slaves to Brazil, and whose descendants gradually returned to Nigeria in the latter half of the nineteenth century. It is interesting to note that in Brazil, many Yoruba worked in the building and architectural trades, and thus influenced Nigerian architecture with the styles and technique they brought back with them from Brazil. See John Michael Vlach, "The Brazilian house in Nigeria: the emergence of a twentieth-century vernacular house type," *The Journal of American Folklore*, vol. 97, no. 383, 1984, pp. 3–23.

16   Zvi Efrat, *Haproyekt Hayisraelee: Bniya ve Adrichalut 1948–1973* [The Israeli Project: Building and Architecture, 1948–1973], Exh. Cat., Tel Aviv: Tel Aviv Museum of Art, 2004, vol. 2, pp. 608–12; Leopold Laufer, "Israel and the Third World," *Political Science Quarterly*, vol. 87, no. 4, 1972, pp. 615–19. Strategically, in the aftermath of the 1956 war between Israel and Egypt, the former maintained new passage through the gulf of Aqaba, which created an important commercial route to Africa (see Ibid., p. 618).

17   Olusola Ojo, *Africa and Israel: Relations in Perspective*, Boulder and London: Westview Press, 1988, p. 8.

18   For detailed accounts of this program see: Mordechai E. Kreinin, *Israel and Africa: A Study in Technical Cooperation*, New York and London: Praeger, 1964; Moshe Decter, *"'To Serve, To Teach, To Leave': The Story of Israel's Development Assistance Program in Black Africa*, New York: American Jewish Congress, 1977; Ojo, op. cit., pp. 18–20; Samuel Decalo, *Israel and Africa: 1956–1996*, Gainesville and London: Florida Academic Press, 1998, pp. 67–94.

19   Kreinin, op. cit., p. 176.

20   Nathan E. Nadelman, "Israel and Black Africa: A Rapprochement?," *The Journal of Modern African Studies*, vol. 19, no. 2, 1981, p. 188.

21   Quoted in Laufer, op. cit., p.619. For a more detailed account of the development of Israeli-Nigerian relations see Nadelman, op. cit., pp. 192–3.

22   Ojo, op. cit., p. 10.

23   Ibid., p. 13; Kreinin, op. cit., pp. 13–14, 120–32.

24   Ojo, op. cit., p. 139. See also Eliyahu Bilzky, *Solel Boneh: 1924–1974*, Tel Aviv: Am Oved, 1974, p. 411.

25   Kreinin, op. cit., pp. 126–8; Ojo, op. cit., pp. 18–21.

26   Kreinin, op. cit., pp. 175–6; Ojo, op. cit., pp. 24–5.

27   Several reasons accounted for this: a less altruistic and more business-like approach adopted by Israel, the continuing Arab-Israeli conflict that affected multilateral relations, and Israel's growing ties with South Africa. In addition, foreign aid on a much larger scale became available from Arab

countries and the Soviet bloc, sources who were interested in discouraging cooperation with Israel. See Ojo, op. cit., pp. 33–54.

28   Ibid.

29   Efrat, op. cit., p. 609; Kreinin, op. cit., pp. 136–7.

30   Interviews with Arieh Sharon's daughter, Ms Yael Aloni, who was employed in her father's office, and Ms Ziva Parnas, who was employed there as well, February 2008, March 2009.

31   Kreinin, op. cit., p. 135; Interviews with Sharon's daughter, Ms. Yael Aloni, who was employed in her father's office, and Ms. Ziva Parnas, who was employed there as well, February 2008, March 2009.

32   Efrat, op. cit., p. 610. It is important to note that with Nigeria's Western Region, two such partnerships were consolidated in 1959, before Nigeria received its independence (in accordance with British provisions made in the 1954 Nigerian Federal Constitution). The two companies were the NigerSol construction company, together with Solel Boneh, and the Nigerian Water Resources Development Company. Similar partnerships were established with the Eastern Region shortly afterwards. See Ojo, op. cit., pp. 139, 141–2.

33   For Solel Boneh's cooperation with other African countries see Kreinin, op. cit., pp. 134–5; Bilzky, op. cit., pp. 403–35. The Afro-Asian Institute worked to instill these socialist ideas as a part of its curriculum. Examples of the various courses are included in Ibid., pp. 126–30, 200–5. For education pertaining to women, as well as a detailed listing of institutions providing education in addition to the Afro-Asian Institute, see: Decter, op. cit., pp. 12–30.

34   Bilzky, op. cit., pp. 410–15.

35   Kreinin, op. cit., p. 198.

36   Arieh Sharon, "Opening speech at the opening ceremony of the Assembly Hall," December 17 1976, p. 1, Arieh Sharon archive.

37   Interviews with Sharon's daughter, Ms Yael Aloni, who was employed in her father's office, and Ms Ziva Parnas, who was employed there as well, February 2008, March 2009. Only scant information regarding Egbor is presently available. He was at a certain point president of the Nigerian Institute of Architects. Le Roux mentions that he received his architectural education abroad. See Le Roux, op. cit., pp. 370, 391, n. 28–9.

38   Interview with Ms Yael Aloni, February 2008.

39   Additional buildings by other architects were also constructed on campus during the 1960s and 1970s, such as Design Group Nigeria, John Harrison, and the firm of James Cubitt, Fello Atkinson and Partners. See Noel Moffett, "Nigeria today," RIBA Journal, vol. 48, no. 6, June 1977, pp. 244–55.

40   These included master plans for the Faculty of Health Sciences at the University of Benin, Bendel State University in Ekpoma, the Rivers State College of Education at Port Harcourt (1983), Apical Hospital and College of Health Sciences in Ife (1978), and the Isaka Resort Hotel in Rivers State (1978). See Curriculum Vitae: Eldar Sharon, Architect and Town Planner, N.D., Sharon Archive. All university projects were commissioned by the respective institutions, and the plans and details carried out in accordance with their specifications and in cooperation with university authorities (correspondence with Ms Yael Aloni, April 9 2009).

41   Nadelman, op. cit., p. 200.

42   Ibid., pp. 214–16.

43   Another important project by Israeli architects in Nigeria was the University of Nsukka, begun 1963 and planned by Alfred Mansfeld (1912–2004) and Daniel Havkin.

44   Sharon, op. cit., p. 126.

45   Ibid., p. 127. The first vice-chancellor, Oladele Ajose, was a doctor. He was a Yoruba, and was the first Black African Professor to be appointed to a full chair in Preventive and Social Medicine at the University College, Ibadan, before taking the position at AOU. See http://news.biafranigeriaworld.com/archive/2003/jul/17/0074.html, retrieved 16 April, 2009. Prof. Ajose and Sharon are photographed in Sharon's book, Kibbutz+Bauhaus, p. 128. The second vice-chancellor, with

whom the architectural team also worked closely, was Professor H. A. Oluwasanmi. See interview with Harold Rubin, January 6 2008. Oluwasanmi, a professor of agriculture, also joined Ife University from the University of Ibadan. See http://www.ui.edu.ng/agrichistory, retrieved June 25 2010.

46 Sharon, op. cit., p. 128; interview with Harold Rubin, January 6 2008.

47 Sharon, op. cit., p. 127.

48 Ibid., pp. 26–43.

49 For the development of international-style architecture in Israel see Alona Nitzan-Shiftan, "Contested Zionism – alternative Modernism: Erich Mendelsohn and the Tel Aviv Chug in mandate Palestine," *Architectural History*, vol. 39, 1996, pp. 147–80; *Tel Aviv Modern Architecture*, 1930–1939, Tubingen: Wasmuth, 1994; Efrat, op. cit., pp. 53–80.

50 Michael Levin, "The Second Generation of Israeli Architects," *Journal of Jewish Art*, vol. 7, 1980, pp. 70–8; Efrat, op. cit., pp. 81–5.

51 Arieh Sharon, *Tichnun Physi be Yisrael* [Physical Planning in Israel], Government Printing Press and Survey of Israel Press, 1951.

52 Sharon, *Kibbutz+Bauhaus*, p. 266.

53 Interview with Ms Yael Aloni; list of recipients of the *Israel Prize* (http://www.education.gov.il/pras-israel/, retrieved June 23 2010. See also http://en.wikipedia.org/wiki/List_of_Israel_Prize_recipients, retrieved June 24 2010).

54 These included the Bat Yam Town Hall (1963–69), distinct for its reverse pyramid structure and diamond-shaped precasts, the Israel Defense Forces Military Academy (1963–67) and several beach resorts along Israel's coasts. See Sharon, *Kibbutz+Bauhaus*, p. 6.

55 Ibid., p. 138.

56 According to Yoruba tradition, Odúduwà, a mythical demiurge believed to have come down from heaven, forged worldly and universal order. See Eva Krapf-Askari, *Yoruba Towns and Cities: An Enquiry into the Nature of Urban Social Phenomena*, Oxford: Clarendon Press, 1969, pp. 1–3. Agricultural circumstances may have also promoted the founding of the university at Ife, as it is located in an area that in the colonial era became very wealthy from the revenues of cocoa crops. See ibid. For a discussion of historical sources and Ife's political status see David D. Laitin, *Hegemony and Culture: Politics and Religious Change among the Yoruba*, Chicago and London: University of Chicago Press, 1986, pp. 110–14; Andrew Apter, *Black Critics and Kings: The Hermeneutics of Power in Yoruba Society*, Chicago and London: University of Chicago Press, 1992, pp. 13–34.

57 Sharon, 'Opening speech at the opening ceremony of the Assembly Hall', p. 1.

58 Sharon, *Kibbutz+Bauhaus*, p. 126.

59 Completed with the Architects' Collaborative in 1950.

60 Nnamdi Elleh, *African Architecture: Evolution and Transformation*, New York: McGraw-Hill, 1997, p. 309; S. Z. Mohammad and S. IK. Umenne, "Socio-cultural and economic aspects of university campus landscape development in sub-saharan Africa," *African Journal of Science and Technology*, vol. 7, no. 2, 2006, p. 32.

61 Krapf-Askari, op. cit., p. 42.

62 Ibid.; Elleh, op. cit., p. 307; Babatunde Lawal, "Some aspects of Yoruba aesthetics," *British Journal of Aesthetics*, vol. 14, no. 3, 1974, p. 246.

63 Sharon, *Kibbutz+Bauhaus*, p. 127.

64 Ibid.

65 Apter, op. cit., p. 100.

66 Sharon, *Kibbutz+Bauhaus*, p. 142.

67 Ibid., p. 128.

68 Ola Uduku, "Modernist architecture and 'the tropical' in West Africa: the tropical architecture movement in West Africa, 1948–1970," *Habitat International*, vol. 30, 2006, pp. 397–98. See also Le Roux, op. cit., p. 366.

69   Uduku, op. cit., p. 397.

70   Krieger, op. cit., pp. 658–9.

71   Uduku, op. cit., p. 404.

72   Sharon, *Kibbutz+Bauhaus*, p. 126.

73   Ibid., pp. 164–5.

74   Ibid., pp. 208–13.

75   Ibid., p. 152.

76   Interview with Harold Rubin, January 6 2008.

77   Sharon, *Kibbutz+Bauhaus*, p. 160.

78   Ibid.

79   Don Rubin, Ousmane Diakhaté, and Hansel Ndumbe Eyoh, *The World Encyclopedia of Contemporary Theatre: Africa*, London: Taylor & Francis, 1997, p. 232.

80   Drewal, op. cit., pp. 12–13.

81   Interview with Harold Rubin, January 6 2008.

82   Rowland Abiodun, "Understanding Yoruba art and aesthetics: the concept of *ase*', *African Arts*, vol. 27, no. 3, 1994, pp. 68–78, 102–3.

83   M. A. Fabunmi, *Ife Shrines*, Ife: University of Ife Press, 1969.

84   The paintings and sculptures are in the collection of Ms Yael Aloni, the architect's daughter, Tel Aviv, Israel.

85   Juan B. Artigas, *UNAM México: Guía de sitios y espacios*, México: Universidad Nacional Autónoma de México, 2006, pp. 51–61.

86   Sharon, *Kibbutz+Bauhaus*, p. 127.

87   Abiodun, op. cit., p. 69.

88   Stephen Foláránmí, "The Importance of Oriki in Yoruba mural art', *Ijele* (Art eJournal of the African World), no. 4, 2002.

89   Abiodun, op. cit., pp. 69–72.

90   Ibid., pp. 68–70.

91   Interview with Harold Rubin, January 6 2008.

92   For the myth of Oranmiyan see Apter, op. cit., pp. 15–17.

93   Ibid., pp. 13–34.

94   For a brief yet poignant discussion of some academic aspects of Yoruba studies see Apter, op. cit., pp. 2–4.

95   Abiodun, op. cit., pp. 71–3.

96   The *opas* of rulers are highly respected and are kept in special shrines. See ibid., p. 78.

97   Chika Okeke-Agulu, "Nationalism and the rhetoric of Modernism in Nigeria: the art of Uche Okeke and Demas Nwoko, 1960–1968," *African Arts*, vol. 39, no. 1, 2006, pp. 26–37, 92–3.

98   Ibid., p. 36. Okeke-Agulu correlates Uche Okeke's use of Igbo motifs with Yoruba author Amos Tutuola's use of traditional Yoruba literature in his writings (written in the English language) (see p. 28).

99   Ibid., p. 37.

100   Ibid., p. 36.

101   See Le Roux, op. cit., Fig. 15. Images of these buildings are also available through the following link: http://www.archnet.org/library/places/one-place.jsp?place_id=6671, retrieved 18 April 2009. Date for the Dominican monastery was retrieved from: Ulrich Clewing, "New art for Nigeria," http://www.culturebase.net/artist.php?1242, retrieved 18 April 2009.

102   Vaughan-Richards cannot be defined as purely Nigerian or expatriate, as he married a Nigerian and Nigeria was his permanent home.

103   Moffett, op. cit., pp. 244–55; Abimbola O. Asojo, "Hybrid forms in the built environment: a case study of African cities," in Toyin Falola, Niyi Afolabi, and Adéronké A. Adésànyà (eds), *Migrations and Creative Expressions in Africa and the African Diaspora*, Durham, NC: Carolina Academic Press, 2008, pp. 140–2; Le Roux, op. cit., pp. 374–80.

104   Le Roux, op. cit., pp. 366–7.

105   See, for example, Loeffler's discussion of the architects of American Embassies abroad. Loeffler cites the architects' intentions of expressing the unique locales of the various countries where the embassies were to be built. As an example of Western Modernism in Third World countries, the degree to which these modernist buildings indeed appropriated local architectural traditions was rather limited and already criticized as such in the late 1950s. See Jane C. Loeffler, *The Architecture of Diplomacy: Building America's Embassies*, New York: Princeton Architectural Press, 1998, pp. 124–6, 182–6. Crinson, in his discussion of Modernist architecture in Ghana in the 1950s and 1960s, dismisses claims that the US embassy in Accra (Henry Weese, 1956) was inspired by elements from local visual culture, as well as similar claims for other buildings constructed in Ghana at the time. He regards only Fry and Drew's tropical architecture as expressing a very subtle relation to local vernacular, and their brise-soleils as attaining something of local design. See Mark Crinson, *Modern Architecture and the End of Empire*, Aldershot: Ashgate, 2003, pp. 138–149.

106   Sharon, 'Opening speech at the opening ceremony of the Assembly Hall', p. 2.

107   Researchers such as Nadelman and Laufer, cited above, assume a priori that Israel is not a Third World country. Migdal, on the other hand, acknowledges the difficulties in situating Israel, and presents some Third World perspectives in analyzing the Israeli condition, stemming from the realities of Israel as a post-British-mandate country. See Joel S. Migdal, *Strong Societies and Weak States: State–Society Relations and State Capabilities in the Third World*, Princeton: Princeton University Press, 1988.

108   For a discussion of the perseverance of Western economic domination of Africa, see Williams and Chrisman, *Colonial Discourse and Post-Colonial Theory*, pp. 3–4, 12; Ania Loomba, *Colonialism/Post-colonialism*, London: Routledge, 1998, pp. 5–7.

109   For a discussion of these terms see: Loomba, op. cit., pp. 104–73; Williams and Chrisman, op. cit., p. 8. For a perspective which problematizes the dichotomies of Self/Other see Homi K. Bhabha, *The Location of Culture*, London: Routledge, 1994, pp. 85–92.

110   Ann McClintock, "The angel of progress: pitfalls of the term 'Post-colonialism'," in Williams and Chrisman, op. cit., p. 293.

Chapter 6

Modernity and Revolution: the architecture of Ceylon's twentieth-century exhibitions

Anoma Pieris

Perry Anderson, in his 1984 critique of Marshall Berman's book, *All That is Solid Melts into Air*, a book that would hitherto shape interpretations of modernity, highlighted the two weaknesses of Berman's thesis as its representation of revolution as a permanent state, a process rather than an episode, and the narcissistic goal of self-development as precluding the formation of community.[1] Anderson was writing on "aesthetics" in 1984, before the fall of the Berlin Wall and under the neo-liberal reforms of Margaret Thatcher. Nationalist sentiment was high following the Falklands conflict and Britain was nostalgically revisiting her past imperial glory. Anderson was one of its most vocal critiques as a representative of Britain's New Left and sensitive to Berman's implicit critique of socialism. But what was Anderson's understanding of the Third World? This essay takes its sur-title from the above mentioned critique focusing on Ceylon where "Modernity and Revolution" was influenced more by the social ideals favored by Anderson, than by the emergence of an individuated and self-conscious modern subject. In fact, we might argue that although the dialectic of a culture radically separated from its past and propelled into a revolutionary future underlay the processes of Ceylonese modernity, it did not necessarily reproduce the cultural visions attributed to Europe or America. In the post-independence decades of the twentieth century, political ideologies, industrialization, and identity politics took a very different turn.

Berman's book made a significant distinction between modernity as a historical experience, mediating between the socio-economic processes of modernization and the originary cultural vision that responded to these processes of change – the modernism of the nineteenth century. His reversion to the classical spirit of modernism, in Anderson's view, was a response to the bourgeois decadence that would follow and become exacerbated by the two world wars. But, argues Anderson, this vision of modernity extended to the early twentieth century and "flowered in the space between a still usable classical past, a still indeterminate technical present, and a still unpredictable political future … it arose at the intersection between a semi-aristocratic ruling order, a semi-industrialized capitalist economy, and a semi-emergent, or -insurgent, labour movement."[2] The human origins of products, the trace of labor and the libidinal investment in such objects had not yet been fully concealed.[3] Following the Second World War, Western Europe would conform to an American economic model of production and consumption resulting in "an oppressively stable, monolithically industrial, capitalist civilization."[4]

Anderson argued that by the postwar period the locus of creativity had shifted to very different sites: environments of extreme instability, pre-capitalist oligarchies, developmental economies, and societies haunted by socialist revolution.[5] They, in turn, were stimulated by visions of utopia. These countries – he mentions Cuba, Nicaragua, Angola and Vietnam – did not produce an autonomous interpretation of modernity fraught by the anxieties of modern self-development, but displayed their ambiguity toward and insecurity with received histories from the West. They offered us art forms that remain inseparable from their subjectivity, some of which, by Latin American authors, are mentioned by Berman. These examples do display the contradictions, self-ironies and inner tensions attributed by Marshall Berman to the modernist avant garde, but are firmly imbricated in the political revolutions of the moment. They were closely linked, moreover, to the politics of postcolonial nationalism.

Modernity was manifested very differently from their European counterparts in the twentieth century Asian nation-states that were undergoing decolonization, revealing the asymmetrical politics of postcolonial state-formation and the extraordinary significance of a rural democratic polity. Although steered by an aristocratic bourgeoisie who were schooled equally in feudal relationships and colonial manners, the violent removal of an inherently racist colonial regime had rekindled an old faith in indigenous culture. Its advocacy would ensure political longevity and rural voters. Ethno-nationalist ideologies based on indigenous histories were written into the language of the nation-state, preventing the forms of social alienation symptomatic of modernity. In fact they strengthened communalism. The cultural forces of kinship, race and religion were exacerbated through citizenship alliances with divisive socio-political outcomes. Virulent anti-colonial sentiments also gave rise to alternative political and economic affiliations in the form of cold war alliances and non-alignment – during the 1960s and 1970s – forging a culture inimical to the West and suspicious of its dialectic. Tense relations between China and India dominated regional politics, and small nations like Ceylon were forced to take sides.

It is possible, this chapter argues, to read the social transformations of the twentieth century through a peripheral site, such as postcolonial Ceylon, where economic change was both radical and modern in dialectical terms. The revolutionary zeal of anti-colonial nationalism had propelled the nascent nation-state from postwar domination by a neo-colonial Commonwealth to the uncharted waters of socialist republicanism. Set adrift due to its political choices, the nation sought alliances with the Soviet Union and China, attempting, however, to maintain its independence through non-alignment. It hosted the 5th non-aligned conference in 1976. One year later, the country would shift to an open economy, far ahead of its neighbor, India, and produce a popular politics for local consumption. These transformations were sharply inscribed on a temporal phenomenon, national exhibitions, a microcosmic representation of national culture, and its revolutionary socio-political transformation. In countries dependent on agricultural production, where urban poverty was constantly fed by rural migrations and urbanization was not imperative, exhibitions were perhaps the only sites where spectacular forms of urban modernity were learned and observed. They were, moreover, the only sites that took local audiences into account. This chapter investigates the history of such exhibitions. To understand their political significance, however, they first need to be contextualized within a longer cultural inheritance of colonial modernity.

Colonial modernity

Colonial exhibitions fall within a larger discourse on colonial and indigenous forms of modernity that have been the preoccupation of scholars of South Asian architecture during the past decade. Scriver and Prakash, William Glover, Gyan Prakash and Swati Chattopadhyay are among those who have explored these issues more generally whereas Jyoti Hosagrahar, Partricia Morton, Mark Crinson and Arindam Dutta have established links between commercial interests and cultural display in the bazaar, the durbar, the colonial exhibitions and the arts and crafts movement in France and in Britain.[6] This discourse and its relevance for a later discussion of nationalism rely heavily on Edward Said's brilliant exposition of the politics of orientalist scholarship.[7] Tim Mitchell's *Colonizing Egypt*, which draws on Said's ideas, is a valuable starting point for any of these investigations of modernism and the divisive colonial culture that resulted.[8] As argued by Tony Bennett, the social display of native bodies, a specular dominance over the whole city, and the world represented as an assemblage of commodities, articulated particular imperial technologies of knowledge and power.[9] Exhibitions crossed the line between scientific inquiry and popular culture, delivering specific forms of nationalist knowledge and prejudice to metropolitan audiences. As observed by Swati Chattopadhyay:

> The Royal Commission in charge of colonial exhibitions hoped that pride in empire could be instilled among the common people who

came to visit these exhibitions. Pride in empire could also forge national identity; visitors would receive a first hand account of the technological achievement of Great Britain clearly juxtaposed against the technological backwardness of Indian crafts.[10]

In her argument, "The modern necessarily required a pre-modern to construct its own identity," and so the modernity claimed by European engineering feats was shaped against "primitive" oriental architecture. European architecture was typically represented as advancing through historical periods, whereas Asia endlessly replicated "timeless" vernacular structures. Such juxtapositions were used quite explicitly to justify Europe's civilizing mission and colonial project, and were also evident in the exhibition's layout.

Whereas in the first great exhibition, held in London in 1851, all exhibits were incorporated into a large industrial building, "the Crystal Palace," by the 1867 exposition in Paris this plan had evolved into a familiar hierarchy: the main building and its adjacent Hall of Industry displayed progressive European technologies while foreign pavilions of Europe's colonies were distributed on its periphery either in designated halls or as separate structures. In the 1889 Paris exposition, the main exposition buildings, designed as halls with interconnected galleries, were located on the Champ de Mars around the Eiffel Tower while the architecture of the colonies represented as villages were scattered throughout the site.[11] Exhibitions during the colonial period served a dual purpose, in expressing the national pride of the hosting nation and providing a diagram of the political geography of Empire.

These distinctions were pervasive, argues Patricia Morton. In the Paris Colonial Exposition of 1931, the reproductions of native architecture were visually distinct from the art deco metropolitan pavilions, maintaining a hierarchy that differentiated between the white and colored worlds – and yet, whereas the native pavilions (for Indochina, for example) were depicted on the outside as untouched or savage, the interiors displayed "the didactic exhibits of civilization's progress."[12] In her view, the hybrid productions that resulted "undermined the separation and differentiation of French culture from colonial culture to the detriment of the mission assigned to architecture."[13]

This dialectical juxtaposition of East and West penetrated architectural production in two ways; indeed, the exhibition was a microcosm of colonial architectural practice. The Victorian inheritance of Indic styles was replacing the Palladian revival of an earlier era, and Hindu, Buddhist and Indo-saracenic architecture was deemed appropriate for colonial institutions at the turn of the century. As described by Tom Metcalf, Edwin Lutyens's design for the Indian capital is exemplary in this regard.[14] In Ceylon, Buddhist decorative motifs were applied onto the neo-classical institutional plans of the Art Gallery, the New University and numerous public buildings of the early twentieth century. Although the political geography of Euro-American expositions had altered with the emergence of private capital, most evident in the New York World's Fair of 1939–

40, the colonies were fixed in the architecture of the past.[15] Moreover, exhibitions increasingly became avant-garde arenas for design experimentation and projections into a futuristic utopia, underwritten by an American brand of capitalism.[16]

Postwar political culture

Such utopian visions would take on new meaning in a climate of postwar reconstruction in the Skylon at London's Festival of Britain in 1951 and the Atomium at Brussels in 1958; and would linger as a design paradigm in the exhibitions of the 1960s, with the Space Needle in Seattle in 1962. By the New York World's Fair of 1964 all buildings would have innovative modernist forms of glass, concrete, and steel.[17] These transformations must also be read in terms of competing economic utopias, a primary site for cold war politics. For example, the American National exposition in Moscow and simultaneous Soviet exposition in New York, both held in 1959, revealed the tensions of that period.[18] Although these two expositions did much to demystify the cold war relationships between the two superpowers by presenting "a social panorama of contemporary life," the events were surrounded by controversy directly related to political differences: for example, the much publicized "kitchen debate" between Presidents Nixon and Kruschev.[19] The everyday life of the USA and USSR had grown to symbolize the successes and failures of opposing political ideologies.

The positioning of exhibitions along cold war battle lines is most revealing of their potential as social technologies and disciplining processes, as argued in the work of Bennett.[20] Whereas during the colonial period an anthropological interest in native practices was exposed to public scrutiny, by the mid twentieth century the panopticism of the metropolitan gaze was being internalized. Exhibitions expanded the scope of state surveillance, reproducing a pervasive political culture as a harmless form of entertainment. Viewed in retrospect, post-independence exhibitions in Colombo can be envisioned similarly, as micro-environments for the playing out of Asia's cold war political alliances. Socialism would play an important role in the initial bid for decolonization, but first, the political and cultural entanglements with the former colonizer needed to be sorted out and the rights of post-independent territories in Asia had to be demarcated. The very first platform for this process was the Colombo Plan, a program that brought seven Commonwealth nations and former British colonies together under a capitalist umbrella, providing funds for development. Framed as an international economic organization, the Colombo Plan was created in 1951 (and inaugurated in Australia) in a cooperative attempt to strengthen the economic and social development of the nations of southeast Asia and the Pacific.[21] It gave assistance in the form of educational and health aid, training programs, loans, food supplies, equipment, and technical aid, and had within its objectives an explicit desire to prevent the spread of communism.

Daniel Oakman, writing on Australia's role in this new organization, observes that it "confirmed a shift in the epicentre of world affairs," with the first meeting of Commonwealth countries in 1950, convened on Asian soil.[22] The Colombo Plan exhibition in 1952, which followed, could be interpreted as the "last hurrah of the British Empire," and as an initial postcolonial submission to its economic dominance.[23] But the location in Asia and objectives of development placed its participants on an equal footing.

The Colombo Plan exhibition of 1952 (Figure 1), held to commemorate the 21st anniversary of Universal Adult Franchise in Ceylon, marked the island's emergence as an independent nation (following independence from British rule in 1948). It consolidated its regional identity, its autonomy from India, and its relative significance despite its small size. Held at Vihara Maha Devi Park (formerly Victoria Park and renamed in the 1950s) opposite the neo-classical Colombo Town Hall, the exhibition occupied Colombo's central axis of local government. The main participants in the exhibition – India, Pakistan, the Maldives, Canada, Australia, and Indonesia – were all former colonies or dominions. Their displays were both regional and progressive in character, emphasizing their common bonds within the British Commonwealth.[24]

The utopia envisioned in this particular context had colonial origins, and in the opinion of the former colonizer released its captives into a dystopian future. This is evident in the pedagogical and patronizing intent of many of the exhibits described in the exhibition brochure. For instance, the Canadian pavilion, by use

Figure 1
**Colombo Plan
Exhibition, aerial view.
Courtesy of Associated
Newspapers Ceylon Ltd.**

of prefabrication, local Canadian materials and exhibits focusing on agriculture, infrastructure and welfare services, hoped to demonstrate local solutions to national problems (to Asian countries). The United Kingdom government's pavilion described the problems of southeast Asia and the part that the United Kingdom could play in their solution.[25] The US pavilion underlined the interests of Americans in the Colombo Plan and in maintaining democracy (in the region). The Australian pavilion featured the exchange of students and experts between the Colombo Plan countries and came with the following cautionary note:

> It is in countries with low living standards and little hope for improvement in the future that extremist political doctrines find fertile ground… This plan is a major part of the answer of the Western world to any questions which may be raised in the minds of the peoples of these countries by Communist influences.[26]

Such overtly political agendas were not confined to the former dominions. Each country would use the exhibition as a stage for competing nationalist lobbies shaped by independence. Ceylon would use it primarily for consolidating its domestic politics and constructing its international profile, and accordingly made various demands on the Commonwealth Relations Office. Ceylon aimed to make the exhibition the largest event ever held in South Asia. A request from Colombo for an Australian circus generated a spate of indignant correspondence between London and its former colonies, where it was observed that the organizing committee in Colombo expected over 10,000 overseas visitors to attend, although the city had no hotel accommodation for them.[27] They wanted a big show in every way or they would drop the idea altogether.[28] Faced with demands and ultimatums of this kind the Commonwealth Relations Office suspected that "the primary intention of the exhibition was to boost Ceylon and provide a jamboree for their own people mainly at other people's expense."[29] They also raised the point that "a spectacular event of this kind would no doubt be of advantage to the UNP (United National Party) during the election year."

The Colombo Plan exhibition gave Ceylon and its ruling United National Party the opportunity to formulate its various national agendas towards defense, agriculture, and development. Unlike in India, independence in Ceylon had been acquired by peaceful means with muted anti-colonial sentiments, and the new government appeared willing to cooperate with its former colonial administration. The Ceylon national pavilion, an E-shaped building with three courtyards and a reception hall at its center, embodied the neo-classical plan and Buddhist-style envelope invented for the colony by the Colonial Public Works Department (Figure 2). The pavilion even repeated a formula of past colonial exhibitions – in London (1920), St Louis (1904) – it was a miniature of the Kandyan King's palace. Yet a section of the pavilion devoted to "Achievements and New Horizons" contrasted sharply with this traditional appearance and featured models of reservoirs, hydro-electric schemes, the university, the harbor and a five-story block proposed for

Figure 2
**Ceylon National
Pavilion. Courtesy of
Associated Newspapers
Ceylon Ltd.**

the General Hospital.[30] Irrigation, education, trade, and healthcare took precedence. The Ceylonese harbored specific modern aspirations underneath the illusion of a colonial order peacefully married to an indigenous past.

The Ceylon pavilion in 1952 offers us a version of the political dialectic forged across numerous colonial exhibitions. While the pavilion resembles the Indo-Chinese pavilion described by Morton, with its modern interior and archaic envelope, the interpretation is different. The replication of the palace, while conceding to past colonial templates, was also nationalistic, a reclaiming of a pre-colonial past for an indigenous polity. Its dialectic was between exterior and interior, between a new-found political self-identity and nascent ambitions for Western-style progress. The importance of irrigation over urban infrastructure signaled the focus on rural agriculture.

The pavilions of other Asian countries were likewise replete with nationalist sentiments filtered through religious and symbolic motifs from the pre-colonial past. Outwardly, they too conformed to the colonial tradition of confining the colonies to their vernacular. But the meaning underlying their vernacular had undergone a change. Its pre-industrial vocabulary constructed a pre-colonial arcadia, which cast the colonizer as polluter.[31] The uneasy reception of these shifting sentiments was voiced by Lord Soulbury (the former Governor General of Ceylon) in a message published in the exhibition brochure. He warned against extreme forms of nationalism, invoking Mahatma Gandhi: "I do not want my house to be walled in on all sides, and my windows stopped up. I want the culture of all lands to be blown about my house as freely as possible. But I refuse to be blown off my feet by any of them."[32]

The Colombo Plan exhibition would be the last event where systems of colonial patronage were aired and tolerated on an international stage. The Commonwealth, which artificially conjoined Britain's Asian colonies and its dominions during the early years of decolonization, was breaking apart by 1952, and the political and economic breach between these two types of colonization was increasingly evident. Such latent asymmetries would be fully articulated and politicized as a division of Third and First World nations in Bandung, Indonesia, only three years later, under the stewardship of Sukarno. A gathering of former colonies seeking to build their self-esteem against a common historical grievance, Bandung would cement the platform for the regional socialist alliances that would follow.[33]

Colombo 1965

The rejection of the colonial past and all its associations by Asian countries coincided with two decades of uninterrupted modernization. The Indianized architecture of the colonial Public Works Departments would be replaced by the new institutions of the independent state, which were cast in a modernist mold. However, the architecture of the period was linked to the former colonizer in two ways. The modernism that was filtering through Indian experiments to Ceylon was being introduced and executed in nationalist architecture by foreign experts. Le Corbusier, Pierre Jeanneret, Maxwell Fry, and Jane Drew were involved in the design of Punjab's new capital, Chandigarh, on the invitation of Jawaharlal Nehru, while Otto Koenigsberger (late 1940s) was planning Bhubaneswar, the capital of Orissa. Louis Kahn designed the Indian Institute of Management in Ahmedabad (1963), a precursor to his capitol in Dhaka (1962–74). A host of architects provided designs for Islamabad's new capital planned by Doxiadis, with the Presidential Palace by Edward Durell Stone. Fry and Drew would later visit Colombo where they designed the Lionel Wendt Theatre and Gallery (1953 and 1959).

The proliferation of Western architects in South Asia during this period was coupled with a new interest in Tropical Modernism, an adaptation of modernism for a tropical climate. Under Fry, Drew, and later Koenigsberger, a Tropical Programme (1954) was inaugurated at the Architectural Association School in London and educated many of Asia's first generation of local architects. The AA School was the nurturing ground for many Ceylonese architects including Minette de Silva and Geoffrey Bawa and the modernist Valentine Gunasekara, who studied there in the Tropical Programme in his final year. Meanwhile in

Australia, at the University of Melbourne, a parallel program commenced in 1962. It provided a similar specialization to Colombo Plan scholars from Asian countries.

The irony of borrowing a nationalist aesthetic from its former colonizer escaped the politicians of postcolonial South Asia, perhaps because their desire to break with the past was so great. Centuries of colonial rule had skillfully emphasized the backwardness of local cultures, and it would take several decades before the pre-colonial past could be reviewed. Although it was not visible in the aesthetics of development, a nationalist spirit of indigenization and communal attitudes was certainly on the rise. In Ceylon it was politicized in Prime Minister S. W. R. D. Bandaranaike's revolutionary "language policy" of 1956, which privileged a Sinhalese ethnic majority and marginalized Tamil- and English-speaking minorities by establishing Sinhalese as the national language. Bandaranaike's self-proclaimed social revolution would inaugurate an era of socialist policies and eventually lead to ethnic conflict. This shift to a pragmatic socialist agenda is evident in the most important exhibition to be held mid-century in Colombo, the industrial exhibition of 1965. Held 17 years after independence, Ceylon 65 deliberately turned its back on the colonial and pre-colonial past.

Largely funded by Russian aid, Ceylon 65 was held at the Colombo race-course, a one-time pleasure ground of colonial sportsmen. However, as evident from its participating countries, it was a site of divisive cold war politics.[34] Nine foreign countries participated, including East Germany, West Germany, Czechoslovakia, Poland, Israel, China, India, Pakistan, and America, and the architecture of their various pavilions competed with those of 18 government corporations and several private entrepreneurs. It was a period when Russia and China loomed large in the Asian imagination, and the de-colonizing nation released from its colonial capitalist history "served as an agent for socialist cosmopolitanism."[35] The 1965 exhibition underscored Ceylon's ultimate bid for non-aligned status, which culminated in a conference held in Colombo in 1976. Non-aligned, that is, with the capitalist West.

Although the presence of America remained peripheral to a government shaped by socialist policies and bent on non-alignment, Jane Loeffler has argued that the American presence in the region dates from President Truman's 1947 doctrine bent on containing Soviet expansion linked to postwar reconstruction.[36] India and Pakistan were seen as "prime targets for Communist infiltration." The first major embassy project was designed for India by Durell Stone in a concrete, steel and glass aesthetic closely aligned with the environmental tenets of Tropical Modernism. Victor Lundy's embassy in Colombo (1961–85) followed similar guidelines. We may assume, therefore, that the political pressures evident in the region had an impact on Ceylon.

The architecture of Ceylon 65 was a world in miniature, a utopian testing ground for new technologies that were being celebrated elsewhere. It comprised a bold display of international-style architectures. The design of the exhibition site as a vast complex of separate and competing pavilions reflected the gradual dissolution of the centralized exhibition hall in the history of international exhibitions. The exhibition demonstrated the gradual transformation of the political economies of Asian nations and the changing sites of industrial production (Figure 3). Rather than blindly imitating Western models, its designers experimented with new technologies on home turf. Folded plate structures, geodetic roofs, and prefabricated building systems prefigured the commitment to concrete technologies symptomatic of modernist experiments of the 1970s and precedents in Chandigarh and Brasilia. These experiments were largely used in the promotion of government industries that had been incorporated into the nationalist agenda and were managed through political appointments and favors. Pavilions of government corporations dominated the landscape of the exhibition. The grand stand was occupied by various departments for local government, marketing, electrical undertakings, agrarian services, irrigation, marketing, labor, post and telecommunications, education, and *shramadana* (self-help). The entire nationalist bureaucracy in all its opacity was being laid bare for public examination.

The exhibition also included cultural activities such as a pigeonry for an aerial orchestra, an international film center and a music and dance center; structures which gave opportunities for technological innovation. The main entrance, a restaurant, a reception hall for the Ministry of Industries, and the Ceylon Pavilion were erected by the State Engineering Corporation (SEC), which played a significant role in the exhibition and was designed by PWD architect Bilimorea and his assistant Tangavale. The star attraction, designed by engineer A. N. S. Kulasinghe and erected by the SEC, was the planetarium, which borrowed its imagery from two recent examples: Sir Frederick Gibberd's Cathedral for Liverpool (1960), and Costa and Niemeyer's Great Cathedral at Brasilia (1960–70). The building, still extant, has a reinforced concrete floor and a pre-stressed concrete folded plate roof, which was pre-cast on site and erected using cranes. It was funded and maintained by East Germany as a gift to the Sri Lankan government.

Both the US pavilion and its exhibits demonstrated prefabricated building systems that would enable the Americans to accelerate the construction

Figure 3
The Colombo Industrial Exhibition site under construction. Courtesy of Associated Newspapers Ceylon Ltd.

of various support facilities during the Vietnam War. The pavilion had steel columns and a geodetic roof structure, and the canvas roof was designed as suspended catenaries with an inverted catenary fabric ceiling. The structure comprised self-supporting right-angled exhibition panels of pre-cast material that folded together concertina-fashion.[37] It was a dismantle-able travelling exhibition module that the Americans would later exhibit in India.[38] In short, labor-saving systems were beginning to enter an industry that was dominated by labor-intensive colonial processes. They brought with it ideas of self-reliance that sat well within socialist ideology. However, private sector firms were few and far between, smaller in size and cast at the periphery, in keeping with the government's economic policies.

The social modernity of the Ceylonese was undoubtedly aided by an inward political orientation and hostility toward western capitalism that limited their exposure to the Western world. This modernity manifested itself in the denial of the orientalized self-image inherited from both the feudal and colonial pasts, and provided new avenues for technological experimentation. As evident in the interior of the Samuel and Sons pavilion, designed by architect Valentine Gunasekara and engineer Jayathi Weerakoon, the subjects of this experiment were Ceylonese men and women dressed in the local fashions of the 1960s: high-heeled shoes, sleeveless sari blouses and bouffant hairstyles (Figure 4). They embodied the spirit of the age and demonstrated an Asian middle-class modernity that had been ignored three decades earlier. This homegrown interpretation of modernity was easily married to a functionalist aesthetic of concrete architectural forms. For the Ceylonese it pre-empted EXPO 1970 in Osaka as the international venue displaying Asia's modernization.

Figure 4
Visitors at the Ceylon Industrial Exhibition 1965. Courtesy of Associated Newspapers Ceylon Ltd.

The shift from a colonial imaginary to a modern one was both radical and self-conscious, an effort on the part of the government to display national progress. Yet the politics underlying the exhibition was far more complex. At the opening in February 1965, in coincidence with Independence Day celebrations, the leader of the socialist coalition government, Sirimavo Bandaranaike, pronounced Ceylon's social and industrial revolutions as well under way.[39] But industries had not developed in a revolutionary manner. Factories were first introduced during the Second World War for the production of essential goods, and were reorganized into corporations during the postwar period. The concrete technologies displayed at the Ceylon Industrial Exhibition originated in the large hydraulic dam projects initiated during this period, which brought large quantities of imported cement for concrete construction. During the late 1950s industrialization became imperative, with a growing population needing both employment and essential goods, but socialist controls on foreign exchange expenditure choked industrial growth. By 1964, there was a shortage of foreign exchange, imports were severely curtailed, and industries were unable to buy either machinery or raw materials.

In fact, Ceylon 65 disguised the achievements of almost two decades of pro-capitalist economic progress in the language of a newly emerging socialist modernism. There is some irony in this sleight of hand at this particular historical moment. The exhibition, which had emerged as a symbol of free market interests and colonial enterprise, was being co-opted in the service of a socialist national agenda proclaiming the centralization of political and industrial development. The country's two domestic political parties, the pro-capitalist United National Party and the pro-socialist Sri Lanka Freedom party, had aligned themselves across cold war political divisions feeding on global insecurities and exploiting the constant see-saw of democratic elections. C. Alagaratnam, Vice Chairman of the National Chamber of Industries, described the exhibition as a last-minute political gambit of an inept government seeking to buttress the flailing confidence of its voters in an election year.[40] As reported in the national press supporting the opposition UNP party:

> They chose to call it the Industrial Exhibition but the National Press and a wide section of the public had a number of other names for it – bad names such as "the great illusion," "an exhibition of ill-timed extravagance," "an industrial tamasha," "a vote-catching stunt performed by the coalition circus"… But the Ceylon Daily Mirror held the pithiest comment when it editorially slanted the triple gemmed Churchillian quotation in order to cast a baleful gleam of editorial insight on this vain effort of industrial exhibitionism, "Never in the field of public hoaxing," it said, "has so much money been squandered by so many to deceive so few!"[41]

The 1965 industrial exhibition in Colombo was the swan song of "modernity as technological progress," at the close of a five-year term under a socialist government. It was also the last of its kind. In retrospect, Ceylon 65 could be viewed as a laboratory for modernism and an expression of its humanist ideals through concrete technologies. Ethnicity, religion, and cultural specificity had no place in the embrace of these concrete giants. Their secular aesthetic and consequent insensitivity to identity-politics was unsustainable long-term. By the 1980s disenchantment with modernist utopias had set in across the region.

The *Gam Udawa* village re-awakening movement

Ceylon's engagement with socialism lasted until 1977, a period that saw considerable economic change. Beginning with the OPEC oil crisis, insular economic policies gradually eroded the country's economy, replacing it with a heavily-subsidized welfare system. Land reform reduced the indigenous capitalist class who had emerged with the colonial economy, and the tea industry (Ceylon's main export) was nationalized under the government. Despite positive political developments such as republican status in 1972 and increasing self-confidence as a non-aligned nation, Sri Lanka's economy had been irrevocably damaged by socialism. Consequently, a bloody Marxist insurrection by the *Janata Vimukthi Peramuna* (JVP: People's Liberation Front) would erupt in 1971 to challenge the socialist government. In 1977, the year following the non-aligned summit in Colombo, the people voted for change. The United National Party returned to government with a resounding two-thirds majority in parliament and a promise to liberalize the economy. It had shed the colonial residue that had stigmatized its political elite and was ready to placate its voters with Buddhist nationalist sentiments.[42]

The opening up of the Sri Lankan economy after a long period of state-led development would impact its society at many levels. First, with the lifting of import restrictions, competitive products would flood the market. New technologies and standards of manufacture became essential for keeping up with international industry. Free trade zones became the sites for new industries predicated on female labor, thus displacing the colonial plantation economy. A new breed of crony capitalists fought over the privileges once reserved for political lackeys, and the centralized structure of the socialist economy was co-opted for a state-led and equally politicized model of economic decentralization.

Following the OPEC oil crisis, the architectural styles of the late 1970s were predicated on import substitution. This strategy not only foregrounded sustainable agendas but also forced the recycling of building elements through necessity rather than choice, reviving an interest in vernacular architecture. The revival of vernacular forms and materials by architects like Minette de Silva and Geoffrey Bawa in Sri Lanka responded to the building practices of the local climatic region and reciprocated the regionalist political sentiments of the time. Whereas its genesis was in the socialist economies of an earlier period, by the

1980s the vernacular style had traveled across economic systems and was being commodified for tourism-led development.

Nihal Perera has argued that in its critical stance against International Style architecture (the modernism of the 1960s) the institutional landscape of Sri Lanka was re-familiarized using an aesthetic derived from local precedent.[43] Certainly its objective was to re-establish continuity with a pre-colonial tradition that was meaningful to the local culture. But the designed vernacular of the 1980s more often took the form of elite residences, resort hotels on the one hand and overtly sentimental renditions of the national narrative in craft museums and village replicas. While the aesthetic revived craftsmanship in trades such as carpentry and plaster work, which has been central to timber and masonry construction, these methods remained labor-intensive and predicated on cheap rural labor. Despite its principles of sustainability and local culture, architectural projects were largely commercially driven by the late 1980s. The scale of these hotel buildings rivaled or exceeded that of local institutions. In fact, the revival of indigenous cultures across Asia during this period was strangely reminiscent of the colonial exhibition tradition reproduced in this case for postcolonial, elite and metropolitan audiences.

According to Arindam Dutta, the successive *Festivals of India* (1983–86) organized by the Indian government and held in the USA, Britain, France, and Japan were ill-concealed economic projects framed in terms of "culture."[44] They coincided with Britain's new-found interest in its imperial past, an outpouring of patriotism around the Falklands conflict, and a reaction to increasing numbers of "Third World" migrants. A thematic approach of dioramas and a focus on artisan cultures was deemed more appropriate than highlighting "history" or "style" in the Western art-historical tradition. This "antidisciplinary" and "ethnofetishistic" bent was evident in the titles of exhibitions, Dutta argues, such as "The Canvas of Culture – Rediscovery of the Past as Adaptations for the Future"; "Vistara – The Architecture of India"; and "From Village to City in Ancient India," etc. The architectural exhibition, Vistara, invoked indigenous themes, traditionally neglected vernacular architecture and buildings from the colonial era, in an unconventional pluralistic approach, observe Bhatt and Bafna.[45] Indian architecture was presented as a series of epiphanies where the various historic epochs, including Vedic, Islamic, and British colonial periods, were presented as a succession of myths or paradigm shifts; and formalized Hindu structures were given mystical and metaphysical meanings.[46] Architects Charles Correa and Ashish Ganju were involved in its manifesto, which placed their own architectural agendas at the centre of a discourse on Indian identity.

The focus on local cultures that followed the Festival of India was encapsulated in craft museums, the Village India Complex, and contributed to a reinvention of the vernacular. In Bombay, the center of postmodern Indian culture, where the colonial urban fabric predominated, culture was reinterpreted as heritage conservation and was articulated through periodic urban festivals.[47] Similarly, indigenous traditions resurfaced as urban artefacts and were used in the recuperation of nationalist positions in Southeast Asia, in the Beautiful Indonesia in Miniature Park (1971), a Disney-type theme park built by Mrs Suharto outside Jakarta where the nation was represented as a colorful and harmonious village.[48] In the Philippines they took the form of the "Nayong Pilipino," sanctioned and produced by Imelda Marcos in 1972.[49]

The history of exhibitions had so far produced two representations of traditional buildings, the first derived from vernacular architecture by British architects and the second a reinvention of the vernacular for contemporary use by local architects trained in the West. Sandwiched between these two positions was the overtly modernist aesthetics of Ceylon 65, which had rejected the vernacular altogether. Yet all of these approaches had been covert metropolitan platforms for furthering particular political-economic agendas, suggesting that aesthetic representations were necessarily urbane. The vast majority of the nation's citizens, who lived in rural areas, were excluded from their rhetoric and could not afford or understand their economic orientation. An endemic fault in the economic agendas projected by each successive national exhibition was their cognitive distance from their most important audience of voters.

Whereas the exhibitions of 1952 and 1965 failed to decolonize both the economy and the society of a post-independent nation, the post-1977 system of governance exposed this very problematic. The *Gam Udawa* (Village Re-awakening) exhibitions that followed would be a symptom of their time, producing eclectic, postmodern sites for historical and political reconstruction (Figure 5). Yet from its genesis, the movement's objectives set it apart from its forebears. It had decentralization as its economic goal and the rural periphery as its primary audience. *Gam Udawa* also reflected a change in the character of political leadership from the elite high-caste politicians educated in colonial ways to an emerging subaltern polity. The scheme was the brainchild of President Ranasinghe Premadasa, who was fired by a genuine desire to alleviate the poverty of the rural majority. An individual from an urban background, without the caste or class advantages of his peers, he rose to be a municipal councilor, prime minister and president, and was a close follower of E. F. Schumacher's ideals.[50] Premadasa hoped to develop the nation's periphery through the provision of low-cost housing.

President Premadasa's Village Re-awakening Scheme, aimed at building 100,000 houses and providing infrastructure to remote villages, was begun in 1979. The projects were executed using explicit and implicit forms of coercion. A workaholic, Premadasa eliminated public sector inefficiency through impulsive retrenchments and compelled private entrepreneurs to contribute to his endeavors. They provided infrastructure for each *Gam Udawa* project, building roads and extending water supply, sewerage, and electricity to remote sites. The official opening of each village would take the form of an exhibition.

The *Gam Udawa* exhibition would commence each year on the 23rd of June, the president's birthday, would continue for ten days, and would include numerous events: competitive sports, singing contests, art competitions, a trade fair, and the opening of the model village. It would attract several thousand visitors from the adjacent towns and villages. The number of houses built in each site would match the president's age at the time. The landscape of the exhibition was designed to capture the popular history of the area; for example, a king who once ruled over the territory would be commemorated with a statue in his honor or a scaled-down replica of an existing stupa. Buddhist pilgrimage sites from all over Sri Lanka and even from abroad – such as Mihintale, Sanchi, and Sri Pada – would be rebuilt in miniature, creating an easy trajectory along which exhibition-goers could consume the religious experience. Described by one visitor as a *Senakaliya* or carnival, the exhibition site typically included numerous trade stalls and entertainment venues such as a sports ground, carousel, and mini zoo in addition to the stalls of government organizations.[51]

Although it is tempting to draw parallels between the *Gam Udawa* projects and the examples in Indonesia and the Philippines cited earlier, a critical distinction needs to be made. As observed by Kusno "Beautiful Indonesia in Miniature" was an attempt at recreating authenticity along the lines of colonial anthropological investigations of the past.[52] The site reduced the nation to a rural utopia and served to educate local tourists. *Gam Udawa* had a very different objective of collapsing the difference between the past and the present. As argued by Hennayake, the exhibition [disarticulated] the "urban-rural and traditional-modern distances within a single bounded space through the use of a wide array of significant symbols representing both categories."[53] It demonstrated Premadasa's goal of people-izing development, in her view.

What were the ideological underpinnings of this process? In the *Arcades Project*, Walter Benjamin describes the re-enchantment of the social world and through it a "reactivation of its mythic powers" under the conditions of capitalism.[54]

Figure 5
Gateway to *Gam Udawa* 90 at Pallekeley. Courtesy of Associated Newspapers Ceylon Ltd.

He writes of the threatening and alluring force of myth underlying the systemic rationalization of social and cultural institutions. Susan Buck-Morss observes that "according to Benjamin, fascism is an extension of the reenchantment of the world and of man's illusory dream state" rather than an extension of modern rationality itself.[55] The *Gam Udawa* exhibitions in Sri Lanka, by clothing expressions of autocracy in populist imagery, re-affirmed old mythologies and constructed new ones within the rubric of a provincially directed capitalism.[56]

For example, *Gam Udawa* 89 at Mahiyangana had as its major axis a path leading from the entrance through a public square to a replica of the Sri Lankan parliament. At one end of the axis was the gallery of heroes and at the other was the *Pattirippuwa* (raised platform) from which the President would make his opening address. A secondary axis to the right took visitors to replicas of the President's House and Temple Trees (the residence of the Prime Minister). Colombo's two major parks, the Vihara Maha Devi Park and Sathutu Uyana (Happy Park) – which the President had built in Colombo – were also represented, followed by a replica of the Colombo Town Hall (Figure 6). Along the periphery of the site were miniature places of Buddhist pilgrimage, Sri Pada, a sacred mountain in Sri Lanka, and Buddha Gaya in India. A field of ripening grain, with a Buddhist stupa in the background, was stylized for the design of the invitation, referring to the rich agricultural bounty for which Mahiyangana was famous. Unlike exhibitions of the past, Premadasa's vision embraced all of Sri Lankan history, its power structure, and even its ethnic communities; many of the exhibition sites included replicas of Hindu temples.

Despite their diversity the exhibitions reflected the violent political transformations that were taking place at that time. Ethnic conflict led to civil war and rising religious fundamentalism. In 1989 the president had brutally suppressed a second insurrection of the resurgent JVP, eliminating its leadership. The climate of rising Buddhist nationalism was evident in the constant reference to sites, personages and traditions in the exhibits and attendant ceremonies, while at Mahiyangana the armed forces occupied a prominent position on the fairground.

Although the utopian community of the re-awakened village presented an insular social vision, Premadasa the statesman was urbane and ambitious. Obsessed by temporality and mortality, he instituted a clock tower in every village, believing that their combined time-keeping would augment his political power.[57] The most significant act of the President was in replicating buildings from Colombo such as the Independence Hall, the old parliament building, architect Geoffrey Bawa's new parliament on the lake, and the Colombo Town Hall, which served to assert the center at the periphery, annually reconstituting the geography of the nation.

At first the traditional vocabulary of the reawakening program gave the exhibition a bucolic appearance, concomitant with the issues of sustainability foregrounded in its ideology. Unfamiliar metropolitan artifacts were surrounded by familiar historical figures domesticating them as part of a collective story. Their romantic building styles responded to regionalist ideals derived from vernacular

Figure 6
**Replica of Colombo
Independence Hall built
at Pallekeley.
Photograph taken by
the author, 2005.**

architecture. However, a shift in this vocabulary occurred during the 1980s that loosened romanticism's ideological hold. Precipitated by the President's visit to an exhibition in Kyoto and facilitated by Jack Kulasinghe, with a doctorate in Visual Communication from Sofia, Bulgaria, the *Gam Udawa* assumed the populist images of international postmodernism. Jack Kulasinghe knew well the power of kinetic sculptures and lighting effects – the industrial technologies of the age. Under his expertise each *Gam Udawa* was given a theme and a color scheme, and the pavilions were designed with detachable façades. They delivered the kind of mass culture described by Benjamin "not merely as the source of phantasmagoria or false consciousness, but as the source of collective energy to overcome it."[58]

The first two exhibitions discussed in this paper had projected very different utopias: the Colombo Plan 52 had revived the specter of empire through the Commonwealth; and Colombo 65 had proclaimed its socialist alliances across cold war battle lines. In contrast, the *Gam Udawa* exhibition educated rural Sri Lankans into citizenship and modernity. During the space of the exhibition, the island's pilgrimage sites and national monuments were inserted into a remote local geography for rural consumption. Unlike the previous exhibitions, which adhered to pre-colonial or modernist ideologies, *Gam Udawa* drew liberally on colonial, vernacular, religious, and international vocabularies, without preference. As the exhibition shifted in content and focus, opening its artifacts to global influences, its symbolisms became far more complex and blurred. Essentialist prejudices regarding culture and indigeneity were deconstructed with each successive pageant. Whereas metropolitan elites saw the designed vernacular as the proper subject of Sri Lankan identity, alternative identities were experimented with on more equitable turf.

The evolution of this approach is most evident in a replica of the familiar palace in Kandy, built for the Buttala *Gam Udawa* in 1992 (Figure 7). Under Jack Kulasinghe's expert hand it was stripped of ornament and reinvented as a Japanese pagoda with a tiered roof and water garden. In its transformation to a complex postmodern cultural symbol the pavilion has abandoned the pastiche of the cardboard façade that haunted the *Gam Udawa*s of the past in order to reappear as a "contemporary" vernacular. The palace's modern manifestation spoke of a different motivation, which left behind its traditional roots to embrace the truly open field of postmodern appropriation. In doing so the pavilion offered a global vision for inhabitants of the rural periphery, releasing them from their timeless reconstitution through a pre-colonial past. The recipients of Premadasa's vision had shed the inhibitions of metropolitan taste.

Gam Udawa exhibitions were held in different parts of the country from 1979 to 1993, until they were halted following the assassination of President Premadasa. Although eagerly embraced by rural audiences, they were ridiculed by urbanites, who described them as "*Gam Rudawa*" (the painful villages).[59] Comparable sentiments had been expressed by architects in the USA in response to *Learning from Las Vegas*, which inserted analyses of popular culture into contemporary architectural discourse.[60] Similarly, the aesthetics of the exhibition presented a messy hybridity at a time when authentic vernaculars were prescribed by regionalist discourses. While this prescribed vernacular, its style and components were central to the capitalist project of social engineering, which installed urban villages in rural wastelands, the myths that grew around it were uneven and irreverent. The contribution of the *Gam Udawa* was forgotten, although the memory of the "carnival," lingered.

Figure 7
Buttala *Gam Udawa* entrance pavilion by Jack Kulasinghe. Courtesy of Jack Kulasinghe, National Housing Development Authority.

Conclusion

Sri Lanka's experimentation through national exhibitions extended for only half a century following independence. The populist cultural vernacular followed its modernist predecessor to the graveyard of creative expression and was replaced by more permanent urban institutions. The "authentic" past in acceptable architectural forms, and disseminated through regionalist debates, presented an alternative postmodernism more palatable to the urban elites and Western consumers. The separation of these two distinct vernaculars within the same time-frame underlined the class distinctions and social hierarchies that were resisting social change. The *Gam Udawa* exhibitions were neither orientalist nor were they sentimental in their eclectic and untroubled appropriation from both the East and the West. Yet they encapsulated the spirit of the age, its people, and its prejudices far more successfully than the aesthetics subscribed to in previous exhibitions. In exposing to public view the architecture of the ordinary, they represented the complexities of an emerging modern consciousness that was not necessarily rooted in urbanity. Despite their careful choreography and their ultimate dismissal as a symptom of one individual's megalomania, the *Gam Udawa* exhibitions captured elements of the unofficial folk culture, the "peculiar second world" within the official order described by Mikhail Bakhtin.[61] It was a form of populism that had been suppressed in the desire for appropriate forms of national representation. Haunted by bloody insurrections and nationalist gyrations from right to left, the exhibitions of Sri Lanka fittingly captured the socio-political sensibilities of specific moments in the twentieth century when Asia first experimented with modernization.

The aesthetics of the *Gam Udawa* genre were not pleasing to the design elite in Sri Lanka's metropolitan circles or to the political adversaries of the UNP. All information on these exhibitions was burnt in the bureaucratic bonfire of a changing political regime, and *Gam Udawa* sites and facilities have been neglected since. Like the exhibitions before them, they too were transient spectacles of the country's path to liberalization. In fact, the lesson of *Gam Udawa*, argues Hennayake, was in its challenge to the modernist dialectic. A journalist is said to have observed that at these exhibitions "people not only literally but metaphorically walk backwards, forwards and just around in circles."[62] Whereas the architectural culture of the era carefully disguised its cosmopolitan influences behind a veneer of vernacular authenticity, the architecture of the people was unpretentious. Yet their emergence in the 1980s, their role in identity construction, and their facile absorption of the capitalist dialectic offer lessons regarding the processes of social modernity in what has been called the third world. R. Premadasa's incongruous matchmaking between urban carnivals and rural polities identified modernization's greatest challenge as not being that of abandoning tradition for modernity, but that of prising them apart.

Notes

1   Perry Anderson, Modernity and Revolution, *New Left Review*, 1984 March–April, 1/144, pp. 96–113. Review of Marshall Berman, *All That is Solid Melts into Air: The Experience of Modernity*, Boston: Simon & Schuster, 1983.

2   Anderson, p. 105.

3   Ibid., p. 107.

4   Ibid., p. 106.

5   Ibid., p.109.

6   See Vikramāditya Prakāsh and Peter Scriver, *Colonial Modernities: Building Dwelling and Architecture in British India and Ceylon*, London: Routledge, 2007, for essays by Chattopadhyay, Hosagrahar and others in this field. William J. Glover, *Making Lahore Modern: Constructing and Imagining a Colonial City*, Minneapolis: University of Minnesota Press, 2008; Gyan Prakash, *Another Reason: Science and the Imagination of Modern India*, Princeton, NJ: Princeton University Press, 1999; Mark Crinson, *Modern Architecture and the End of Empire*, Aldershot: Ashgate Publishing, 2003; Patricia Morton, *Hybrid Modernities: Architecture and Representation at the 1931 Colonial Exposition, Paris*, Cambridge MA: The MIT Press, 2000; Arindam Dutta, *The Bureaucracy of Beauty: Design in the Age of its Global Reproducibility*, Routledge: 2006.

7   Edward Said, *Orientalism*, London: Pantheon, 1978.

8   Timothy Mitchell, *Colonizing Egypt*, New York: Cambridge UP, 1988.

9   Tony Bennett, *The Birth of the Museum: History, Theory, Politics*, London; New York: Routledge, 1995, pp. 83–4.

10 Swati Chattopadhyay, "A Critical History of Architecture in a Post-Colonial World: A View from Indian Architectural History," *Architronic*, vol. 6, no. 1 (May 1997).

11 Eric Mattie, *World's Fairs*, New York: Princeton University Press, 1998, pp. 77 and 82.

12 Patricia Morton, op. cit., pp. 195–97.

13 Ibid.

14 Thomas R. Metcalf, *An Imperial Vision: Indian Architecture and Britain's Raj*, Berkeley: University of California Press, 1989.

15 Eric Mattie, op. cit., 1998.

16 Ibid., p. 199.

17 Ibid., p. 222.

18 Marilyn Kushner, "Exhibiting art at the American National Exhibition in Moscow, 1959: domestic politics and cultural diplomacy," *Journal of Cold War Studies*, Winter 2002 Vol. 4 (1), pp. 6–26.

19 (http://aaa.si.edu; Introduction) [19 June 2010]; http://www3.sympatico.ca/robsab/debate.html [10 December 2007].

20 Bennett, op. cit.

21 See Daniel Oakman, *Facing Asia: A History of the Colombo Plan*, Pandanus Books, 2003.

22 Ibid., p. 33.

23 Ibid, p. 37. Oakman describes the American view of the 1950 conference in these terms.

24 Colombo Plan Exhibition Brochure, 1952.

25 Ibid., p. 46.

26 Ibid., p. 52. The pavilion was former Minister for External Affairs Percy Spender's brainchild.

27 CO 825-89/2, 3, May 1951, NUS Central Library archives 264–7, Outward telegram from Commonwealth Relations Office to Canada, Australia, New Zealand, India, and Pakistan, and inward telegram to Commonwealth Relations Office from UK High Commission in Ceylon.

28 Report made by Sir Oliver Gunatileke, mentioned in the above correspondence.

29 Ibid.

30 Brochure, 1952, p. 43.

31 Ibid., p. 3.

32 Ibid.

33   See Jamie Mackie, *Bandung 1955: Non-alignment and Afro-Asian Solidarity*, Singapore: Select Books, 2005.

34   Even though the United States had agreed in early 1958 to provide the country with technical assistance (and a grant of about $780,000) for economic projects, the Soviet Union and Ceylon had signed trade and economic agreements at about the same time. Shortly afterwards Ceylon accepted a loan of about $10.5 million from China.

35   Pheng Cheah describes this historical process in Bruce Robbins and Pheng Cheah (eds), *Cosmopolitics: Thinking and Feeling beyond the Nation*, Minneapolis: University of Minnesota Press, 1998, p. 29.

36   Jane Loeffler, *The Architecture of Diplomacy: Building America's Embassies*, NJ: Princeton Architectural Press, 1998, pp. 37–8.

37   Communication from Jayathi Weerakoon, Engineer for the pavilion, August 9 2004.

38   Interview of Valentine Gunasekara by author, Bedford Massachusetts (May 28 – June 1 2003).

39   *Ceylon Daily News*, 2 February 1965, Tuesday, vol. 49 (28).

40   C. Alagaratnam (Vice Chairman of the National Chamber of Industries), "The exhibition: politics not industry," Editorial, *Industrial Ceylon*, December 1964, Vol. 4, no. 4.

41   *Times of Ceylon Annual* 1965 edited by Subbiah Muttiah, printed and published by P. Don Nichols for the *Times of Ceylon*, "News pictures of the year…their stories by Winston Rodrigo (no page numbers given). Picture by Oliver Seneviratne, "Ceylon Daily Mirror," February 17 1965.

42   See Deborah Winslow and Michael D. Woost (eds), *Economy, Culture and Civil War in Sri Lanka*, Indiana University Press, 2004.

43   Nihal Perera, *Society and Space: Colonialism, Nationalism, and Postcolonial Identity in Sri Lanka*, Boulder, Colorado: Westview Press, 1998, p. 147.

44   Aridam Dutta, op. cit., p. 268.

45   Ritu Bhatt and Sonit Bafna, "Post-Colonial Narratives of Indian Architecture," *Architecture+Design*, Vol XII No. 6 (November–December 1995), pp. 85–89.

46   Ibid.

47   See Rahul Mehrotra, "Learning from Mumbai," http://www.india-seminar.com/2003/530/530%20 rahul%20mehrotra.htm [21 January 2009]; Rahul J. Mehrotra (1992), "Bazaars in Victorian arcades [transformation and conservation in historic environments]', *Places*, Vol. 8, No. 1, Article. http://repositories.cdlib.org/ced/places/vol8/iss1/RahulJMehrotra [21 January 2009].

48   Abidin Kusno, *Behind the Postcolonial: Architecture, Urban Space, and Political Cultures in Indonesia*, London: Routledge, 2000, p. 74.

49   Gerard Lico, *The Edifice Complex: Power, Myth and Marcos State Architecture*, Ateneo de Manila University Press, 2003, p. 69.

50   E. F. Schumacher, *Small is Beautiful: A Study of Economics as if People Mattered*, Blond and Briggs, 1973.

51   Interview with Sumangala Jayatileke, January 2005.

52   Abidin Kusno, op. cit., pp. 83–4.

53   Nalani Hennayake, *Culture, Politics and Development in Postcolonial Sri Lanka*, UK: Lexington Books, 2006, p. 147.

54   Walter Benjamin, *The Arcades Project*, trans. Howard Eiland and Kevin McLaughlin (paperback edition), Harvard University Press, 2000 in Susan Buck-Morss, *The Dialectics of Seeing: Walter Benjamin and the Arcades Project*, MIT Press, 1989, pp. 253–255.

55   Ibid., footnote 3, 454.

56   Ibid.

57   Based on private communication with R. Obeyesekere, 15 January 2005.

58   Susan Buck-Morss, op. cit.,, p. 253.

59   A commonly held criticism among Colombo residents.

60   Robert Venturi, Denise Scott Brown, and Steven Izenour, *Learning from Las Vegas*, Cambridge, Mass., MIT Press, 1972.

61   Mikhail Bakhtin, *Rabelais and His World*, translated by Hélène Iswolsky, Bloomington, Ind.: Indiana University Press, 1984, p. 154.

62   Hennayake, op. cit., p. 148. L.S. Palansuriya and Jack Kulasinghe of the NHDA provided much of the material on Gam Udawa Programs during an interview in February 2006. Material on Ceylon 65 was previously discussed in Anoma Pieris, Modernity at the Margins: Reconsidering Valentine Gunasekara, in *Grey Room*, 28 (Summer 2007), pp.56–85.

Chapter 7

This is not an American House: good sense modernism in 1950s Turkey

Elâ Kaçel

In memory of Şevki Vanlı

In 1958, the architect and critic Şevki Vanlı (1926–2008) coined the term "Hiltonculuk" to describe a fad among prominent Turkish architects who uncritically modeled their buildings after the Istanbul Hilton Hotel (1952–5), designed by Gordon Bunshaft of Skidmore, Owings and Merrill (SOM) and Sedad Hakkı Eldem (Figure 1). Vanlı's criticism was directed at the easy reproduction of the "perfect mediocrity" of 1950s American architecture à la International Style in postwar Turkey.[1]

In the same year, the architect Maruf Önal designed a house located in Bayramoğlu, a small resort town 50 kilometers southeast of Istanbul (Figure 2). Unlike other houses Önal designed for his clients in the 1950s, this vacation house for his own family was minimal, modest, and unpretentious. Although built at the peak of "Hiltonculuk," the house does not fit under the categories either of a formulaic Americanism or of a "perfect mediocrity."

Overlooked by historians and critics for almost 50 years, Önal's house recently found a place in Vanlı's last book, a critical study of twentieth-century Turkish architecture. Though not a historian by profession, Vanlı has historicized ordinary practices of architecture in Turkey, the historical legitimacy of which has been downplayed by professional historians until recently. While bringing dozens of Turkish architects to light whose works have been written out of mainstream history because of their ordinariness, Vanlı raised his 50-year-old criticism of "Hiltonculuk" again and questioned the extents of ordinariness in design. Alongside a critical analysis of architectural discourse, the book displays a new approach to historiography that is non-historicist, expandable, and open-ended.

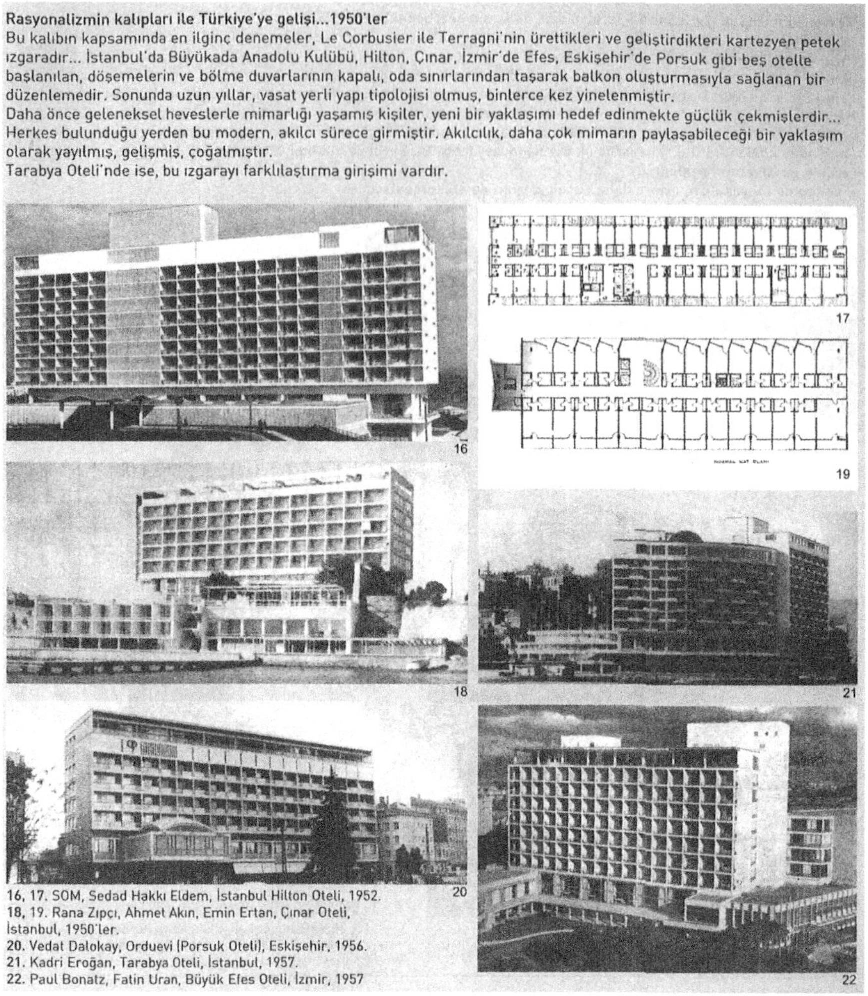

Rasyonalizmin kalıpları ile Türkiye'ye gelişi...1950'ler

Bu kalıbın kapsamında en ilginç denemeler, Le Corbusier ile Terragni'nin ürettikleri ve geliştirdikleri kartezyen petek ızgaradır... İstanbul'da Büyükada Anadolu Kulübü, Hilton, Çınar, İzmir'de Efes, Eskişehir'de Porsuk gibi beş otelle başlanılan, döşemelerin ve bölme duvarlarının kapalı, oda sınırlarından taşarak balkon oluşturmasıyla sağlanan bir düzenlemedir. Sonunda uzun yıllar, vasat yerli yapı tipolojisi olmuş, binlerce kez yinelenmiştir.

Daha önce geleneksel heveslerle mimarlığı yaşamış kişiler, yeni bir yaklaşımı hedef edinmekte güçlük çekmişlerdir... Herkes bulunduğu yerden bu modern, akılcı sürece girmiştir. Akılcılık, daha çok mimarın paylaşabileceği bir yaklaşım olarak yayılmış, gelişmiş, çoğalmıştır.

Tarabya Oteli'nde ise, bu ızgarayı farklılaştırma girişimi vardır.

16, 17. SOM, Sedad Hakkı Eldem, İstanbul Hilton Oteli, 1952.
18, 19. Rana Zıpcı, Ahmet Akın, Emin Ertan, Çınar Oteli, İstanbul, 1950'ler.
20. Vedat Dalokay, Orduevi (Porsuk Oteli), Eskişehir, 1956.
21. Kadri Eroğan, Tarabya Oteli, İstanbul, 1957.
22. Paul Bonatz, Fatin Uran, Büyük Efes Oteli, İzmir, 1957

Figure 1

"Hiltonculuk" featured in Vanlı's last book on a full page. Vanlı let the Istanbul Hilton (top left) confront its replicas, that is, other hotels in Turkey built in the late 1950s. The comparison of the typical floor plan of the Hilton (top right) to the plan below of the Çınar Hotel is noteworthy. Source: Vanlı, *Mimariden Konuşmak*, vol. 1 (2006), p. 211. Used with permission of the Şevki Vanlı Architecture Foundation.

The discussion of Önal's house in Vanlı's book is a good illustration of such an open-ended historiography that allows the reader to participate and refine. While interpreting the house as "one of the most sensitive and original buildings of Turkish rationalism," Vanlı does not thoroughly explore where this sensitivity and originality come from.[2] The implication is that the house is an antithesis of Hiltonculuk, yet he isolates it from the context of its design: Önal was one of three founding members of İnşaat ve Mimarlık Atölyesi (İMA), the first corporate architectural office in Turkey. How is it possible that Önal's house is a critical, "sensitive and original" counterexample within İMA's "perfect mediocrity?" Given the absence of avant-gardism in Turkish architecture (in the Western sense), can one categorically isolate creative individualism in architectural practice from "bureaucratic architecture"?[3]

Both Vanlı's criticism and Önal's house prove to be crucial tools for two tasks at hand: first, to question historical narratives of postwar modernism

that take for granted the "Americanization of modernism" in Third World countries without contextualizing the International Style within local discourses of architecture. And secondly, to further explore what "perfect mediocrity" and ordinariness entail in the context of Turkish postwar modernism. Rather than challenging Henry-Russell Hitchcock's argument of the 1960s that modern architecture is synonymous with American architecture, most historians have tried to justify Hitchcock's argument – that icons of postwar American architecture initiate mainstream histories of modernism in developing countries such as Turkey, as illustrated by the case of the Istanbul Hilton. Thus, architectural exchanges among the USA, Europe, and Third World countries during the cold war have been reduced to an export-import rhetoric that assumes that the process of change went unchallenged.[4] I suggest, on the other hand, that the process of the "Americanization of modernism" should be read as a contentious, multi-directional exchange rather than a unidirectional flow.[5] The appropriation of the International Style modernism as common sense in 1950s Turkey, like Vanlı's criticism of "Hiltonculuk," hints at the contentions that are in play in the United States as much as in Turkey.

In order to differentiate between critical and uncritical practices of architecture and map the cultural shifts of postwar modernism in Turkey, I use Antonio Gramsci's distinction between common sense and good sense. Common sense, for Gramsci, is the uncritical, passive, and unconscious way of being in the world that becomes commonly accepted. And yet it needs to be criticized, not only by the philosopher but by the common man: anyone has the capacity to recognize "the healthy nucleus that exists in 'common sense,' the part of it which can be called 'good sense' and which deserves to be made more unitary and coherent."[6] Good sense arises from within common sense, neither in isolation nor in opposition to it, and can generate a second thought on common sense.

In this chapter, I analyze and critique just how vulnerable to common sense architects became in everyday life, as well as how they created a "common sense" within architecture. In modernizing countries like Turkey, however, the uncritical appropriation and practice of the so-called International Style (which I will call common sense modernism) was propagated under the postwar sponsorship of the United States as *modern culture* and *modernity* itself. Advocates of modernization theory also believed that the acquisition of modernism as a "style of life" in the form of the International Style was a legitimate sign of modernization in developing countries.[7] The questioning of common sense was all that much harder when both the political and sociological views on what modern culture should be overlapped.

Turning to Gramsci's distinction between common sense and good sense, I explore how "ordinary" architects make use of the relational knowledge networks into which they are embedded to critique their own common sense practice of architecture and popular clichés of postwar modernism such as the "American house," the "Hilton-style washbasin," and the "ready-made house," transforming them into good sense. Rather than claiming absolute autonomy (as in the example of sole practitioners like Eldem), architects working in the first multi-partner offices in 1950s Turkey based their practices on relational knowledge as a design incentive and a group ideology.[8] In this chapter, Önal's house and Vanlı's history of common sense modernism will be my cases for rethinking modernism and its historiography respectively.

Modernization via good life

In August 1957, *Dostluk*, the biweekly Turkish newspaper of the United States Information Service (USIS), announced the opening of the American Pavilion at the 26th Izmir International Fair. The focus of that year's exhibits was on American domestic life, and the novelty, the article claimed, was a new model house built adjacent to the pavilion building. Built of Californian redwood, this fully furnished bungalow was presented to Turkish visitors as the "Modern American house" (Figure 3).[9]

An earlier issue of *Dostluk* showed a photograph of the house under construction (Figure 4). If a reader had examined this photograph closely, though, it would be obvious that the image belies the caption's claim that it is "one of the 'ready-made' houses that are mass-produced like cars and refrigerators … in a variety of colors, forms and plans in a factory."[10] Merely considering the wasted plywood and other materials lying on the ground, even a lay person would not imagine that what was being built on the site of the American Pavilion in Izmir was a mass-produced American house.

Figure 3

The American model house displayed on the site of the American Pavilion at the 26th Izmir International Fair, 1957. Source: *Dostluk*, no. 19 (28 August 1957), p. 6. Unknown photographer.

Figure 4

The model house under construction next to the American Pavilion seen on the right, 1957. Source: *Dostluk*, no. 18 (14 August 1957), p. 3. Unknown photographer.

Neither mass-produced in a factory nor prefabricated, the haphazard construction of this house is simply the production of a publicized image of the "modern American house." While representing grand ideologies such as freedom, welfare, and the good life as absolutes, the model house became a place where modernism was ideologically equated to Americanism. In other words, the house bears a double function: both objective and ideological.[11] While concealing the political ideologies of Americanization architecturally, the house also became the visual embodiment of the concepts of prefabrication, consumerism, and modernism, which were perceived by Turkish visitors as objective knowledge. It is through the appropriation of these concepts without question that the model house turns into an image of common sense in visitors' minds.

Without doubt, the image of the United States as the enabler of modernization, development, and modernity in Turkey accompanied this image of common sense. In the wake of a series of mutual aid agreements in 1945, new relations between the United States and Turkey started to emerge in various spheres including the economy, the military, technical assistance, education, the arts, and culture, reaching its peak with the Marshall Plan. The anti-protectionist economics and large investment plans of the governing Democrat Party and the Prime Minister's own vision of Turkey as "little America"[12] further perpetuated a popular curiosity and desire to attain the good life through modernity as depicted in the "modern American house" at the Izmir International Fair.

The "good life" is a convincing catch-all to summarize the visions of modernity advocated by disparate groups in the 1950s, whether those of house speculators, journal editors, reform-minded architects, or social scientists. In his critical analysis of the American house, Mark Jarzombek defines "Good-Life Modernism" as a popular, mass movement that constructs a consumerist ideology of modern living and residential architecture, respectively. Perpetuated by the media, museums, and manufacturers, this movement compelled hundreds of builders, architects, and even some avant-garde architects (such as Philip Johnson and Charles and Ray Eames) to design significant prototypes of "Good-Life Modernism."[13]

Even though architects were critical of speculative housing, that is, of "Good-Life Modernism," they were also pondering the question of how to define the notion of the good life architecturally and how to provide it to the public. "Architecture for the Good Life" was the theme of the convention of the American Institute of Architects (AIA) in 1956. As a remedy for "the monotonous repetitive patterns stamped out by the builder's machine," Clarence Stein proposed to develop "community architecture," and Carlos Contreras suggested that the "two-thirds of the population of the world, who live below the right level of living conditions" should fall under the protectorate of architecture.[14] He argued that architects' primary role is to improve living standards in underdeveloped areas of the world via architectural amenities suggestive of the good life. For Contreras, the ideal built form of the good life was a single-family home "that satisfies the minimum requirements of size, cleanliness, water, light, air, a small garden for the average human family," that is, an ideologically stripped-down version of mainstream, commercialized modernism in America in the 1950s. Shared by speculative builders and reform-minded architects alike, the single-family house was indeed an image of common sense in America.

It was precisely this image of common sense specific to America that was projected onto developing countries. Daniel Lerner, sociologist and advocate of modernization theory, even argued that the Sears mail-order house would become the ideal house for modern living in developing countries.[15] Indeed, even though the relative scales of the housing markets and building industries in postwar America and Turkey were vastly different, the experts of modernization, bureaucrats of both states, and administrators of mass media persistently created a version of "Good-Life Modernism" in Turkey, albeit contrived and nonfunctional.

Learning from common sense

Communication and mass media were the two keys that modernization programs used to generate the physical, social, and psychological mobility of individuals. Lerner explains how mass media was seen as an essential, multi-functional tool of modernity:

> The media teach new desires and new satisfactions. They depict situations in which the "good things" of life – of which most Middle Easterners never dreamed before – are taken for granted. They portray roles in which these richer lives are lived, and provide clues as to how these roles can be enacted by others.[16]

Media participation is the most questionable phase of the modernization process because of its social, cultural, yet manipulative influence over the public. Media-stimulated imaginations and desires would, in return, make individuals demand a better life: more modern, more urban, and more consumerist in nature. In this process, modernization theory's own function was to legitimize the controversies that arose from the functioning of mass media in modernizing countries.

Whether for the purposes of information, culture, or propaganda, the fact is that public and private agencies both in Turkey and the United States came to unconditionally agree on the essence of "Good-Life Modernism, " that is, the single-family house, through its promotion in mass media. Even though no infrastructural preconditions existed for proper "Good-Life Modernism" in 1950s Turkey, individuals were still stimulated by the narratives, images, myths, and stereotypes, and schooled themselves in home ownership, domesticity, and do-it-yourself. Especially for city dwellers of all social strata, the imagination was kept alive through movies, radio, newspapers, and magazines where the advertisements repeated the same images in every issue: a plot of land, a single house in the suburb, or an apartment flat in the city.

Through popular and professional publications and advertising, images of common sense prevailed in postwar architectural culture. Most savings banks prepared annual lotteries for plots, houses, or flats and promoted the idea of the single-family house with a garden. Architects were enlisted to design houses for suburban housing which were financed and developed by these banks. The trade journal *Arkitekt* continually advertised the aforementioned lotteries, even while failing to engage in any substantive (rather than descriptive) discourse of modernism. House projects were published with great enthusiasm but little editorial restraint. *Ev İş*, a home journal for women, began a series on single-family house design, publishing one architect-designed house in each issue. The single-family house – whether with pitched or terrace roof, traditional or modern, modest or pretentious – was promoted as the ultimate commodity in Turkey, in contrast to Jarzombek's analysis of the postwar housing situation in Europe, where "the house is rarely interpreted as an affordable consumer item."[17]

The dilemma is that even though state agencies and the media stimulated new desires and wants like the single-family house, those desires were never completely met. Thus, the "revolution of rising expectations" of the 1950s turned into the "revolution of rising frustrations" – not in the 1960s, as Lerner suggests, but even at the same time in the 1950s. More crucial to my discussion, however, are the aftereffects of the stimulation of empathy in media participation. Taking into account various experiences of "being modern," I argue that the stimulation of empathy ultimately generated two sensations in individuals facing modernity: the negative frustration; and the positive sense visual knowledge.[18]

Consider, for example, a bank advertisement for a home savings plan in the popular monthly *Bütün Dünya* (a Turkish version of *Reader's Digest*).[19] The illustration with the accompanying script "Always on my mind!" [Hep Zihnimde] clearly demonstrates how empathy was stimulated by the media to promote homeownership and attract customers to a new home savings plan (Figure 5). Readers were intended to understand the dramatic face of the woman illustrated on the ad as a self-portrait and to internalize her desire to be a homeowner. Yet if media-stimulated needs, desires, and targets could not be met in social, economic, and political terms, media participation would then easily turn into "the traumatic source of individual frustration."[20] Indeed, this was an impasse of the media and, in a wider sense, of freedom, welfare, and democracy, as well.

Considering the vast accumulation of images of common sense in everyday life, I suggest that even though it may have ended in frustration, the stimulation by the mass media still provided everyone with some positive sense, namely, visual knowledge. What I would like to emphasize is this: visual exposure to common sense is not negative by nature; it is not merely frustrating and destructive. Even though it negates the freedom of individuals in mass culture (as Theodor W. Adorno would argue), it provides a common basis that is shared by visitors to fairs, magazine buyers, film and theater audiences alike. What I mean by visual knowledge is exactly such a cultural contact with common sense and, in particular, with common sense modernism that is shared by architects and laymen alike.

Let me exemplify the prevalence of visual knowledge in the architectural culture of 1950s Turkey. The interest that many young, practicing architects of the time had in American modernism was not something that the Fine Arts Academy nor the Istanbul Technical University formally cultivated among students. Rather, it was the young assistants of well-established,

Figure 5
**Bank advertisement for
a home savings plan.
Illustration by Ihap
Hulusi.** Source: *Bütün
Dünya*, no. 94
**(November 1955), p.
627.**

Figure 5
**Bank advertisement for
a home savings plan.
Illustration by Ihap
Hulusi.** Source: *Bütün
Dünya*, no. 94
**(November 1955), p.
627.**

conservative design professors who surreptitiously added modern architecture to the curriculum. Ironically, the subjective interests of those individuals coincided with the formal agenda of the USIS in Turkey, which aimed to disseminate "objective" knowledge of American architecture via its various cultural programs. The self-education undertaken by many young architects and architectural students equipped them with bits and pieces of architectural knowledge that were information, culture, and propaganda, all at once.

The piecemeal sources of American architecture available to architects in Turkey came in various forms: blown-up photographs of American cities and buildings at the USIS exhibitions in Istanbul; articles on American architecture translated in *Arkitekt* (which the editor received from the USIS in the 1950s, and from Nezahat Arıkoğlu, an architect practicing in the US, in the 1960s); books and journals on American art and architecture at the USIS library (which were "browsed," since few could read English); special editions of European journals like *L'Architecture d'aujourd'hui* dealing with American architecture; a USIS and

MoMA exhibition entitled "Skyscrapers, USA" in 1957; and the "Modern American House" displayed adjacent to the American Pavilion at the 26th Izmir International Fair in 1957. It is crucial to note that most of these forms popularized modernism for professionals and the general public alike. Although it is difficult to ascertain the significance of each source, one can draw the conclusion that contact with American architectural modernism was always visual as well as mediated.[21]

The paradoxes in the production of this visual and mediated knowledge on American modernism are clearest in the pages of *Arkitekt*, where Turkish architects directly encountered architectural clichés about America. High-rise buildings and the detached single-family house were the most featured building types in *Arkitekt*. Brief, proscriptive texts on prefabrication and standardization were translated from *Architectural Forum* but were given little due in comparison to the lengthy tracts and eye-catching photographs taken from the pages of *House Beautiful* and *Journal of Home Economics*. As a result, domesticity and modern living were highlighted over the technical and theoretical concerns of the architectural discourse. Through these articles, the suburban house, the prefabricated house, and the mechanized kitchen – even values and habits of producing, consuming, and enjoying – were taken out of their American context and exported to the everyday discourse of *Arkitekt*'s readers. Thus, the journal had a considerable role in establishing a common sense regarding American architecture.

The one exception to the rule of short-shrifting the technical aspects of American housing construction was a comprehensive article on the Acorn house, which warranted a three-page spread complete with perspective photographs, sections, elevations, plans, and also narrative descriptions of the interior layout and design features of the house including kitchen and bathroom facilities, cabinet spaces, and shelving (Figure 6).[22] Yet, still, the name of the architect of the well-known Acorn House – a factory, ready-made house type designed by Carl Koch – was missing. The only reference to its origin was simply: the United States.

When the article was published in *Arkitekt* in 1950, more than a year after it had been originally published in *Life*, the implication was that this form of house was widespread in the USA. In fact, the focus of the *Life* article had been on the impracticality of the house as a model, as well as the bureaucratic, stylistic, and technical difficulties that mass production of such a house would entail. While the columnist admitted that the house was a rare gem among ordinary prefabricated houses, the concluding words sum up the inescapable reality: "The U.S. generally may never see it except in pictures like these."[23]

The Acorn house was interpreted by the Turkish editor and his audience as common sense American Modernism, even though it bore no relation to the real American house. Ironically, however, common sense was the very basis for rejecting the self-same house in the USA. A whole range of attempts made by architects to "modernize" the living experience in an American

Figure 6
**Acorn House featured in
Arkitekt as a typical
American prefabricated
house. Source: *Arkitekt*,
vol. 19, no. 3–4 (1950),
p. 71.**

house did not last long – including the most popular ones such as the Lustron House or the Acorn House – because of the lack of a public affirmation of such a modernist scheme.

"I am no historian"

In the absence of constructive criticism, only one architect directly engaged with the question of how International Style modernism was appropriated in Turkey. In 1958, just three years after the opening of the hotel, Şevki Vanlı was quick to observe and comment on the aftereffects of the Istanbul Hilton. He coined the term "Hiltonculuk" and mocked local architects who started to take the Hilton as a typology and reproduce it all around the country. It was precisely this *common sense* modernism and the underlying anti-intellectualism which frustrated Vanlı at the time. "Hiltonculuk" was thus a contemporaneous criticism of common sense modernism targeted both at the designers of the hotel and at the majority of Turkish architects who were acritical of their own practices.

In Vanlı's view, the ordinariness of the Hilton was directly related to the fact that it was designed by a corporate architectural firm. The temporary partnership between Gordon Bunshaft of SOM and Sedad Hakkı Eldem set the standard for common sense modernism in Turkey in the same fashion as it was set by SOM in the United States under what the historian Henry-Russell Hitchcock called "bureaucratic architecture."[24] For Vanlı, neither Eldem's nor Bunshaft's individual fame mitigated the ordinariness of the building. Indeed, he suggests that the Bunshaft–Eldem collaboration created a legion of "experts of Hiltonculuk."[25]

Vanlı was also critical of the Turkish architectural discourse. None of the architects, critics, or editors in architectural circles were questioning the hotel's design and the resultant Hiltonculuk. His sharp criticism targeted mainstream architects for their "mediocre" and "uncreative" work, as well as critics (including the juries of design competitions) for their "affirmative silence" of mediocre production. It is unsurprising that Vanlı's op-ed piece on the subject appeared in a weekly news magazine, *Kim*, which was geared towards a broader readership and focused on contemporary politics and culture. It was far too radical to be published in the mainstream architectural journal, *Arkitekt*, though Vanlı himself had written several analytical articles for that journal.

Having started at the margins of architectural practice and discourse in Turkey, Vanlı could step out of the prevalent common sense and develop a critical view. Vanlı's introduction to modernism was less, or more accurately, differently, mediated. While studying architecture in Florence from 1947 to 1953, he became acquainted with the architecture of Frank Lloyd Wright, Alvar Aalto, and the members of the Association for Organic Architecture (APAO). Especially Sigfried Giedion's and Bruno Zevi's books on modern architecture and the Wright Exhibition in Florence in 1950 were influential in Vanlı's intellectual formation in early 1950s. Later, in 1960, he wrote the first scholarly Turkish work on Wright that, as he acknowledges, was marginal to the Turkish discourse of the time.[26] Just as Zevi challenged the modernist tradition of the architect–historian pairing and called for a historical and cultural revision in postwar modernism, Vanlı tried to do the same for the Turkish context with his book on Wright.[27]

While Vanlı's attempt to introduce a non-historicist, pluralist history of modernism escaped most of his contemporaries, he saw such history as the essential basis for architectural culture and knowledge. In Turkish architectural discourse, Vanlı strove to be a provocateur calling architects to "think" and "criticize," not as an intellectual activity as historians and critics do by profession, but as part of their everyday practice as designers. In the preface to his three-volume opus, *Talking Architecture: A Critical View of 20th Century Turkish Architecture that No One Wants to Know About*, he eschews the role of historian:

> This publication is not a history book. Perhaps we might say it is the observation of a designer on the context in which he lives. It has no pretensions to being unbiased or comprehensive, but it also does not rely on previous works of history. Anyway, I am no historian. I have long believed that because designers practice, they have different things to say and explain than historians. Thinking is everyone's responsibility…[28]

While a proper dilettante, Vanlı's concern for historiography is serious, and indeed, the prevailing interpretation of history within architectural discourse is what motivated Vanlı to pick up the pen. His purpose is a more public, democratic discussion of subjects like tradition, vernacularism, and identity, which have heretofore been the exclusive domain of intellectual circles. Vanlı writes a history of common sense modernism, which he argues that professional historians have neglected because of its ordinariness and insignificance in light of assumed, universal standards of modernism. What sets Vanlı apart, however, is his invitation to reflexivity, which springs from his practical involvement with architectural discourse over the last 50 years. Vanlı's common sense knowledge leads to good sense historiography. Reminiscent of Gramsci's proposition that "all men are intellectuals," this is clearly an attempt to redefine intellectualism, opening it up to ordinary, practicing architects who are neither historians nor avant-garde.

Individualism within common sense

Established in 1951, İMA was the first corporate architectural office in Istanbul, and Maruf Önal was one of three founding partners, who immediately grew to five. Their idealism, the willingness to collaborate with other partnerships, and the relational knowledge generated in a think tank of likeminded architects resulted in a number of significant design competition prizes. But these achievements did not suffice either to hold the five partners of İMA together or to prevent their work from being subjected to "perfect mediocrity." Although it introduced a new understanding of architectural practice based on relational knowledge, the firm ultimately set the bar for both common sense and "perfect mediocrity" in postwar Turkey until it dissolved in 1959. Some of the partners, like Önal, became conscious of the firm's contribution to common sense modernism and recognized the fact that architectural practice in the 1950s was turning into a profit-making business: architects had to perform fiduciary duties to both clients and building contractors. The individuality of an architect also became vulnerable to such changes. "In the process of business-making," as Önal indicates, "the architect turns into an ordinary man from a creative, artistic person."[29]

During the time of his partnership with İMA, from 1951 to 1959, Maruf Önal designed only four one-off houses for clients, only one of which was commissioned to İMA itself. The next two were completed on his own (apart from the partnership), and the last was the vacation house for his family in Bayramoğlu. Önal was also involved in a number of cooperative housing projects during this same period (Figure 7), and the single-family houses he designed for these larger İMA projects are manifestly different from the houses he designed on his own.

While researching the firm, the dialogue between these two forms of practice caught my attention. Whereas the work for İMA falls within my framework of common sense modernism, the houses he designed in his own name seem to be situated within an architectural language that is more individual and disconnected, but still intricate. In one of many interviews, Önal elucidated

Figure 7
Plan and perspective drawings of Izmir TARIŞ Cooperative Houses. Designed by Maruf Önal, IMA, 1953. Courtesy of the Istanbul Metropolitan Branch of UTCEA.

the design process of his vacation house. He gave the following explanation for his reservations about taking his design to İMA: "I designed the house by myself at home, not in the office; besides, if I showed it to my colleagues, they would interfere." The statement is a contradiction given that İMA, along with two other partnerships, constituted a think tank that intended to be a unique, intellectual form of practice where all the partners, associates and interns alike were involved in a democratic, collaborative process of design punctuated by group discussion and critique. For many interns and young graduates, İMA was as much about education as about work. Why would Önal not want to benefit from this process for the design of his own home, even when it was a common and familiar practice for the projects developed in the office? Why was collaboration sometimes deemed "interference"?

While distinguishing the house from its contemporaries and suggesting its belated inclusion into the repertoire of postwar modernism, Vanlı overlooked the organic link between Önal and İMA in his last book and treated them as separate histories. Although he was concerned with the easy, uncritical reproduction of the bureaucratic character of 1950s American architecture in Turkey, he did not take the changing form of architectural practice into consideration – namely the impetus for turning architecture into a multi-partnered, business-like profession. It was not merely imitation, but economic pressures and the need to join forces in order to meet the demands of more complex buildings and building types, that laid the foundation for even larger partnerships in Turkey.

This is not an American house

Considering Önal's consciousness that he functioned within the confines of common sense modernism, how can one explain the fact that Önal's house is distinct from the typical houses of the time? The design may transcend common sense, and Önal claims to have situated it on a different set of values, but *how?*[30]

These dilemmas lead me to a further analysis of the house. In my view, the house exemplifies four issues with regard to Önal's own exposure to common sense: 1) Önal's disconnection from İMA and, hence, from relational knowledge; 2) his vulnerability to the images of common sense modernism, to visual knowledge, and to consumerist habits which he unavoidably shares with his clients; 3) his silent criticism of common sense modernism which, in return, generates good sense; and 4) the critical forms of cultural contact which ordinary people (in this case, his circle of friends and neighbors) establish to modernism and to his house.

While defining "Good-Life Modernism" as the antithesis of avant-garde modernism in the 1950s and 1960s, Jarzombek suggests that it is possible to draw a line between the populist and avant-gardist buildings of an architect. Following Jarzombek's approach, the Izmir TARİŞ co-op house plans (1953) cannot be compared with the Önal house (1958) or the Anka House and Studio he designed for a sculptor (1957). This poses no problem for Jarzombek's analysis of postwar modernism, because only an architect's avant-garde production is relevant for the history of modernism, while contributions to "Good-Life Modernism" are mere biographical footnotes.

Önal's self-reflexive challenge to common sense modernism insists on a subtler framework for historical analysis. Rather than manifesting individuality as autonomy, as avant-gardes would claim to do, he participated in common sense in a non-affirmative manner. While he sought some separation from his typical, collaborative mode of practice, the individualism of the design is the product of a self-consciousness of his own relation to architecture, practice, common sense, and his collaborators.

The process of organizing the construction of the house came to play a significant role in shaping Önal's aesthetic and spatial concerns. To build the 36 square meter house economically, Önal had all the necessary components of its construction prefabricated in workshops in and around Istanbul. On the morning of the ground breaking, he rented a truck and collected the raw materials, rebar, and wooden formwork for the house, found a couple of builders along the way, and drove to the [then] remote site.

The house was built of concrete. The entrance level was completely open: only the stair, four columns, and a single massive wall touched the ground (Figure 8).[31] The upper floor provided a space for minimum living; and yet the open layout secured flexibility as much as possible for several functions in the house such as living, eating, sleeping, studying, cooking, and bathing (Figure 9). Construction lasted only a few days, and none of the material was wasted (including the wooden formwork, which was applied to the ceiling). Whatever came to the site on the truck found itself incorporated into the house.

Because Önal's intention was to design a minimal, yet livable house on a small budget, he invented his own scrappy form of prefabrication. Unlike the

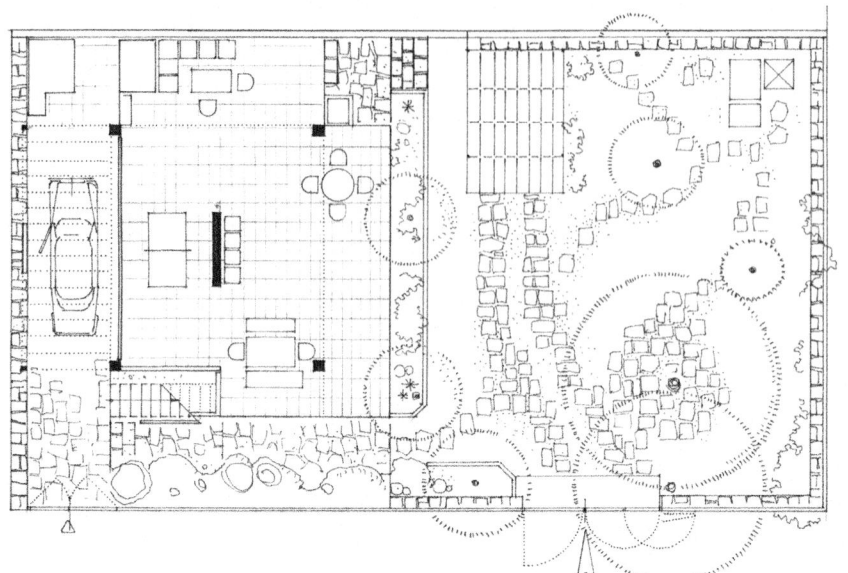

Figure 8
**Ground floor plan of the
Önal House,
Bayramoğlu. Drawings
by Maruf Önal. Courtesy
of the Istanbul
Metropolitan Branch of
UTCEA.**

Acorn House, whose high-tech manufacture allows it to unfold on site, Önal's house was poured and molded – even furniture like the table and benches were poured from concrete as organic outgrowths of the concrete structure (Figure 10). Indeed, only a single element of the Önal's house is attached ex post: a moveable wooden brise-soleil mounted on a steel rail.

This illustration of Önal's practice on site brings me to a crucial point. Unlike the editors of *Arkitekt* who uncritically disseminated architectural clichés on America, Önal's intellectual practice generates a number of criticisms, and yet not of all them become visible to himself. If there is a silent criticism of Americanism in this house, the fact that it is unwitting does not make Önal less legitimate or less intellectual. It demonstrates that Önal's cultural contact with American modernism had always been visual and mediated, as was the case with the majority of his colleagues in the country.[32]

If a critique of American domesticity is the criterion for being critical of "Good-Life Modernism," such a critique is also apparent in the fact that there were no popular consumer additions to the house, only a handful of avant-garde pieces: curtains designed by the painter Bedri Rahmi, a mosaic coffee table by the artist Füreya Koral, and wire chairs designed by the sculptor Şadi Çalık for the Karametal Studio. But these pieces were not designed specially for this house – rather they were the "leftovers" of these designers' commissions. The table, for instance, was a prototype designed for the Istanbul Hilton and was given to Önal as a gift by the designer.

With his own house, Önal tries to separate himself from his clients' consumerist habitus and from his colleagues' relational knowledge at the same time. Although this two-way criticism is important, it also complicates the nature of his criticism. On the one hand, he is the founder of a design firm that has to

Figure 9
Upper floor plan of the Önal House, Bayramoğlu. Drawings by Maruf Önal. Courtesy of the Istanbul Metropolitan Branch of UTCEA.

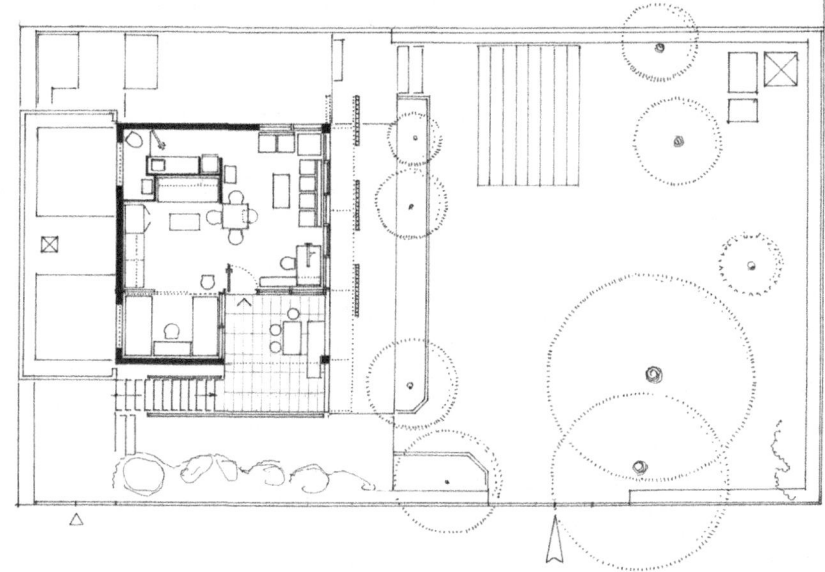

operate within common sense with regard to the mechanization of design and its bureaucratic structure. On the other hand, he shares the same visual knowledge with his clients and rejects reproducing any clichés that exemplify American architecture in the pages of *Arkitekt*. In my view, this double bind in Önal's criticism embodied in the house explains why this is not an American house.

In interviews, Önal has revealed his intentions and the inherent contradictions involved in the design. His cultural references for the house

Figure 10
Cast concrete table and benches in the patio of the Önal House, Bayramoğlu. Photo by Maruf Önal. Courtesy of the Istanbul Metropolitan Branch of UTCEA.

included the "images" of modernism propagated through the discourse of architecture but also his personal experience of the serander typology, a vernacular wooden structure raised on pilotis common to the plateaus of Trabzon.[33] Önal believes that the serander, which he had experienced while summering along the Black Sea as a child, influenced the design even more than its obvious referent, Albert Frey's Kocher Weekend House (1934), which he had came across in a book by Le Corbusier.[34]

Önal's various referents – the Frey house, the serander, the Acorn House, and others – become secondary to what I argue is the real success of the design: that it had become a living model house. Whether intended or not, the house engages those who interact with it. Architect friends disliked and disputed the design; neighbors found the concrete table on the porch uncanny; another colleague attempted to clone the house in the same neighborhood; the daughter of a close friend, Şadi Calık, vividly recalls fond memories of the house and the time she spent there as a child (mirroring Önal's own experience of the serander). What such lived experiences illustrate is a milieu created around the house which enabled several people to establish cultural contact with the house in various forms. The tactile qualities of this contact are significant in making individuals conscious of their alienation as much as their empathy. For example, neighbors visiting the Bayramoğlu House get familiar with the space, objects etc. while sitting on a wire armchair or eating on a concrete table. This means that getting familiar with modernism and developing a personal knowledge of it is a process in itself and does not automatically emerge right away after the first view of a modern object (which can be a house or a piece of furniture).

Good sense modernism: a silent criticism

Good sense is not the antithesis of common sense modernism. Rather, it is a common sense modernism that is critical of itself – that is, self-reflexive. Reflexivity, rather than criticism, sets good sense modernism apart. It rejects "Good-Life Modernism," but not in the form of an elitist, avant-garde attack.

Good sense also requires one to detach and disconnect oneself from common sense. Such disconnection is even more crucial for intellectuals who contribute to establishing common sense while producing and reproducing "objective" forms of knowledge on modernism. But it is also crucial for historians/ critics because good sense can provide them with a new analytic tool for differentiating between the practices of intellectuals (that is, the subjects of historical studies). Whether an architect, a historian, a critic, or an editor, there will be a significant difference between intellectuals who start their mediating functions with common sense that is uncritical and taken-for-granted or with good sense that is critical. In history writing, for example, while the first one would reproduce common-sense histories of modernism, only the second one would be more likely to initiate self-reflexivity and a reflexive historiography that in return proposes a more democratic milieu for knowledge production.

That is precisely how Önal's and Vanlı's disconnection from common sense – whether in the practice or the discourse of architecture – resulted in a criticism of common sense modernism. Though silent and partly unintentional, this criticism was generated by Önal's design for his house but came alive in practice when his family and friends started to comment on the house during their everyday interactions with it. Similarly, Vanlı's criticism of "Hiltonculuk," which initially failed to generate any reflexivity among the "experts of Hiltonculuk," now opens up the history of postwar modernism in Turkey as well as the Americanization of modernism to its own intricacies and to its own common sense, while making us, historians and critics, self-critical of our common-sense practices.

Acknowledgements

Early versions of this paper were presented at Cornell University (Ithaca, NY) and the Middle East Technical University (Ankara) in April 2007 and December 2009 respectively. I am grateful to Chris Otto, Sibel Bozdoğan, Robert Gassner, and Duanfang Lu for their valuable comments in various stages of its development.

Notes

1   The suffixes in Vanlı's made-up word "Hiltonculuk" imply two meanings. First, the word connotes a professional practice and its ideology of designing Hilton-like buildings. And secondly, it alludes to a game in which participants (architects, in this case) pretend to be "experts of Hiltonculuk." Ş. Vanlı, "Hiltonculuk", *Kim*, 28 November 1958, pp. 21–2.

2   Ş. Vanlı, *Mimariden Konuşmak: Bilinmek Istenmeyen 20. Yüzyıl Türk Mimarlığı Eleştirel Bakış*, Ankara: Şevki Vanlı Mimarlık Vakfı, 2006, vol. I, p. 220.

3   The historian Henry-Russell Hitchcock differentiates between special buildings and regular buildings – the former being a work of art by a genius architect and the latter being an ordinary building by an architect of a multi-partnered office with a more bureaucratic character. H.-R. Hitchcock, "The architecture of bureaucracy and the architecture of genius," *Architectural Review*, January 1947, pp. 3–6.

4   For narratives based on export-import rhetoric, see A. J. Wharton, *Building the Cold War: Hilton International Hotels and Modern Architecture*, Chicago: Univ. of Chicago Press, 2001; J. W. Cody, *Exporting American Architecture, 1870–2000*, London: Routledge, 2003. For Hitchcock's advocacy of the International Style, see H.-R. Hitchcock, *The Rise to World Dominance of American Architecture* (vol. 1) and *Looking Forward* (vol. 12) in *Voice of America Forum Lectures: Architecture Series*, Washington, DC: United States Information Agency, 1961.

5   For various depictions of the "Americanization of modernism," see J. Ockman, *Architecture Culture 1943–1968: A Documentary Anthology*, New York: Rizzoli, 1993, pp. 16–19; S. Bozdoğan, "Democracy, development, and the Americanization of Turkish architectural culture in the 1950s," in S. Isenstadt and K. Rizvi (eds), *Modernism and the Middle East: Architecture and Politics in the Twentieth Century*, Seattle: Univ. of Washington Press, 2008.

6   A. Gramsci, *Selections from the Prison Notebooks*, New York: International Publishers, 1971, p. 328.

7   I refer to the sociologist Daniel Lerner's understanding of modernism as a "style of life." (D. Lerner, *The Passing of Traditional Society: Modernizing the Middle East*, New York: Free Press of Glencoe, 1958, p. 60.) For modernizing countries including Turkey, Lerner suggests that "the most cosmopolitan Turks … are at home with the 'international' (shall we say, late-Bauhaus) style

in personality as in architecture." (D. Riesman and D. Lerner, "Self and society: reflections on some Turks in transition," *Explorations* 5, 1955, p. 77.)

8 Borrowing from Karl Mannheim, I understand architectural knowledge as "relational knowledge" because of its non-autonomous (that is, objective) nature, its reciprocal operation, and its dynamism (K. Mannheim, *Ideology and Utopia: An Introduction to the Sociology of Knowledge*, trans. L. Wirth and E. Shils, London: K. Paul, Trench, Trubner, 1936).

9 "26.ıncı İzmir Fuarında Amerikan Pavyonu," *Dostluk* 19, August 28 1957, p. 6.

10 "Bu Haftanın Resimleri," *Dostluk* 18, August 14 1957, p. 3. Translated by the author.

11 Antonio Gramsci points to the double functioning of architecture. On the one hand, architecture is part of the "material structure of ideology," that is, the material means by which intellectuals transmit ideas (and also ideologies) to the public. But on the other hand, the discipline of architecture has also "a special objective" character. A. Gramsci, *Prison Notebooks*, vol. 2, trans. and ed. J. A. Buttigieg, New York: Columbia Univ. Press, 1996, p. 125.

12 This catchphrase became popular because of the Democrat Party's pro-American foreign politics. For a discussion of Americanism and Anti-Americanism in political and popular discourses of Turkey in historical perspective, see Tanıl Bora, "Amerika: 'En' Batı ve 'Başka' Batı," in U. Kocabaşoğlu (ed.), *Modernleşme ve Batıcılık*, vol. 3, *Modern Türkiye'de Siyasi Düşünce*, Istanbul: İletişim Yayınları, 2002.

13 M. Jarzombek, "Good-life modernism and beyond: the American house in the 1950s and 1960s: a commentary," *The Cornell Journal of Architecture* 4, Fall 1990, pp. 76–93.

14 C. Stein, "Communities for the Good Life," *Journal of the AIA* 26, no. 1 (1956), pp. 11–18; Carlos Contreras, "Architecture for the Good Life, Part II," *Journal of the AIA*, 1956, vol. 26, no. 6, pp. 263–6.

15 According to modernization theory, via literacy, consumption would spread out of city limits. "The great symbol of this phase," Lerner argues, "is the Sears-Roebuck catalogue." Obviously, having the image of an average American consumer living in suburbia in his mind, he even goes further and states: "The mail-order house replaces the peddler only when enough people can read catalogues and write letters." Lerner, *The Passing of Traditional Society*, pp. 61–2.

16 Ibid., p. 400.

17 Jarzombek, op. cit., p. 81.

18 Even though it is Lerner himself who mentions frustration as an outcome of the process of modernization, he does not discuss any positive sense in particular. Visual knowledge is a concept that I develop in order to account for the condition of being exposed to common sense in everyday life and for its value and significance in the appropriation of modernism in the professional lives of architects alongside relational knowledge.

19 *Bütün Dünya* 94, November 1955, p. 627.

20 D. Lerner, "Changing social structure and economic development – reflections on a decade of international experience," in J. R. Hopper and R. I. Levin (eds), *The Turkish Administrator: A Cultural Survey*, Ankara: USAID Public Administration Division, 1968, p. 108.

21 My use of the term "mediated" refers to the fact that any knowledge Turkish architects had about American architecture was the product of the mediating roles that intellectuals (such as editors, cultural affairs officers, historians etc.) undertook between their agencies/fields and the public/target audience. For further discussion, see E. Kaçel, *Intellectualism and Consumerism: Ideologies, Practices and Criticisms of Common Sense Modernism in Postwar Turkey*, unpublished dissertation, Cornell University, 2009.

22 "Amerika Birlesik Devletlerinde Fabrika Mamulü Hazir Ev Tipi," *Arkitekt*, 1950, vol. 19, no. 3–4, pp. 71–3.

23 "Unfolding house: Acorn Houses, Inc.", *Life*, vol. 26, January 24 1949, p. 72.

24 Hitchcock exemplified the best of bureaucratic architecture in the work of SOM. However, it was the figure of Gordon Bunshaft of SOM and the Istanbul Hilton project that problematized such a rigid separation between the genius and the bureaucratic by redefining the term genius (in

Hitchcock's terms) as bureaucratic and vice versa outside of the American context. (Hitchcock, op. cit., pp. 3–6.)

25   Vanlı, "Hiltonculuk", p. 22.

26   Ş. Vanlı, *Frank Lloyd Wright: Insana Dönüş*, Ankara: Dost Yayınları, 1960. Şevki Vanlı, interview by the author, November 7 2005, Ankara.

27   When Zevi pioneered organic architecture and its institutionalization in Italy via the Associations for an Organic Architecture (APAO), he emphasized that it was not "any manner of Wrightism" that was being disseminated (B. Zevi, "A message to the Congrès International d'Architecture Moderne: concerning architectural culture", *Metron*, 1948, vol. 4, nos. 31–32, p. 29). With this statement, he was clearly trying to challenge the troubled position of a historian as an advocate of a certain architectural ideology. Zevi concerned himself with the significance of a particular building for architectural culture less than with its significance for its creator, or later, for the historian.

28   Vanlı, *Mimariden Konuşmak*, vol. 1, p. xii. Translated by the author.

29   Maruf Önal, interview by the author, December 28 2005, Istanbul.

30   This house is also documented in a recent collection of interviews made with Önal. See M. Önal, *Maruf Önal. Oda Tarihinden Portreler 2*, interview by M. Yapıcı, Istanbul: TMMOB Mimarlar Odası İstanbul Büyükkent Şubesi, 2006, pp. 104–6.

31   Later, when the family needed more space for their two children, Önal enclosed half of the ground floor from the massive wall to the edge of the garage and added rooms.

32   Economic constraints prevented most of these architects from traveling to see American buildings in their physical and cultural contexts in the 1950s and 1960s. Thus, there was little direct interaction with counterparts in the United States. A few architects who collaborated with Americans (like Eldem) or worked in the United States (like Ali Kolsal, Nezahat Arıkoğlu, and Enis Kortan) were uncommon exceptions.

33   Built on the site of a country house, serander is an additional structure used for storage purposes. For an analysis of the plans, building materials, and the social context of this structure, see O. Özgüner, *Köyde Mimari Doğu Karadeniz*, Ankara: ODTÜ Mimarlık Fakültesi, 1970.

34   This house was co-designed by the architects A. Lawrence Kocher and Albert Frey in Long Island, New York. For more information on the Weekend House, see A. Roth (ed.), *La Nouvelle architecture: présentée en 20 examples*, Zürich: Girsberger, 1940, pp. 11–16.

Part III

Entangled modernities

Chapter 8

Modernity Transfers: the MoMA and postcolonial India

Farhan Sirajul Karim

While working on the mid-century design shows in India, after hearing that a cache of MoMA (Museum of Modern Art, New York) design objects of the late 1950s had ended up somewhere in Gujarat, I started my quest to trace the journey of these objects. It was on a sunny day in early April 2009 – around the end of Gujarat's tantalizingly short spring – that I arrived at the National Institute of Design in Ahmedabad. My friend Professor Ranjan ushered me to another part of the campus; after traversing a long pathway we finally arrived at the door of their storehouse. Through its glass wall, I could barely see the silhouette of a heap of piled objects inside the room. Humming to myself, I walked into the storeroom, which was located beneath the central cafe of the school. This was the tomb of the 400 objects that MoMA sent half a century ago to hail the greatest achievers of their time – Gropius, Le Corbusier, Jeanneret, Perriand, Nelson, Saarinen, Mies, Thonet, and Ray and Charles Eames (Figure 1). All of the objects were dusty and smeared with numerous fingerprints – a poignant satire on the belief that nothing truly modern grows old. I could hear the tumultuous sound of students in the cafe over my head: the objects appeared to me as if they were messengers from a bygone time, still heralding the un-kept promise of an industrial utopia, a vanished culture, one in which visions of and strategies for modernization – and its global and local variants – overlapped. I was fascinated after realizing that after all these years these objects were still performing in an exhibition in this Ahmedabad design school. They were being studied as case study objects in design studios and being exposed to the critical gaze of both students and teachers. In order to impart knowledge about structural integrity and construction methods, several times each year they are taken apart piece-by-piece and then re-assembled. I realized I had found a story to tell.

This chapter will observe three strategies of modernization at work: (1) The first was the promotion of a modernity of affluence, modeled and promoted by

Figure 1

A portion of NID's store where they keep most of the objects reminiscent of MoMA's 1959 design exhibition. These objects are now used as classroom examples of the modernist aesthetic and production techniques. Photo by the author.

America as part of its cold war cultural strategy that sought to demonstrate a fantastic view of future domesticity before an Indian audience. Cold war dynamics affected the flow of the Euro-American model of modernity that was predicted to become dissipated in India. But now the Indian camp proved that it would not merely play a role of passive receptor as was previously the case with colonial modernity and was assumed to be the "norm."[1] Rather, this pro-active new sense of India's agency in its own development championed the uninterrupted flow of modernity from the West. The old linear model of cultural imperialism could not explain this form of flow. Modernity was no longer merely an imposition, that is, a one-way flow from West to East, but the result of a two-way process. (2) The second strategy was the self-promotion of this Indian agency to the West as a model of a non-industrial material world. Although the dominant discourse of modernity may tend to identify this model as regressive – in the way that the architects of nineteenth-century colonial India sketched the country as a feminine body of craft[2] – immediate post-independence India's post-colonial ideology was dialectically complex, opting to retain its image of a country constrained by non-industrial aesthetics whilst striving hard to attain a socialist form of state-controlled industrialization at the same time. (3) Yet a third strategy was represented in the approach of Pierre Jeanneret, who tried to reconcile the previous two streams by synthesizing the modernist trope of machine-made, luxurious consumer goods with the asceticism of a Gandhian material culture in a bid to forge a true hybrid of ascetic modernity. Jeanneret investigated the potential of vernacular materials to be manifested in a functionalist rhetoric of modernist aesthetics that could go far beyond the tentative moves of adapting cutting edge modern objects within the vernacular lifestyle but referred to a very different possibility of modernity to be realized in a non-affluent model.

The ambivalence and mutual tension that emerged from the exchanging of modernity – the to-and-fro from the West to India and from India to the West – is studied through two exhibitions that were organized by MoMA during the 1950s, one featuring *India* mounted in New York and titled "Textile and Ornamental Arts of India" and the other featuring the *West*, mounted in India and titled "Design Today in Europe and America." When it comes to any assessment of the effect that these exhibitions may have had, it might be seen as asymmetric: the course that the West rendered may become more visible. But my aim here is to identify the historical context that made the exchange possible.

"Glitter and gilt dazzles the eyes"

As Harold Isaac[3] once pointed out, for the postwar American there were only four kinds of Indian: (1) the *fabulous* Indians, the maharajas and magicians in tandem with their exotic animals; (2) the *mystical* and *religionists*, a people who were "deep, contemplative, tranquil, profound"; (3) the *benighted heathen*, who venerated animals and worshipped many-headed gods; and (4) the *lesser breed*, trampled by poverty and crippling disease – "shriveled bellies, corpses, children with fly-encircled eyes, with swollen stomachs, children dying in the streets, rivers choked with bodies." In contrast, the Indian perspective of the USA was one of "war-mongers and so on and so forth" as mourned by Secretary of State John Foster Dulles during the visit of leading Indian industrialist Birla to the USA in October 1954.[4] Indian–US relations had been long afflicted by mutual distrust, suspicion and acrimony. In the wake of global transference of western modernity as a particular way of perceiving domesticity, consumer goods, and visual culture, such mutual "misinterpretation"[5] ought to have been obliterated by both parties. They needed to identify a negotiable third space from which both countries could benefit reciprocally, the newly decolonized receiver by receiving Modernity and adapting it to its specific context, and the maker of Modernity by spawning it in the new world and claiming it within its ideological bloc. "Textile and Ornamental Arts of India," organized by the Museum of Modern Art NY from April 13 to September 25 1955, made a move to reconcile the reluctance, to conciliate mutual *misinterpretation*, and to broaden the possibilities of postwar cultural exchange beyond a "developed-nation modernity" vs. "underdeveloped antimodernity" binary. In doing so, MoMA explored ways in which to revive tropes of a fabulous, dazzling Orient.

This show was the result of efforts to collect and present pieces of India's past from a range of sources to create an ideal image of India as a homogenous formation. A significant number of exhibits came from private collections – from India, England and the USA. These included the collection of Edgar Kaufmann, Jr. and Alexander Girard. The partnership of these two key figures of American high modernity proved successful in constructing the Indian image in a western land. Kaufmann and Girard embarked upon a six-week tour of Great Britain and India to collect exhibit artifacts ranging from Indian textiles to various craft objects, creating a "prototype"[6] for the exhibition. Sir Leigh Ashton and John Irwin, of London's Victoria and Albert Museum, helped them to select from their vast range of Indian objects to build up an authentic version of Indian material culture that was to be presented in the USA. The Indian assistance came through the "All India Handicraft Board," particularly with the personal involvement of Kamaladevi Chattopadhyaya and Pupul Jayakar – the two most prominent figures of the post-independence craft movement. During the 1950s, both became concerned at the possibility of the introduction of western methods of factory-based mass production in India as part of Nehru's vision for India's development.[7] However, the show was conceived of as "a celebration of the revival under India's new commonwealth status of some of her oldest native crafts."[8] The physical installation of the show was devised to invite the audience to conjure up the lost world of fantastic objects of the East (Figure 2). Alexander Girard, a renowned architect, textile designer and famous folk art collector, designed the exhibition in the form of an "imaginary bazaar,"[9] a prototype of an Indian market place that seemed self explanatory of its setting. The exhibition site included three consecutive rooms. A 50-foot-long water pool surrounded by 12 towering golden columns embellished the main exhibition hall. Over the pool, a dazzling array of saris hung from the ceiling, creating a sky canopy resembling those of Indian fables – rich gold and silver brocades, intricately hand woven and tie-dyed silks, Kashmir shawls, gossamer cottons, vigorous muslins, feather short wools, and beautifully patterned embroideries. However, the objects of everyday use presented in this show were somewhat underscored since the main objective of the exhibition was to emphasize the quality of the ornaments, the vibrant colors and patterns, all of which – when it comes to Indian objects – are historically regarded as an envelope exclusive to its use value.[10] Elsewhere, Girard expressed his notion that an exhibition of objects exclusive to its context vitiates its meaning. As Kate P. Kent argues, it is imperative to construct a context for the objects that will create a certain theatricality of presentation,[11] instead of inferring its true place of origin by constructing such contexts as Girard proposes, that is, "a fantasy setting based on relationships perceived by Girard between it and certain other objects, perhaps from other parts of the world."[12] Notwithstanding, the intention of the installation was to introduce the myth of Indian exoticism and to spur the curiosity of both public and press. And to this end it was an out-and-out success. As noted journalist Betty Pepis wrote in *The New York Times*: "Glitter and gilt dazzle the eye as one enters the native Indian bazaar just installed on the first floor of the Museum of Modern Art."[13] Lester Gaba, writing in *Woman's Wear Daily*, implored his reader to "Go west, young displayman, go west on 53rd Street to see the town's most exciting display."[14] The 1955 MoMA exhibition was effectively contrived to convey the spectacle of Indian craft, a magical setting for equally exotic and magical objects amidst the concrete "jungle" of Manhattan's modernity.

While it was difficult to determine the impact that the show made on the American mind, one could confidently suggest that India appeared as a piece of

Figure 2
US textile and fashion designer Nancy Kenealy, posed for a local "hybrid" design in the 1958 exhibition mounted by the Institute for Industrial Design. Designed by "Rangoli" – an Indian boutique house – this dress showed the adaptability of Rajasthan cotton for Western skirts. Source: *Art in Industry Magazine*, **vol. 6, no. 3, 1958, p. 23. Courtesy of the British Museum, London.**

fantasy amidst the modernity of American life. Alice Hughes wrote in the *Times*: "The American beholder is swept with admiration for the 'fantasy' now displayed in the 'Arts of India' show."[15] The exhibition drew in excess of 300,000 visitors: public demand resulted in the prolongation of the exhibition for five months, during which time the press became aware of the increasing news value of the show.[16] Optimistic comments echoed the American wish image: "The arts and crafts of India are already influencing both fashions and home furnishing in this country … [W]hat's important to American eyes in viewing this handsome exhibit is the shadow of the future it casts on our latest fashion for living."[17] The show reflected the postwar faith in a future of open exchange – an avenue that would make cultural transference possible among the seemingly asymmetric segments of the world. MoMA saw the trade potential of this show as its highest stake. As Wheeler maintained: "Its purpose is to guide the millions of skilled native craftsmen in the way of traditional design and to publicize and market those folk arts in India and other countries."[18] India's post-independence international trade potential was an important consideration for the National Planning Committee's pre-independence scheme.[19] A propos the historical fracture of sovereign trade over two centuries when India was about to make her independent trade debut with the West and embrace the notion of a modern democratic nation state, the question at hand was forming a rhetoric of *Indianness*, the semantic construction of a free India within a free market of consumer goods. When it came to *Indian Object*, in the world's eyes postwar India wanted to retain her exotic persona.[20] The Indian magazine *Life*, describing this exhibition, declared with immense pride that: "The East has been inching up on the US for several years."[21] At the Indian end it was the superiority of India's long tradition of crafts and art that was going to take over the global trade market. K. Balaram, an eminent journalist, wrote a series of articles in the *Hindu* (Madras), the *Nagpur Times*, and the *Capital* (Calcutta) about the potential of India's trade with the USA, expressing the hope for a growing demand for the "saree-dress." Several articles that appeared in the *Journal of Art for Industry* expressed the view that the Indian *saree* would soon find its place among global female dress.[22] Although periodic statements of intent of progressive socialization were issued from India, and some industries were reserved only for the public sector, the government of India tried to attract American capital by promising equal treatment, full remittance of profit, and fair compensation in case of eventual nationalization.[23] During the late 1950s and early 1960s the USA, which had previously regarded India as little more than "a scratch on our minds,"[24] started to promote it as a democratic counterweight to communist China.[25] In the view of the US State Department:

> South Asia became a testing ground for the free world; in this will be determined whether nations can surmount tremendous economic and social problems, can achieve far reaching changes in their entire pattern of life without resorting to the totalitarian system of communism.[26]

In a bid to prove the triumph of the free market and the free world over the communist bloc, US assistance towards making India a consumer society reached its peak between 1954 and 1964 when US aid totaled US$10 billion.[27] This signaled an attempt to assuage the negative schema that the USA and India had long held towards each other. Also it provided an opportunity to explore their potential mutual relationship in the future free market, a possibility to sample the blessing of a consumer society that America had long imbibed and India had yet to relish.

"Blend beauty with utility"

In the same year, George Nelson's office mounted the epochal American National Exhibition in Moscow. The NSIC (National Small Industry Corporation – a corporate alumni of Indian businessmen and a part of the Ministry of Commerce of India) asked MoMA to mount a similar show in India.[28] With the sponsorship of the Ford Foundation and the USIA (United States Information Agency), along with objects selected by Associate Curator Greata Daniel, MoMA engaged the same design team as the Nelson office to mount their first ever and largest show in southeast Asia. Lasting for two years from 1959 to 1961, the show traveled through nine major cities and pulled more than a million visitors from all over India. Even though they used the same design team and the same geodesic dome, the two MoMA exhibitions were fundamentally dissimilar: one was produced by the USIA as a way of undermining the Soviet state by depicting the USA as a consumer paradise;[29] the other, which generated from a request by local businessmen operating under the umbrella of government bureaucracy, aimed to spur the development of the national economy. NSIC's expectations of this show were that it would channel local artisans' and designers' tastes into producing objects that by virtue of having a modern appearance would heighten the taste of the Indian consumer class, resulting in a concomitant expansion of the Indian home market for certain consumer goods.[30] In effect, local businessmen interpreted MoMA's aesthetic mission as a trade potential. Thus the 1959 Indian show was not solely an American diplomatic push but more of an Indian economic pull. On the one hand, the USA seized the opportunity to explore India as a "testing ground"[31] for the promotion of a capitalist culture; on the other, it sought to harness the potential of India as a future consumer (Figure 3). In MoMA's words, this endeavor was "a result of [a] unique venture in[to] international cooperation by public and private agencies."[32] This show proved a classic example of the symbiotic transference of mid century modernity from one part of the globe to another.

The general setting of the exhibition was intended to portray an image of western progress as well as illuminate the neutral appearance of the machine-made modern product that stood in opposition to the vivid and colorful Indian objects.[33] Housed as it was in Buckminster Fuller's geodesic dome,[34] architect Gordon Chadwick of the Nelson office had conceived the entire site as a monochrome backdrop with the exception of the bright orange letters at the entrance depicting the title of the exhibition, "Design Today in America and Europe." Upon entering the dome, the viewer saw an Indian-style brick courtyard: in the centre were variously-shaped, cocoa-matted, wooden platforms on which the exhibit materials were placed, each tagged with a general number signifying its catalog entry. The 400 household objects included chairs, lamps, glassware, kitchen utensils, textiles and tools from New York, all representative of a time span from the 18th century to contemporary times and ranging in origin from Europe to the USA. As an exhibition release by Pupul Jayakar suggested, the objective of the exhibition was to draw the attention of the visitor to the place of materials and tools and their function in the creation of objects for daily use – not to replicate the object directly as part of Indian life nor to adopt the way of life that the aforesaid objects demanded.[35] The brown-stained deodar beams and white plywood panels, illuminated by the diffused ambient light that streamed through the dome, created a live domestic setting for the modern western goods. This was MoMA's aim – to draw a hard line between the eastern and western modes

Figure 3
A long queue of people
awaiting their turn to
attend the opening
ceremony in New Delhi,
1959. Source: VII.
SP-ICE-17-57.6, MoMA
Archives, NY. Courtesy
of MoMA, NY.

of conceiving everyday objects. As Dr Ensminger (who represented the Ford Foundation[36]) commented to Susan Cable Senior (associate director of the international program) and architect Gordon Chadwick at the inauguration ceremony: "This show is absolutely going to stand this country right on its ear – which is precisely what we want."[37] Like the presentation style adopted at the 1959 Indian show of good design, MoMA opted not to exhibit household objects by live demonstration in a virtual ideal American home, a style they had followed in Europe.[38] Rather than attempting to sell the American way of life, MoMA's project in India seemed to dissolve the modern object and its aesthetic into Indian production and consumption. It then became India's responsibility to produce and accommodate these modern objects in everyday life. MoMA counted on the active participation of Indian agencies for the transference of modernity to India. Nevertheless, the internal dissonance of these two catalysts *vis-à-vis* transnational dissemination of modernity questioned the over-determined portrayal of the Americanization effort.

The involvement of the Ford Foundation as sponsor of this exhibition should be understood within the Foundation's broader Cold War era role as a transnational catalyst transferring[39] "the best thought available in the United States"[40] to the developing regions of the world.[41] The Foundation advised the Indian government of its new development strategy, that is, the advancing of its small-scale industries on the basis of an outline proposed by an American experts team.[42] During their visit to India in 1953, the team identified the scope for Indian goods to create a "quality market" as soon as modern requirements of production and supplies were met. Taking as its point of departure the setting up of a National School of Design and Fashion,[43] it represented a call to integrate India into a culture of mass production and mass consumption (Figure 4). Integrated development, as perceived by the Foundation, was only achievable through the mass transmission of US technical expertise, mainly in the form of Foundation grants that would essentially emphasize American achievements in technology and progress,[44] either in the guise of exhibitions or otherwise. After six years of the Foundation's policies, Indian businessmen felt the need for similar development, a need that would be realized in the newly-developed design sector by harnessing the small sector industry that would lead to perceived integrated development. Placing it in a broader context, this design show exemplified the pull factor generated by local demand pairing up with the global rise of consumerism to become part of global technical development.

Influential mid-century design critic Arthur Drexler wrote in the exhibition catalogue: "In the western world there is one object in which all problems of design come to a sharp focus: Chair."[45] During the mid-century cultural politics of visual display performed at various design exhibitions, *chair* became an agent to define the human subject by the framing of its body in it,[46] just as *kitchen* became the very site of defining postwar consumer domesticity.[47] In this 1959 show, chair was central to demonstrating the notion of physical comfort, that is, of working or resting the body paradoxically at a time when chair – in MoMA's sense – was a relatively novel product for India and was even less known to her masses.[48] In

Figure 4
The strangeness of MoMA's domestic modernity becomes more than a subject of curiosity, Delhi, 1959. Source: VII.SP-ICE-17-57.7, MoMA Archives, NY. Courtesy of MoMA, NY.

MoMA's perception, western man's pursuit of understanding the methodology of any system directed his inquiry into how man's life on Earth could be made ever more comfortable. This inquiry would ultimately equip him with the novel tool of technology.[49] By presenting a survey of the evolution of western design, MoMA's exhibition in India thus served to showcase the end means by which contemporary western man could make his life more enjoyable on Earth.

MoMA presented western civilization in India as a progressive spirit seeking the methodological formation of the physical world by asking the question *How?*[50] This model had its western postwar detractor in Hannah Arendt, who argued that excessive emphasis on work itself, and on achieving methodological perfection of end means, makes the human akin to a beast of burden, a drudge condemned to daily routine – the *Animal laborens*.[51] Notwithstanding, the European longing for physical comfort reached its peak during the Victorian age. As John Gloag observed: "Victorians loved comfort without shame, as the Georgians before them had loved pleasure without apology."[52] Yearning for domestic comfort and an aversion to a hostile outside created a much-exaggerated form of luxurious furnishing together with the notion of interiority.[53] The love for interiority spawned a queer domestic narrative of introverted reclining bodies reposing quite anxiously, conscious of the vulnerability of their bodies.[54] By the end of the nineteenth century, the development of the furniture industry in the USA reflected socio-economic changes attributable to the industrial revolution – domestic space appeared as a site for the privatization of social norms.[55] Focus was now more on mass production of comfort and luxury, what Penny Sparkle terms "the democratization of comfort."[56] By turning the Victorian construct of individual comfort into consumable en masse, the narrative of comfort heightened comfort as a public discourse. The 18th-century consumer revolution in Europe and America recast the meaning of comfort by synthesizing its new physical dimension with the previous form of "comfort as moral support."[57] Since then, comfort has in the main become a concern of cultural progress – not merely physically natural. At the beginning of the twentieth century, in an attempt to explain the notion of comfort in a contemporary machine age situation, Edgar Kaufman Jr., director of MoMA's good design show, wrote: "The truly comfortable person was the one reclining. The attitude gradually became the model of general comfort in public."[58] In another place describing the room of William Morris as the origin of comfortable modern living, Kaufman said: "This room speaks to the eye of relaxation, of pampering the individual, and of friendly association between individuals who share its atmosphere."[59] MoMA's modernity relates the culture of comfort with the consumption pattern in domesticity that requires the household to increase its technological specialization and lessen its primary production for subsistence so that within the newer "modern" environment, domestic activities and their associated patterns of consumption can take place free from traditional elemental constraints. The vision of modernist design showcased by the 1959 show is one that uses physical comfort and advanced technology as icons of a vision of postwar modernity defined by Western middle class leisure and consumption

(Figure 5). In other words, these artifacts prescribe a specific vision of postwar modern life, of which America was at the cutting edge in 1959.

MoMA's show established that mass submission to comfort and pleasure was achievable through a methodological change of production of objects, that is, from craft to industrial. Referring to Plato's notion of *ideal* and Thomas Aquinas's notion of perfection, MoMA contended that the newly invented "art form" presented solutions that the West had evolved to accommodate the mechanical production, new materials and energy potentials that scientific research had made available and new consumer demands that had arisen over the last 50 years.[60] By discarding the relevance of the non-industrial, the domestic working body of the craftsman was rendered subterranean amidst a mass of reproducible objects. In MoMA's words:

> [S]ince [the] middle of the nineteenth century, Western handicrafts have steadily diminished in importance until they are no longer the chief source of our common implements … [T]he crafts man has found a new role in the useful arts. The prototypes for many machine-made objects are first developed by the individual crafts man, particularly in such fields as textiles and glass.[61]

Figure 5
A page from the exhibition catalogue. Source: VII.SP-ICE-17-57.8, MoMA Archives, NY. Courtesy of MoMA, NY.

Regarding the conflicting concepts of crafts and industrial objects, MoMA argued two points. First, mass produced objects do not lose their artistic quality: they are still representative of western verity – irrefutable fundamentals of Classical purity and ideals; secondly, modern living is essentially an artistic task since individual crafts have been replaced by mass artistic proliferation, reproduced on the factory line and recycled in consumer houses. Living in a modern era is essentially practicing art amidst smoldering comfort, not practicing life to its bitter end.

Indian bureaucratic expectations of this exhibition – as described by Manubhai Shah, Union Minister of Industry – were to learn how the visual appearance of Indian objects could be made more appealing as mass consumption goods.[62] The Indian bureaucracy's major concern was that the primary task of design should be to make the objects more presentable on the global market. Such a pragmatic role of design was closely linked to the synthesis of India's home market of consumer goods with its global dissipation. Manubhai, writing in the introduction to the exhibition catalogue, stated: "The degree of success in making a product depends greatly on the extent to which a fusion of technical quality, functional excellence and visual design is achieved … [Design must create] an immediate and overwhelming appeal to a buyer." [63] Vice President Dr. S. Radhakrishnan, in his opening remarks, beseeched the industrialists and craftsmen of India to adopt "quality above cheapness," calling on the local manufacturers, designers and artisans to act under the rubric of "Blend Beauty with Utility,"[64] an approach notoriously similar to the Victorian revivalist attitude towards industrial products.[65] The immediate post-independence Indian bureaucracy was troubled by its bid to locate itself among global cultural politics. While on the one hand the nation's collective memory was still enthralled by the Gandhian spirit of asceticism, on the other, Nehru's sympathy for Soviet-style socialism paired with a counter demand for a free market[66] created a complex situation. This complexity resulted in the local businessman's selection of MoMA's cutting edge exhibition artifacts, a careful selection of industrially produced, transatlantic consumer goods that would inform both vernacular craftsmen and community-based small industry (Figure 6).

The new role of mass produced, machine-made household objects as a producer of everyday domestic experience contested the Indian notion of domesticity as a personalized and contextualized experience that had its profound connection with Gandhi's alternative form of domesticity of ashram life.[67] The exhibited objects heralded a way of life forged on comfort, the lessening of human labor on daily household tasks by means of the machine. This was quite different from the Gandhian way of life that emphasized incorporating gender-unspecified human labor as much as possible into all aspects of household work[68] at a time when overwhelmingly, mass media and women's magazines were promoting an image of the picturesque home[69] wherein the Indian woman's extended dual role was one of Indian and Western housewife at the same time.[70] In nineteenth-century colonial exhibitions, machines were displayed as a single entity, a single animated force bent upon producing a new phase of civilization:

Figure 6
The MoMA show at Amritsar, 1959. Exhibit objects being inspected at close range. One of the major objectives of this show was to evoke demand for modern household goods – the installation was considered a site for virtual consumption. Source: VII.SP-ICE-17-57.6, MoMA Archives, New York. Courtesy of MoMA, NY.

modernity.[71] Working bodies were almost erased from the scene other than being depicted as the "human exotic." Tim Barringer describes this as a "fantasy of production without labour, a world without a working class."[72] Throughout the first half of the twentieth century, Gandhi assiduously promoted a material culture[73] – perhaps impossible to realize in a consumer society but at least sounding more ethical to the Indian ear – that took effort to retain the value system embedded in objects, a value system which the capitalist market reduced to exchange value and freely floated as an independent, value free commodity.[74] Gandhi's challenge to the material culture of the modern West soon became a challenge for his own countrymen when post-independence India recanted his ascetic way of living. Gandhi, with his ascetic material culture, resisted independent India's ambition to become modern. After a decade of independence, the century-long debate surrounding craft versus industrial product[75] transformed into a debate over accepting a different form of domesticity forged on a different material culture. As Pupul Jayakar wrote in the flyer circulated at the 1959 exhibition: "It is a challenge to democracy and an industrial society whether or not within its contours a great artisan tradition can flourish."[76] By 1959 it was well established in India that the old way of producing objects, representative of a bygone political order, was no longer acceptable. In fact, in decolonized India it was confronting. But the fundamental incompatibility of the two forms of domesticity led to an arbitrary juxtaposition, a soft form of modernity or lumpy aggregates that would allow certain reminiscences of a bygone culture that India had shown four years earlier in Manhattan or that Girard and Eames continued to strive for.

In its global transference of mid century modernity, while modernism was championed by MoMA for its aesthetic superiority, it was imported by Indian culture brokers as a potential business asset. As I have shown, comfort was a key trope of this particular iteration of postwar modernism. But more often the promotion mechanism used only the myth of comfort – far from its actual realization. As Gaelen Cranz notes:

> Ideas about what is comfortable ... seem to vary from one historical era to another ... People seem to respond more to their *ideas* about comfort than to their actual physical experience of it. Advertisers, of course, capitalize on the difference between the reality of comfort and its image in the marketing process. The most likely illusions and allusions are to luxury, power, and prestige.[77]

Considering that the MoMA canon of modernist exemplars shown in India took shape in the USA as part of Edgar Kaufmann Jr.'s Good Design project to market modernism to American furniture consumers, it becomes clear that what is encoded in this culturally constructed notion of comfort is luxurious mass consumption. MoMA's collection of canonic objects of "good design," shipped by the USIA throughout Western Europe as strategic assets of a "charm offensive" intended to convince postwar Europeans that the USA wasn't just an uncultivated land of vulgar consumption, presents a transatlantic portrait of modernism in which the USA is the tradition's most recent and accomplished heir. Manubhai Shah, expressing the view of Indian businessmen who established their opinions of modernism as an aesthetic vs. a profitable commodity, stated:

> The small entrepreneur generally possesses a creative mind besides some business acumen and the necessary technical know-how. I am sure such a person and other technicians will be able to draw ideas from the articles that will be displayed and try to adapt the improvements for their own products.[78]

This vision of modernism presents as the domestic material culture of transatlantic capitalism. Indian businessmen became the driving force behind bringing this "style" to India as a springboard for the development of the nation's manufacturing and trade capacities.

Domestic modernity of the minimum: the ascetic hybrid of Jeanneret

A very different strategy of modernist cultural transmission was evident in the ideology of architect Pierre Jeanneret, who in attempting to inject Gandhian values and a Gandhian world view into the functionalist aesthetic of European modernism, arrived at a true hybrid – marrying the thesis of luxurious, modernist material consumption with the antithesis of Gandhian ascetic modernity to yield an ascetic hybrid, a specifically Indian modernism reminiscent of the militant and highly polemical modernism of Hannes Meyer.[79] In other words, it was the creation of an internally consistent hybrid culture. Jeanneret, who arrived in India along with Le Corbusier in February 1951, was appointed senior architect. Later, in his career in the Punjab – from 1958 to 1965 – he worked as Chief Architect and Town Planner of the new capital city.[80] Unlike Le Corbusier, Jeanneret related closely to the native population, trying to grasp their culture of dwelling.[81] Subsequently, at his home studio in Chandigarh he designed a number of furnishings, ascetic in spirit but modern in look.[82] In the face of India's aspiration to become modern, and the state's bureaucratic demand for cutting edge modernity in technology, affluence and material abundance, Jeanneret tried to find a middle ground that would reconcile Gandhian material culture with the culture of industrial modernity (Figure 7).

In the Chandigarh project Jeanneret increasingly became involved in designing low-cost housing for low-income groups. Le Corbusier, his long-time collaborator and perhaps the most prominent architect of the modern movement, confined himself to designing monumental civic buildings, deeming it impossible to reconcile modernist ideas with the Third World condition.[83] Jeanneret's

Figure 7

Jeanneret's synthesized modernity – an image from the *Simple Furniture and Interior*, a government publication circulating the new form of Indian domesticity. Source: D. N. Anand, *Simple Furniture and Interior Decoration*, New Delhi, Directorate of Extension and Training, Ministry of Food and Agriculture, 1959. Courtesy of National Library of India, Kolkata.

experiments in low-cost housing types were displayed later at the "International Exhibition on Low Cost Housing" in Delhi, January 1954.[84] The furniture that he developed for his own personal use during his stay at Chandigarh played the central role in his scheme for new Indian domesticity. Figure 7, from a 1959 government publication,[85] illustrates a series of mock-up rooms designed by Jeanneret, furnished according to his design of interior furnishing that employed a vernacular form, element, and material as its principal inspiration.[86] Jeanneret's chair expresses a fundamental incompatibility with the modernist chair displayed in the MoMA exhibition in terms of production process and notions of comfort. Instead of using industrial materials such as steel, plywood or industrial textiles,[87] he employed bamboo for the frame and a naturally woven surface as upholstery. The image of the chair in effect is an effort to overturn the state of disembodied human labor in the modernist chair. The woven surface and the employment of a natural element in its natural state suggest that this chair allows a certain degree of human error that is natural in any human production. But at the same time its standard fabrication suggests that it is reproducible on a mass scale and might prove consumable on a mass scale. Instead of following the central image of the modern chair – the comfort-giving device displayed in the MoMA exhibition – Jeanneret's design was an attempt to produce the new Indian body as comfortable albeit in a very different way, like the comfort embedded in the seated/working body of Gandhi. Although the bodily posture that this stylized, Indian, low height chair would demand may seem uncomfortable in the modern sense, this state of discomfort is not the lumpy insertion of the psychological comfort of Girard or Eames;[88] rather, it is candidly suggestive of a culture of ascetic poverty – a voluntary dispossession akin to Myer and Gandhi. Under the sway of the mid-century government slogan for a new Indian domesticity, "Poverty can sometimes give an impression of greater dignity than riches,"[89] Jeanneret envisioned his synthesized modernity as part of the Gandhian material culture that agreed with the Indian reality in which labor-saving mass production and mechanically reproducible objects were less affordable. Describing his experience of working in India, Jeanneret wrote:

> My greatest concern now is to employ as many men as possible on the work sites which I supervise. After having for years tried my hardest to find ways of replicating human labor with machinery for economic reasons, I never thought I would, one day, be reconsidering the problem from a different angle: that of trying to give work to the greatest possible number of men.[90]

Jeanneret's chair stands for a synthesis of human engagement and mass production, austerity and consumption, discomfort and luxury. Providing an alternative vision to postwar modernism, Jeanneret calibrated to a Gandhian political economy that championed austerity, asceticism, poverty, and the spiritual importance of physical labor.

Figure 8

A bamboo chair designed by Professor M. P. Ranjan, NID. The chair demonstrates an industrially reproducible bamboo joinery system. Courtesy of National Institute of Design, NID, Ahmedabad, India.

At the end of this chapter I would like to go back to the design school at Ahmedabad from where I started. After the MoMA show ended in 1961, the objects were presented to the Indian government to form the nucleus of a permanent collection so that the people of India could benefit from access to them over a longer period of time. These objects were handed over to the NID for presentation to students as examples of what could be the point of departure for creating a new Indian modernity (Figure 8).[91] For over four decades now, these objects have been a source of inspiration for generations of Indian designers. The guardian of these objects (the NID) is still exploring forms of synthesis. Over the last two decades, their "Centre for Bamboo Initiatives" has been experimenting with the possibility of turning traditional bamboo and cane furniture into mass reproducible objects. In 2001 they published the results of their experiments along with pieces of designs and with their production methods.[92] While designing mass reproducible bamboo trusses, folding chairs and vertical partitions, Professor Ranjan, who is heading this project, developed a unique joinery system for bamboo structures, which can be used as a universally applicable model for industrially-produced bamboo furniture. It is a classic example of breaching the modern attitudes towards objects using natural materials and direct human involvement. Hitherto, while such processes could not have been considered democratic, the masses were denied access to objects because they were not produced on a grand scale. Nevertheless, at the crossroads of the mid-century global transference of modernity and its homegrown synthesis, the discursive formation of a new material culture has been gradually opening up over MoMA's tomb that by sharing a common discourse of the Third World underdevelopment pursued a very different trajectory of modernity.

Acknowledgement

I am grateful to Greg Castillo for the many conversations and insights that helped shape this chapter. I owe particular thanks to Duanfang Lu, Gay Mcdonald and two anonymous reviewers for their constructive criticism and invaluable suggestions.

Notes

1 Peter Scriver and Vikramāditya Prakāsh, "Between modernity and representation, framing and architectural critique of colonial South Asia," in Peter Scriver and Vikramāditya Prakāsh (eds), *Colonial Modernities: Building, Dwelling and Architecture in British India and Ceylon*, New York: Routledge, 2007.

2 Peter H. Hoffenberg, *An Empire on Display: English, Indian, and Australian Exhibitions from the Crystal Palace to the Great War*, California: University of California Press, 2001.

3 Harold R. Isaac, *Scratches on Our Minds, American Images of China and India*, New York: The John Day Company, 1958, pp. 243–4, 249, 259, 271.

4 "Interview with Hon. John Foster Dulles", in Ramachandra Guha, *India after Gandhi, the History of the World's Largest Democracy*, London: Picador 2007, p. 160.

5 Ibid., p. 161.

6 Monroe Wheeler, "Forward" in Monroe Wheeler (ed.), *Textiles and Ornaments of India*, New York: Museum of Modern Art, 1956, p. 11.

7 Kamaladevi Chattopadhyaya and Yusuf Meherally, *At the Cross-roads*, Bombay: National Information and Publications Ltd., 1947; Kamaladevi Chattopadhyaya, *America, The land of Superlatives*, Phoenix Publications, 1946.

8 International Council/International Program Exhibition Records. *Textile and Ornamental Arts of India:* VI.ICE-D-5-54.2. New York, The Museum of Modern Art Archives, New York.

9 Wheeler, op. cit., p. 11.

10 Abigail S. McGowan, "'All That Is Rare, Characteristic Or Beautiful', Design and the Defense of Tradition in Colonial India, 1851–1903," *Journal of Material Culture*, 2005, vol. 10, pp. 263–87.

11 Kate P. Kent, "The Girard Foundation Collection at the Museum of International Folk Art", *African Arts*, November 1983, vol. 17, no. 1, pp. 60–4.

12 Ibid., p. 64.

13 VI.ICE-D-5-54.2. MoMA Archives, NY.

14 Ibid.

15 Ibid.

16 Ibid.

17 Ibid.

18 Ibid.

19 Ananda Gopal Mukherjee and Vinod Tagra (eds), *Jawaharlal Nehru – The Architect of Modern India (A Documentary Account of Nehru's Concept of Planning Development)*, New Delhi: Reliance Publishing House, 1989, p. viii.

20 *India's Chances in the German Market, Indian Ties with Germany: A Supplement to the Times of India*, 1959, September 30.

21 VI.ICE-D-5-54.2. MoMA Archives, NY.

22 Dinesh Dutt, "Traditional designs and their modern implication," *Art in Industry Magazine*, vol. 2, no. 1, Dec 1950, pp. 25–32. Ajit Mokerjee, "Sari: its role in international publicity and contemporary fashion," *Art in Industry Magazine*, vol. 2, no. 1, Dec 1950, pp. 32–9; D. P. Ghosh, "Industrial application of ancient Orissan design," *Art in Industry Magazine*, vol. 3, no. 1, Jan 1952, pp. 20–3; Subrata Banerjee, "Indian influence on western design," *Art in Industry Magazine*, vol. 3, no. 1, Jan 1952, pp. 16–20.

23 Surjuit Mansingh, "India and the United States", in B. R. Nanda (ed.), *Indian Foreign Policy, The Nehru Years*, New Delhi: Radiant Publishers, Nehru Memorial Museum and Library 1976, p. 156.

24 Isaac, op. cit.

25 Arthur Robinoff, "Incompatible objectives and shortsighted politics", in Sumit Ganguly, Brian Shoup and Andrew Scobell (eds), *US–Indian Strategic Cooperation into the 21st Century, More than Words*, NY: Routledge, 2006, p. 46.

26 US Department of State, *The Subcontinent of South Asia*, Near and Middle Eastern Series no. 41, Washington Department of State, 1959, p. 6. Quoted in Robinoff, op. cit., p. 43.

27 Guha, op. cit.

28 John Elderfield (editor in chief), *The Museum of Modern Art in Mid-Century At Home and Abroad*, The Museum of Modern Art, 1994, p. 138.

29 Greg Castillo, "Domesticating the cold war: household consumption as propaganda in Marshall Plan Germany," *Journal of Contemporary History*, April 2005, vol. 40, no. 2, pp. 261–88.

30 International Council/International Program Exhibition Records. *Design Today in America and Europe*: VII.SP-ICE-17-57.8. MoMA Archives, NY.

31 Robinoff, op. cit., p. 43.

32 VII.SP-ICE-17-57.2. MoMA Archives, NY.

33 "Design show opens in India, 1959," *Industrial Design*, March 1959, p.14.

34 Fuller's dome was used by USIA for erecting exhibition pavilions within short periods of time, which was also a symbol of the USA's engineering marvel. See Jack Masey and Conway Lloyd Morgan, *Cold War Confrontations, US Exhibitions and Their Role in the Cultural Cold War*, Baden: Lars Muller Publishers, 2008, pp. 58–67.

35 VII.SP-ICE-17-57.2. MoMA Archives, NY.

36 For the Ford Foundation's role in India, see Leonard A. Gordon, "Wealth equals wisdom? the Rockefeller and Ford Foundations in India," *Annals of the American Academy of Political and Social Science*, vol. 554, The Role of NGOs: Charity and Empowerment, November 1997, pp. 104–16.

37 VII.SP-ICE-17-57.7: New Delhi. MoMA Archives, NY.

38 Castillo, op. cit.; Gay Mcdonald, "Selling the American Dream: MoMA, Industrial Design and Post-War France," *Journal of Design History*, 2004, vol. 17, no.4. Gay McDonald, *Homemakers, Domestic Wares and the Cold War: Exhibitions of US Design and the Construction of the Domesticated Consumer Body*, International Association of Societies of Design Research, The Hongkong Polytechnic University, December 12–15 2007.

39 Kathleen D. McCarthy, "From cold war to cultural development: the international cultural activities of the Ford Foundation, 1950–1980," *Daedalus*, vol. 116, no. 1, Philanthropy, Patronage Politics, Winter, 1987, pp. 93–117. India as a rising economic force won American attention during the 1950s. C. Douglas Dillon, Secretary of State for Economic Affairs, described the problem of

India's future development as the "most important economic project we have anywhere in the world." See VII.SP-ICE-17-57.2. MoMA Archives, NY.

40   Peter D. Bell, "The Ford Foundation as a transnational actor," *International Organization*, vol. 25, no. 3, Summer, 1971, pp. 465–78.

41   A program commonly known as the "Point Four Program" was initiated by President Truman for underdeveloped countries to preempt the Marxist appeal to poverty-torn newly decolonized countries by making American achievements available for their development. Mansingh, op. cit.

42   VII.SP-ICE-17-57.8. MoMA Archives, NY.

43   Ibid.

44   McCarthy, op. cit.

45   VII.SP-ICE-17-57.8. MoMA Archives, NY.

46   Galen Cranz, *The Chair*, New York: W. W. Norton and Company, 1998, pp. 79–89.

47   Greg Castillo, "The American 'fat kitchen' in Europe: postwar domestic modernity and Marshall Plan strategies of enchantment," in R. Oldenziel and K. Zachmann (eds), *Cold War Kitchen: Americanization, Technology, and European Users*, New York: MIT Press, Cambridge, 2009.

48   Rustam J. Mehta, *The Handicrafts and Industrial Art of India*, Bombay: Taraporevala's, 1960; Ananda Coomaraswamy, *The Arts and Crafts of India and Ceylon*, New York: Farrar, Straus, 1964; K. Krishna Murthy, *Ancient Indian Furniture*, Sandeep Prakashan, 2004.

49   Arthur Drexler, "Design today in America and Europe," in *Design Today in America and Europe*, exhibition catalogue, 1959, pp. 9–10.

50   VII.SP-ICE-17-57.8. MoMA Archives, NY.

51   Hannah Arendt, *The Human Condition*, Chicago: University of Chicago Press, 1958.

52   John Gloag, *Victorian Comfort: A Social History of Design from 1830–1900*, London: Adam and Charles Black, 1961, p. xv.

53   Katherine C. Grier, *Culture and Comfort: People, Parlors, and Upholstery, 1850–1930*, Rochester, NY, Strong Museum; Amherst, 1988, pp. 287–8.

54   Joyce Henry Robinson, "'Hi Honey, I'm home,': weary (neurasthenic) businessman and the formulation of a serenely modern aesthetic," in Andrew Ballantyne (ed.), *What is Architecture?*, NY: Routledge, 2002, pp. 112–28.

55   Victoria Rosner, *Modernism and the Architecture of Private Life*, New York: Columbia University Press, 2005, p. 121.

56   Penny Sparke, *Furniture*, London: Bell and Hyman, 1986, pp. 21–5.

57   John E. Crowley, *The Invention of Comfort: Sensibilities and Design in Early Modern Britain and Early America*, Baltimore: Johns Hopkins University Press, 2001, p. 292.

58   E. Kaufman Jr., *What is Modern Interior Design?*, New York: The Museum of Modern Art, 1953, p.5.

59   VII.SP-ICE-17-57.8. MoMA Archives, NY, p.4.

60   Ibid.

61   Ibid., p. 34.

62   Ibid.

63   Ibid., p. 6.

64   *The Times of India*, January 16 1959.

65   Arindam Dutta, *The Bureaucracy of Beauty: Design in the Age of its Global Reproducibility*, NY: Routledge, 2006.

66   Guha, op. cit., pp. 692–3.

67   Mark Thompson, *Gandhi and His Ashrams*, Bombay: Popular Prakashan, 1993, pp. 91–173.

68   Lisa N. Trivedi, *Clothing Gandhi's Nation: Homespun and Modern India*, Bloomington: Indiana University Press, 2007, pp. 16–17.

69   Rajni Chadha, *The Emerging Consumer, A Changing Profile of the Urban Indian House-wife and its Implications*, New Delhi: New Age International Publishers, 1995, p. 32.

70   Ursula Sharma, *Women's Work, Class, and the Urban Household: a Study of Shimla, North India*, New York: Tavistock Publications, 1986, p.82.

71   Hoffenberg, op. cit., pp. 166–71. Terry Smith, *Making the Modern: Industry, Art, and Design in America*, Chicago: University of Chicago Press, 1993, pp. 6–11.

72   Tim Barringer, *Men at Work: Art and Labour in Victorian Britain*, London: Yale University Press, New Haven, 2005, p. 8.

73   Mohit Chakrabarti, *The Gandhian Philosophy of the Spinning Wheel*, New Delhi: Concept Publishing Company, 2000, pp. 11–13.

74   Andrzej Piotrowski, "The spectacle of architectural discourses," *Architectural Theory Review*, vol. 13, no. 2, August 2008, pp. 130–44.

75   Abigail McGowan, *Crafting the Nation in Colonial India*, New York: Palgrave Macmillan, 2009, pp. 187–91.

76   VII.SP-ICE-17-57.2. MoMA Archives, NY.

77   Cranz, op. cit., pp. 112–13.

78   "Blend beauty with utility, call to industrialists," *The Times of India*, January 1959.

79   Modernity's incarnation in vernacular furnishing was first endeavored by the forgotten European tradition of ascetic modernity between the 1920s and the end of the 1940s. In the wake of wartime economic construction, the immediate postwar European notion of dwelling, especially as formulated by Werkbund and Bauhaus alumni, sought to formulate a low-consumption living pattern that would discard any "false abundance." They aestheticized poverty as a form of redemption and promoted a minimal way of living furnished by *ascetic objects* – a mood that was killed off by the West German economic miracle of the later 1950s. See Paul Betts, *The Authority of Everyday Objects, A Cultural History of West German Industrial Design*, Berkeley: University of California Press, 2007, pp. 82–3.

80   For a discussion of Jeanneret's stay and work at Chandigarh see Surinder Bhaga, *Le Corbusier and Pierre Jeanneret: Footprints on the Sands of Indian Architecture*, New Delhi: Galgotia Pub, 2000, pp. 23–37.

81   M. L. Malik, *Guide to Chandigarh*, Chandigarh: Navjeewan News Agency, 1968.

82   Jeanneret's connection to the ascetic mood of objects can be traced back to his early career during 1927, when he jointly designed with Le Corbusier three houses for the Deutscher Werkbund in Stuttgart. This particular exhibition explored the possibility of post World War reformation of European housing with the limited resources Europe could afford at that time. See Karin Kirsch, *The Weissenhofsiedlung, Experimental Housing Built for the Deutscher Werbund, Stuttgart, 1927*, New York: Rizzoli, 1989, pp. 100–19.

83   Kenneth Frampton, *Le Corbusier*, London: Thames and Hudson, 2001, p.187.

84   *Model Houses Constructed in the International Exhibition on Low Cost Housing 1954*, New Delhi: Government of India, Ministry of Works, Housing and Supply, 1954.

85   D. N. Anand, *Simple Furniture and Interior Decoration*, New Delhi: Directorate of Extension and Training, Ministry of Food and Agriculture, 1959.

86   This small booklet was divided into two sections; the first section has the series of mock-up rooms design by Jeanneret and the second section consists of the work of local designers that employs more traditional forms.

87   The legendary US modern designers Ray and Charles Eames's experiment with vernacular materials and primitive motifs were criticized as anti-modern. And Ray Eames was often accused as the bad influence on her partner Charles Eames for having made him stray from the pure modernist expression of steel, plastic etc. Pat Kirkham, "Humanizing modernism: the crafts, 'functioning decoration' and the Eameses," *Journal of Design History*, 1998, vol. 11, no. 1, pp. 15–29.

88   Kent, op. cit.; Kirkham, op. cit.

89   Anand, op. cit.

90   Helene Cauquil, "Pierre Jeanneret in India," *Architecture in India*, Paris: Electa Moniteur, 1985, quoted in Bhaga, op. cit., p. 29.

91   In conversation with Professor Ranjan in April 2009.

92   M. P. Ranjan, *Katlamara Chalo: A Design for Development Strategy, Design as a Driver for the Indian Rural Economy*, Ahmedabad: Centre for Bamboo Initiative at NID, National Institute of Design, 2001.

Chapter 9

Building a Colonial Technoscientific Network: tropical architecture, building science and the politics of decolonization

Jiat-Hwee Chang

The past few years have seen the emergence of an interesting body of new research on tropical architecture. This scholarship focuses mainly on the work of British architects in Africa during the mid-twentieth century. It examines a broad range of social, political, and cultural issues in the production of tropical architecture and engages in important debates on themes such as (post)colonialism and the politics of (de)colonization, and internationalization versus regionalism.[1] The emergence of tropical architecture was linked to key figures such as Maxwell Fry, Jane Drew, and Otto Koenigsberger, important metropolitan institutions such as the Department of Tropical Architecture at the Architectural Association, and also landmark events such as the 1953 Conference on Tropical Architecture. There is no doubt that the best of this scholarship situates the production of tropical architecture in the context of complex socio-political relations between the metropole and the colonies, the British Empire and the postcolonial nations. It is, however, largely silent on the technoscientific dimensions of tropical architecture. This oversight is significant given the technical nature of most of the discourses on tropical architecture in the mid-twentieth century.[2]

It has been argued that science and technology are social constructions.[3] I share this view, though not in the epistemologically relativist sense, but in the sense that science and technology are what Donna Haraway calls "situated knowledge"[4] in that what is assumed to be universally true and objective scientific knowledge is necessarily local, mediated, situated, and partial to begin with.[5] In other words, the production of technoscientific knowledge could never be understood in isolation from the socio-politico-cultural context. Recent scholarship on (post)colonial technoscience has argued that the significance of socio-politico-cultural context is even more accentuated in the production of colonial technoscience. In that context, the asymmetrical development in scientific knowledge and technological power between the colonizer and the colonized was overlaid with similarly lopsided socio-politico-cultural power-relations in colonial societies.[6] However, it has also been argued that science and technology are inadequately understood through the vagaries of socio-cultural interpretations.[7]

Actor-Network-Theory (ANT), as put forth by Bruno Latour and others, offers a theoretical framework for understanding such a moderate social constructivism. Unlike some other social constructivist views, ANT does not privilege the social in understanding how science and technology are constructed. ANT emphasizes the heterogeneous ensemble that shapes science and technology, taking into account both the social and the non-social forces, the human and the non-human actants.[8] In doing so, ANT addresses the accusation of relativism as raised in the controversies surrounding the social constructivist view of technoscience.[9] Furthermore, it also provides a way to account for how specific technological infrastructures of instruments, tools, and manuals are deployed to facilitate the production of technoscientific facts. Drawing on these insights, I hope to add to the scholarship on modern tropical architecture in the mid-twentieth century by examining how architectural technoscience was shaped by, as well as shaped, the complex socio-political configurations at the end of the British Empire. In this chapter, I will focus on the technoscientific dimensions of tropical architecture by studying what has, at best, been peripheral in recent scholarship on tropical architecture – the work of the Tropical Building Division (TBD) of the Building Research Station (BRS).

In the first part of the chapter, I study the 1945 proposal to set up the Colonial Liaison Unit (CLU), the predecessor of the TBD, for the purpose of conducting research on colonial housing and building problems. I show that the proposal, in terms of its organizational structure, research methodologies, and underlying assumptions, was based on the established model of colonial scientific research in tropical medicine and tropical agriculture. I also show that the proposal was an inextricable part of a colonial development regime, in which technoscience became an instrument of development. I will then focus on the work of the CLU and the TBD in the second part of the chapter. Their work in producing and maintaining technical standards for tropical building in the British Empire/Commonwealth entailed what is conceptualized as network building in ANT. ANT and the idea of network building rework certain entrenched assumptions in the understanding of modern tropical architecture, particularly the local versus global, universal science versus local crafts binaries. Specifically, this paper problematizes the regionalism discourse that views tropical architecture as a place-based architecture rooted in the cultural-climatic specificities of a region. Likewise, this paper also interrogates the universalizing and diffusionist discourse of modern architecture that sees tropical architecture as no more than a "natural" variant, acclimatized to the tropics.[10] I also argue that the network built has Foucauldian power-effects, in that it enabled the metropole to become a center of calculation in the network through the accumulation of power-knowledge. In the third section of the chapter, I illustrate the specificities of how such a network actually facilitated the accumulation of knowledge and the attendant power through the production of immutable mobiles by studying CLU and TBD's research on climatic design and thermal comfort. I argue that by privileging climate in the knowledge of place, the research on climatic design facilitated "action at a distance."

The colonial research model: the proposal for colonial housing research

The Tropical Division of BRS had its origin in the recommendations put forward by the Colonial Housing Research Group in 1945.[11] The Group was formed in around 1944 to advise the CO on housing in the colonies.[12] It was chaired by I. G. Evans, the acting director of BRS, and it involved key colonial experts such as Professor D. B. Blacklock of Liverpool School of Tropical Medicine, who authored a book on the "empire problem" of housing in the 1930s,[13] and Major Granville St. John Orde Browne, the labor advisor to the CO and a renowned expert on colonial labor issues.[14] In their report, the Group recommended making a coordinated effort in housing research to deal with the immense housing problems in the colonies. Valuable work on housing research was being carried out in many of the colonies, they noted, but those efforts were dispersed and uncoordinated. The knowledge gained from these efforts in a colony was thus not available to those in other colonies, leading to the inefficient and uneconomical duplication of work. To deal with this problem, the Group made two recommendations – the establishment of a center, which the Group called the Colonial Housing Bureau, for the collection and dissemination of information concerning colonial housing research in the metropole, and the setting up of regional research establishments in the colonies. The center in the metropole was to be a depository in which data such as "type plans, reports on various materials and on the performance, cost and suitability from various points of view of various designs might be accumulated and be available for consultation."[15] The center would also be disseminating the knowledge accumulated to the various colonial departments through the publication of periodical digests. A Colonial Liaison Officer was subsequently appointed by the Colonial Secretary to take charge of this metropolitan center, that is, the CLU. Besides establishing the metropolitan center, the Group also recommended the setting up of four regional research centers in the periphery, with the West Indies, East Africa, West Africa, and Malaya being mentioned as the probable locations for the regional centers.[16]

These recommendations were significant in several different ways. First, they were the first time that a major coordinated effort matched by a large sum of funding was made by the Colonial Office (CO) to deal with the much-neglected problem of colonial housing. Of course there had been earlier efforts that addressed the colonial housing problems. For example, in the early twentieth century, various initiatives were undertaken by the municipal and colonial governments in different parts of the British Empire to improve housing conditions for certain segments of the "native" population through the Improvement Trusts.[17] However, the earlier efforts were smaller scale local initiatives at the municipality level which tended to be underfunded and/or were not supported by strong political will. The new concerted effort taken to address the colonial housing problem prompted a senior staff member of CO to remark in 1947 that: "Colonial Housing and Building, hitherto a Colonial Office Cinderella, has suddenly come very much on the tapis here."[18] Alongside the efforts of the Colonial Housing Group, other housing initiatives, such as the appointment of Professor William Graham Holford as the Honorary Town Planning Advisor to the Secretary of State for the Colonies and the setting up of a Housing Advisory Panel, were also made in the 1940s.[19] The position on housing taken by the Colonial Housing Research Group that the "general economic development must be pursued concurrently with improved housing" reflects the official view following the passing of the Colonial Development and Welfare Act (CDWA) in 1940.

The equal emphases on both economic development and the welfare of the natives, through provision in areas such as health, education, and housing, was seen by the British officials as a disavowal of any intention to merely exploit the colonies more efficiently.[20] This emphasis on welfare and its implementation through comprehensive provision set the CDWA apart from earlier development schemes. Previously, development priorities had been unambiguously economic in focus, although the British administrators did pay lip-service to their mandate of taking care of the welfare of the natives and "civilizing" them as a way to legitimize colonial rule.[21] But the new post-1940 concern for the welfare of the natives did not merely arise from the "benevolence" of the British imperial government. Rather, welfare was seen as an antidote to the "disorder" in many colonial territories. After all, the CDWA was formulated primarily to deal with what the British called "disturbances" – both labor unrest and anti-colonial nationalist movements – in the colonies.[22] Central in this shift was the report of the West India Royal Commission, which was submitted in 1939 but it was so controversial that it was not published until 1945. The recommendations of the West India Royal Commission led to the establishment of CDWA. Some of the earliest large scale colonial housing initiatives, including research, were undertaken in the West Indies in the early 1940s under Sir Frank Stockdale, the Comptroller for Development and Welfare, and his town planning advisor Robert Gardner-Medwin.[23]

Secondly, the recommendations made by the Colonial Housing Group were shaped by prior models of colonial scientific research. This is perhaps not unexpected, as the Group consisted of members from the CO, the Crown Agents, and also experts from organizations that had previously been engaged in colonial research, such as the Liverpool School of Tropical Medicine, the Imperial Institute, and the Department of Science and Industrial Research (DSIR).[24]

Following the practice adopted for the Imperial Agricultural Bureau, the proposed Colonial Housing Bureau was to be attached to an existing metropolitan institution working on similar problems. In this case, the Bureau was to be attached to BRS, which was first established in 1921 as part of the DSIR to carry out scientific research on building materials and construction methods in order to address post-First-World-War housing shortages.[25] The regional research establishments in the colonies were also to be modeled after the metropolitan model. After the group's report, two BRS officers, at the request of the CO, visited the British West African colonies from December 1946 to January 1947. They submitted a comprehensive proposal on the establishment of a West African Building Research Station along the lines of the BRS.[26]

Methodologically, the Group proposed that colonial housing research follow that of colonial nutrition. Michael Worboys has noted that British colonial nutrition research in Africa followed the technical problem-solving approach in which the problem of undernourishment was isolated from the larger socio-economic conditions of poverty and turned into a specialized medical problem that required professional expertise to solve.[27] As a result, the prescribed solution for the colonial nutrition problem overlooked the larger structural conditions that caused poverty and undernourishment in the first place.[28] In a not dissimilar manner, the Group proposed that housing research be compartmentalized into different spheres of specialization and the colonial housing bureau should concentrate on the "study of the more physical and material aspects."[29] This was despite the Group's recognition that "[h]ousing research ... is not a mere matter of materials and construction" and "without a broad medico-sociologico-economic background of knowledge, house design and the planning of housing schemes are bound to suffer."[30]

Even though the colonial model of research was derived from the metropolitan model, there was a major difference between them. It has been noted in the case of tropical medicine that there was a division of labor between the specialist research work in the metropolitan institutions to discover the causes of tropical diseases and the general practitioners in the colonies treating the diseases.[31] A similar hierarchical division of labor was also assumed between the center and the periphery in the proposed organization of building research institutions.[32] It was stated in the Group's report that the primary roles of the regional centers would be to "act as local centres of information, and to carry out those investigations which must necessarily be done on the spot." In contrast, "[c]ertain other investigations of a specialist character or of a more long-term or general nature might well be undertaken in [Britain]" at metropolitan institutions such as the BRS and the Imperial Institute.[33] This center–periphery division of labor in scientific research corresponded to the prevailing view of center–periphery economic relations, in which tropical colonies in the periphery produced raw materials for industrial production in the temperate metropole.[34] From the perspective of world system theory, such a welding of peripheral tropical production to metropolitan temperate industrialization means that the tropical economy was caught up in a relationship of dependency on the temperate economy – not only subjected to their economic exploitation and vulnerable to the fluctuations of their economic cycles, but also perpetually relying on their capital and expertise.[35]

Thirdly, underlying the Group's recommendation is a fundamental faith in the transformative power of science and technology, especially in terms of how the application of technoscientific knowledge would enable socio-economic development and provide for welfare. Recent scholarship in social studies of science, especially in relation to colonial technoscience, has argued that scientific research has never been a disinterested pursuit for its own sake.[36] Instead, colonial technoscience has been understood as an instrument of economic development; to further the exploitation of natural resources by increasing the productive capacity of soil and identifying the properties and potential commercial uses of natural resources. State-sponsored colonial scientific research was first initiated in a systematic manner in the late nineteenth century after Joseph Chamberlain became Colonial Secretary in 1895. Chamberlain championed "constructive imperialism" to develop the "immense estate" of Britain's colonial territories. His years as Colonial Secretary marked the beginning of the shift from the *laissez-faire* approach towards colonial economies in the Victorian era to a more systematic approach of economic planning and development that subsequently shaped the CDWA.[37] Other than providing loans and grants to the colonies for infrastructural projects of railway, port, and road construction, the CO under Chamberlain also organized and funded scientific research in tropical medicine and agriculture to alleviate colonial health and agricultural problems. Initiatives related to Chamberlain included the founding of the Liverpool and London Schools of Tropical Medicine, the Imperial Department of Agriculture, and the appointment of Patrick Manson as medical advisor to the CO.[38]

Later in the mid-twentieth century, with more funding from the CDWA and following the recommendations of Lord Hailey's *African Survey*, technoscientific research on British colonial problems was further intensified and broadened. Its scope expanded beyond the traditional fields of medicine, agriculture, and geology to include, among other areas, social sciences, economics, veterinary, fisheries, road building, and, of course, building. Colonial housing research was thus part of the broader expansion in colonial research in the mid-twentieth century.[39] Furthermore, with the beginning of the end of the British Empire, and the shift into a new "world order" defined by Cold War politics and the division into "developed" and "underdeveloped" countries, development expanded beyond the confines of the British Empire. Development was internationalized under the aegis of the United States and new development agencies, such as the World Bank, the International Monetary Fund, and the various United Nations development organizations.[40] The faith in science and technology of this new development regime was even greater than before. This was exemplified in United States president Harry Truman's Point Four Program in which he promised that the developed countries, as led by the United States, would use their technical knowledge to help the underdeveloped countries eradicate poverty and its attendant social problems. That became manifested in the many technical assistance and technology transfer schemes rendered by the developed world to the developing one. The faith in technoscience brought about the expansion of technoscience into every possible social field, creating new forms of knowledge where there were none, elaborating new objects, concepts, and theories, so much so that these technoscientific development discourses "colonized reality."[41]

Network building: the work of the Tropical Building Division

After an almost-three-year search, George Anthony Atkinson was appointed as Colonial Liaison Officer in June 1948. After Atkinson's appointment, each British colony was to assign a technical officer as his correspondent in order to facilitate his work of collecting, organizing, and disseminating information on colonial housing and building. Atkinson was also appointed as housing advisor to the CO. Atkinson's appointment was for an initial period of three years and it was funded by the CDWA and administered through the Social Service Department. Atkinson was deemed suitable because of his overseas work experience, specifically his war-time experience working with the Royal Air Force Airfield Construction Service in West Africa, North Africa and the Middle East.[42] (Figure 1) Atkinson's scope of work extended beyond the original proposed focus on colonial housing to include colonial building in general. That was because, besides social housing,

Figure 1

The bungalow George Atkinson designed and built for himself at the Waterloo Airfield in Sierra Leone, 1941. Source: George Atkinson.

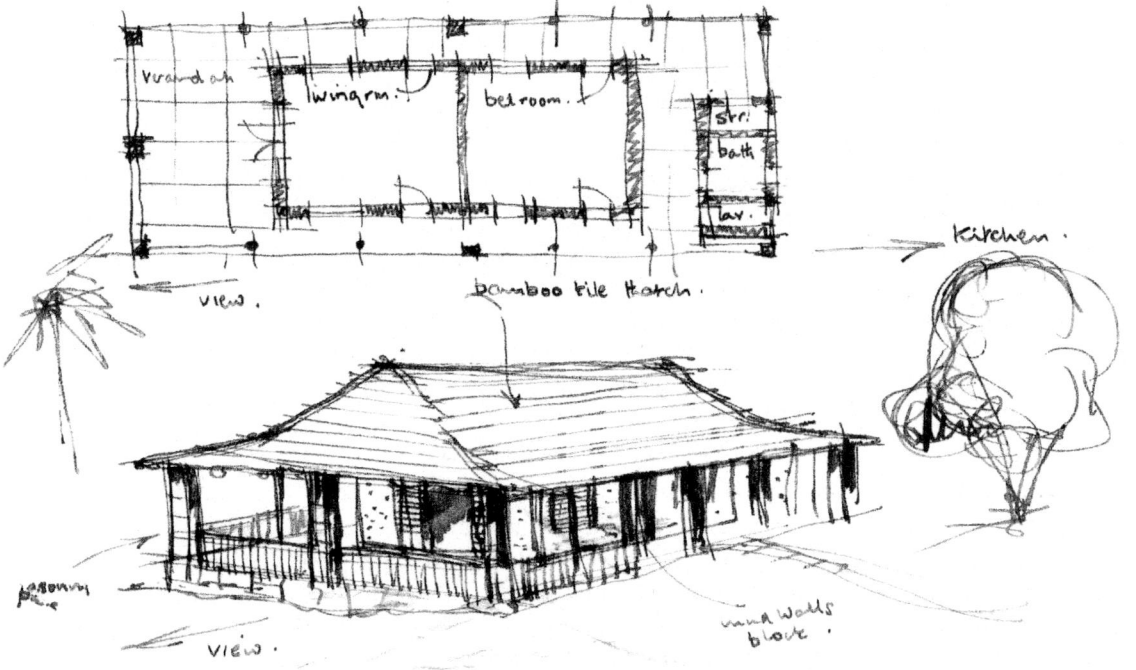

CDWA was also funding other schemes that involved the building of schools, hospitals, and offices. Moreover, there was the "recognition of the difficulty of separating the physical problems of building from those of general housing and planning policies in the overseas territories."[43]

Other than the aforementioned "discovery" of colonial housing problems in the 1940s, another impetus behind the appointment of a Colonial Liaison Officer was the need to control the escalating costs of building construction in the colonies, especially those sponsored by CDWA funds.[44] Although the escalating costs of building construction could be partially accounted for by the shortage of building materials in the immediate postwar years, the CO also attributed the cause to the lack of well-defined minimum building standards, which led "imperceptibly to somewhat extravagant schemes." To reduce cost, the Secretary of State went as far as expressing his anxiety that "colonies should avoid the error of constructing buildings of a more permanent character than circumstances warrant."[45] As a result, one of the earliest tasks for Atkinson was to formulate minimum standards for building in the tropics.[46] Here, standards referred not to standard plans for building types such as bungalows and barracks, which have been in existence in the British Empire since the nineteenth century.[47] Standards here should rather be understood in relation to building science research. According to Sir Frederick Lea, the director of BRS from 1946 to 1965, scientific methods were first systematically applied to building research from the 1920s with the establishment of the BRS in order to overcome the limitations of a building industry that was largely craft-based.[48] Traditional craft which depended on rules of thumb established through generations of trial and error was deemed inadequate in keeping up with the array of new construction materials that industrialization brought about. Lea argued that "[w]ith new materials tradition could be no guide and its blindfold application to them was a gamble"[49] that supposedly caused many building failures. In contrast to craft, the application of scientific methods to building research sought to achieve *predictability* in performance and *replicability* in different sites and contexts.[50] To accomplish that, not only were new building standards required, it also "infer[red] the dissemination of the knowledge gained, a new outlook and new methods in architectural and technical training and a new conception of the fundamentals of architecture on the part of its practitioners."[51]

Building standards would be useless if they were not adhered to outside the building research stations where they were formulated or if they were not adopted by people besides the building scientists who formulated them. For standards to work, the knowledge gained from building research has to be disseminated, the building industry has to be trained to follow established norms of practices, and new tools and instruments may be required. In other words, building standards have to remain constant when circulating between different sites and situations – such as building research stations, construction sites, architectural studios, and building material factories – and different people – such as building scientists, architects, building contractors, and building material suppliers. In many ways, a building standard approximates what Bruno Latour calls immutable mobile, an entity that is mobile, stable, and combinable in that it is an entity that could circulate without distortion, corruption or decay. According to Latour, immutable mobile only remains immutable and combinable *inside* the network.[52] Producing building standards thus entails network building, that is, bringing the heterogeneous elements of people and things, institutions and practices from different sites, which were needed to sustain the standard, into alignment.[53]

The work undertaken by Atkinson after his appointment as Colonial Liaison Officer could be understood along the lines of network building. Besides acquiring information from his correspondents, Atkinson also traveled extensively to visit the different colonial territories. At these places, he would carry out diverse activities, such as survey and advise on the colonial building developments, lecture and publicize the work undertaken in colonial building research, and encourage the setting up of building research stations.[54] Besides that, Atkinson also publicized the work of colonial building research by publishing extensively in different periodicals linked to the building industry – from metropolitan architectural journals such as the *RIBA Journal*, the *Architectural Association Journal*, and the *Architectural Review*,[55] to trade journals such as *Prefabrication*,[56] to regional architectural journals such as *Quarterly Journal of the Institute of Architects of Malaya*,[57] to journals on society and politics such as *African Affairs*.[58]

One of Atkinson's main tasks as Colonial Liaison Officer as spelt out in the Secretary of State's circular was the publication of a periodical digest disseminating the information and knowledge of colonial building gathered at the Unit. The periodical digest later took the form of *Colonial Building Notes* (1950–8), which was renamed *Overseas Building Notes* (1958–84) (Figure 2) in 1958 in view of the changing geopolitical landscape of the decolonizing British Empire. These periodicals, which were published at irregular intervals varying from a month to a few months, consist of various types of article that covered a wide range of topics. They range from description of various exemplary building schemes in the British Empire/Commonwealth, to summaries of the latest building research findings, to bibliographies and reference lists on key subjects, to technical guides on various topics. The topics covered could be classified into three main overlapping areas – information on exemplary building and planning schemes in the tropics; building construction materials and building methods for the tropics; and climatic design, especially in terms of sun-shading, natural ventilation and thermal comfort.[59] By 1984, when *Overseas Building Notes* ceased publication, 191 issues had been published and widely circulated. For example, in 1961, the circulation for each issue was about 1400 copies.[60] The Unit also published five issues of *Tropical Building Studies* from 1960 to 1963, each of which was an in-depth research report on a particular aspect of building in the tropics.

Atkinson took on educational initiatives too. From around 1950 to 1961, he helped to organize short courses for overseas officers – architects, civil engineers, and quantity surveyors – in government service.[61] Atkinson also taught at the Department of Tropical Architecture at the Architectural Association.[62] In addition, the Unit provided advisory services to the different colonial governments and to special committees working on building projects funded by the CDWA. They included the Inter-University Council for Higher Education in the Colonies and the Colonial University Grants Advisory Committee, which were building universities in colonies like the Gold Coast, Uganda, the West Indies, and Nigeria, including the well-known example of University College at Ibadan. The Unit also provided consultancy services to British architects and builders who wished to work or were already working in the colonial territories. For example, Architects Co-Partnership in Nigeria collaborated with the Unit to make a "strenuous enquiry into the performance of each successive building" it designed.[63]

One of the most important aspects of the Unit's and Atkinson's network building entailed assisting the establishment of regional building research

Figure 2
Cover of *Colonial Building Notes.*

stations in the colonies, as envisioned in the Colonial Housing Group's recommendations, and also maintaining contacts and sharing research findings with these research stations. As discussed earlier, the West African Building Research Institute was established in Accra in 1952 following the recommendations of two BRS officers. A proposal was put forward in 1948 to establish a building research station in the West Indies but the lack of funds in the CDWA ended any hope of its establishment.[64] A similar proposal in Malaya was at least partially fulfilled in the form of a Design and Research Branch within the Public Works Department, but not an autonomous building research station.[65] Other than the building research stations in the colonies, two other building research stations were established in the British dominions in the early 1940s following the BRS model – the National Building Research Institute in South Africa in 1942, and the Commonwealth Experimental Station in Australia in 1944.[66] The other prominent building research station then was India's Central Building Research Station, established in 1947 under the Council of Scientific and Industrial Research and initially based at the Thomason College of Engineering at Roorkee.[67]

Network building was more than gathering and disseminating information through publication, training expertise through educational work, or establishing a technical infrastructure through the building of research stations. According to Latour, network building also entails a series of translations of interest and the enrollment of allies so that more entities (both human actors and nonhuman actants)[68] participate in the construction of fact, slowly transforming "a claim into a matter of fact." By translation, Latour meant "the interpretation given by fact-builders of their interests and that of the people they enroll" so that associations and alliances can be formed to control the actions of others and make them predictable.[69] Latour's articulation of interest tends to refer narrowly to only economic self-interest. Although that is problematic,[70] we could easily expand on the notion of interest by being more attentive to how there are other forms of vested socio-politico-cultural interests, which according to Pierre Bourdieu are often interconvertible to economic interests.[71] Active translation of interest and enrollment of allies is quite apparent in Atkinson's various writings and published speeches. Atkinson articulated the benefits of building research in different ways, catering specifically to the interests of his targeted audience. In his famous speech to an audience consisting mainly of British architects at the Architectural Association in April 1953, Atkinson impressed on his audience the abundant building opportunities available in the tropics and the importance of acquiring the appropriate technical expertise of building in the tropics if they wished to seize these opportunities.[72] However, when Atkinson was lecturing in Singapore, he shifted his earlier emphasis on how technical knowledge would privilege the metropolitan architects to show that it would instead benefit the local building scene. He noted that the establishment of a regional building research center in Malaya would mean that "results of research and technical development throughout the World can be applied to Malayan conditions" and the station could also be "where problems, particular to Malaya [could] be studied."[73] In another instance, when Atkinson was writing in a trade journal for the building prefabrication industry, he reviewed the existing building techniques and the state of the building industry in the colonies and advised on the opportunities available to the British manufacturers for exporting their prefabricated buildings to these places.[74]

Other than enrolling human actors, Latour also argued that nonhuman actants are crucial to the construction of facts. By nonhuman actants, Latour referred to entities such as tools, instruments, or even something as simple as a graph. These tools or instruments might be critical in the conduct of an experiment so that a hypothesis could be proven, and the graph might help one visualize particular data and facts. In the case of building science and the work of the CLU of the BRS, instruments such as the heliodon and graphical representations such as the sun-path diagram and thermal comfort charts were especially important in the attempt to enroll more architects in the construction of tropical building science. As Henry Cowan, the self-professed first professor in building science, noted, "the average architect is receptive to visual demonstrations, but that he does not respond well to mathematical treatment."[75] The heliodon (Figure 3), which was invented by A. F. Dufton and H. E. Beckett of the BRS in 1928,[76] is one such instrument that provides effective visual demonstration. It is a powerful "device for determining the natural lightings of rooms, and the shadows cast on, and by, buildings."[77] It shows the daylight level and the shadow cast three-dimensionally by simulating the sun with a light bulb, the Earth's surface with an adjustable flat board, and the building with a model. The heliodon was designed to allow it to simulate the sun's position for all latitudes for all days of the year and all the sunlight hours of a day. It is thus a useful design aid that could be used to predict various aspects of building performance related to sun-shading and sunlight penetration.

Most of the works described above were of course not undertaken by Atkinson alone, as the CLU expanded fairly rapidly after his appointment as Colonial Liaison Officer in 1948. In 1951, an assistant architect and an experiment officer were appointed. Later on in 1954, a senior architect and a town planner were added to the Unit. Three years later, a tropical paint research fellow was

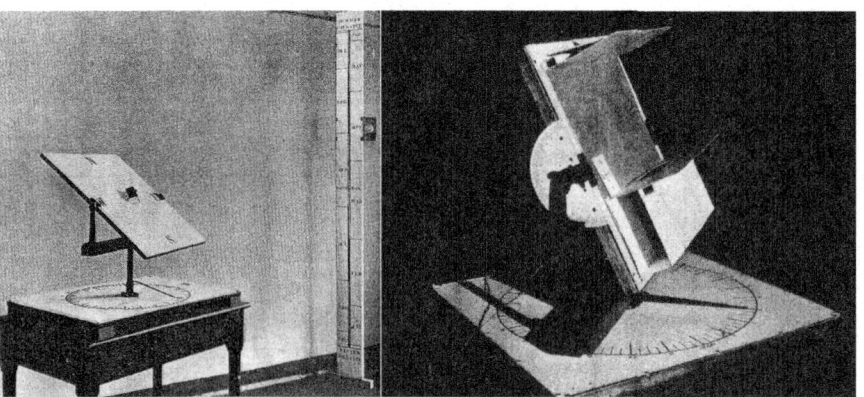

Figure 3
View of the components of a heliodon (left) and close-up view of the heliodon with a model attached (right). Source: *Colonial Building Notes.*

appointed to specifically investigate the performance of paints suitable for tropical buildings. In 1956, the Unit applied unsuccessfully for funds to expand and carry out research in areas such as building climatology, thermal conditions, natural ventilation, daylighting, and the use of solar energy in the tropics. In 1959, it made another failed application for funds to study the field conditions of thermal discomfort. However, in the same year, the Unit was renamed as TBD, one of the three tropical units in DSIR. The other tropical units were the Tropical Products Institute and the Tropical Unit in Road Research Laboratory.[78] The change in name reflected the change in emphasis from a "colonial" focus on dependent countries and countries in the British Commonwealth to a broader "tropical" coverage that included countries newly independent and even those outside the Commonwealth. In 1960, the unit came under the administration of the Department of Technical Cooperation as it took over the former functions of the CO. In the same year, the division expanded from wholly advisory work to conducting some research work of its own.[79] Due to changes in British foreign policy and its administration of development aid as the Empire gradually dissolved in the 1960s, the TBD similarly underwent many changes in the 1960s. In 1964, it came under the administration of the Ministry of Overseas Development, and the division was renamed as the Overseas Division in 1966.[80] These changes signaled the shift of the division's focus away from the tropics and perhaps marked a decline of its influence on tropical architecture. As noted earlier, a great amount of work is involved in building and sustaining a network. "Vigilance and surveillance have to be maintained," or the contingent alignment of heterogeneous "elements will fall out of line and the network will crumble."[81] Despite its subsequent decline, the Overseas Division of BRS and its predecessors nevertheless played an important part in providing the technoscientific foundation for tropical architecture in the British Empire/Commonwealth for about two decades. At this point, it is perhaps pertinent to ask, what did the network achieve besides enabling the circulation of immutable mobiles? What were the other effects of the network?

Spatially, as Latour noted, a network "indicates [that] resources are concentrated in a few places – the knots and the nodes – which are connected with one another – the links and the meshes: these connections transform scattered resources into a net that may seem to extend everywhere."[82] Within the network, events, places and people could be turned into abstract, transportable, and combinable information – that is, immutable mobiles. This information could then be circulated from one point of the network to another, often from the edges or peripheries of the network to the nodes or centers, facilitating the accumulation of knowledge at these centers. According to Latour, the accumulation of knowledge is also the accumulation of power because it allows a point, or a few points, in the network to become center(s) of calculations which can act on distant places because of its familiarity with things, people, and events there. Cycles of accumulating knowledge will create and reinforce an asymmetry of power between the centers and the peripheries of the network, thus allowing the centers of calculation to dominate others. Even as such an understanding of the working of the technoscientific network reinforces the insight of the world system theory on center–periphery relations, this understanding is not based on the capitalist logic of production but on technoscientific practices. Moreover, unlike the world system theory, ANT does not conceive the center as a fixed or static entity. As the center of calculation is formed through network building, theoretically it could be surpassed or replaced by another center emerging from the periphery of the original network that builds a better and stronger network. In the case of the TBD, its role as a center of calculation in the field of tropical architecture declined in the 1960s, when the British Empire was coming to an end with many of its former colonies gaining independence. The original technoscientific network became much weaker, if not disintegrated, with decolonization. Without the accumulation of knowledge through the network, TBD could not function as a center. In the next section, I will use case studies of the TBD's work on climatic design and thermal comfort to illustrate how immutable mobiles actually work in the technoscientific network of tropical architecture to facilitate the accumulation of power at the center of calculation.

(Im)mutable mobiles: the case of climatic design and thermal comfort

Climatic design came into common usage in the architectural discourses of North America and Europe during the mid-twentieth century. Prominent among those discourses were the "Weather and the Building Industry" conference organized by the Building Research Advisory of the United States National Academy of Science in 1950,[83] and other publications such as Jeffrey Ellis Aronin's *Climate and Architecture* (1953), Olgyay Brothers' *Design with Climate*, and B. Givoni's *Man, Climate and Architecture* (1969). These developments in North America represented some the earliest attempts to establish climatic design on a seemingly neutral technoscientific basis devoid of the moral and racist undertones of earlier colonial discourses on climate and design. These North American developments paralleled the European – that is, primarily British, French and German – development of modern tropical architecture. Tropical architecture was seen by many as the natural extension of climatic design to the conditions of the tropics. The common rhetoric of both tropical architecture and climatic design states that the primary function of architecture is to serve as a shelter for man from the elements of nature. Thus, the need to design in response to climate is an ontological truth. Normative history of tropical architecture does not question this rhetoric. Instead it adds to it by tracing the emergence of tropical architecture to the formal precedents in the works of the masters of modern architecture – from Stamo Papadaki and Le Corbusier's use of the *brise soleil* (sun breaker) in their works in the hotter climates, to Lucio Costa and Oscar Niemeyer's Brazilian architecture, to Paul Rudolph's Florida Houses.[84] In this narrative of diffusion, tropical architecture as pioneered by these masters then came to influence

British architects such as Maxwell Fry and Jane Drew through publications and the networks of associations such as MARS (Modern Architecture Research Group) and CIAM (*Congrès International d'Architecture Moderne*).

There are a few problems with this normative narrative. First, it ignores the prior history of "climatic design" in the British Empire. Climate, especially the hot and humid tropical variant, and its influence on the built environment has featured prominently in British colonial architectural discourses for more than a century prior to the mid-twentieth century. For much of the nineteenth and early twentieth centuries, the prevalence of miasmic theories of disease transmission and other related environmentalist discourse meant that a lot attention was channeled towards modifying the built environment in order to mitigate the supposedly pernicious effects of the torrid tropical climate on white men. As a result, systematic bodies of knowledge on building in the colonial tropics were developed from the early nineteenth century and they were especially apparent in the design of building types such as bungalows, barracks, and hospitals.[85] The colonial environmentalist discourse on climate was not simply a neutral scientific knowledge describing natural phenomena, it was entwined with the politics of colonial governance and the related constructions of race, culture, and civilization.[86]

Secondly, climatic design, as we know it in the mid-twentieth century, was a new concept, premised on the availability of comprehensive climatic data and not the discovery of some ontological truth. For example, in North America, the comprehensive climatic data – hourly readings of wet and dry bulb temperatures and wind velocities at 110 weather bureau stations – used in a climatic design manual was only available in 1935, and the raw climatic data only became useful in 1938 when they were recorded on IBM punch cards and analyzed.[87] For the British colonial context, gathering and analyzing such comprehensive climatic data from such vast territories and varied geographies was difficult. As late as 1955, a technical officer of the Colonial Liaison Section, BRS, reported that they, along with other Colonial Liaison Sections under the DSIR, were "handicapped by the lack of climatological information for overseas territories."[88] The technical officer was reacting to the responses to their circular sent out to the various colonial meteorological organizations requesting climatological data for the colonies.[89] Most of the colonies replied that they did not have consistent meteorological and climatological data. In extreme cases like the Western Pacific and the Leeward Islands, they had "neither the staff nor the instruments to supply the data required."[90] Even for the colonies where there were summaries of existing data, those data presented many limitations. For example, effective temperature, required to ascertain thermal comfort, could not be calculated because "the summarized records of the different variables do not refer to the same observation hour."[91] In order to obtain proper climatological data, CLU tried to collaborate with the other colonial sections in DSIR. Initiatives were also made to coordinate and collaborate between the meteorological services of the different territories, both within the British Commonwealth, and between the French, Belgian, and British colonies in Africa.[92]

Despite the lack of comprehensive and precise climatological data, more systematic climatological data collection did take place through the technoscientific network that the CLU and George Atkinson built. With the preliminary data, they were able to produce a simple overview of the idea of climatic design in the tropics by putting together existing knowledge on climatology and the limited climatological data, as summarized in a graph (Figure 4).[93] Atkinson classified the tropics into three principal climatic types – warm and humid, hot and dry, and upland. In the graph, the three climatic types were represented by the examples of Freetown in Sierra Leone, Kano in Nigeria, and Nairobi in Kenya. Juxtaposed onto the graph is a zone that represents that of the thermal comfort zone. The thermal comfort standard used in the graph was based on studies done on summer conditions in the United States, presumably because no conclusive study had been done in the tropics yet. Based on the differences between the three climatic zones and the thermal comfort standard, Atkinson provided basic design guidelines on the features of buildings in the three climatic zones. For example, for the hot and humid climate, high humidity was the main cause of discomfort. Thus, the design guidelines called for buildings in the hot and humid tropics to be as open as possible, well-ventilated, and oriented towards the direction of the prevailing wind.

This effective overview of climatic design seems to do a few things. First, the complex tropics seem to become "knowable" through three principal climatic types. In privileging climate, the complex socio-political conditions of the tropics, especially the highly politicized problems regarding anti-colonial struggles, emerging nationalism, and problems of development, could seemingly be overlooked as part of this technical focus on climate. Knowing the climate almost

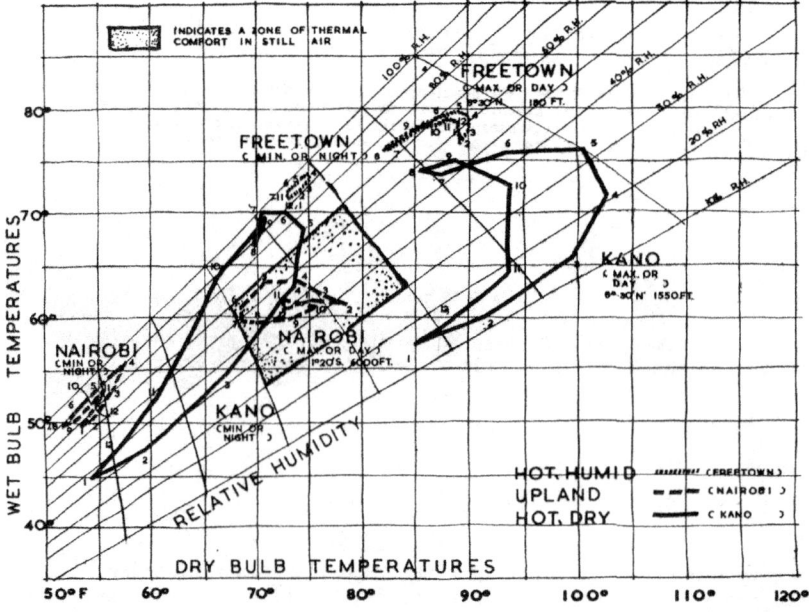

Figure 4
Thermal comfort graph.
Source: *Colonial Building Notes*.

takes the place of knowledge about the locality through the reduction, simplification, and standardization of a complex life-world into a set of climatic parameters. Secondly, knowing locality through climate might peculiarly mean that socio-politically diverse entities such as Freetown and Singapore could be conveniently grouped together because they both share the characteristics of hot and humid tropical climate. Thirdly, by representing the climate and the question of climatic design through a simple graph, which works like an immutable mobile in that it is highly transportable and is stable, climatic design facilitates "action at a distance on unfamiliar events, places and people."[94] In other words, for the British architects in the metropole, this graph, along with the related expertise on tropical building science available in what ANT would call the "center of calculation," allowed them to produce tropical architecture without even needing to travel to the colonies. Given this, it is no wonder that the special issue of *Architectural Review* focusing on Commonwealth architecture in the tropical Commonwealth featured mainly tropical architecture "*designed in England* by English architects (as in the case of many of those in West Africa) or designed by architects of English origin, largely trained in England or America, who practice locally."[95]

A postcolonial network of power-knowledge

By studying the formation and transformation of the TBD at the BRS in this chapter, I traced how building science research on tropical building problems was organized – especially how housing problems were framed and solutions proposed, and how building science research activities expanded in the British Empire. I focused on what was previously a peripheral institution in the history of tropical architecture and I explored the roles played by the much overlooked non-human actants, that is, the instruments, graphs, and numerical standards of tropical architecture. In doing so, not only did I rectify the tendency to ignore technoscientific knowledge and practices in architectural history, I also demonstrated how an imperial technoscientific infrastructure facilitated the emergence of tropical architecture in the British Empire. Besides the aforementioned, this chapter also overlaps with and, I hope, contributes to two key current discussions related to the fields of tropical architecture and Third World modernism.

The first discussion concerns what I called the "geopolitics" of tropical architecture and critical regionalism.[96] In the past few years, certain accounts have hailed tropical architecture as a variant of critical regionalism and endowed it with a capacity to resist the homogenizing forces of globalization.[97] In these accounts, climate is seen as a key attribute of a place and thus an important part of any place-based culture. As a subset of climatic design that deploys strategies of passive cooling, that is, non-mechanical means of cooling, tropical architecture is thus seen as an expression of the distinctively rooted culture of the tropics, just as the hermetically sealed architecture mechanically cooled by the air-conditioner is deemed to be the homogenizing force that erodes the place-conscious culture.[98] In contrast to the above view, it has also been argued that tropical architecture was a product of mid-twentieth century internationalism.[99] According to this view, mid-twentieth century tropical architecture in places such as West Africa was made possible by an international network of architects, institutions, and publications, with their attendant knowledge regime.

From the ANT perspective, such a conception of the global and local/ regional as opposing forces, with the former seen as the macro homogenizing structural forces imposed from above and the latter understood as the micro resisting forces countering from below, is flawed. This a priori conception of the global and local ignores how the global and local are interconnected via a network.[100] As Latour has argued, all knowledge is local. Even the purportedly universal, abstract technoscientific knowledge, or what James Scott called *episteme*,[101] started off as local knowledge in that it was produced in a specific site using specific instruments, deploying carefully calibrated techniques and under particular conditions. This local knowledge was then made "global", that is, it became an immutable mobile and could circulate to other sites and situations without distortion, through network building and a series of translations. As I have shown earlier, building standards produced by BRS only became "global" after much work. To ensure the *predictability* in performance and *replicability* in different sites and contexts, regional building research centers with the required testing facilities and measuring instruments were established, and local correspondents with the necessary expertise were assigned to provide Atkinson with local information. Atkinson also had to travel extensively to survey and understand different colonial situations, and he had to translate interests and enroll allies in his various talks and writings addressing the different groups of people connected with the building industry. It was only after all this work that locally produced building standards could behave like immutable mobiles. Latour compares such a network to the railroad model. He notes that the railroad is neither entirely local nor global. On the one hand, it is local at all points in that it has the same infrastructure of railway stations, tracks, and workers at the different locations in the network. On the other hand, it is global in that it could take one from a city or town to another city or town. However, it is not sufficiently global to take one anywhere, as there has to be railway track and stations for the train to travel and stop.[102] Seen as such, tropical architecture is only global insofar as an existing socio-technical infrastructure is in place. Tropical architecture, however, could not be considered strictly local because it is also, to a certain extent, an immutable mobile that could be replicated elsewhere within the socio-technical network.

The second discussion concerns our understanding of power in relation to colonial and postcolonial architecture. I have earlier situated the work of the TBD in relation to the larger changes in the relationship between the metropole and the colonies/periphery in the British Empire/Commonwealth in the mid-twentieth century because of decolonization and the attendant geopolitical shifts. I have argued that, in spite of the depoliticized technoscientific discourse, mid-twentieth century tropical architecture recast prior asymmetrical power-relations between the metropole and the colonies in new ways, through the production and accumulation of technoscientific knowledge. Using ANT, I showed that, through network building and attendant accumulation of technoscientific knowledge and power, the metropole became a center of calculation. I further illustrated this using the specific case of climatic design and thermal comfort. Power has become a key analytical theme in the scholarship on many colonial and postcolonial architectural histories following the emergence of postcolonial studies and its use of Foucauldian theories. However, the scholarship, as rooted in traditional art history's approach, relies mainly on formal analysis; and social, cultural and political effects are too easily correlated with formal causes. The focus tends to be on buildings as what Sibel Bozdoğan has called "visible politics"[103] in another context, that is, a highly visible and politicized image of power. As a consequence, this scholarship directs its attention towards the more visible, spectacular, and monumental public buildings – the train stations, town halls, banking headquarters, and exhibition pavilions. This scholarship tends to fall into what Arindam Dutta described as "the linear theme of power-display-knowledge ... [which] is patently inadequate to understanding the *informal* skeins of power."[104] In addition to an emerging body of scholarship on the built environment that attends more closely to the more nuanced Foucauldian conception of how power is spatialized, for example in relation to biopolitics and governmental rationality,[105] I propose that the combination of the ANT approach with the Foucauldian notion of power-knowledge in this chapter constitutes another way in which power could be conceptualized in relation to postcolonial architecture.

In short, this chapter contributes to the understanding of Third World modernism in two main ways. First, critical regionalism, which has hitherto been the conceptual category deployed in standard modern architecture history to incorporate Third World modernism into what is essentially still a Eurocentric narrative, is seen as inadequate for grasping the complex geopolitics of how Third World modernism could be understood. I am not advocating that local–global, Third World–First World and other related geopolitical binaries be simply discarded or transcended. Rather, what is necessary for understanding Third World modernism is to rethink the binaries through the concepts of network, circulation, and translation. Next, this chapter argues that Third World modernism should be studied based on a more nuanced understanding of power. Power should not be simply conceptualized as something that resides with certain political entities and is typically displayed as a form of oppressive dominance in highly visible nationalist projects, as is common in the current scholarship on Third World modernism. Power should also be understood as something more pervasive, ubiquitous and productive, shaping knowledge and practices linked to the production of the larger built environment.

Acknowledgements

I am grateful to Greig Crysler and Anthony D. King for their insightful comments on the earlier version of this chapter.

Notes

1   Notable among this scholarship are Mark Crinson, *Modern Architecture and the End of Empire* (Aldershot: Ashgate, 2003); Hannah Le Roux, "The networks of tropical architecture," *The Journal of Architecture*, 8 (2003); Rhodri Windsor-Liscombe, "Modernism in late imperial British West Africa: the work of Maxwell Fry and Jane Drew, 1946–56," *Journal of the Society of Architectural Historians*, 65, no. 2 (2006).

2   See the many technical textbooks and manuals of tropical architecture produced in the mid-twentieth century, for example Miles Danby, *Grammar of Architectural Design, with Special Reference to the Tropics* (New York: Oxford University Press, 1963), Maxwell Fry and Jane Drew, *Tropical Architecture in the Dry and Humid Zones* (London: Batsford, 1964), Georg Lippsmeier, Walter Kluska, and Carol Gray Edrich, *Tropenbau/Building in the Tropics* (Munchen: Callwey, 1969), David Oakley, *Tropical Houses: A Guide to Their Design* (London: Batsford, 1961).

3   David J. Hess, *Science Studies: An Advanced Introduction* (New York: New York University Press, 1997).

4   Donna Haraway, "Situated knowledges: the science question in feminism and the privilege of partial perspective," *Feminist Studies*, 14, no. 3 (1988).

5   Latour made a similar argument, stating that all knowledges are local, except that the purportedly "universal" knowledge is one that has the "shape of a network transporting back and forth immutable mobiles to act a distance." Bruno Latour, *Science in Action: How to Follow Scientists and Engineers through Society* (Cambridge: Harvard University Press, 1987), p. 229. Such a standpoint epistemology seeks to negotiate between the dichotomy of objectivism and relativism. It objects to the reductive idea of objectivity-as-transcendence, or the "god trick of seeing everything from nowhere." Haraway, op. cit., p. 581.

6   Warwick Anderson, "Introduction: postcolonial technoscience," *Social Studies of Science*, 32, no. 5/6, Special Issue: Postcolonial Technoscience (2002); Michael A. Osborne, "Introduction: the social history of science, technoscience and imperialism," *Science, Technology & Society*, 4, no. 2 (1999); Gyan Prakash, *Another Reason: Science and the Imagination of Modern India* (Princeton: Princeton University Press, 1999).

7   Stephen J. Collier and Aihwa Ong, "Global assemblages, anthropological problems," in *Global Assemblages: Technology, Politics, and Ethics as Anthropological Problems*, Aihwa Ong and Stephen J. Collier (eds), (Malden, MA: Blackwell Publishing, 2005).

8   Actant is used in place of actor of the classical social theory of Parsonian functionalism so that the non-human actants could be attributed with the agency of shaping technological outcomes.

9   The recent so-called "Science Wars" between the natural scientists and the social scientists is a case in point. A group of natural scientists accused social scientists in STS of assaulting rationality and objectivity, caricaturing it as an "antiscience movement" and its exponents as "postmodern" relativists and "science bashers." For an overview of the "Science Wars," see Andrew Ross, "Introduction," *Social Text* 46/47, Science Wars (1996).

10   For a related critique of tropical architecture as a "natural" variant, see Jiat-Hwee Chang, "Tropical variants of sustainable architecture: a postcolonial perspective," in *Handbook of Architectural Theory*, Greig Crysler, Stephen Cairns, and Hilde Heynen (eds), (London: Sage, forthcoming).

11   "Housing research in the colonies: report by the Housing Research Group" enclosed in CO dispatch dated 4 December 1945. PRO CO927/6/7, *Housing Research in the Colonies: Proposal to Establish a Housing Research Centre in West Africa*.

12   PRO CO1005/1, *Colonial Housing Research Group: Minutes and Papers*.

13   D. B. Blacklock, *An Empire Problem: The House and Village in the Tropics* (London: Hodder & Stoughton Ltd, 1932).

14   Anthony Clayton, "Browne, Sir Granville St John Orde (1883–1947)," in *Oxford Dictionary of National Biography* (Oxford: Oxford University Press, 2004). An example of the type of detailed report Browne published on colonial labor problems is G. St. J. Orde Browne, *Labour Conditions in Ceylon, Mauritius, and Malaya* (London: HMSO, 1943).

15   CO927/6/7, Housing Research.

16   Ibid.

17   For the work of the Bombay and Calcutta Improvement Trust, see Robert K. Home, *Of Planting and Planning: The Making of British Colonial Cities* (London: Spon, 1997), pp. 85–116. For the Singapore Improvement Trust, see J. M. Fraser, *The Work of the Singapore Improvement Trust 1927–1947* (Singapore: Singapore Improvement Trust, 1948).

18   J. G. Hibbert in a letter dated December 19 1947. CO927/6/7, *Housing Research*.

19   Ibid.

20   Frederick Cooper, "Modernizing Bureaucrats, Backward Africans, and the Development Concept," in *International Development and the Social Sciences: Essays on the History and Politics of Knowledge*, Frederick Cooper and Randall M. Packard (eds), (Berkeley: University of California Press, 1997).

21   For a history of British colonial development, see Michael A. Havinden and David Meredith, *Colonialism and Development: Britain and Its Tropical Colonies, 1850–1960* (London: Routledge, 1993).

22   Frederick Cooper and Randall M. Packard, "Introduction," in *International Development and the Social Sciences: Essays on the History and Politics of Knowledge*, Frederick Cooper and Randall M. Packard (eds), (Berkeley: University of California Press, 1997).

23   PRO CO927/7/1, *Proposals for Building Research Programme in the British West Indies and British Guiana*. Frank Stockdale, Robert Gardner-Medwin, and S. M. de Syllas, "Recent planning developments in the colonies," *RIBA Journal*, 55 (1948). Gardner-Medwin was to become an expert on housing in the tropics and the Roscoe Professor of Architecture at Liverpool University. Norman Kingham, "Obituary: Professor Robert Gardner-Medwin," *The Independent*, July 8 1995.

24   Besides Evans, Blacklock, and Browne, the Group consisted of Mary Blacklock of Liverpool School of Tropical Medicine; R. H. Burt of CO; C. Y. Carstairs, secretary of the Colonial Research Committee; S. E. Chandler and S. J. Johnstone of the Imperial Institute; R. W. Foxlee, deputy chief engineer to the Crown Agents for the colonies; and W. H. Kauntze, deputy medical advisor, CO. For the work of the Crown Agents, see "Work of the Crown Agents," *The Crown Colonist*, Preliminary Number (1931). For the Imperial Institute's involvement in colonial research, see Michael Worboys, "The Imperial Institute: the state and the development of the natural resources of the colonial empire, 1887–1923," in *Imperialism and the Natural World*, John M. Mackenzie (ed.) (Manchester: Manchester University Press, 1990). For British imperial research on tropical medicine, see Douglas Melvin Haynes, "The social production of metropolitan expertise in tropical diseases: the Imperial State, Colonial Service and Tropical Diseases Research Fund," *Science, Technology & Society*, 4, no. 2 (1999).

25   BRS, *The Building Research Station: Its History, Organization and Work* (Garston, Watford: BRS, 1954); F. M. Lea, *Science and Building: A History of the Building Research Station* (London: HMSO, 1971).

26   The two BRS officers were R. W. Nurse and A. W. Pott. CO927/6/7, *Housing Research*, PRO DSIR4/2524, *Establishment of a Building Research Station on the Gold Coast*.

27   Michael Worboys, "The Discovery of Colonial Malnutrition between the Wars," in *Imperial Medicine and Indigenous Societies*, David Arnold (ed.) (Manchester: Manchester University Press, 1988).

28   Arturo Escobar also makes a similar argument about the development discourses and practices in the mid-twentieth century. See Arturo Escobar, *Encountering Development: The Making and Unmaking of the Third World* (Princeton: Princeton University Press, 1995).

29   "Housing Research in the Colonies." CO927/6/7, *Housing Research.*

30   Ibid.

31   Haynes, op. cit.

32   This insistence on the division of labor between "pure science" research in the metropole and the "applied science" research in the colony was also evident in the tense relationship between the two agencies created to advance and apply science in British India – the Indian Advisory Committee of the Royal Society based in the metropole and the Board of Scientific Advice of the Government of India. See Roy MacLeod, "Scientific advice for British India: imperial perceptions and administrative goals, 1898–1923," *Modern Asian Studies*, 9, no 3 (1975). Such a division between the center and the periphery is never really stable, however much the imperialist would like to maintain it, because it is subjected to contestations and internal contradictions. See David Wade Chambers and Richard Gillespie, "Locality in the history of science: colonial science, technoscience, and indigenous knowledge," *Osiris*, 15, special issue on nature and empire: science and the colonial enterprise (2000).

33   CO927/6/7, *Housing Research.*

34   This economic relation is best expressed by Leo Amery, the British Secretary of State for the Colonies in the 1920s. He said: "One of the most striking features of modern industrial development is the marriage of tropical production to the industrial production of the temperate zone. They are essentially complementary regions, and owing to their character and the character of their inhabitants they are likely to remain so." Quoted in Havinden and Meredith, op. cit., 169.

35   For world system theory, see Immanuel M. Wallerstein, *World-Systems Analysis: An Introduction* (Durham: Duke University Press, 2004). For world system theory in relation to architecture and urbanism, see Anthony D. King, *Urbanism, Colonialism, and the World-Economy: Cultural and Spatial Foundations of the World Urban System* (London: Routledge, 1990).

36   See, for example, Roy MacLeod, "Introduction to special issue on nature and empire: science and the colonial enterprise," *Osiris* 15 (2000); Paolo Palladino and Michael Worboys, "Critiques and Contentions: Science and Imperialism," *Isis* 84, no. 1 (1993).

37   Havinden and Meredith, op. cit.

38   Ibid., Worboys, "The Imperial Institute."

39   Sir Charles Joseph Jeffries (ed.), *A Review of Colonial Research, 1940–1960* (London: HMSO, 1964).

40   Cooper and Packard, op. cit.

41   Escobar, op. cit., p. 10. See also Wolfgang Sachs (ed.), *The Development Dictionary: A Guide to Knowledge as Power* (London: Zed Books, 1992).

42   PRO CO927/35/5, *Proposed Colonial Housing Bureau: Appointment of Colonial Liaison Officer to Dsir.*

43   Lea, op. cit., p. 163.

44   See Secretary of State for the Colonies' circular, "Cost of buildings in the Colonies," dated July 27 1948. CO927/35/5, *Proposed Colonial Housing Bureau.*

45   Ibid.

46   George Anthony Atkinson, "Tropical architecture and building standards," in *Conference on Tropical Architecture 1953: A Report of the Proceedings of the Conference Held at University College, London, March 1953*, Arthur Foyle (ed.) (London: University College London, 1953).

47   For the case of the bungalow, see Anthony D. King, *The Bungalow: The Production of a Global Culture*, 2nd edn (New York: Oxford University Press, 1995 [1984]). For the hospital, see Jiat-Hwee Chang, "Tropicalising technologies of environment and government: the Singapore General Hospital and the circulation of the pavilion plan hospital in the British Empire, 1860–1930," in *Re-Shaping Cities: How Global Mobility Transforms Architecture and Urban Form*, Michael Guggenheim and Ola Söderström (eds), (London: Routledge, 2009). For British India's PWD standardization, see Peter Scriver, "Empire-building and thinking in the Public Works Department of British India," in *Colonial Modernities: Building, Dwelling and Architecture in British India and Ceylon*, Peter Scriver and Vikramāditya Prakāsh (eds) (London: Routledge, 2007).

48   According to Atkinson, prior to the establishment of BRS, building research was carried out in a fragmentary and unrelated manner. Some of the results were published in journals such as *The Builder* and *The Civil Engineer*, etc. Building research was fragmentary because the building industry was dominated by small firms that were resource-poor. Moreover, the industry was characterized by the diversity of fields and it was also further split by the division of labor into different specializations. See George Anthony Atkinson, "Thoughts during the Building Research Establishment's 75th anniversary," *Construction History*, 12 (1996).

49   Lea, op. cit., p. 2.

50   "The Building Research Station: its origin, work and scope," *Journal of the Royal Institute of British Architects*, 43 (1936).

51   Ibid., p. 790. Scientific research in building during the mid-twentieth century should also be understood in relation to the institutionalization of the sub-field of "building science" at the same time. See chapter 4 of Jiat-Hwee Chang, "A genealogy of tropical architecture: Singapore in the British (post)colonial networks of nature, technoscience and governmentality, 1830s to 1960s" (unpublished Ph.D. dissertation, University of California at Berkeley, 2009).

52   Latour, op. cit., pp. 215–57.

53   John Law and John Hassard, *Actor Network Theory and After* (Malden, MA: Blackwell, 1999).

54   See, for example, Atkinson's visit to Singapore. George Anthony Atkinson, "The work of the colonial liaison building officer and building in the tropics," *The Quarterly Journal of the Institute of Architects of Malaya*, 2, no. 1 (1952).

55   George Anthony Atkinson: "British architects in the tropics," *Architectural Association Journal*, 69 (1953), "Building in the tropics," *RIBA Journal*, 57 (1950), "Principles of tropical design," *Architectural Review*, 128 (1960), "West Indian houses," *Architectural Association Journal*, 67 (1952).

56   George Anthony Atkinson: "Building techniques overseas," *Prefabrication*, 1, no. 9 (1954), "Building techniques overseas – II," *Prefabrication*, 1, no. 10 (1954).

57   Atkinson, "The work of the colonial liaison building officer and building in the tropics."

58   George Anthony Atkinson, "African housing," *African Affairs*, 49, no. 196 (1950).

59   Lea describes the research on climatic design as work on "the functional efficiency of buildings in the tropics." See Lea, op. cit., 165.

60   PRO DSIR4/3361, *Tropical Building Division*.

61   Ibid.

62   He was included in the list of lecturers and critics of the 1954 and 1955 Prospectuses for Department of Tropical Architecture at the Architectural Association.

63   D. C. Robinson, "Towards a tropical architecture: the work of Architects Co-Partnership in Nigeria," *Architectural Design*, April (1959).

64   PRO CO927/35/2, *Trinidad: Proposed Establishment of Building Research Station*.

65   DSIR4/3361, *Tropical Building Division*.

66   Natal Regional Research Committee and the University of Natal, *Symposium on Design for Tropical Living* (Durban: The University of Natal, 1957).

67   See PRO DSIR4/3647, *Council of Scientific and Industrial Research: Establishment of a Building Research Station in India*.

68   Bruno Latour, "On recalling ANT," in *Actor Network Theory and After*, John Law and John Hassard (eds), (Malden, MA: Blackwell, 1999).

69   Latour, *Science in Action*, p. 108.

70   For an overview of some of the problems of articulating interest narrowly as economic self-interest not covered in this paper, see Corinne P. Hayden, *When Nature Goes Public: The Making and Unmaking of Bioprospecting in Mexico* (Princeton: Princeton University Press, 2003), pp. 19–29.

71   Pierre Bourdieu, *Practical Reason: On the Theory of Action* (Stanford: Stanford University Press, 1998), pp. 92–123.

72   Atkinson, "British architects in the tropics."

73   Atkinson, "The work of the colonial liaison building officer and building in the tropics," p. 36.

74   Atkinson: "Building techniques overseas", "Building techniques overseas – II."

75   Henry J. Cowan, "The Architectural Science Laboratory," *Royal Institute of British Architects Journal*, 66, no. 12 (1959). Cowan claims that he is the first professor of building science in his autobiography. See Henry J. Cowan, *A Contradiction in Terms: The Autobiography of Henry J. Cowan* (Sydney: Hermitage Press, 1993).

76   The RIBA Joint Committee on the Orientation of Buildings, *The Orientation of Buildings, Being the Report with Appendices of the RIBA Joint Committee on the Orientation of Buildings* (London: RIBA, 1933).

77   George Anthony Atkinson, "Construction and erection of the heliodon," *Colonial Building Notes*, 26, January (1955): 12.

78   DSIR4/3361, *Tropical Building Division*.

79   Ibid.

80   Lea, op. cit.

81   John Law, "Technology and heterogeneous engineering: the case of Portuguese expansion," in *The Social Construction of Technological Systems: New Directions in the Sociology and History of Technology*, Wiebe E. Bijker, Thomas P. Hughes, and T. J. Pinch (eds), (Cambridge, MA: MIT Press, 1987), p. 114.

82   Latour, *Science in Action*, p. 180.

83   Building Research Advisory Board, *Weather and the Building Industry; a Research Correlation Conference on Climatological Research and Its Impact on Building Design, Construction, Materials and Equipment, National Academy of Science, January 11 and 12, 1950* (Washington: Building Research Advisory Board, Division of Engineering and Industrial Research, National Research Council, 1950).

84   See Le Roux, op. cit.; Alexander Tzonis and Liane Lefaivre, "The suppression and rethinking of regionalism and tropicalism after 1945," in *Tropical Architecture: Critical Regionalism in the Age of Globalization*, Alexander Tzonis, Bruno Stagno, and Liane Lefaivre (eds), (Chichester: Wiley-Academic, 2001).

85   See Chang, "A genealogy of tropical architecture"; King, *The Bungalow*.

86   See, for example, David Arnold, *The Problem of Nature: Environment, Culture and European Expansion* (Oxford: Blackwell, 1996), pp. 141–68; Felix Driver and Brenda S. A. Yeoh, "Constructing the tropics: introduction," *Singapore Journal of Tropical Geography*, 21, no. 1 (2000).

87   Walter A. Taylor, "Regional climate analyses and design data," in *The House Beautiful Climate Control Project: Regional Climate Analyses and Design Data*, American Institute of Architects (ed.) (Washington: American Institute of Architects, 1949–52), p. 556.

88   PRO CO937/365, *The Role of Meteorology and Climatology in Tropical Building and Housing.*

89   Ibid.

90   Ibid.

91   Ibid.

92   Ibid.

93   George Anthony Atkinson, "Warm climates and building design," *Colonial Building Notes*, 12, April (1953).

94   Latour, *Science in Action*. See also the literature in science technology studies and actor network theory, for example, T. J. Pinch, Thomas Parke Hughes, and Wiebe E. Bijker (eds), *The Social Construction of Technological Systems: New Directions in the Sociology and History of Technology* (Cambridge, MA: MIT Press, 1987).

95   Editors, "Editorial: Commonwealth 2," *Architectural Review*, 127 (1960).

96   Much has been written about the problems of critical regionalism. Especially notable for critical regionalism in the context of the developing countries are Mark Crinson, "Singapore's moment: critical regionalism, its colonial roots and profound aftermaths," *The Journal of Architecture*, 13, no. 5 (2008); Keith L. Eggener, "Placing resistance: a critique of critical regionalism," *Journal of Architectural Education*, 55, no. 4 (2002).

97   See, for example, the essays in Alexander Tzonis, Bruno Stagno, and Liane Lefaivre (eds), *Tropical Architecture: Critical Regionalism in the Age of Globalization* (Chichester: Wiley-Academic, 2001).

98   Kenneth Frampton, "Towards a critical regionalism: six points for an architecture of resistance," in *The Anti-Aesthetic: Essays on Postmodern Culture*, Hal Foster (ed.) (New York: New Press, 1998 [1983]).

99   See, for example, Le Roux, op. cit.

100   Bruno Latour, *Reassembling the Social: An Introduction into Actor-Network-Theory* (Oxford: Oxford University Press, 2005), pp. 173–90.

101   James C. Scott, *Seeing Like a State: How Certain Schemes to Improve the Human Condition Have Failed* (New Haven: Yale University Press, 1998).

102   Bruno Latour, *We Have Never Been Modern* (Cambridge, MA: Harvard University Press, 1993), p. 117.

103   Sibel Bozdoğan, *Modernism and Nation Building: Turkish Architectural Culture in the Early Republic* (Seattle: University of Washington Press, 2001).

104   Arindam Dutta, "Review of Mark Crinson, Modern Architecture and the End of Empire (Aldershot: Ashgate, 2003)," *Journal of the Society of Architectural Historians*, 67, no. 2 (2008), p. 293.

105   See, for example, Chang, "Tropicalising technologies of environment and government"; Stephen Legg, *Spaces of Colonialism: Delhi's Urban Governmentalities* (Malden: Blackwell, 2007).

Chapter 10

Otto Koenigsberger and the Tropicalization of British Architectural Culture

Vandana Baweja

Climate responsive design was central to the Third Worldist practice of Tropical Architecture during the 1950s and 1960s. However, climate responsiveness, which meant designing a building climate specifically so that it could function with minimum or no mechanical conditioning, seemed redundant to European and North American architects. In particular, Peter and Alison Smithson, who established themselves as the new generation of British postwar architects with the Hunstanton School in 1949, were critical of the climate responsive design method of Tropical Architecture. In 1960, in an article titled "The function of architecture in cultures-in-change" in the journal *Architectural Design*, they addressed the problem of generating architectural form in the tropics, which were going through rapid modernization. They wrote:

> It is no good looking to the climate and the physical environment to give the form of the building. Technically, a glass box and a mass-concrete cave can produce the same comfort conditions, if one can afford the right mechanical equipment. It all depends what you are after. The shape of the culture can only be built up by separate individual form-giving decisions towards a common ideal – however vague this ideal may seem at the present.[1]

In a complete reversal of the Smithsons' 1960 criticism of climatic design, in 1994 a retrospective exhibition of their work, titled *Climate Register*, opened at the Architectural Association (AA) School of Architecture in London. Lorenzo Wong, their associate, defined *Climate Register* as "The notion to uncover particular environmental resonances and qualities of space and place in four projects by Alison and Peter Smithson: the Economist Building, London; Second Arts Building, Bath; Kuwait-mat Building; and Alexandria Library."[2]

The projects showcased in *Climate Register* underscored climate responsiveness as a characteristic of the Smithsons' architecture. In this chapter, I address the following questions: How did the Smithsons transform from hubristic believers in the power of technology to control indoor climate, to designers who believed in climate responsiveness as an act of place making? How did they develop climate responsiveness in their designs? And what was their notion of climate responsiveness, and how did it differ from the climatic design method of Tropical Architects? I argue that the discourse and practice of Tropical Architecture at the AA School of Architecture in London introduced the Smithsons to climate responsive design in the 1960s. The Smithsons collaborated with Otto Koenigsberger (1909–99), the director of the department of Tropical Architecture at the AA, as the tropical advisor for their unbuilt tropical projects: the British Embassy in Brasilia (1964) and the Kuwait Mat-Building (1969). These tropical projects transformed their architectural thinking to include climate responsiveness in their later domestic works, such as the Second Arts Building in Bath, England (1979–81). This chapter rests on the premise that climate conscious design, the paradigm central to Tropical Architecture, developed through the interaction of European modernist architects with colonial architectural cultures in the tropics, which were reconstituted as the Third World after the Second World War.[3]

Tropical Architecture: from hygiene to architecture

The practice of Tropical Architecture has its origins in the discipline of hygiene in the British and French colonies, which constituted a significant portion of the climatic zone that we call the tropics. In order to understand how Tropical Architecture was transformed from a colonial hygiene practice into a Third World Modern architectural movement, I begin with the definition of the tropics in colonial histories. As scholars have noted, the tropics were not only a physical climatic zone enclosed by the tropics, but a discursive construct that were produced by knowledge from several disciplines, including geography, anthropology, zoology, botany, medicine, and hygiene.[4] David Arnold argues that the foundational principle on which the discourse of tropicality rested was the notion that in the tropics, nature dominated all spheres of life and could not be controlled.[5] This orientalist belief defined disciplinary tropical practices in fields such as medicine, hygiene, and eventually architecture. In the sphere of architecture, tropicality translated as climate responsive design. Tropical Architecture as an architectural discipline developed somewhat belatedly at the end of the British Empire after the Second World War.

In the late nineteenth and early twentieth centuries, the discourse of Tropical Architecture developed in the discipline of hygiene and circulated through colonial hygiene manuals. From the 1930s through the 1950s, Tropical Architecture established its disciplinary home in the field of architecture through a number of inter-colonial conferences held globally, not only in the imperial capitals such as Paris, Lisbon, Washington, D.C., and London, but also in the former and existing colonies, such as India, Uganda, and Nairobi. The first conference on Tropical Architecture was organized in Paris under the chairmanship of Henri Prost and Marshall Lyautey.[6] The International Federation organized the next conference on Tropical Architecture for Housing and Planning in Mexico.[7] These interwar conferences served as a forum of exchange for colonial architects and planners and facilitated the establishment of Tropical Architecture as an institutionally endorsed architectural discipline.

In the 1950s, Tropical Architecture completely migrated from the discipline of hygiene to architecture and was recast as Modernism for the tropics, which were largely the decolonizing and decolonized zones of the British and French Empires. In its 1950s and 1960s incarnation, Tropical Architecture became a Modernist movement that was based largely on the notion that Modern Architecture in the Third World tropics should be based on climate responsive design. Architects practicing in the Third World tropics were aware that they could use mechanical means of climate control, but the economic conditions in the Third World tropical countries made mechanical conditioning unaffordable. The most significant practicing architects and educators in the field of postwar Tropical Architecture included Otto Koenisgberger, Jane Drew and Maxwell Fry, Geoffrey Bawa, Fello Atkinson, George Atkinson, and Leo De Syllas.

In 1954, the AA School of Architecture in London became the first school of architecture to establish a department dedicated to Tropical Architecture. In the 1950s and 1960s, as most of the former colonial tropics were reconstituted as the "Third World," Tropical Architecture flourished as a climate responsive design movement in the Third World along the networks of the British Empire.[8]

This chapter shows how ideas developed through a Third Worldist architectural movement impacted the work of Peter and Alison Smithson in London long after the demise of the Empire and Tropical Architecture movement in the early 1970s. I propose that Otto Koenigsberger, one of the key players in the Department of Tropical Architecture at the AA, influenced the Smithsons in changing their ideas about the relationship between climate and architecture.

Otto Koenigsberger

Climate responsiveness had different and changing meanings for Koenigsberger and the Smithsons. In order to convey the impact of Tropical Architecture on the Smithsons, I would like to present Koenigsberger's career trajectory to show how it intersected with the Smithsons' career, *vis-à-vis* the relationship between climate and architecture. As one of the founders of the Department of Tropical Architecture at the Architectural Association, Koenigsberger established himself as an expert on climate responsive architecture in the tropics in the 1960s. In the following section, I establish how Koenisgberger became an expert on Tropical Architecture.

Otto Koenigsberger was trained as an architect at the Technical University of Berlin as a student of Hans Poelzig from 1927 to 1931. His mentors included Bruno Taut and Heinrich Tessenow. He worked briefly with Ernst May and won the Schinkel Prize in 1933 for a design for the forthcoming 1936 Olympics in Berlin. He was dismissed from service by Hitler's government in 1933, at which point he proceeded from Berlin to Egypt and worked as an archeologist. During his work in Egypt, he produced his doctoral thesis on the construction of the ancient Egyptian door. Koenigsberger's thesis was accepted in Berlin in 1935. [9]

In 1939, Koenigsberger had the choice of two jobs: teaching hieroglyphics at the University of Michigan in Ann Arbor or becoming the chief architect of the Mysore State in India. Koenigsberger chose India, arriving in Mysore in 1939 as an émigré architect at the invitation of Sir Mirza Ismail, the *Dewan* (Prime Minister) of Mysore State. Mysore was a South Indian province under indirect British rule, which meant that the Maharajah of Mysore paid a subsidy to the British for military protection. In 1956, Princely Mysore was territorially subsumed into the larger Mysore state, and in 1973, it was renamed Karnataka.

Koenigsberger served as Chief Architect of the Public Works Department (PWD) in Mysore from 1939 to 1948. While in India, Koenigsberger also served as a planner to corporate houses, such as the Tatas, and to the government of India. In 1945, Koenigsberger prepared the third-phase plans for the industrial town of Jamshedpur. [10] In 1948, he also served as planner for Bhubaneswar, the capital of Orissa. [11]

In 1948, as India became independent and Princely Mysore became part of the Union of India, Koenigsberger moved to Delhi and became the Federal Director of Housing (1948–51) for the Ministry of Health in Nehru's government. His work for Nehru involved both planning and architecture projects to resettle partition refugees. From 1948 to 1951, Koenigsberger served as planning advisor to the New Towns of Faridabad, Rajpura, Gandhidham, and Sindri, which were developed to resettle partition refugees. [12]

To solve this massive housing demand problem posed by partition refugees under Nehru, Koenigsberger proposed a pre-fabricated housing module for resettling the refugees. The housing units did not succeed, and Koenigsberger subsequently resigned from his position as the Federal Director of Housing and went to England. In 1951, he moved to London and in 1954 founded the Department of Tropical Architecture (1954–71) at the AA. Koenigsberger headed the Department of Tropical Architecture from 1957 until its closure in 1971. In 1970, Koenigsberger established the Development Planning Unit (DPU) at University College London (UCL), which he led until he retired in 1988. He died in London in 1999.

Koenigsberger is best known for his treatise on Tropical Architecture called *Manual of Tropical Housing and Building*, a textbook on climate responsive design for the tropics.[13] As a student in India, I studied Koenisgberger's textbook in my second year in the architecture school in a mandatory class on climatology. This book continues to be prescribed for undergraduate architectural curricula in most Third World tropical countries and also appears on reading lists for Green Architecture. Based on Koenigsberger's writings, I define Tropical Architecture paradigmatically as climate responsive and energy conservative design that makes the best possible use of locally available resources.

Koenisgberger in Mysore, India

Koenigsberger began theorizing Tropical Architecture in Mysore. The project through which he began to formulate Tropical Architecture as a climate responsive design was the Mysore *Akashvani* Building (Mysore Broadcasting House, 1942), now the All India Radio Building (AIR) at Mysore (Figure 1). In an article on the Broadcasting House Building at Mysore, Koenigsberger wrote how he derived the form of the building purely from the climatic requirements. Even though Mysore has a pleasant climate, the contradictory requirements of acoustics and thermal comfort posed a challenge for Koenigsberger. Acoustics demanded a hermetically sealed building, while thermal comfort demanded either openable windows or air-conditioning in the studios. Due to cost and energy constraints, the building could not be air-conditioned.

Koenigsberger began to develop and theorize climate responsive design through passive techniques in Mysore. He devised a building section by

Figure 1
Mysore Broadcasting House. Photograph taken by the author.

which the building would be ventilated during the hours when the studio was not on air. The studio has double glazed ventilators placed at high level, yet accessible by attendants. The shutters were opened when the studio was off air, but closed for the brief time that the studio went on air. He recorded his AIR project as an example of how architectural form ought to be generated according to climatic requirements. This project furthered Koenigsberger's interest in theorizing climate responsive architecture as a balancing act between contradictory design requirements, such as how to let in light and fresh air without compromising the acoustical requirements. In India, he was forced to work with what we now call passive technologies, using renewable sources of energy such as wind and natural light.

To use passive techniques in order to design for conflicting requirements, such as letting in breeze without excessive light, would be a recurring theme in Tropical Architecture later in London. This kind of contradiction frequently constituted studio design problems at the AA later. After his experience in India, Koenigsberger would always practice universal energy conservation as a principle, not just as a specific design requirement. Even in places like Kuwait, where energy was abundant and cheap, he always recommended passive design techniques to conserve energy.

Climate responsive design in architectural historiography

Climate responsive design constitutes an important phase in the development of passive technology, solar architecture, and Green Architecture.[14] From the early 1930s to the end of the 1960s, climate responsive design matured as a global phenomenon, developing as Bio-Climatic Architecture in the United States and as Tropical Architecture in Asia and Africa along the networks of the British and French Empires. In the United States, the Hungarian-born twins Victor and Aladar Olgyay produced a significant corpus of knowledge on Bio-Climatic design.[15]

Tropical Architecture occupies a marginal position in Euro-centric modernist architectural historiography both because of its engagement with the tropics and because energy conservative design seemed redundant to European and American architects prior to 1970s. In the 1950s and 1960s, the cheap and abundant availability of energy sharply decreased interest in climatic design and energy conservative design practices.[16] Only after the OPEC oil crises in 1973 did energy conservation and climate responsiveness emerge as significant environmental concerns in American and European mainstream architectural discourses.[17]

Existing postcolonial histories of modern architecture view Tropical Architecture as a colonial orientalist construct and as a British neo-colonial project in the tropics at the end of the Empire.[18] Environmental discourses construct Tropical Architecture as a value-neutral scientific climatic design discourse.[19] My larger project addresses how Tropical Architecture exists in separate historiographies of Modern Architecture and environmental architecture and how the two intersect.[20] While Tropical Architecture was undoubtedly a discursive construct to reinforce the colony-metropole relationships at the end of the Empire, there is little or no scholarship that examines the impact of Tropical Architecture on architects in London and the location of Tropical Architecture in the environmental histories of architecture. To address this gap in scholarship, in this chapter I will focus on how the Smithsons adopted certain aspects of Tropical Architecture and climate responsiveness in their domestic work. In other words, how did the orientalist construct of Tropical Architecture impact the thinking of London architects such as the Smithsons? What was the afterlife of Tropical Architecture once it died as a movement in the colonial tropics, which became the Third World? In this chapter, I look at how Koenigsberger's ideas about climate responsiveness in the field of Tropical Architecture impacted the Smithsons.

I propose that although Tropical Architecture was intended to be a neo-colonial project at the end of the Empire, it also paradoxically became a platform for the development of climate responsive design and architectural practices that were critical of reckless energy and resource consumption.

The Smithsons and Tropical Architecture

Tropical Architecture at the AA began as a regionalist discourse for the tropics and evolved into energy conscious design. Tropical Architecture meant architecture climatically appropriate for the tropical context. The term "climate" referred not only to the physical climate, but also to both the local technological capacity and the socio-economic context. By the mid-1960s, Koenigsberger specifically used climate responsiveness to achieve what Rayner Banham called "selective mode" to conserve energy.[21] Selective mode translated, in Koenigsberger's vocabulary, into "naturally conditioned," which he defined as selecting and controlling the environmental features to minimize exposure to unwanted climatic conditions and maximize exposure to desirable climatic features.[22] By the 1960s, for Koenigsberger climate consciousness had become synonymous with energy consciousness. By the late 1990s, climate responsive architecture was subsumed into Green Architecture.

The Smithsons established themselves with the winning entry for the competition of the Hunstanton School in 1949. The Smithsons' brutalist expression of exposed mechanical services in Hunstanton and their liberation from climatic constraints through mechanically conditioned buildings forms the prehistory of their 1960 criticism of climatic determinism. In the 1950s, with lowered energy costs due to tropical oil, the interest in developing climate responsive low energy buildings in Europe and the USA declined in the absence of a market for these design technologies.[23] European and American architects, who felt liberated from climate as the source of architectural form, were busy experimenting with the formal expression of mechanical services, which ranged from invisibility, as in the pure glass box, to Kahn's formal experiments with servant and served spaces.[24] At this point in history, Tropical Architects in London and the tropics were acutely aware of the prohibitive costs of mechanical conditioning. In response, they developed a climate conscious and energy conservative architecture, which constituted Tropical Architecture. By the 1960s, energy conservation through passive design became central to Tropical Architecture and was implemented irrespective of cost constraints, long before energy consciousness was taken seriously in the European and American architectural cultures.

The Smithsons' relationship with climatic responsiveness and Tropical Architecture evolved over their career. I argue that prior to collaborating with Koenigsberger, the Smithsons were apprehensive of the application of Tropical Design principles. As their career evolved, they developed a more nuanced approach to climatic design. Initially, they appreciated Tropical Architecture for its cultural sensitivity, but they feared that the dominance of climatic design over other aspects of architecture was problematic. The Smithsons began engaging with Tropical Architecture in 1955 when they regarded ATBAT-Afrique's Moroccan housing project as a "fine" example of Tropical Architecture in terms of its cultural and climatic sensitivity.[25] Revisionist histories of postwar modernism establish how Team X's notion of "habitat" was shaped by ATBAT-Afrique's Tropical Urban experiments in the Moroccan housing project.[26]

In an essay titled "An alternative to the garden city idea," the Smithsons proposed three principles that would result in better towns. They suggested that climate responsiveness practiced by Tropical Architects could be used to establish a "positive relationship with site and climate."[27] They began by defining Tropical Architecture as climate responsive design, in the following words:

> For the design of buildings and layout of towns in tropical areas, it is an accepted method to establish the general principles of design by considering the ways in which the bad effects of the climate can be ameliorated and its beneficial effects exploited.[28]

At the level of the home, the Smithsons elaborated how English architecture could be tropicalized or follow the principles of Tropical Architecture through climate responsiveness. They wrote:

> The English climate is not characterized by intense rain or cold but by changeability. The house, therefore, should be capable of grasping what fine weather it can get, grasping solar heat through south windows into the rooms and giving easy access to sheltered patios, roof gardens, or terraces which can be arranged in a moment to catch the pleasures of our climate and then closed up in a moment so that we can ignore it.[29]

However, the Smithsons' translation of climate responsiveness into urban form was naïve. To them, urban forms such as town squares were suited to warmer climates, where people could be comfortable outdoors. However, the wet and cold English climate placed severe limitations on the use of urban forms such as pedestrian streets and squares. To ameliorate the effects of the English climate, the Smithsons proposed a covered indoor urban space. They wrote:

> But our climate would seem to demand that the circulation between such things as shops, places of entertainment, municipal offices, etc. should take place under cover. And if we have cars we want to be able to use them for just those things that take place at the centre. The big hotel with its foyers, shops, restaurants, palm courts, etc. under centralized control and with adequate parking arrangements is the prototype for this type of indoor centre.[30]

By climate responsive, they did not mean energy conservative buildings or architectural form determined by climate. Their notion of climate responsiveness in England was a hotel with foyer and shops, protected from the cold climate through mechanical conditioning and suited to an automobile intensive lifestyle. They confused climate responsiveness with energy intensive protection from climate. Their notion of climate differences between temperate and tropical living translated simplistically into indoor and outdoor living. They later retracted their idea of a central hotel as a climate responsive structure. In a footnote in the article, they claim to have revised their notion of the hotel with a foyer as an urban form responsive to England's climate.

What made the Smithsons appreciative of regional aspects of Tropical Architecture, yet critical of climatic design? They were dismissive of climate as the *only* consideration in the generation of architectural form, as is evident in their 1960 criticism of climatic determinism.[31] At the AA's Tropical Department, climate and pragmatic technological considerations were privileged over the emotional, intellectual, and painterly aspects of architecture.[32] The Smithsons were critical of this "form follows climate" approach of Tropical Architecture because they felt that the climate responsive design approach suppressed cultural functions of architecture. They perceived a split between architecture as an object of physical protection from the climate, and architecture as a form of cultural expression of the spirit and time of a place. They proposed that although Tropical Architecture functioned well as physical protection, its architects did not pay any attention to the cultural aspects of architecture in the tropics. They appreciated Tropical Architecture insofar as it served as a means of place making and as a critique of Modernism's universalist tendencies.

The Smithsons began to dwell on climate responsiveness as a substitute for mechanical conditioning and as a source of architectural form with the designs for the British Embassy in Brasilia (1964–8), the Kuwait Mat-Building (1969–70), the Pahlavi master plan and National Library (1977–8), and the

Alexandria Library (1990). Koenigsberger served as a climate consultant for the British Embassy in Brasilia and the Kuwait Mat-Building as the head of the Tropical Advisory Service (TAS) at the AA. The Smithsons revised their idea of climate responsiveness through their collaboration with Koenigsberger. Through their work in the unfamiliar cultural and climatic terrain of the tropics, the Smithsons not only evolved their ideas on the relationship between architectural form and climate, but also established a dialogue between construction details and climate.

I propose that it is through the unbuilt projects in the tropics that the Smithsons began to theorize climate as the connection between the site and materiality of the building. The Smithsons interpreted climate responsiveness in terms of an abstract disembodied relationship between the materiality of the building and physical impact of the climate on the building over time, while for Tropical Architects the objectives of climatic design were to achieve physiological bodily comfort with minimum energy expenditure. These two interpretations of climatic design intersected in the Smithsons' unbuilt tropical projects and in the process, sensitized the Smithsons to explore the relationship between temporality of climate and materiality of architecture through climatic design.

Kuwait Mat Project

Koenigsberger served as a consultant to Peter and Alison Smithsons for the Kuwait Mat Project (1969), which was a mixed-use government office project. This project was never built, but it demonstrates a point that I want to make about the paradigmatic differences between Tropical Architecture and the mainstream of English architecture represented by Peter and Alison Smithson. There were no financial or energy constraints in Kuwait on the use of air-conditioning in public buildings, yet Koenigsberger recommended a series of climate responsive design features which would cut down energy consumption.[33] I argue that Koenigsberger proposed to cut down energy consumption because Tropical Architecture had evolved into a paradigm of universal energy conservation and resource maximization, *irrespective* of the cost constraints. Tropical Architects did not merely argue for energy conservation in contexts where energy was scarce, but followed universal energy conservation even in places like Kuwait that had abundant supplies of energy.

The Smithsons designed the government complex on a grid of 20 by 20 m, interspersed by courtyards and open interstitial spaces, which made it look like a mat of open and covered spaces, hence the name "Mat-Building" (Figure 2). The building was raised on *pilotis* to provide shaded walkways and parking. The stepped profile of the building was designed to shade the external walls (Figure 3). The plan comprises stair and service hooded towers placed diagonally at 40 m intervals. These towers were supposedly in a visual dialogue with the existing minarets in the city.

In the Kuwait project, Koenigsberger proposed to cut down sun exposure and sun penetration through a north–south orientation, a clustered

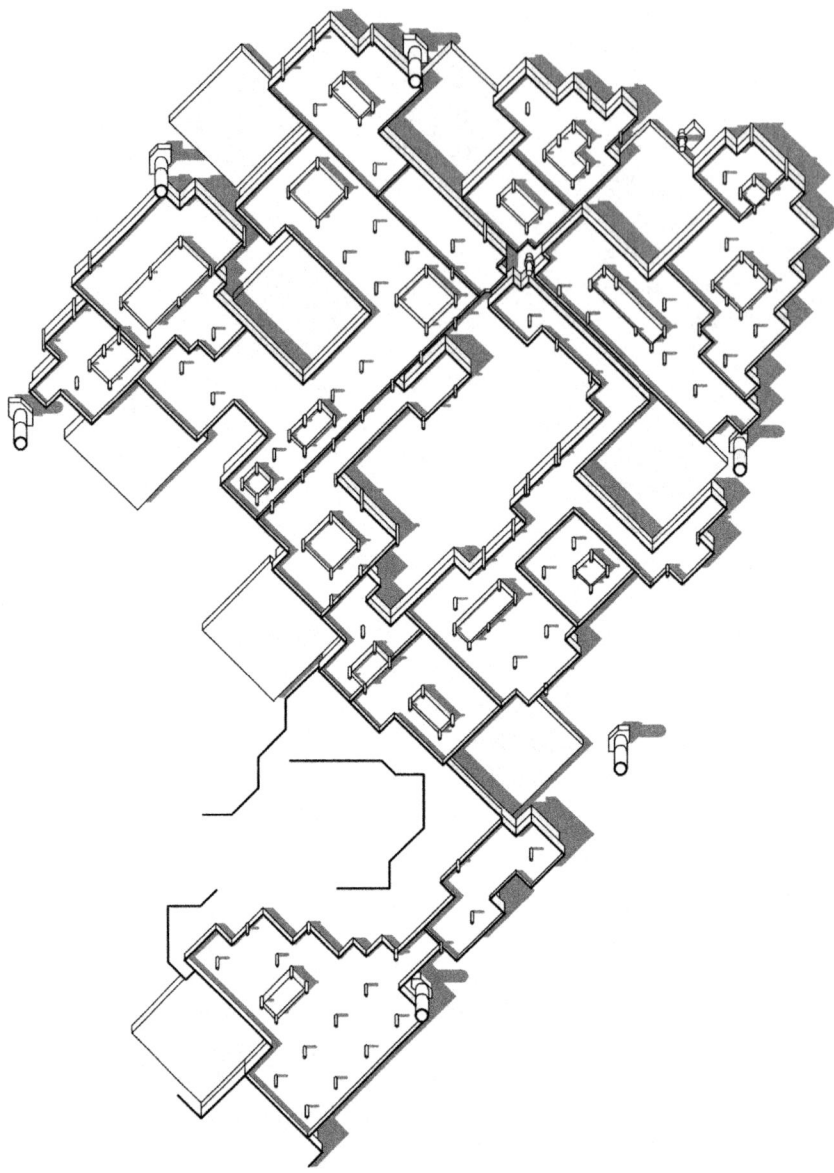

Figure 2
Axonometric of Kuwait Mat-Building showing the courtyards. Source: Redrawn by Simon Barrow based on an axonometric of the Kuwait Mat-Building published in Alison and Peter Smithson, *The Charged Void – Architecture* (New York: Monacelli Press, 2001).

layout organized around courtyards, restricted openings on the north–south walls, and heavily insulated external walls and roofs.[34] In addition, he proposed shaded walkways and parking spaces. The Smithsons followed these recommendations to a large extent in preparing their designs.

These suggestions made by Koenigsberger were backed by precise calculations based on sun diagrams. In the early 1950s, Tropical Architects merely suggested passive techniques at a theoretical level, but by the 1960s they had developed precise methods to quantify what we now call passive design. For example, in determining the best possible orientation for the galleries,

Figure 3
A sketch of a section through the courtyard showing the stepped profile of the Kuwait Mat-Building, 1969. Source: Redrawn by Simon Barrow, based on a sketch by Peter and Alison Smithson published in Alison and Peter Smithson, *The Charged Void – Architecture* (New York: Monacelli Press, 2001).

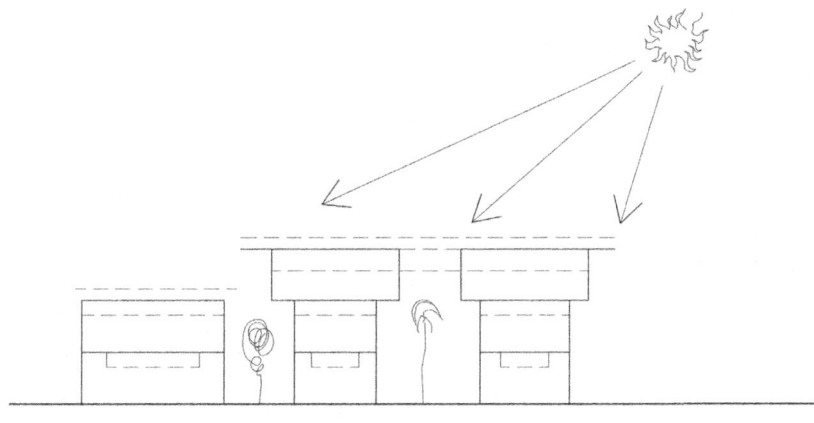

Koenigsberger calculated the sun penetration into the interstitial spaces within the building for four possible orientation angles: 0°, 22.5°, 40°, and 67.5°. These calculations were made by a series of sun diagrams which calculated the width of the sun-patch for each angle to determine the best possible orientation for the Kuwait complex (Figure 4).

Students of the Tropical Department used climatic data to calculate wall thickness, window openings, ventilation methods, and other passive methods to arrive at architectural solutions. The climatic data included geographical coordinates such as latitude, longitude, and altitude, and meteorological data such as annual range of temperature, daily range of temperature, rainfall pattern, and wind flow patterns.[35] The architectural presentations of the tropical students were distinguished from the other AA students' work by the juxtaposition of visual representations of climatic data in the form of solar path diagrams, wind flow diagrams, and rainfall charts, which rationalized architectural form in terms of climate and gave Tropical Architecture its distinct identity as climate responsive design.

In the case of the Kuwait Mat project, the Smithsons claimed that they approached the design problem with the intention of grounding the building in its Kuwaiti context through cultural and climatic responsiveness, which was a departure from their reliance on total mechanical conditioning. Koenigsberger's design objective as a climate consultant to the Kuwait Mat project was to cut down on energy expenditure. The Smithsons followed Koenigsberger's advice to approach design as a climatic problem and adopted most of the design solutions suggested by him, including orientation, the stepped profile of the buildings, and shaded walkways. In the process, the Smithsons privileged climate responsiveness to determine architectural form and contradicted their 1960 statement, in which they had remarked that any building form could be mechanically conditioned to achieve physiological comfort anywhere, so long as it responded to the *culture* of the place. Their notions of climate responsiveness and cultural responsiveness had somewhat merged in the Kuwait Mat project.

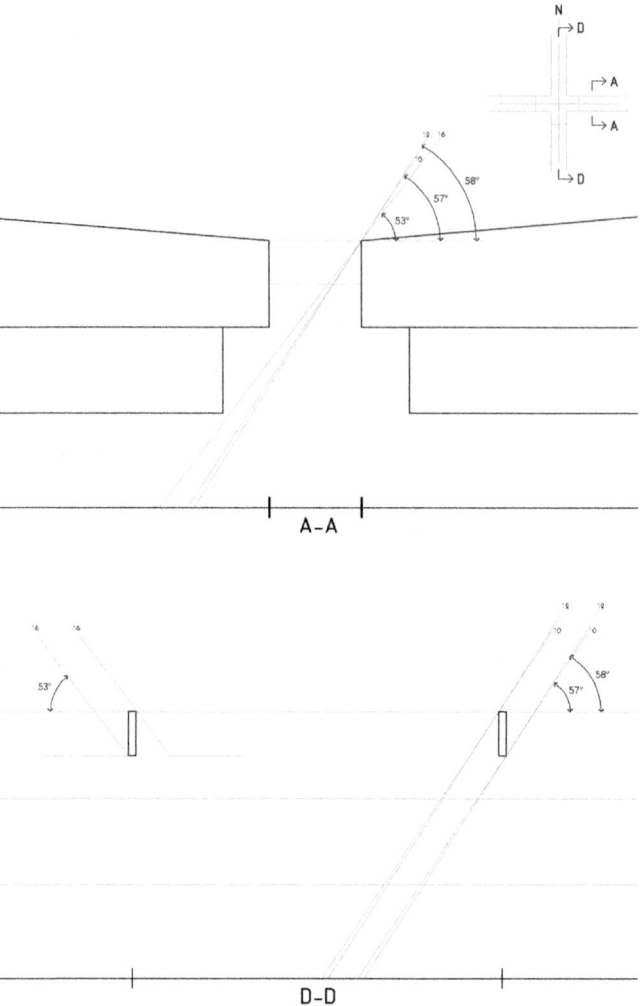

Figure 4
Sun diagrams for Kuwait Mat-Building. Source: Redrawn by Simon Barrow, based on sun diagrams published in Tropical Advisory Service, "Climate analysis and design recommendations for Kuwait Old City" (London, prepared for Peter and Alison Smithson by Tropical Advisory Service, Department of Tropical Architecture, Architectural Association School of Architecture).

Koenigsberger's recommendations relied heavily on developing the building sections in relation to the temporality of the climate, that is, the changing sun positions throughout the day and the year.[36] This method of design, in which changing climatic, solar, and light conditions were deployed to determine architectural form, was the normative practice in Tropical Architecture.

Although the Smithsons' tropical projects were never built, these projects sensitized them to the temporality of climate and the interactions between the climate and the buildings. They used the weathering of the building materials over time as an aesthetic expression for registering the temporal effects of climate on buildings. Koenigsberger engaged with the changing rhythms of the day and seasons through climatic design to create energy conservative architectural solutions. The Smithsons were enamored with the temporality of the climate and its relationship with architecture at the level of the building form and at the micro-level of architectural detail.[37] They disembodied climate responsiveness to establish an abstract relationship with the building as an object that would be transformed by climatic action over time, while for Koenigsberger, physiological bodily comfort and energy conservation remained prime objectives of climatic design. Eventually, the Smithsons completely changed their perception of climatic design, as is evident in the Second Arts Building at Bath (1978–81).

The change in the Smithsons' attitude to climate responsiveness was documented in the exhibition *Climate Register*. In this exhibition, their unbuilt tropical projects and their built domestic projects were collapsed into a single discursive space of the relationship between architecture and climate. The exhibit included their Kuwait Mat project and the Second Arts Building at Bath, which was constructed in 1978–81 on the same principles that Tropical Architects developed in the mid-twentieth century.[38] The untold story in *Climate Register* is the story of how the Smithsons engaged with tropicality through their career.

Second Arts Building at Bath

The Second Arts Building was built for the University of Bath on a hillside just outside the city of Bath. The Second Arts Building program comprised the School of Modern Languages, specialist rooms for the School of Education, the Centre for European Industrial Studies, and part of the School of Management. Segregated vertically, each school occupies a separate floor and has two kinds of space: small teacher's rooms and larger teaching rooms.

The Smithsons were concerned with a climatic design that enabled natural light to enter the building. Their design began with sun diagrams that were typical of Tropical Architecture. Describing their Bath project design, they wrote:

> We concerned ourselves (almost from the very beginning) with the movement of the sun first to ensure that the two existing residential towers to the south did not put the site into permanent shadows and second to see what the effects would be if the immediately adjacent sites to the east and the west were developed northwards at their existing heights to their natural limit. [39]

The sun diagrams of the Bath project determined the orientation and the location of rooms within the building (Figure 5). The Smithsons adopted what they called a "delta" plan, which would let in the sun into the southeast and southwest facing rooms. In sun-facing rooms, the Smithsons located the teachers' and administrators' rooms, where people were likely to spend more time. In the zig-zag surface of the building, facing northeast and northwest, the Smithsons located large teaching rooms, in which teaching time was short and the sun would interfere with activities of the classroom.

In the Second Arts Building, University of Bath, the Smithsons presented solar path diagrams in a presentation style which was typical of

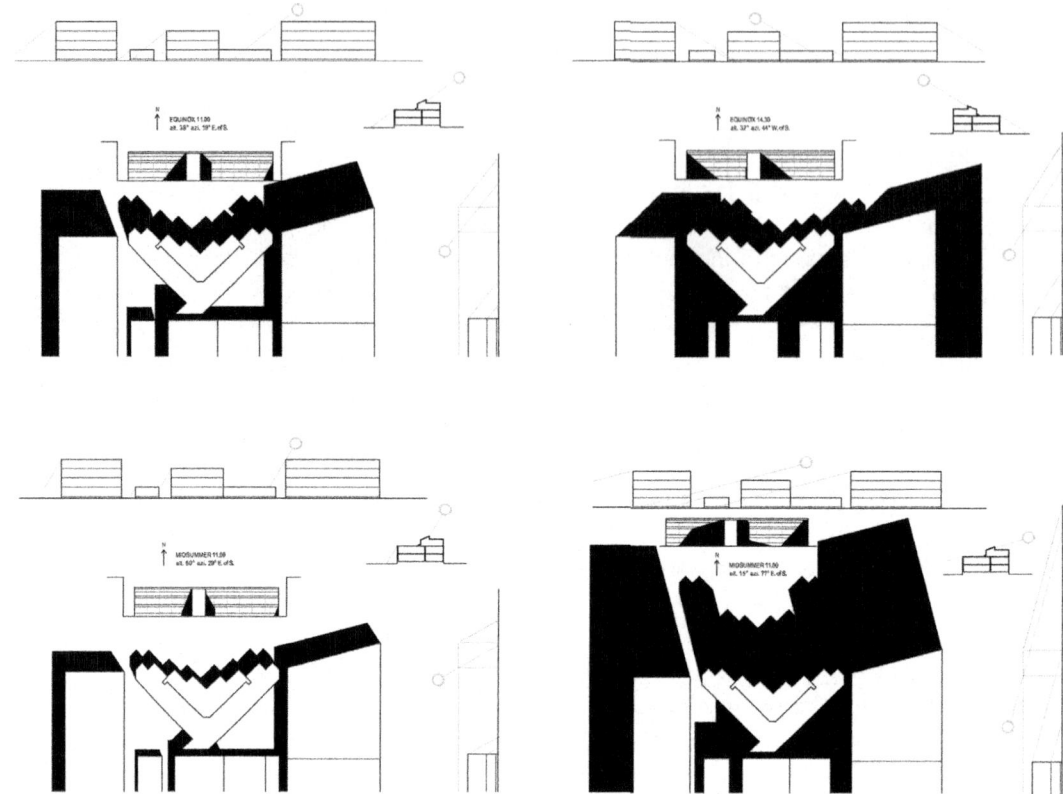

Tropical Architects. They claimed that they chose the orientation of the building after careful analysis of the sun diagrams to ensure that the building got the maximum amount of sun. Clearly, the Smithsons had adopted the climatic responsive design methods of the Tropical Department. Although there was no objective to conserve energy in the Second Arts Building, and no compulsion to design with the climate, the Smithsons nevertheless made extensive sun diagram studies to determine the location of the rooms based on their function and building orientation.

Likewise, in their 1986 project for the Lutzowstrasse housing in Berlin, the Smithsons used the term "sun consciousness" and placed the terraces on the south side of the building to get the maximum amount of sun. The Smithsons' idea of climatic design changed over the course of their career and eventually aligned with that of the Third Worldist praxis of Tropical Architecture.

While I have focused on the work of the Smithsons and their relationship to Tropical Architecture, I want to end this chapter by addressing how a Third Worldist discourse such as Tropical Architecture was eventually subsumed into global discourses such as Solar Architecture and Sustainable Architecture.

Figure 5

Sun diagrams for second arts building at Bath. Source: Redrawn by Simon Barrow based on sun diagrams published in Lorenzo Wong, *Climate Register: Four Works by Alison and Peter Smithson* (London: Architectural Association, 1994), p. 47.

The afterlife of Tropical Architecture

Tropical Architects at the AA and in the tropics built a body of knowledge on design techniques which would minimize energy consumption through climate responsive design. The Tropical Department closed at the AA in 1971. By this time, Koenigsberger's interest had shifted to planning, and he inaugurated the Development Planning Unit (DPU), a department dedicated to planning in the Third World at University College London (UCL). The DPU still exists at UCL. With the demise of the Tropical Architecture Department at the AA and its reconstitution as Third World Planning, the discourse of nineteenth-century tropicality was transformed into twentieth-century "Third Worldism." The idea of an energy conservative and climate responsive architecture did not diminish with the closure of the Tropical Department at the AA, but entered the dominant architectural discourse of energy conservation through Solar and Sustainable Architecture globally.

In the early 1970s, as Tropical Architecture began to diminish as a Third World movement, Koenigsberger collaborated with T. G. Ingersoll, Alan Mayhew, and Steven Szokolay to describe tropical design methods in the *Manual of Tropical Housing and Architecture*, which was published in 1974.[40] After the Tropical Department at the AA closed down in 1971, and as environmental discourse became a popular concern after the OPEC crises, many of Koenigsberger's students and co-authors of the *Tropical Manual* shifted their practice to various aspects of environmentalism in architecture. People who trained or taught at the Tropical Architecture Department went on to practice Solar, Green, and Sustainable Architectures, and that is no coincidence. I have argued elsewhere that one of the origins of Sustainable Architecture lies in the discourse of Tropical Architecture.[41] This is evident from the career trajectories of architects who left the AA at the closure of the Department of Tropical Architecture and transformed their practice from Tropical Architecture to "Solar Architecture." To cite a few examples, T. G. Ingersoll, who co-authored the *Tropical Design Manual* with Koenigsberger, practiced in Massachusetts with a firm called "Massdesign" which specialized in solar-heated houses. Steven Szokolay, who also co-authored the *Tropical Design Manual* with Koenigsberger, established his career in academia in Australia to become a solar energy and Sustainable Architecture expert.[42] In 1964, Szokolay began his academic career at Liverpool University as a lecturer. His job got him to Nairobi, where Liverpool University was helping the University of East Africa to start a course in architecture. Szokolay attended a course run by Koenigsberger at the AA on teaching in developing countries. He spent two years in Nairobi and did some field work on tropical building, which he used for a Master of Architecture degree. Just as Koenigsberger's work in India got him interested in energy conservation, Szokolay's work in Nairobi got him interested in Solar Architecture and low energy design. In 1975, right after the OPEC energy crises, Szokolay's book *Solar Energy and Building* moved beyond the tropics to engage with knowledge on energy conservative practices on a global scale. Szokolay authored several books on Solar Architecture and Sustainable Architecture. In the progression of books authored by Szokolay, which includes books on Tropical Architecture prior to the OPEC crises, on Solar Architecture in the 1980s, and on Sustainable Architecture in the 1990s and 2000s, we can trace how the knowledge produced in the field of Tropical Architecture was gradually subsumed into the spheres of Solar and Sustainable Architecture. Harris Sobin, an AA Tropical alumnus, became devoted to teaching environmental design in the United States in Arizona.[43] K. K. Mumtaz, another alumnus of the AA Tropical Department who has written extensively about architecture in Pakistan, practices Green Architecture there.[44] Carl Mahoney, who collaborated with Koenigsberger to develop the Mahoney Tables, established himself as an expert in Passive and Low Energy Architecture (PLEA).[45] The Mahoney Tables, a tool used for climate responsive design, facilitate the quick calculation of correlation between climatic data and architectural design appropriate for a given climate. It is no coincidence that Carl Mahoney is also an expert in Sustainable Development.

Canonical architectural histories treat Tropical Architecture as an export commodity that traveled from the metropole to the tropics. In the process of "exporting" architectural knowledge overseas to the tropical Third World, British architects in London and Third World architects unwittingly developed a body of knowledge which was eventually subsumed into the global praxis of Sustainable Architecture.

Acknowledgments

I would like to thank Robert Fishman at the University of Michigan for his advice; Duanfang Lu for her patience and generosity with her feedback; the Architectural Association School of Architecture for letting me access their archives; Renate Koenisgberger, the widow of Otto Koenisberger, for letting me access the private papers of Otto Koenisgberger in London; and Mary Daniels and Ines Zalduendo at the Special Collections Department at the Frances Loeb Library in the Graduate School of Design at Harvard University, for letting me access the Smithson archive.

Notes

1   Alison and Peter Smithson, "The function of architecture in cultures-in-change," *Architectural Design*, vol. 30, no. 4 (April 1960), pp. 149–50.

2   Lorenzo Wong, *Climate Register: Four Works by Alison and Peter Smithson* (London: Architectural Association, 1994), p. 7.

3   Vandana Baweja, *A Pre-History of Green Architecture: Otto Koenigsberger and Tropical Architecture, from Princely Mysore to Post-Colonial London* (University of Michigan, 2008). It should be noted that not all tropical zones were part of the Third World. For instance, the Tropical Architecture movement in Florida, best represented by the work of Paul Rudolph, was based on a completely different set of ideas.

4   Felix Driver and Brenda Yeoh, "Constructing the tropics: introduction," *Singapore Journal of Tropical Geography*, 21, no. 1 (2000), pp. 1–5.

5   David Arnold, "'Illusory riches': representations of the Tropical World, 1840–1950," *Singapore Journal of Tropical Geography*, 21, no. 1 (2000), pp. 6–18.

6   Jean Royer, *L'Urbanisme aux colonies et dans les pays tropicaux; communications et rapports du Congrès International de l'Urbanisme aux Colonies et dans les Pays de Latitude Intertropicale*, Congrès International de l'Urbanisme aux Colonies et dans les Pays de Latitude Intertropicale (La Charité-sur-Loire: Delayance, 1932).

7   International Federation for Housing and Planning, *Papers and Reports: XVI International Housing and Town Planning Congress, Mexico, 1938* (Bruxelles: International Federation for Housing and Planning, 1938).

8   Hannah Le Roux, "The networks of Tropical Architecture," *The Journal of Architecture*, 8, no. 3 (2003), pp. 337–54.

9   Otto H. Koenigsberger, *Die Konstruktion der Ägyptischen Tür* (Glückstadt: Verlag von J. J. Augustin, 1936).

10   See Otto H. Koenigsberger, "Jamshedpur Development Plan" (Bombay: Tata Iron and Steel Company, 1945).

11   See Ravi Kalia, *Bhubaneswar: From a Temple Town to a Capital City* (Carbondale: Southern Illinois University Press, 1994).

12   Otto H. Koenigsberger, "New Towns in India," *The Town Planning Review*, 23, no. 2 (1952), pp. 94–132.

13   Otto H. Koenigsberger *et al.*, *Manual of Tropical Housing and Building* (London: Longman, 1974).

14   Jeffrey Cook, "Six evolutionary phases toward solar architecture: thermal application of solar energy in buildings," in *Solar World Congress: Proceedings of the Eighth Biennial Congress of the International Solar Energy Society, Perth, 14–19 August, 1983*, ed. International Solar Energy Society and S. V. Szokolay (Oxford [Oxfordshire]; New York: Pergamon Press, 1984), pp. 4–15.

15   Victor Olgyay, *Design with Climate: Bioclimatic Approach to Architectural Regionalism* (Princeton, N.J.: Princeton University Press, 1963).

16   See Adam Ward Rome, *The Bulldozer in the Countryside: Suburban Sprawl and the Rise of American Environmentalism*, Studies in Environment and History (Cambridge; New York: Cambridge University Press, 2001).

17   See *Journal of Architectural Education*, vol. 30 no. 3, Energy and Architecture (1977).

18   Mark Crinson, *Modern Architecture and the End of Empire* (Aldershot, England; Burlington, VT: Ashgate, 2003); Hannah Le Roux, op. cit.

19   Cook, op. cit.

20   Vandana Baweja, "A Pre-History of Green Architecture: Otto Koenigsberger and Tropical Architecture, from Princely Mysore to Post-Colonial London (University of Michigan, 2008)."

21   Reyner Banham, *The Architecture of the Well-Tempered Environment* (London; Chicago: Architectural Press; University of Chicago 1973), pp. 18–28.

22   Tropical Advisory Service, "British High Commission, Islamabad: Climatic Design Report" (London, prepared for the Ministry of Public Building and Works, London by Tropical Advisory Service, Department of Tropical Studies, Architectural Association School of Architecture 1965–6).

23   Colin Porteus, "Green trail to now – ecology vs economy," in *The New Eco-Architecture: Alternatives from the Modern Movement* (London and New York: Spon Press, 2002), pp. 121–5.

24   Banham, op. cit.

25   Alison and Peter Smithson, "Collective housing in Morocco," *Architectural Design*, 25 (January 1955), pp. 2–7.

26   Monique Eleb, "An alternative to functionalist universalism: Ecohard, Candilis, and Atbat-Afrique," in *Anxious Modernisms: Experimentation in Postwar Architectural Culture*, ed. Sarah Goldhagen and Rejean Legault (Cambridge: MIT Press, 2000), pp. 25–54.

27   Alison and Peter Smithson, "An alternative to the garden city idea," *Architectural Design*, 26, no. 7 (July 1956), pp. 229–31.

28   Ibid.

29   Ibid.

30   Ibid.

31   Alison and Peter Smithson, "The function of architecture in cultures-in-change."

32   W. A. Henderson *et al.*, "Annual exhibition of school work," *Architectural Association Journal*, vol. 71 (September/October 1955), pp. 66–73.

33   Tropical Advisory Service, "Climate analysis and design recommendations for Kuwait Old City" (London, prepared for Peter and Alison Smithson by Tropical Advisory Service, Department of Tropical Architecture, Architectural Association School of Architecture 1969).

34   Ibid.

35   George Anthony Atkinson, "Mass housing in rapidly developing tropical areas," *Town Planning Review*, vol. 31, no. 2 (1960), pp. 85–102.

36   Tropical Advisory Service, op. cit.

37   Wong, *Climate Register: Four Works by Alison and Peter Smithson.*

38   Ibid.

39   Peter Smithson, "Bath walks within the walls: a study of Bath as a built-form taken over by other uses," *Architectural Design*, 39, no. 10 (Oct 1969), pp. 554–64.

40   Koenigsberger *et al.*, op. cit.

41   Vandana Baweja, "A Pre-History of Green Architecture: Otto Koenigsberger and Tropical Architecture, from Princely Mysore to Post-Colonial London (University of Michigan, 2008)."

42   See S. Szokolay, *Solar Energy and Building* (London, New York: Architectural Press; Halsted Press Division Wiley, 1975), *World Solar Architecture* (London, New York: Architectural Press; Halsted Press, 1980), *Architecture and Climate Change* (Red Hill A.C.T.: Royal Australian Institute of Architects Education Division, 1992), *Introduction to Architectural Science: The Basis of Sustainable Design* (Amsterdam; London: Architectural 2008); Cook, op. cit.

43   See Harris J. Sobin, "3 museums," *Architectural Association Journal*, vol. 77, no. 860 (March 1962), pp. 209–15.

44   Salman S. Minhas, "Kamil Khan Mumtaz: the grand master of traditional & green architecture in Pakistan," *The-south-asian.com*, October 2004, 1–4.

45   Koenigsberger *et al.*, op. cit.

Chapter 11

Epilogue: Third World Modernism, or Just Modernism: towards a cosmopolitan reading of modernism

Vikramāditya Prakāsh

Recently, with the much talked about rise of China and India, and their imminent location in the pantheon of super-powers, I have increasingly found that conversations between Indian origin "native informants" such as myself and my Chinese counterparts often turn to speculation and contestation on issues such as: "Is globalization good for the cities of India and China?", "Is there a genuine local architecture and urbanism emerging in Asia?", "Must sustainability and energy efficiency be the new mantras of development?", "Who is doing better – China or India?" and, of course, "What can our role be as US-based architect-academics in influencing and participating in this new development?"[1] In one such conversation, when I was bemoaning the need for us to break free of the persistent circuit of debates of the "global versus the local," the "universal versus the regional" type, a Chinese colleague suggested that what he was interested in was thinking about architecture of the "New Third World."[2] While our conversation did not advance into specifics, I was intrigued by his renewal of the term "Third World" with the prefix "New" – a move to re-don that tattered old title, that generally signals economic deprivation, as the title for asserting new found power under globalization. As the act of recasting a former slur as a badge of honor, the idea of a "New Third World" could be understood as a genuinely postcolonial act, if being postcolonial is described as the work of inverting and reinscribing colonial ideologies in the service of the postcolonies rather than the metropolitan centers. The backwardness of the colonized world was described by colonial ideology as a consequence of the inherent civilizational backwardness, rather than the specific cause of two-plus centuries of colonial deprivation that had resulted in the creation of the poverty of the postcolonial Third World. Re-wearing the badge of poverty with the "New" prefix, thus, insists on seeing the postcolonial world's new accession to power on the world stage as a revising of history, rather than a completion of the colonial project by discarding that supposed backwardness and "opening up" to Western style capitalism/civilization.

The project of what the architecture of this "New Third World" might specifically look like must remain latent in this essay. By way of preparation for this project, here I am interested in unpacking aspects of the term "Third World" and in particular its relationships with its suffix "modernism." The term "Third World Modernism" purports to describe a "modernism" that is specific to, or belongs to, the "Third World." I am interested in "modernism" as a term and an ideology because from the very outset it signals a civilizational claim, authorized by the European Enlightenment, about the superiority and accomplishments of modern Western civilization. What does it mean to claim "modernism" for the "Third World"? While I recognize that "modernism" is hardly a term that is uncontested, in this essay I am using "modernism" as the normative that is usually used to describe the modern movement in architecture or just modern architecture.[3] I am in sympathy but in contestatory relationship with the claims of "alternative modernisms" or "many modernisms," the claim that modern architecture took many forms world-wide each of which must be recognized for its own, unique distinctiveness.[4] While I am sympathetic to critiques of metropolitan discourses that inevitably locate non-Euro-American modernism as only secondary derivatives of a mythologized Eurocentric canon, I am here interested in describing not so much the distinctiveness of a Third World Modernism (which it inevitably always possesses) but rather in tracking the manner in which modernism "itself" is deployed in the various theaters of decolonization, including the so-called Third World.

In this essay I begin by reviewing a history of the term "Third World" as a political claim, and then offer a reading of a Third World Modernism using the making of Chandigarh as a case study. Finally, I hazard some notes on the theoretical work that would be needed to develop a more generalized theory of what might be called a New Third World modernism.

The Third World

If as its name suggests, the term Third World were to be distinguished from a presumed First/Second World, and if one were to begin to know such a stream by searching for its beginnings, one would in fact encounter a mis-attribution. In common parlance, the "Third World" is not a geographical descriptor, but one that is indexed to economic development. It purports to describe those nations of the world that are generally considered to be economically underdeveloped, as compared to the nations of a presumed "First" and "Second" World. The latter nations, however, are never attributed by those descriptors but others such as "The West," the "Developed World," "G8," and so on. The reason why the developed nations of the First/Second worlds are not known by those terms is because the term "Third World" did not come into being as a derivative of a First and Second Worlds, but as its own third alternative. It came into being in the context of the Cold War, as a global marker of resistance and difference. In the 1950s, when the Cold War was heating up between the USA and the former USSR and their allies, the geo-politics of the world were often described in terms of the "Two Worlds" theory,[5] that is, as being split up between two political perspectives, that of the capitalist world and the communist world, both vying for legitimacy and domination in the post Second World War, postcolonial world. As a new kind of world war, from which no nation on Earth could strictly be said to be immune as a consequence of the global or "inter-continental" reach of new weaponry, all the nations of the world were expected to align with one "world" or the other. It was in this context that a series of nations first met in Bandung, Indonesia on April 18–24 1955 and by rejecting the bi-polar choices of the two world theory, chose to remain non-aligned with either of the capitalist or the communist worlds. Instead, they proposed the creation of a third perspective, a third alternative against the bi-polar choices of the two-worlds theory. This third alternative came to be known as the "Third World" alternative.[6]

The Bandung Conference, also known as the Afro-Asian Conference, was convened collectively by Indonesia, Burma, Sri Lanka, Pakistan, and India, with Indonesia's President Sukarno the instigator and host of the event. The immediate cause for the conference was the continued occupation of West New Guinea by the Dutch, which Sukarno claimed, with the support of convening countries, as belonging to Indonesia.[7] The official stated goal of the Bandung Conference was to promote collaboration and cooperation amongst the older and recently independent nations of Asia and Africa, thereby encouraging self-reliance and reducing their continued dependence on the former colonial powers. Quickly, however, the agenda of the conference turned to broader issues, instigated by the West New Guinea issue. The majority of the conference was dedicated to denouncing the acts of what were perceived as new colonial powers of the time, that is, the USA and the USSR. The conference delegates denounced the non-consultative, dictatorial policies of what were described as the "neo-colonial" powers that were seen as using their undisputed status as rival military powers to coerce and bully the rest of the world to join their respective blocs.[8] The conference broadly condemned "colonialism in all of its manifestations" and adopted a set of ten principles based on those of the UN Charter emphasizing national sovereignty and negotiated resolution of disputes and abjuring arrangements of collective defense of the kinds sought by the USA and the USSR.[9]

The Third World therefore began essentially as a theory or a statement of principles whose main purport can be described as being pacifist and anti-big power alliances. The kernel for the principles of the Bandung Conference was based on an agreement over Tibet between China and India that was crafted between Zhao En-lai, the Premier of the new Republic of China, and Jawaharlal Nehru, the first Prime Minister of the newly independent India. Known as the "Five Principles of Peaceful Coexistence" or Panchsheel, these principles stood at the head of a more detailed treaty on trade and cultural exchanges between Tibet and India. The principles were: mutual respect for each other's territorial integrity and sovereignty, mutual non-aggression, mutual non-interference in domestic affairs, equality and mutual benefit and, most importantly, peaceful co-existence.[10] In June 1954, just a year before the Bandung Conference, Jawaharlal Nehru and Zhou En-lai met for three days in New Delhi. The value of extending the Panchsheel agreement beyond India and China into a generalized "area of peace" based on non-aggression and neutrality, was first developed in their conversations at this meeting.[11] Both Nehru and Zhou En-lai were deeply cognizant of the regional "big power" status of their respective nations, and committed themselves to developing an "area of peace" in South-East Asia by not building defensive alliances in the region and by offering similar treaties to the other countries in the region, especially Burma, Indonesia, Cambodia, Ceylon, and Afghanistan. They envisioned that this zone could emerge as a bulwark against Cold War alliances, and project China and India as leaders in an alternative global perspective.[12]

Fresh from his conversations with Zhou En-lai, Nehru played an important part in laying down the ideological framework at the Bandung Conference. When a proposal was also advanced that a new power under India's leadership be created, Nehru refused, underlining his commitment to non-alignment as a principled stance rather than a political alliance.[13] For Nehru, the very concept of "pacts" was questionable. "I submit to you," he noted:

> [E]very pact has brought insecurity and not security to the countries which have entered into them. They have brought the danger of atomic bombs and the rest of it nearer to them than would have been the case otherwise. They have not added to the strength of any country, I submit, which it had singly. It may have produced some idea of security, but it is a false security. It is a bad thing for any country thus to be lulled into security...[14]

Nehru articulated his position as that of not wishing to align with any one group, not just in terms of defensive alliance, but also in terms of ideological positions. "We do not agree with the communist teachings," he noted, and "we do not agree with the anti-communist teachings, because they are both based on wrong principles." For Nehru, the critical thing was to truly assert independence from the former colonial powers, to no longer be "hangers-on," and make a show of independent thinking:

> [A]re we, the countries of Asia and Africa, devoid of any positive position except being pro-communist or anti-communist? Has it come to this, that the leaders of thought who have given religions and all

kinds of things to the world have to tag on to this kind of group or that and be hangers-on of this party or the other carrying out their wishes and occasionally giving an idea? It is most degrading and humiliating to any self-respecting people or nation. It is an intolerable thought to me that the great countries of Asia and Africa should come out of bondage into freedom only to degrade themselves or humiliate themselves in this way...[15]

In 1961, at a conference held in Belgrade, the principles of the Bandung Conference were formalized into an organization called Non Aligned Movement (NAM). Josef Broz Tito of the former Yugoslavia, Abdel Nasser of Egypt, Kwame Nkrumah of Ghana, Sukarno of Indonesia and Jawaharlal Nehru of India came to be known as the Group of Five who initiated NAM. NAM began with an initial membership of 29 nations and slowly grew over the years to 118 member states as of 2006, consisting of two-thirds of the members of the United Nations representing about 55% percent of the world's population. Since NAM was based on the Bandung Conference, its principles and positions can be described as that of the Third World alternative. As a political group, NAM remained committed to pacifism and non-Cold War competitive thinking as its core agenda. Increasingly over the years, however, its agenda turned to economic development and collaboration between member states, without recourse to the West.

Though China was not one of the initiators of the Bandung Conference, Zhao En-lai did attend.[16] A major point of contention at the conference, raised by several Asian nations, questioned China's own territorial intentions. Although Nehru strongly defended China at Bandung, China maintained its distance from the Non Aligned Movement, only joining as an observer in 1993. Through the 1950s, Nehru had invested deeply in the idea that India and China, in spite of their significant differences, could collectively define the identity of the Third World. But the Tibet issue, in spite of Panchsheel, continued to be a major bone of contention between the two countries. In 1959 Nehru accepted the Dalai Lama as a refugee into India, and in 1962 a series of border skirmishes led to a full-out war between China and India over territorial disputes. China prevailed in this war, seriously souring relations between the countries.[17]

By the early 1960s, NAM came to be dominated by India, with China increasingly carving out its singular identity in world politics. Nehru defined the more centrist position for the Third World, one that was an amalgamation of the best of both the capitalist and communist blocs, while Chairman Mao and Zhao En-lai steered China towards their own post-Soviet peasantist conception of Communism. Nehru died in 1965 and after that, NAM began to wane as political force on the global stage as the Cold War continued to escalate. In 1974, Chairman Mao is reputed to have said: "I think the United States and the Soviet Union was the First World. Centrist, Japan, Europe, Australia, Canada, is the Second World. We are the Third World," completely removing the Two Worlds theory as a reference.[18]

While its principled stance made heroes out of its initiators in their home countries such as India, NAM had negligible influence on the development and eventual victory of the capitalist bloc. As it was, it was mostly the largely under-developed nations that joined the Non Aligned Movement, so that, in common parlance, the term "Third World," from being an explicitly political term that expressed a stance of principled opposition, came to be known as an economic term, descriptive of the poor or under-developed, often euphemized as the "developing" world.

Today, the Third World is usually referred to as the "Global South," an alternate reference produced to counter the discourses, generally organized around the rubric "globalization," that describe the new economic logics of the post-Cold War world. The Global South, thus, can be said to be the new name of the Third Worldist position, used primarily as an economic descriptor. Discourses on globalization tend to traverse familiar themes such as neo-imperialism, transnationalism and regionalization, while those of the Global South generally tend to focus on the local, in particular the role of the not-for-profit non governmental sector and their work in stewarding "change from below."[19] In both of these, the status of the autonomous, independent nation state is routinely undermined, a long way from the principled alliance of the kind proposed by NAM.[20] In this global versus local context, a renewed focus on a New Third World, which by now must be clear that it begins as a historical project, offers the possibility of re-thinking the status of the nation state, and alliances of nation states, not as an economic alliance negotiating at Davos, but as something of a not global–local entity, responsible to its citizenry.[21]

Modernism and the Third World: the view from India

NAM as a global movement, and India's leadership role in it, was well recognized in the popular urban culture of India as part of the independent, centrist and ambitious stance of the Nehruvian nation state.[22] The new Indian nation state, under Nehru's tutelage, was also fashioned along the contours of his Third-Worldist attitude. While some of the core capitalist institutions such as democracy, private property, and free markets (carefully regulated) were allowed to stand, large industries such as power, steel, and transportation were centralized under the state. Imports and exports, and movement of goods across states within the country were also carefully regulated, creating a developmentalist model. Seeking to access the "best of both worlds," US expertise was sought to build gigantic hydroelectric power stations, while the Soviet Union helped India build its steel plants. The elite Indian bureaucracy, inherited from the British civil service, was put in charge of executing the Soviet-style five-year plans that were supposed to chart India's growth, which was often compared to Franklin Roosevelt's New Deal. The making of Chandigarh (and other cities such as Bhubaneshwar and Gandhinagar) was part of this enterprise.

The defining moment in the history of the modern architecture of India is usually taken to be the yoking of the Nehruvian nation state to modern architecture in the making of Chandigarh in the 1950s. There was an existing discussion (dating back to the colonial period) in Indian architectural circles that debated the value of developing an identifiably Indian architectural style through reference to historical architecture (parallel to the development of neo-classicism as a modern European architectural style) versus adopting modern architecture as an expression of the new India (since modern architecture was conceived as being expressive of the new aspirations of the times).[23]

Nehru's mandate for Chandigarh decided the debate in favor of the modernists. As the new capital of the partitioned state of Punjab, Chandigarh, the replacement for Lahore, was not only made to house refugees, but conceived as a metonym of state, as described by Nehru's mandate "Let this be a new town, symbolic of the freedom of India, unfettered by the traditions of the past, a expression of the nation's faith in the future."[24] In this context new meant "modern."[25] To a certain extent, Nehru's perspective was historicist. He believed that the weight of history had stifled Indian progress, leading to India's colonization, and therefore independence must continue the colonial project of modernizing India.[26] At the same time, expression of independence and independence of thought was central to Nehru. Here, we can contextualize Nehru's decision by referencing his more famous architectural metaphor calling his new hydroelectric dams (such as Bhakra Nangal with which Chandigarh was closely associated) "the temples of modern India."[27] Dams as temples of a modern India yokes the secularism of the Indian nation state to the new works of state.[28] Secularism was enshrined in the Indian constitution from its very inception. It was a keystone in the Nehruvian nation state's self-definition, conceived on the one hand as an acceptance of one of the core constituent elements of the Western constitution of its nation states. At the same time, it was also a repudiation of the West as colonizers' historicist reading of identity that gave to religion the status of the primary index of identity of the colonial subjects, who were considered to have not yet advanced to the level of citizenship attained by the Euro-American citizens. This "not-yet" reading of Indian identity authorized the partition of India into Islamic Pakistan, and non-Islamic or largely Hindu India. Although the European nations had not constructed themselves explicitly as religious states, the colonial creation of Pakistan as an explicitly religious country was precipitated by the colonialist belief that India's citizens were not yet ready to truly be modern citizens, since their identities, both public and private, were primarily constructed through their religious affiliations. Repudiating this colonialist reading of identity, the Nehruvian nation state bound the Indian constitution to an explicitly secular code.[29]

This is the context in which Chandigarh came into being. Since the state of Punjab had been partitioned and its historic capital lost to Pakistan, and since a large number of Muslims and Sikhs had lost their lives trying to cross the border as a consequence of religious violence, Nehru's decision to not build Chandigarh through a historicist reading as a "Sikh" or "Hindu" city was designed to not perpetuate this colonialist reading of identity. In its place he accepted modernism, because it offered the most expedient and progressive position at hand.

Chandigarh's modernism as secularism can be brought into focus by comparing it with New Delhi.[30] The making of New Delhi was of course part of the final act in the colonial enterprise to try to legitimize Empire as the instituting of the superiority of the Western/English civilization as the natural inheritors of the Enlightenment. New Delhi's stripped neoclassicism was not just an embodiment of English architecture, but was the latest installment of what used to be called "the eternal style," that is, the architectural style whose aesthetic qualities embodied European civilization's privileged access to the principles of the Enlightenment as the progeny of the classical age (verified through the Renaissance).

This is the context in which modern architecture emerged as a counter-claimant style of the Enlightenment. In the nineteenth and early twentieth centuries, while the colonial discourse of national styles was being played out in the various capitals of Europe, modernism was constructed in the context of the European Enlightenment not as a Western or, say, European construct, but specifically as a non-identitarian, that is, universal and transnational, construct.[31] Rightly or wrongly, modernism made its claims not as a historically or locally defined architecture, but rather as an ahistorical and foundational reading of the purposes of architecture. What is important here is not whether or not modernism in fact was ahistorical and foundational but that it constructed itself as such. This construction authorized a full-fledged discourse on modernism in the West as a universal "fact," with all its claims and counter-claims. "Facts" were expressly divorced from questions of national styles, which was thus an expressly counter-nationalist and, in our context, counter-colonial position. So, the adoption of stripped neo-classicism by Lutyens in New Delhi was specifically an expression of Eurocentrism, or the expression of the Enlightenment as the West and as the modern superiority of the West. The rejection of New Delhi as the prerequisite of the architectural style of Chandigarh can thus be understood as the newly independent postcolonial nation state's rejection of Eurocentrism, or of modernism as the West. And Chandigarh's modern architecture, therefore, can be understood as the adoption of a non-Western, or non-Eurocentric, modernism.

In other words, modernism's self-construction as an ahistorical style, and as such as a counter-Euro-nationalist style, made it ideal for adoption as expressive for the aspirations of the newly constituted secular Nehruvian nation state – not because modernism in any particular sense embodied Nehru's vision of an Indian architecture, but because it married well with his modern-Enlightenment-based anti-colonial political stance. Thus it is no surprise that when Nehru was asked whether he liked Chandigarh or not after it was completed, he said:

It is totally immaterial whether you like it or not. It is the biggest thing in India of this kind. That is why I welcome it. It is the biggest thing because it hits you on the head and makes you think...[32]

Nonetheless, "Chandigarh style" became the referential model for new architecture and urbanism in postcolonial India, particularly in state-sponsored projects, spawning the first generation of easily recognizable Indian modernists (Figures 1 and 2).[33]

Here I would simply extrapolate and suggest that it was modern architecture's expressly anti-Euronationalist stance that is likely a significant part of the reason why modern architecture was adopted worldwide in the post-colonies as their national "style" such as in Australia, Brazil, Turkey, Israel, Pakistan, Bangladesh, and Indonesia as well as in India. Thus while the Western nations clothed their national capitals in various styles designed to create links to a mythologized historical past, the postcolonial nations adopted modernism with its tabula rasa, utopian promises for the future. Indeed, even in colonial times, modern architecture at times found greater purchase in the colonies than in their metropolitan centers. Indeed, one can argue that even in colonial times modern architechture at times found greater purchase in the colonies than in their metropolitan centres. This is because the colonies, as Jean Louis Cohen has shown was the case in Casablanca, were considered to be frontier outposts that a cause of their non-metropolitan character were prime sites for experimental architecture, as modernism proffered itself as being.[34] As such, one can argue that the history of the rise of modern architecture can be seen not as the spread

Figure 1
Hostel of the Panjab Agricultural University, Ludhiana by Aditya Prakash, 1964, in "Chandigarh style" Indian modernism. Courtesy of The Aditya Prakash Foundation, Chandigarh.

Figure 2
**Nehru visiting the PAU
Hostel, c. 1964.
Courtesy of The Aditya
Prakash Foundation,
Chandigarh.**

of the European sun that shone its light throughout the world, but as a global process that lumbered into being as a polycentric network, rather than a unifocal spread.[35] Conceived as such, an Indian modernism is both inextricably linked to global modernism and is uniquely located in the history of India and its Third-Worldist non-aligned aspirations. As a global event, verified more in the colonies than in the metropolitan centers, it is a decentered rendition of the history of modernism, that makes modernism a global heritage, at once as much, and in the counter-colonial register, more Indian than Western.

Notes towards a more general theory of a New Third World Modernism

Modernism's universalism as a reading of the Indian nation state through a secularist repudiation of colonialist historicism sees universality as something that is simultaneously universal and local.[36] Nonetheless, there is inescapably the sense that modernism is essentially Western because it is inescapably, as Partha Mitter puts it, the sense that the intellectual property rights of modernism, specifically its claimed universality, belong to the West.[37] Inescapably then, in the Third World, modernism cannot not be construed as a Western event, and this therefore suggests that it has to be re-legitimized, not as a simple import, but as a secondary derivative construct, one that self-consciously localizes and transforms the claimed universality of modernism.

Here it is important to note that the localization of Third World as the tributary or derivative case must be distinguished from what one might describe as the "particularization" of the universal case, as for instance, in the discourses of what is sometimes called Regional Modernism. Regional Modernisms, such as those used to describe the secondary practices of places such as the Pacific Northwest, are constructed as that of the carefully bracketed particularization of universal epistemic categories such as climate, materials, soil, and sometimes, in the same bracketed sense, culture and history. The master trope at work here is geography as the binding or subtending frame, not only of verifiable "facts" such as climate and materials, but also culture and history construed as similarly cognizable facts with geographic origins. Thus, the close link of this discourse to the notion of region or regionalism, as mediated in particular by the "natural" body at work, as in notions of craft and construction.[38] Now, interpreted through the lens of "regional modernism," the idea of a "third world" modernism can also be quickly sketched out in geographical terms whereby the question of the Third World becomes the question of the map; the Third World becoming a bio-climatic zone whose poverty and inequity are also similarly seen as "facts" of their geographic condition, to be appropriately addressed in the designs. This is often located under the rubric "tropical modernism," a consequence of the location of many of the regions of the Third World in the "tropical" south. As a "tropical" construct, one can quite persuasively build a vocabulary or a typology of a modern architecture – with emphasis on elements such as sunscreen, pergolas, open-to-sky spaces, verandahs, local earthy materials, and so on – that can be said to be an alternative to the modernism of, say, the International Style.

This geographic reading of Third World modernism of course flattens the historical specificity of the colonial exploitation that generated the economic conditions of the Third World, as also it denies the potential for a radical rethinking of global power of the type proposed by the NAM reading of Third World. So it is not alternative in the explicitly political sense, but only in the intra-disciplinary sense of an alternative formal expression.[39] But if one wants to preserve the political import of an architecture of the Third World (economic asymmetry, political alternative), it would be necessary to insist on the reading of the Third World first as a historical category and only then in formal and other terms. This history-first reading of the "Third World" can of course lead us back to the discourses of economic marginality and/or alternative world visions, but here I would like to move towards another reading by returning to the discussion of modernism and universality.

One of the implications of situating modernism's universality as the specific inheritance of the West is that it produces asymmetry in readings of universality. When one views it from the "First World" or non-Third World context, the universal can surely be particularized as in Regional Modernism. But when one views it from within the context of the Third World, universal modernism as just-modernism, is first Western modernism. It is as such already "localized" or particularized. Universality itself is already localized, a consequence of the fact that modernism was conceived in the crucible of colonization. It is, in other words, already a "local modernism" and inevitably so. Thus from the point of view of the Third World, the task of defining a Third World modernism as a postcolonial act, I would argue, can simply be construed as the project of creating symmetry (or of undoing colonial asymmetry): as there is a Western modernism, there can also be a Third World modernism, not as a derivative project, but as an equivalent project. As an equivalent project, modernism claimed universality does not have to be bracketed with a nod towards an insistent localism. Rather, by seeing all modernisms as always already local, we can instead bracket the discourse of primary and derivative modernisms, and move towards a new horizon where the universal only exists as the particular, not as the derivative particularization of a universal type, but as the universal itself.

The point here, in terms of a globalized reading of the history of modern architecture, is to try to move towards a horizon where the asymmetries in the postcolonial reading of modernism can be productively drawn into dialogue with the more disciplinary reading of modernism as the negotiation between the universal and the particular. This work, I would suggest, points towards the direction of what in recent art history is being called cosmopolitan modernism. As Partha Mitter describes it, this is an effort to "shift the center of gravity from the original discourse to a more heterogeneous definition of global modernism … this calls into question the purity of the modernist canon and the consequent imputation of the derivative character of the periphery."[40] Rather than thinking of modernism as a "closed system of discourse," which can admit new modernist discourses at best only as derivative discourses derived from a master narrative, it is more productive, I would suggest, to think of "just modernism" itself as the concatenation of multiple local discourses that enumerates and promotes a worldwide modernism replete with "plurality, heterogeneity and difference."[41] In this work it is precisely modernism's core claim to universality that is its crucial component; that is, not universality that has been circumscribed, sublated or transformed through a negotiation with locality or the region or the individual, but universality as such. Or, what Anthony Appiah celebrates as everyone's "right to share the common human heritage."[42] This is not however to champion the abstract universal individual as an ideal, but rather to attach the notion "universality of the human experience," like that of universal human rights; to precisely assert the right of local lives to take control of their very local lives, not against universality, but precisely in the name of universality – a process that James Clifford calls "cosmopolitanism from below."[43]

Acknowledgements

I would like to thank Cheryl Gilge, Jiawen Hu, and Tyler Sprague, dedicated Ph.D. students, for reading this paper and making valuable suggestions. Thanks also to Duanfang Lu for the thankless task of compiling this volume.

Notes

1   Elsewhere I have offered an opinion on globalization and the Western academy in "Engaging Asia: The Ear of the Other", *JAE: Journal of Architectural Education*, 2010, vol. 61, no. 3, p. 78. Duanfang Lu has suggested that the present essay be published as something of an "Epilogue" to this book. Accordingly, I have inserted a more conversational tone into this essay, to keep things open-ended.

2   Conversation with Yang Ho Chang, during the Critical Practice in a Globalizing World Symposium held at the University of Washington, October 2006.

3   See for instance "Coda: Reconceptualizing the Modern" in Goldhagen, Sarah Williams, and Réjean Legault, *Anxious Modernisms: Experimentation in Postwar Architectural Culture*. Montréal: Canadian Centre for Architecture, 2000.

4   See for instance Fraser, Valerie, *Building the New World: Studies in the Modern Architecture of Latin America 1930–1960*. London: Verso, 2000.

5   See Dan Diner, *Cataclysms: A History of the Twentieth Century from Europe's Edge*, University of Wisconsin Press, 2007, p. 201.

6   Apparently the term "Third World" was first used by the French demographer Alfred Sauvy, in an article published in *L'Observateur*, August 14 1952, where he used the term as derived from the conception of the Third Estate, the commoners of France who, during the French Revolution, opposed both priests and nobles, who were said to define the First and Second Estates. Discussed in Mason, Mike, *Development and Disorder: A History of the Third World since 1945*. Hanover N.H.: University Press of New England, 1997, p. 30.

7   The Bandung Conference was preceded by a series of Asian Relations Conferences: The Asian Relations Conference, New Delhi, 1947; the Second Asian Relations Conference (on Indonesia), New Delhi, January 1949; the First Colombo Powers Conference, Colombo, April 1954, and the Second Colombo Powers Conference, Bogor, Indonesia, December 1954. Muthiah Alagappa, *Asian Security Order: Instrumental and Normative Features*. Stanford, California: Stanford University Press, 2003, p. 216.

8   Certainly the huge shadow at the Bandung Conference were the CENTO (Central Treaty Organization) and SEATO (South East Asian Treaty Organization) that, at the initiative of the USA, bound West Asian and South East Asian allies of the USA into a NATO style collective defense agreement. CENTO was signed by Iraq, Turkey, Pakistan, Iran, and the UK. CENTO was dissolved in 1979. SEATO was signed by the US, the UK, France, Thailand, the Philippines, Australia, New

Zealand, and Pakistan. SEATO was of course designed to counter the US perception of the Communist threat in South East Asia, with Korea and Vietnam (Indo-China) as the focal theaters of confrontation. SEATO was dissolved in 1977. For a discussion of the treaties and their role in shaping the Third World see E. J. Hobsbawm, *The Age of Extremes: A History of the World, 1914–1991*. New York: Pantheon Books, 1994, pp. 357–9.

9 These were: 1. Respect for fundamental human rights and for the purposes and principles of the charter of the United Nations; 2. Respect for the sovereignty and territorial integrity of all nations; 3. Recognition of the equality of all races and of the equality of all nations large and small; 4. Abstention from intervention or interference in the internal affairs of another country; 5. Respect for the right of each nation to defend itself, singly or collectively, in conformity with the charter of the United Nations; 6. (a) Abstention from the use of arrangements of collective defense to serve any particular interests of the big powers; (b) Abstention by any country from exerting pressures on other countries; 7. Refraining from acts or threats of aggression or the use of force against the territorial integrity or political independence of any country; 8. Settlement of all international disputes by peaceful means, such as negotiation, conciliation, arbitration, or judicial settlement as well as other peaceful means of the parties' own choice, in conformity with the charter of the United Nations; 9. Promotion of mutual interests and cooperation; 10. Respect for justice and international obligations. See Odd Arne Westad, *The Global Cold War: Third World Interventions and the Making of Our Times*. Cambridge: Cambridge University Press, 2005, p. 102.

10 From "Agreement between the Republic of India and the People's Republic of China on Trade and Intercourse between Tibet Region of China and India," http://www.claudearpi.net/maintenance/uploaded_pics/ThePancheelAgreement.pdf accessed on March 4 2010.

11 From "Talks between Nehru and Zhou, June 1954," http://www.claudearpi.net/maintenance/uploaded_pics/195406VisitZhouinDelhi.pdf accessed on March 4 2010. This is the record of the five sessions of conversation between Nehru and Zhou En-lai held from June 25 to 27 1954 in New Delhi. The minutes of the conversations were maintained by T. N. Kaul, Joint Secretary, Ministry of External Affairs, Government of India.

12 For Nehru similar areas of peace could be developed in postcolonial Africa and West Asia, similar postcolonial areas of the world facing an uncertain future in the Cold War climate. "Talks Between Nehru and Zhou," op. cit.

13 Darryl C. Thomas *The Theory and Practice of Third World Solidarity*. Westport, Connecticut: Praeger Publisher, 2001, p. 72.

14 Jawaharlal Nehru, "Speech to the Bandung Conference Political Committee, 1955" in *The Asian-African Conference*, ed. G. M. Kahim, Ithaca, NY: Cornell University Press, 1956, pp. 64–72.

15 Ibid.

16 Famously the aircraft taking him to Bandung was sabotaged, killing all the members of his team. Zhao En-lai had luckily boarded another aircraft.

17 The Indo-Chinese War made Panchsheel a symbol of mockery for the opposition in India.

18 See "Third World – Origins", Science Encyclopedia, http://science.jrank.org/pages/11447/Third-World-Origins.html, accessed March 5 2010.

19 Of course, the newest co-efficient of globalization is the environment, with climate change and sustainability increasingly being defined as the new modernism of our times, with their sense of a global human crisis with redemption offered by a technological fix authored by the West.

20 NAM conferences now actively have to address the question of their continued relevance, now that the Cold War is deemed to have ended.

21 As I noted before, this work of course remains to be done.

22 When I moved to the United States in the 1980s, I was constantly surprised how often even my academic audiences had never heard of NAM, far less of India's role in it, just as they were not well aware of any legitimate Third World Modernism, other than the great works of Le Corbusier and Louis Kahn etc., which were largely conceived simply as extensions of their personal oeuvre.

23   One of the best summaries of the plurality of these discussions is captured in Lang, Jon T., Madhavi Desai, and Miki Desai, *Architecture and Independence: the Search for Identity – India 1880 to 1980*. Delhi: Oxford University Press, 1997. The specific reference is on pp. 194–5, but discussion from pp. 114–210 chronicles the various positions.

24   Quoted in S. C. Bhatt and Gopal K. Bhargava (eds), *Land and the People of Indian States and Union Territories, Chandigarh*. Delhi: Kalpaz Publications, p. 54. Also quoted in the newspaper *Hindustan Times*, New Delhi, July 8 1950. Though this quote by Nehru, in various iterations, can be found on every pamphlet and publication on Chandigarh, I have still not been able to locate an authoritative source from Nehru's papers.

25   Similar synonymity between "modern" and "new" is found in multiple other sources, including Fraser, op. cit., p. 4.

26   In a speech given at the Indian Institute of Engineers in 1959, for instance, Nehru claimed that the British had managed to colonize India because Indian civilization had become fossilized. See Jawaharlal Nehru, "Mr. Nehru on architecture," *Urban and Rural Planning Thought*, vol. 2.2, April 1959, p. 49.

27   See C. V. J. Sharma (ed.), *Modern Temples of India: Selected Speeches of Jawaharlal Nehru at Irrigation and Power Projects*. Delhi: Central Board of Irrigation and Power, 1989, pp. 40–9.

28   But not a reading of secularism as equality of the state with respect to all religions, which is how secularism came to be defined in Nehruvian India, but in the more French or Western sense, in that secularism means the disassociation and even public suppression of religious identity, particularly as an expression of state.

29   For the "not yet" of historicism see the Introduction in Chakrabarty, Dipesh, *Provincializing Europe: Postcolonial Thought and Historical Difference*. Princeton, N. J.: Princeton University Press, 2000, pp. 3–26.

30   One could juxtapose New Delhi and Chandigarh on the same page, as Stanislos von Moos does, and suggest graphically a direct continuity between the colonial and the postcolonial acts, both as expressions of Western architectural identities imported into Indian soil. And to a certain extent this is of course certainly true, and one can simply note that New Delhi and Chandigarh are just another chapter in the unfolding drama of global influences playing themselves out in the Indian theatre. Moos, Stanislaus von,. *Le Corbusier, Elements of a Synthesis*. Cambridge, Mass: MIT Press, 1979, p. 259.

31   Later this claim to universality was re-presented as the highly disputed "International Style" which came to stand for a certain contextless formalism. International as the transnational, I would suggest, must be rigorously distinguished from international as the contextless.

32   Nehru, op. cit., p. 49.

33   That flourished until the mid-1970s, until postmodernism came into vogue, insisting on the non-Indianness of modern architecture.

34   Cohen, Jean-Louis and Monique Eleb, *Casablanca: Colonial Myths and Architectural Ventures*. New York: Monacelli Press, 2002.

35   An example of approaching architectural history from alternate "positions" can be found in Upton, Dell, "Starting from Baalbek," *JSAH*, December 2009, v. 68, n. 4, pp. 457–65.

36   Interestingly enough, the preliminary work of Matthew Nowicki in India was described by Lewis Mumford as "a genuine universalism in which the warm, the intimate, the personal attributes of a local culture would have mingled with the ideas and forms that are common to all men in our time," in "The Life, Teaching and Architecture of Matthew Nowicki," Part III, *Architectural Record*, August 1954, v. 116, p. 169.

37   Mitter, Partha, "Interventions – decentering Modernism: art history and avant-garde art from the periphery," *The Art Bulletin*, 90 (4): p. 535.

38   Which connects to attendant discourses on "tectonics" and such.

39   The mechanics that connect a formal expression to a politics, is of course something that remains un-discussed here.

40   Mitter, op. cit., p. 544.

41   Ibid., p. 540.

42   Ibid., p. 542.

43   Ibid., p. 542.

Selected Bibliography

Adorno, Theodor W. and Max Horkheimer (1979 [1947]) *Dialectic of Enlightenment*. Tr. John Cumming. London: Verso.

Anderson, Warwick. (2002) "Introduction: Postcolonial Technoscience," *Social Studies of Science* 32, no. 5/6, pp. 643-58.

Arnold, David (1996) *The Problem of Nature: Environment, Culture and European Expansion*. Oxford: Blackwell.

AlSayyad, Nezar (ed.) (1992) *Forms of Dominance: On the Architecture and Urbanism of the Colonial Enterprise,* Aldershot: Avebury.

——— (ed.) (2001) *Hybrid Urbanism: On the Identity Discourse and the Built Environment*. Westport, Connecticut: Praeger.

Andreoli, Elisabetta and Adrian Forty (eds) (2004) *Brazil's Modern Architecture*. London: Phaidon.

——— (ed.) (2004) *End of Tradition?* New York: Routledge.

Appadurai, Arjun (1996) *Modernity at Large: Cultural Dimensions of Globalisation*. Minneapolis, Minnesota: University of Minnesota Press.

Arnold, Dana, Elvan Altan Ergut and Belgin Turan Özkaya (eds) (2006) *Rethinking Architectural Historiography*. New York: Routledge.

Asojo, Abimbola O. (2008) "Hybrid forms in the built environment: a case study of African cities," in Toyin Falola, Niyi Afolabi, and Adéronké A. Adésànyà (eds), *Migrations and Creative Expressions in Africa and the African Diaspora,* Durham, NC: Carolina Academic Press.

Bell, Peter D. (1971) "The Ford Foundation as a transnational actor," *International Organization,* 25, 3: 465-78.

Benevolo, Leonardo (1971) *History of Modern Architecture*. Cambridge, Massachusetts: MIT Press.

Berman, Marshall (1982) *All that is Solid Melts into Air: The Experience of Modernity*. New York: Simon and Schuster.

Betts, Paul (2004) *The Authority of Everyday Objects: A Cultural History of West German Industrial Design*. Berkeley, California: University of California Press.

Bhatt, Ritu and Sonit Bafna (1995) "Post-Colonial narratives of Indian architecture," *Architecture+Design*, 12, 6: 85-89.

Bourdieu, Pierre (1998) *Practical Reason: On the Theory of Action*. Stanford: Stanford University Press.

Bozdogan, Sibel (1999) "Architectural history in professional education: reflections on postcolonial challenges to the modern survey," *Journal of Architectural Education*, 52, 4: 207-16.

——— (2001) *Modernism and Nation Building: Turkish Architectural Culture in the Early Republic*. Seattle: University of Washington Press.

Burian, Edward R. (ed.) (1997) *Modernity and the Architecture of Mexico*. Austin: University of Texas Press.

Cairns, Stephen (ed.) (2004) *Drifting: Architecture and Migrancy*. London: Routledge.

Carranza, Luis (2002) "Editor's introduction: expressions of modernity in Latin American architecture," *Journal of Architectural Education* 55(4):199-200.

Castillo, Greg (2005) "Domesticating the Cold War: household consumption as propaganda in Marshall Plan Germany," *Journal of Contemporary History*, 40, 2: 261-88.

Selected Bibliography

Çelik, Zeynep (1992) *Displaying the Orient: Architecture of Islam at Nineteenth-Century World's Fairs*, Berkeley, California: University of California Press.

——— (1997) *Urban Forms and Colonial Confrontations: Algiers under French Rule*, Berkeley, California: University of California Press.

——— (2005) "The ordinary and the third world at CIAM IX," in *Team Ten: 1953-1981, in Search of a Utopia of the Present*. Rotterdam: NAi.

Chakrabarty, Dipesh (2000) *Provincializing Europe: Postcolonial Thought and Historical Difference*. Princeton: Princeton University Press.

Chaliand, Gerard (1977) *Revolution in the Third World: Myths and Prospects*. New York: Viking.

Chang, Jiat-Hwee (2009) "Tropicalising technologies of environment and government: the Singapore general hospital and the circulation of the pavilion plan hospital in the British Empire, 1860-1930," in *Re-Shaping Cities: How Global Mobility Transforms Architecture and Urban Form*, edited by Michael Guggenheim and Ola Söderström, London: Routledge.

Chattopadhyay, Swati (2005) *Representing Calcutta: Modernity, Nationalism, and the Colonial Uncanny*. London: Routledge.

Cody, Jeffery W. (2003) *Exporting American Architecture, 1870-2000*. London: Routledge.

Colquhoun, Alan (1997) "The concept of regionalism," in Gülsüm Baydar Nal-bantoglu and Wong Chong Thai (eds) *Postcolonial Space(s)*, New York: Princeton Architectural Press, pp. 13-23.

Collier, Stephen J., and Aihwa Ong (2005) "Global assemblages, anthropological problems," In *Global Assemblages: Technology, Politics, and Ethics as Anthropological Problems*, edited by Aihwa Ong and Stephen J. Collier, Malden: Blackwell Publishing, pp. 3-21.

Cohen, Jean-Louis and Monique Eleb (2002) *Casablanca: Colonial Myths and Architectural Ventures*. New York: Monacelli Press.

Conrads, Ulrich (1970) *Programs and Manifestoes on 20th-Century Architecture*. Tr. Michael Bullock. Cambridge, Massachusetts: MIT Press.

Crinson, Mark (2003) *Modern Architecture and the End of Empire*. London: Ashgate.

Cronon, William (1996) *Uncommon Ground: Rethinking the Human Place in Nature*. New York: W.W. Norton & Co.

Crowley, John E. (2001) *The Invention of Comfort: Sensibilities and Design in Early Modern Britain and Early America*. Baltimore: Johns Hopkins University Press.

Crysler, Greig (2003) *Writing Spaces: Discourses of Architecture, Urbanism, and the Built Environment, 1960–2000*. New York: Routledge.

Curtis, William J. (1982) *Modern Architecture Since 1900*. Englewood Cliffs, New Jersey: Prentice-Hall.

Dal Co, Francesco (1990) *Figures of Architecture and Thought: German Architecture Culture, 1880-1920*. New York: Rizzoli.

Decter, Moshe (1977) *"To Serve, to Teach, to Leave": The Story of Israel's Development Assistance Program in Black Africa*. New York: American Jewish Congress.

Dirlik, Arif (2007 [2006]) *Global Modernity: Modernity in the Age of Global Capitalism*. Boulder: Paradigm Publishers.

Driver, Felix, and Brenda S. A. Yeoh (2000) "Constructing the tropics: introduction," *Singapore Journal of Tropical Geography* 21, 1, pp. 1-5.

Dutta, Arindam (2006) *The Bureaucracy of Beauty: Design in the Age of Its Global Reproducibility*. New York: Routledge.

Escobar, Arturo (1995) *Encountering Development: The Making and Unmaking of the Third World*. Princeton: Princeton University Press.

Eggener, Keith L. (2002) "Placing resistance: a critique of critical regionalism," *Journal of Architectural Education* 55(4): 228-37.

Eisenstadt, Shmuel N. (ed.) (2002) *Multiple Modernities*. New Brunswick: Transaction Publishers.

Elleh, Nnamdi (1997) *African Architecture: Evolution and Transformation*. New York: Macgraw-Hill.

Fletcher, Sir Banister (1897) *A History of Architecture on the Comparative Method*, London: B.T. Batsford.

Frampton, Kenneth (1983) "Prospects for a critical regionalism," *Perspecta* 20:147-62.

———— (1992 [1980]) *Modern Architecture: A Critical History*. 3rd ed. London: Thamesand Hudson.

———— (1998 [1983]) "Towards a critical regionalism: six points for an architecture of resistance," in Hal Foster (ed.) *The Anti-Aesthetic: Essays on Postmodern Culture*. New York: The New Press, pp. 17-34.

Fraser, Valerie (2000) *Building the New World: Studies in the Modern Architecture of Latin America, 1930–1960*. New York: Verso.

Fry, Maxwell, and Jane Drew (1964) *Tropical Architecture in the Dry and Humid Zones*. London: Batsford.

Fuller, Mia (2007) *Moderns Abroad: Architecture, Cities and Italian Imperialism*. New York: Routledge.

Gaonkar, Dilip Parameshwar (1999) "On alternative modernities," *Public Culture* 11(1):1-18.

———— (ed.) (2001) *Alternative Modernities*. Durham, North Carolina: Duke University Press.

Gidion, Siegfried (1941) *Space, Time and Architecture: The Growth of a New Tradition*. Cambridge, Massachusetts: Harvard University Press.

Gloag, John (1961) *Victorian Comfort: A Social History of Design from 1830-1900*. London: Adam & Charles Black.

Glover, William J. (2008) *Making Lahore Modern: Constructing and Imagining a Colonial City*. Minneapolis: University of Minnesota Press.

Goldhagen, Sarah Williams and Réjean Legault (eds) (2000) *Anxious Modernisms: Experimentation in Postwar Architectural Culture*. Montréal: Canadian Centre for Architecture.

Gramsci, Antonio (1971) *Selections from the Prison Notebooks*. Eds and tr. Quintin Hoare and Geoffrey Nowell-Smith. London: Lawrence & Wishart.

Grier, Katherine C. (1988) *Culture & Comfort: People, Parlors, and Upholstery, 1850-1930*. Rochester, N.Y.Strong Museum; Amherst.

Gropius, Walter (1965) *The New Architecture and the Bauhaus*. Cambridge, Massachusetts: MIT Press.

Guillén, Mauro F. (2004) "Modernism without modernity: the rise of modernist architecture in Mexico, Brazil, and Argentina, 1890–1940," *Latin American Research Review*, 39(2): 6-34.

Habermas, Jurgen (1981) "Modernity versus postmodernity," *New German Critique* 22:3-14.

Haraway, Donna (1988) "Situated knowledges: the science question in feminism and the privilege of partial perspective." *Feminist Studies* 14, 3, pp. 575-99.

Hartoonian, Gevork (1997) *Modernity and Its Other: A Post-Script to Contemporary Architecture*. College Station, Texas: Texas A&M University Press.

Havinden, Michael A., and David Meredith (1993) *Colonialism and Development: Britain and Its Tropical Colonies, 1850-1960*. London: Routledge.

Hays, K. Michael (1992) *Modernism and the Posthumanist Subject: The Architecture of Hannes Meyer and Ludwig Hilberseimer*. Cambridge, Massachusetts: MIT Press.

Herf, Jeffrey (1984) *Reactionary Modernism: Technology, Culture, and Politics in Weimar and the Third Reich*. Cambridge: Cambridge University Press.

Hernandez, Felipe (2002) "On the notion of architectural hybridization in Latin America," *Journal of Archi-tecture*, 7, 1: 77-86.

Heynen, Hilde (1999) *Architecture and Modernity: A Critique*. Cambridge, Massachusetts: MIT Press.

Heynen, Hilde and Gülsüm Baydar (eds) (2005) *Negotiating Domesticity: Spatial Productions of Gender in Modern Architecture*. London: Routledge.

Hitchcock, Henry R. (1955) *Latin American Architecture since 1945*, New York: MoMA.

Hitchcock, Henry-Russell and Philip Johnson (1932) *The International Style*. New York: Norton.

Hoffenberg, Peter H. (2001) *An Empire on Display: English, Indian, and Australian Exhibitions from the Crystal Palace to the Great War*. Berkeley, Caifornia: University of California Press.

Holston, James (1989) *The Modernist City: An Anthropological Critique of Brasília*. Chicago: University of Chicago Press.

Home, Robert K. (1997) *Of Planting and Planning: The Making of British Colonial Cities*. London: Spon.

Hudson, Hugh D., Jr. (1994) *Blueprints and Blood: the Stalinization of Soviet Architecture, 1917-1937*. Princeton, New Jersey: Princeton University Press.

Selected Bibliography

Hvattum, Mari and Christian Hermansen (eds) (2004) *Tracing Modernity: Manifestations of the Modern in Architecture and the City*. New York: Routledge.

Ike, Vincent Chukwuemeka (1976) *University Development in Africa*, Ibadan: Oxford University Press.

Isenstadt, Sandy and Kishwar Rizvi (2008) *Modern Architecture and the Middle East: Architecture and Politics in the Twentieth Century. Seattle:* University of Washington Press.

Isaac, Harold R. (1958) *Scratches on Our Minds: American Images of China and India*. New York: The John Day Company.

Jacobs, Jane M. (1996) *Edge of Empire: Postcolonialism and the City*. London: Routledge.

Kalm, Mart and Ingrid Ruudi (eds) (2005) *Constructed Happiness: Domestic Environment in the Cold War Era*. Tallinn: Estonian Academy of Arts.

King, Anthony D. (1990) *Urbanism, Colonialism, and the World-Economy: Cultural and Spatial Foundations of the World Urban System*. London: Routledge.

—— (1995 [1984]) *The Bungalow: The Production of a Global Culture*. 2nd ed. New York: Oxford University Press.

Kirsch, Karin (1989) *The Weissenhofsiedlung: Experimental Housing Built for the Deutscher Werkbund, Stuttgart, 1927*. New York: Rizzoli.

Kreinin, Mordechai E. (1964) *Israel and Africa: A Study in Technical Cooperation*, New York: Praeger.

Kusno, Abidin (2000) *Behind the Postcolonial: Architecture, Urban Space, and Political Cultures in Indonesia*. London: Routledge.

Lane, Barbara Miller (ed.) (2007) *Housing and Dwelling: Perspectives on Modern Domestic Architecture*. London: Routledge.

Lang, Jon, Madhavi Desai, and Miki Desai (1997) *Architecture and Independence: The Search for Identity–India 1880 to 1980*. Delhi: Oxford University Press.

Latour, Bruno (1987) *Science in Action: How to Follow Scientists and Engineers through Society*. Cambridge: Harvard University Press.

——. (1993) *We Have Never Been Modern*. Cambridge, MA: Harvard University Press.

Law, John (1987) "Technology and heterogeneous engineering: the case of Portuguese Expansion," in *The Social Construction of Technological Systems: New Directions in the Sociology and History of Technology*, edited by Wiebe E. Bijker, Thomas P. Hughes and T. J. Pinch, Cambridge, MA: MIT Press, pp. 111-34.

Le Corbusier (1927) *Towards a New Architecture*. Tr. Frederick Etchells. London: John Rodker.

Le Roux, Hannah (2003) "The networks of tropical architecture," *Journal of Architecture* 8: 337-54.

Lefèbvre, Henri (1991) *The Production of Space*. Cambridge: Basil Blackwell.

Lea, F. M. (1971) *Science and Building: A History of the Building Research Station*. London: Her Majesty's Stationary Office.

Lippsmeier, Georg, Walter Kluska, and Carol Gray Edrich (1969) *Tropenbau/Building in the Tropics*. Munchen: Callwey.

Loeffler, Jane C. (1998) *The Architecture of Diplomacy: Building America's Embassies*. New York: Princeton Architectural Press.

Lu, Duanfang (2000) "The changing landscape of hybridity: a reading of ethnic identity and urban form in late-twentieth-century Vancouver," *Traditional Dwellings and Settlements Review* 11(2): 19-28.

—— (2006) *Remaking Chinese Urban Form: Modernity, Scarcity and Space, 1949–2005*. London: Routledge.

—— (2007a) "Third World modernism: modernity, utopia and the people's commune in China," *Journal of Architectural Education* 60(3): 40-8.

—— (2007b) "Architecture and global imaginations in China," *Journal of Architecture* 12(2): 123-45.

—— (forthcoming) "Entangled modernities in architecture," in Greg Crysler, Stephen Cairns and Hilde Heynen (eds) *Handbook of Architectural Theory*, London: Sage.

McCarthy, Kathleen D. (1987) "From Cold War to cultural development: the international cultural activities of the Ford Foundation, 1950-1980," *Daedalus*, 116, 1: 93-117.

Mcdonald, Gay (2004) "Selling the American dream: MoMA, industrial design and post-war France," *Journal of Design History*, 17, 4: 397-412.

McGowan, Abigail (2009) *Crafting the Nation in Colonial India*. New York: Palgrave Macmillan.

Metcalf, Thomas R. (1989) *An Imperial Vision: Indian Architecture and Britain's Raj*, Berkeley, California: University of California Press.

Mackie, Jamie (2005) *Bandung 1955: Non-alignment and Afro-Asian Solidarity*. Singapore: Select Books.

MacLeod, Roy (2000) "Introduction to special issue on nature and empire: science and the colonial enterprise," *Osiris* 15: 1-13.

Masey, Jack and Conway Lloyd Morgan (2008) *Cold War Confrontations, US Exhibitions And Their Role In the Cultural Cold War*. Baden: Lars Muller Publishers.

Mason, Mike (1997) *Development and Disorder: A History of the Third World since 1945*. Hanover, NH: University Press of New England.

McNeil, Donald (2009) *The Global Architect: Firms, Fame and Urban Form*. New York: Routledge.

Mitter, Partha (2008) "Interventions - decentering modernism: art history and avant-garde art from the periphery," *The Art Bulletin*, 90 (4): 531-48.

Morton, Patricia (2000) *Hybrid Modernities: Architecture and Representation at the 1931 Colonial Exposition, Paris*. Cambridge MA: The MIT Press.

Nitzan-Shiftan, Alona (1996) "Contested zionism – alternative modernism: Erich Mendelsohn and the Tel Aviv Chug in Mandate Palestine," *Architectural History*, 39: 147-80.

Mindlin, Henrique E. (1956) *Modern Architecture in Brazil*, New York: Reinhold.

Mohammad, S.Z. and S. IK. Umenne (2006) "Socio-cultural and economic aspects of university campus landscape development in sub-Saharan Africa," *African Journal of Science and Technology*, 7, 2.

Noobanjong, Koompong (2003) *Power, Identity, and the Rise of Modern Architecture: From Siam to Thailand*. Florida: Universal Publishers.

Norwine, Jim and Alfonso Gonzalez (1988) *The Third World: States of Mind and Being*. Winchester, Mass.: Unwin Hyman, Inc.

Ojo, Olusola (1988) *Africa and Israel: Relations in Perspective*, Boulder: Westview Press.

Ockman, Joan (1993) *Architecture Culture 1943-1968: A Documentary Anthology*, New York: Rizzoli.

Overy, Paul (2005) "White walls, white skins: cosmopolitanism and colonialism in inter-war modernist architecture," in Kobena Mercer (ed.) *Cosmopolitan Modernisms*. London: Institute of International Visual Arts, pp. 50-67.

Pevsner, Nikolaus (1968) *The Sources of Modern Architecture and Design*. New York: Praeger.

Pieris, Anoma (2006) "Is sustainability sustainable? interrogating the tropical paradigm in Asian architecture," in Joo-Hwa Bay and Boon Lay Ong (eds) *Tropical Sustainable Architecture: Social and Environmental Dimensions* (Oxford: Architectural Press), pp. 267-86.

Pinch, T. J., Thomas Parke. Hughes, and Wiebe E. Bijker (eds) (1987) *The Social Construction of Technological Systems: New Directions in the Sociology and History of Technology*. Cambridge, MA: MIT Press.

Prakash, Gyan (1999) *Another Reason: Science and the Imagination of Modern India*. Princeton: Princeton University Press.

Prakāsh, Vikramāditya (2002) *Chandigarh's Le Corbusier: The Struggle for Modernity in Postcolonial India*. Seattle: University of Washington Press.

Perera, Nihal (1998) *Society and Space: Colonialism, Nationalism, and Postcolonial Identity in Sri Lanka*. Boulder, Colorado: Westview Press,

Rabinow, Paul (1989) *French Modern: Norms and Forms of the Social Environment*. Cambridge, Massachusetts: MIT Press.

Radhakrishnan, Rajagopalan (2000) "Postmodernism and the rest of the world," in Fawzia Afzal-Khan and Kalpana Seshadri-Crooks (eds) *The Pre-Occupation of Postcolonial Studies*. Durham: Duke University Press, pp. 37-70.

Robinson, Jennifer (2005) *Ordinary Cities: Between Modernity and Development*. New York: Routledge.

Robinson, Joyce Henry (2002) "'Hi Honey, I'm home', weary (neurasthenic) businessman and the formulation of a serenely modern Aesthetic," in Andrew Ballantyne (ed.) *What is Architecture*, New York: Routledge, 2002, pp. 112-128.

Selected Bibliography

Rosner, Victoria (2005) *Modernism and the Architecture of Private Life*. New York: Columbia University Press.

Roux, Hannah Le (2004) "Modern architecture in post-colonial Ghana and Nigeria," *Architectural History*, 47: 361-92.

Rowe, Peter G. and Seng Kuan (2002) *Architectural Encounters with Essence and Form in Modern China*. Cambridge, Massachusetts: MIT Press.

Sachs, Wolfgang (ed.) (1992) *The Development Dictionary: A Guide to Knowledge as Power*. London: Zed Books.

Sachsenmaier, Dominic, Jens Riedel and Shmuel N. Eisenstadt (2002) *Reflections on Multiple Modernities: European, Chinese and Other Interpretations*. Leiden: Brill.

Said, Edward W. (1978) *Orientalism*. London: Routledge.

Sand, Jordan (2003) *House and Home in Modern Japan: Architecture, Domestic Space, and Bourgeois Culture, 1880-1930*. Cambridge, Massachusetts: Harvard University Press.

Scott, James C. (1998) *Seeing Like a State: How Certain Schemes to Improve the Human Condition Have Failed*. New Haven: Yale University Press.

Scriver, Peter and Vikramāditya Prakāsh (2007) *Colonial Modernities: Building, Dwelling and Architecture in British India and Ceylon*. London: Routledge.

Therborn, Göran (2003) "Entangled modernities," *European Journal of Social Theory* 6(3): 293-305. Thomas, Darryl C. (2001) *The Theory and Practice of Third World Solidarity*. Westport, Connecticut: Praeger Publisher.

Tzonis, Alexander and Liane Lefaivre (1981) "The grid and the pathway," *Architecture in Greece* 15:164-78.

Umbach, Maiken and Bernd Hüppauf (eds) (2005) *Vernacular Modernism: Heimat, Globalization, and the Built Environment*. Stanford, California: Stanford University Press.

Uduku, Ola (2006) "Modernist architecture and 'the tropical' in West Africa: The tropical architecture movement in West Africa, 1948–1970," *Habitat International*, 30: 397-98

Upton, Dell (1991) "Architectural history or landscape history?" *Journal of Architectural Education* 44 (4):195-9.

Vlach, John Michael (1984) "The Brazilian house in Nigeria: the emergence of a 20th-century vernacular house type," *The Journal of American Folklore*, 97, 383: 3-23.

Wharton, A. J. (2001) *Building the Cold War: Hilton International Hotels and Modern Architecture*. Chicago: Univ. of Chicago Press.

Williams, Patrick and Laura Chrisman (1994) *Colonial Discourse and Post-Colonial Theory: A reader*. New York: Columbia University Press.

Williams, Richard J. (2009) *Brazil: Modern Architectures in History*. London: Reaktion Books.

Windsor-Liscombe, Rhodri (2006) "Modernism in late imperial British West Africa: the work of Maxwell Fry and Jane Drew, 1946-56," *Journal of the Society of Architectural Historians* 65, 2: 188-213.

Wolf, Eric R. (1997 [1982]) *Europe and the People without History*. 2nd ed. Berkeley, California: University of California Press.

Wright, Gwendolyn (1991) *The Politics of Design in French Colonial Urbanism*. Chicago: University of Chicago Press.

Zhu, Jianfei (2009) *Architecture of Modern China: A Historical Critique*. London: Routledge.

Zou, Denong (2001) *Zhongguo xiandai jianzhu shi* [Modern Chinese Architectural History]. Tianjin: Tianjin kexue jishu chubanshe.

Contributors

Vandana Baweja is Assistant Professor of Architecture in the School of Architecture, and the Sustainability Program in the College of Design Construction and Planning at the University of Florida, USA. She was trained as an architect in New Delhi, India, and holds masters from the Architectural Association School of Architecture and a Ph.D. from the University of Michigan-Ann Arbor. Her research focuses on the history of Sustainable Architecture and Modern South Asia.

Jiat-Hwee Chang is Assistant Professor at the Department of Architecture, National University of Singapore. He holds a PhD in Architecture from the University of California, Berkeley. His writings on colonial and postcolonial architectural history, sustainability and the built environment, and design cultures appear in various edited volumes and journals, including *Journal of Architectural Education* and *Docomomo Journal*. He is the author of a book on new design culture in cosmopolitan Singapore (Pesaro, 2010) and the co-editor of a forthcoming special issue of *Singapore Journal of Tropical Geography* on "tropical architecture."

Aziza Chaouni is Assistant Professor in the John H. Daniels Faculty of Architecture, Landscape, and Design at the University of Toronto, Canada. She has a M. Arch. from the Harvard Graduate School of Design and a B.Sc. from Columbia University. She is Director of the research board of DOCO.MO.MO Morocco and Principal of Bureau E.A.S.T. She is currently researching on the work of Jean-François Zevaco and Elie Azagury. Her research "Hybrid urban sutures: filling the gaps in the medina of Fez" received the 2007 Progressive Architecture Award.

Inbal Ben-Asher Gitler teaches modern art and architectural history at Tel Aviv University, Ben Gurion University and Sapir Academic College, Israel. Her research has concentrated upon modern Israeli architecture and urbanism, and Orientalism in the arts. She has published papers on British Mandatory art and architecture and urbanism in Israel/Palestine.

Elâ Kaçel is Assistant Professor at the Bahçeşehir University, Istanbul. She received her Ph.D. in the History of Architecture from Cornell University. Drawing on case studies from postwar Turkish modernism, her research considers the role of intellectuals in the context of social change, taking into regard the role of cultural politics, consumerism and knowledge production in professional life. Her publications include *Ingiltere'de Konut Standartlarının Değişen Bağlamı* (1998), "Fidüsyer: Bir Kolektif Düşünme Pratiği" in Müge Cengizkan (ed.), *Haluk Baysal – Melih Birsel* (2007) and articles in *Cogito, Arredamento Mimarlık, Domus m* and *Candide: Journal for Architectural Knowledge*.

Sharif S. Kahatt holds a Master's degree in Architecture and Urban Design from Harvard GSD, a Master's degree in Theory and History of Architecture from the ETSAB, Barcelona, and a professional degree in Architecture from Ricardo Palma University, Lima. He is currently completing a doctoral dissertation on design strategies for collective housing in Lima at the ETSAB, Barcelona. He is an architect, urban designer and founder of K+M Arquitectura y Urbanismo, and has taught in Peru, Spain, and the United States.

Farhan Sirajul Karim is Lecturer in Architectural History at the Bangladesh University of Engineering and Technology. His research work intersects the history of built environment and the history of political emancipation. He is currently a Ph.D. candidate in the Faculty of Architecture, Design and Planning at the University of Sydney. His dissertation examines an array of colonial and post-colonial design and home exhibitions – a site of contesting notions of a national home and an ideological desire for modernity in India.

Duanfang Lu is Senior Lecturer in the Faculty of Architecture, Design and Planning at the University of Sydney, Australia. She holds a Bachelor of Architecture from Tsinghua University, Beijing and a Ph.D. in Architecture from the University of California, Berkeley. She has published widely on modern Chinese architectural and planning history. She serves on editorial boards of the journals *Architectural Theory Review* and *Traditional Dwellings and Settlements Review*, and has been a recipient of many prestigious research grants and awards.

Anoma Pieris is Senior Lecturer in the Faculty of Architecture, Building and Planning at the University of Melbourne, Australia. She is the author of *Hidden Hands and Divided Landscapes: the Penal History of Singapore's Plural Society* (University of Hawaii Press, 2009); *Imagining Modernity: The Architecture of Valentine Gunasekara* (2007); *JCY: The Architecture of Jones Coulter Young* (2005) and co-author (with P. Goad) of *New Directions in Tropical Asian Architecture* (2005). She has a B.Sc. (Built Env.) from the University of Moratuwa, Sri Lanka; M.Arch. and S.M.Arch.S. from the Massachusetts Institute of Technology, and a Ph.D. from the University of California, Berkeley.

Vikramaditya Prakāsh is Professor of Architecture at the University of Washington, USA. He grew up in Chandigarh, India, received his B.Arch. from the Chandigarh College of Architecture, Panjab University, and an M.A. and Ph.D. in History and Theory of Architecture and Urbanism from Cornell University. Prakāsh has published several papers and books including *Chandigarh's Le Corbusier: The Struggle for Modernity in Postcolonial India* (2002), *A Global History of Architecture* (with Francis D. K. Ching and Mark Jarzombek, 2006) and *Colonial Modernities: Building, Dwelling and Architecture in British India and Ceylon* (co-edited with Peter Scriver, 2007). Professor Prakāsh is currently working on "A New History of the Architecture of India," a multi-media, multi-format project intended to put colonial histories of India finally to rest.

Daniela Sandler is Assistant Professor in the Department of the History of Art and Visual Culture at the University of California, Santa Cruz, USA. She has a Ph.D. in Visual and Cultural Studies from the University of Rochester, and a professional degree in architecture and urbanism from the University of São Paulo, Brazil. She has published on modern architecture, urbanism, and memory in Brazil and in Germany.

Index

Page references to Figures are in *italic* print, while references to Notes are followed by the letter 'n'

Aalto, Alvar, 81, 122, 176
Abiodun, Rowland, 139n
Accra: US embassy in, 140n; West African
    Building Research Institute in, 215, 221
Achebe, Chinua, 113, 135n
Acorn House, 174, 175, 180
active urbanism (evolving housing), 76
Actor-Network-Theory (ANT), 212, 224, 228, 229
Adam, André, 83n, 84n
adapted housing, 67
Ade Ajayi, J. F., 136n
Adésànyà, Adéronké A., 139n
Adorno, Theodor W., 20, 28n, 172
Adrianzén, Alberto, 107n
aesthetic-economic theories (Le Corbusier and
    Gropius), 37
Afolabi, Niyi, 139n
Africa: Israeli technical assistance programs to,
    115–19; Yoruba art, 126, 129, 130, 132, 133;
    see also Morocco/Moroccan modernism;
    Nigeria
Afro-Asian Institute, Israel, 116
Afzal-Khan, Fawzia, 28n
Agadir: earthquake in, 58, 72; Evolving Housing
    project, 79; housing block in, 68;
    reconstruction of, 58; social housing project,
    77–8
Agricultural Cooperatives Headquarters, Tel Aviv,
    126, 127
Agrupación Espacio, 86, 89, 103, 105; and
    challenge of CIAM-Peru Group, 99–101; end
    of, 101–4; and search for modern city, 94–9;
    significance of, 106
Agurto, Santiago, 86, 89, 95, 102, 104, 106, 107n
Ahmedabad design school, 189, 205
Aix-en-Provence, CIAM 9 meeting at, 61, 64, 65,
    69, 78
Ajose, Oladele, 137n
Alagappa, Muthiah, 267n
Alagaratnam, C., 153, 163n
"All India Handicraft Board," 192
All That is Solid Melts into Air (Berman), 141
Almandoz, Arturo, 54n
Aloni, Yael, *112, 121, 125, 128, 131,* 135, 137n,
    138n
AlSayyad, Nezar, 26n, 27n
Alva, Eduardo Neira, 107n, 109n
Álvarez Calderón, Augusto, 109n
Amarel, Aracy, 53n
ambiguous modernism, Brazil, 33–42; in Rua
    Santa Cruz house, 32, 38
ambivalent modernism, Brazil, 32, 43–50, 52n
American Institute of Architects (AIA), 170

Amery, Leo, 232n
Amzallag, Armand, 72, 77, 79
Anand, D. N., *203,* 209n
de Andrade, José Oswald, 53–4n
de Andrade, Mario, 53–4n
Anderson, Benedict, 27n
Anderson, Perry, 141, 142, 162n
Anderson, Stanford, 56n
Anderson, Warwick, 230n
Andreoli, Elisabetta, 25n, 54n
Anelli, Renato, 47, 56n
AnkoǦlu, Nezahat, 185n
ANT (Actor-Network-Theory), 212, 224, 228, 229
anthropological approach, development (Group
    GAMMA), 73–8
APAO (Association for Organic Architecture),
    176, 185n
Appiah, Anthony, 267
Apter, Andrew, 138n
Aquinas, Thomas, 199
Arab-Israeli conflict, 117, 136n
Arabo-Andalousian courtyard, Morocco, 81
Arantes, Pedro Fiori, 43–4, 55n, 56n
Arcades Project (Benjamin), 157
Architectural Association (AA), 149, 221;
    Department of Tropical Architecture, 17, 211,
    220, 237, 238
Architectural Forum, 23, 174
Architectural Journal (Jianzhu xuebao), 23
Architecture + Urbanism (A+U), 58, *72,* 73, 76,
    78
Architecture d'Aujourd'hui, 58, 66, 69
"Architecture for the Good Life," 170
"Architecture without architects" (exhibition), 78
Arendt, Hannah, 198, 208n
ArikoǦlu, Nezahat, 173
Arkitekt (trade journal), 171, 173, 174, 176, 180,
    181
Arkush, R. David, 28n
Arnold, David, 234n, 237, 253n
Aronin, Jeffrey Ellis, 224
Artigas, Juan B., 139n
ascetic modernity, 190, 209n
Ashton, Sir Leigh, 192
Asojo, Abimbola O., 139n
Association des Architects, 73
Association for Organic Architecture (APAO),
    176, 185n
ATBAT-Afrique, Morocco, 61, 67, 83n, 243;
    Candilis as head of, 65–9; housing project,
    243
Athens Charter, 61, 62, 63, 69; hygiene concerns,
    66

Atkinson, Fello, 17, 137n, 238
Atkinson, George Anthony, 217–21, 226, 228,
    232n, 233n, 234n, 254n; as CLO, 219, 222
Atlas Mountains, 66
Australia: and Colombo Plan, 145–6, 147, 150;
    Commonwealth Experimental Station, 221
auto-construction, 103
avant-garde, 35, 86, 92, 142, 179; and Turkey,
    166
Avenida Paulista, Brazil, 44, 46, 47; see also
    Museum of Art, São Paulo (MASP)
Avermaete, Tom, 83n
Awokoya, Stephan, 114, 115
Awolowo, Jeramiah Obafemi, 115
Azagury, Elie, 61, 62, 64, 65, 67, 68, 71, 75, 76,
    78, 82n, 84n
Azikiwe, Nnamdi, 114, 136n

Bafna, Sonit, 155, 163n
Bakhtin, Mikhail, 161, 164n
Bakra Nangal dam, 261
Balaram, K., 194
Ballantyne, Andrew, 208n
Ballent, A., 93
Bandaranaike, S. W. R. D., 150, 153
Bandaranaike Memorial International Conference
    Hall, Colombo, 7, 8
Bandung Conference (Afro-Asian Conference),
    1955, 2, 267n; principles, 257–8, 268n
Banerjee, Subrata, 207n
Bangladesh, National Assembly, Dacca, 129
Banham, Reyner, 253n
Bank of Israel, Jerusalem, 127
Bardi, Lina Bo, 11–12, 32, 43–50, 53, 56n;
    immigration to Brazil, 43, 44, 50, 51
Bardi, Pietro Maria, 44, 46, 52, 52n
Barnitz, Jacqueline, 55n
Barreto, Samuel Pérez, 107n
barriadas, 86, 102, 106
Barringer, Tim, 201, 209n
Barrow, Simon, 246, 247, 248, 250
Bath, Second Arts Building, 249–50
Batsford, B. T., 28n
Bauhaus school, Dessau, 113, 119
Bawa, Geoffrey, 149, 154, 158, 238
Baweja, Vandana, 18, 236–52, 253n, 254n
Baydar Nal-bantoglu, Gülsüm, 28n
BayramoĞlu House, 182
"Beautiful Indonesia in Miniature," 156, 157
Beaux Arts School, Casablanca, 71, 79, 84n
Beaux-Arts principles, 34
Beckett, H. E., 222
Belaúnde, Fernando, 89, 90, 91–2, 94, 95, 97, 98,
    100, 101, 104, 107n, 108n, 109n, 110n; "four
    city functions," 88, 89
Belgrade conference (1961), 259
Belkahia, Farid, 79
Bell, Peter D., 208n
Ben Embarek, Mourad, 72, 73, 84n
Benevolo, Leonardo, 26n
Benítez, Juan F., 98, 109n
Benjamin, Walter, 157–8, 159, 163n
Bennett, Tony, 143, 144, 162n
Beraud, 84n
Bergamo, CIAM 7 project in, 61, 97
Berman, Marshall, 4, 26n, 141–2, 162n
Bertram, 107n

Betts, Paul, 26n, 209n
Beunard, Yannick, 59
Bhabha, Homi K., 27n, 140n
Bhaga, Surinder, 209n
Bhargava, Gopal K., 269n
Bhatt, Ritu, 155, 163n
Bhatt, S. C., 269n
Bhubaneswar, planning of, 149
Bianco, Mario, 100, 107n, 109n
Bijker, Wiebe E., 234n
Bilimorea (architect), 151
Bilzky, Eliyahu, 136n, 137n
Bio-Climatic Architecture, United States, 241
Birla (Indian industrialist), 191
Black, Adam and Charles, 208n
Blacklock, D. B., 213, 231n
Blacklock, Mary, 231n
Bloc, André, 69
Bo Bardi, Lina, 56n
Boaventura, Maria Eugênia, 53n
Bodiansky, Vladimir, 61, 63, 83n, 84n
Bogéa, Marta, 55n
Bonet, Luis, 99
Bonillo, Jean-Lucien, 81, 84n
Bora, Tanil, 184n
Borj Al Omar, Meknes, 73–4
Bosman, Joe, 82n
Bourdieu, Pierre, 221, 233n
BozdoĞan, Sibel, 25n, 26n, 27n, 229, 235n
Brasília, 10, 37, 42, 45, 151; British Embassy in,
    237, 244, 245
Brayer, Marie-Ange, 82n
Brazil/Brazilian modernism, 11–12, 31–52;
    ambiguous modernism, 32, 33–42;
    ambivalent modernism, 32, 43–50, 52n;
    developmentalism, 42–3, 45; Ministry of
    Health and Education, 36, 37, 41, 42;
    Modernist House (Casa Modernista), 11, 32,
    33, 34, 36–42, 39, 51; modernist movement,
    34, 35, 38; Museum of Art, São Paulo, 32,
    44–50; and Nigeria, 115, 136n; Pampulha
    complex, 36, 37, 41; political context, 48;
    traditional houses, layout, 38, 39, 40; "unique
    visage" of architecture, 33
Brazilian Pavilion, 41
Bretton Woods Agreements (1944), 8
Bridgewater Congress, 61, 63
Brion, Edmond, 83n
brise-soleil, 67, 224
British architectural culture, 236–52; climate
    responsive design, in architectural
    historiography, 241–2; Kuwait Mat Project,
    245–9; Second Arts Building, Bath, 249–50;
    Tropical Architecture, 237–8, 251–2
Browne, Sir Granville St John Orde, 213, 231n
BRS see Building Research Station (BRS)
Buck-Morss, Susan, 158, 163n
Buddhism, Ceylon, 144, 154, 157, 158
Building Research Station (BRS), 6, 221, 222;
    Tropical Building Division, 17, 212, 213,
    217–24, 228
building standards, 218–19
buildings, regular vs special, 183n
Bullock, Michael, 26n
Bunshaft, Gordon, 110n, 165, 175, 176, 184n
bureaucratic architecture, 175
Burian, Edward R., 25n

Burt, R. H., 231n
Bustamante y Rivero, José Luis, 87
Buttigieg, J. A., 184n
Bütün Dünya, 172

Cable Senior, Susan, 196
Cage, John, 48
Cairns, Stephen, 27n, 28n, 230n
Çalik, Şadi, 180, 182
Calvo, Santiago Agurto, 109n, 110n
Can Our Cities Survive? (Sert), 92
Canclini, Néstor García, 85, 106n
Candilis, George, 60–4, 71, 74, 76, 77, 80, 83n,
    84n; and Group GAMMA, 65–9; as head of
    ATBAT Afrique, 65
Carrières Centrales (Casablancan shantytown),
    63, 66, 69, 80
Carstairs, C. Y., 231n
Casa Huiracocha (Quesada's house in Lima), 93
Casablanca, 263; Beaux Arts School, 71, 79, 84n;
    Carrières Centrales (shantytown), 63, 66,
    69,80; Derb Jdid housing project, 74–5, 76;
    population, 83n
Castelnau, Elaine, 79, 84n
Castillo, Greg, 206, 207n, 208n
Cauquil, Helene, 210n
Cayo, Javier, 107n, 109n
CDWA (Colonial Development and Welfare Act),
    214, 217–18, 220
Çelik, Zeynep, 26n, 83n
CENTO (Central Treaty Organization), 2, 267n
Central Building Research Station, India, 221
Centre for Bamboo Initiatives (NID), 205
Centro Vacacional Huampaní project, Peru, 89
CERF (research center), 75
Ceylon/Sri Lanka, 8, 141–61; colonial modernity,
    143–5; exhibition of 1965 (Colombo 65), 15,
    150–1, *152*, 153, 154, 156, 159; *Gam Udawa*
    (Village Re-awakening) movement, 156–60,
    161; language policy (1956), 150; national
    pavilion, 147, 148, 151; postwar political
    culture, 145–9; social modernity of, 152; Sri
    Lanka Freedom Party, 153; United National
    Party, 147, 153, 154, 161; Universal Adult
    Franchise in, 21st anniversary (1952), 146;
    see also Colombo
Chadha, Rajni, 208n
Chadwick, Gordon, 195
chair, and physical comfort, 197, 204
Chakrabarti, Mohit, 209n
Chakrabarty, Dipesh, 9, 24, 26n, 28n, 269n
Chaliand, Gerard, 25n
Chamberlain, Joseph, 216
Chambers, David Wade, 232n
Chandigarh, 13–14, 149, 151, 203, 256, 260–3,
    264; and New Dehli, 14, 262, 269n
Chandler, S. E., 231n
Chang, Jiat-Hwee, 6, 17–18, 211–29, 230n, 233n,
    234n, 235n
Chang, Yang Ho, 267n
Chaouni, Aziza, 12, 57–81
Charter of Machu Picchu, 104
Chateaubriand, Assis, 44
Chattopadhyay, Kamaladevi, 192, 206n
Chattopadhyay, Swati, 26n, 143–4, 162n
Chemineau, J., 63, 71
Chiclayo Housing Complex, Peru, 104

Chimbote project, Peru, 87–8, 91, 97
China, 7, 10, 19, 255, 257, 258, 259
Chrisman, Laura, 135n, 140n
CHU (Circumscription of Urbanism and Habitat,
    formerly Service of Urbanism), 73, 74, 75, 79;
    see also Service of Urbanism, Morocco
Chukwuemeka Ike, Vincent, 135n
Churchill, Winston, 133, 134
CIAM (*Congress International d'Architecture
    Moderne*), 4, 7, 57, 58, 86, 225; CIAM 7
    (Bergamo), 61, 97; CIAM 8 (Hoddesdon), 60,
    61, 82n; CIAM 9 (Aix-en-Provence), 61, 64,
    65, 69, 78; CIAM 10 (Dubrovnik), 71, 102;
    CIAM 11 (Otterlo), 71; *CIAM Chapter for
    Relief and Postwar Planning*, 91; CIAM-Peru
    Group, 99–101; council, 61; end of, 101–4;
    evangelization and Peruvian pioneers of
    modern architecture, 90–3; formation of
    groups, 59–60; four functions, 89; grid, 62,
    64, 66, 73, 83n; Maroc Group, 61; Team 10,
    57, 69, 81, 101; *see also* Group GAMMA
    (Groupe d'Architectes Modernes Marocains),
    Morocco; Morocco/Moroccan modernism;
    Peru
Cité Radieuse, 69
civilizing mission, concept, 57, 65, 82n, 117
Clayton, Anthony, 231n
Clewing, Ulrich, 139n
Clifford, James, 16, 27n
Climate Register, 236–7, 249
climatic design/climate responsive design, 224–7,
    241–5, 247, 251
CLU (Colonial Liaison Unit), 212, 213, 222, 226
CNV (*Corporación Nacional de la Vivienda*), Peru,
    89, 95, 103
Cody, J. W., 26n, 27n, 183n
Cohen, Jean-Louis, 82n, 83n, 84n, 263, 269n
Colabora la Agrupación Espacio, 95
Cold War, 3, 6, 145, 257
Coldefy, Pierre, 74
collaboration, 178
Collier, Stephen J., 230n
Colombo, 149–54; Bandaranaike Memorial
    International Conference Hall, 7, *8*; Colombo
    65, 15, 150–1, *152*, 153, 154, 156, 159;
    Colombo Plan 52, 145, 146, 147, 149, 159;
    embassy in, 150; Lionel Wendt Theatre and
    Gallery, 149; parks in, 158; post-
    independence exhibitions in, 15, 145, 146,
    149; *see also* Ceylon
Colomina, Beatriz, 55n
Colonial Development and Welfare Act (CDWA),
    214, 217–18, 220
Colonial Housing Bureau, 6, 213, 215
Colonial Housing Research Group, 213, 214, 216,
    221
Colonial Liaison Officer, 213, 218, 219
Colonial Liaison Unit (CLU), 212, 213, 222, 226
Colonial Office (CO), 213, 214, 217
colonial research model, 213–17
colonial technoscientific network building, 211–29
colonialism, 13, 69, 114; anti-colonial sentiments,
    65, 142; colonial modernity, 143–5
Colonizing Egypt (Mitchell), 143
Colquhoun, Alan, 28n
comfort, 197, 198, 199, 202
Commission II, Sitguna preparatory meeting, 61

common sense modernism, 167–8, 170; criticism, 183; individualism within, 177–8; learning from, 171–5
Commonwealth Experimental Station, Australia, 221
Commonwealth Relations Office, and Colombo Plan, 147
Communism, image of, 48
community structuring, 103
concrete, use of, 36, 37, 41, 45, 46, 126
Conkin, Alice, 82n
Conrads, Ulrich, 26n
consumption, 170, 184n
Contreras, Carlos, 170
Cook, Jeffrey, 253n
Coomaraswamy, Ananda, 208n
Cooper, Frederick, 231n, 232n
Córdova, Adolfo, 86, 94, 102, *104*, 106, 107n, 108n, 109n
CORPAC (*Corporación Peruana de* Aeropuertos y Aviación Comercial), Peru, 87
Correa, Charles, 1, 155
cosmopolitan modernism, 18, 255–67
Costa, Lucio, 33, 34, 40, 44, 53n, 54n, 151, 224
courtyard, Morocco, 79–80, 81
Cowan, Henry J., 222, 234n
CPA (*Corporación Peruana del Amazonas*), Peru, 87
CPS (*Corporación Peruana del Santa*), Peru, 87
crafts and industrial objects debate, 200, 201
Cranz, Gaelen, 202, 208n
Crinson, Mark, 25n, 26n, 27n, 140n, 143, 162n, 230n, 234n, 253n
critical regionalism, 21, 22, 227, 234n
Crowley, John E., 208n
Cruchaga, Miguel, 106
Crysler, Greg, 28n, 230n
Crystal Palace, 144
cubic forms, 37
Cubitt, James, 137n
Cueto F, Carlos, 107n
Curtis, William J., 28n

Da Costa Meyer, Esther, 44, 49, 55n
Dai Nianci, 7, *8*
Dalai Lama, 259
Dammert, Alfredo, *98*
dams, hydroelectric, 261
Danby, Miles, 230n
Daniel, Greata, 195
Daniels, Mary, 106
Dasso, David, 108n
Dawson, Layla, 64, 84n
De Syllas, Leo, 238
Deckker, Zilah Quezado, 54n
Declaration of Human Rights, 71
decolonization of Asian nation-states, 142
Demazière, Morocco, 66, *67*, 72, 78
democratization of comfort, 198
Department of Science and Industrial Research (DSIR), 214, 215, 223
Department of Tropical Architecture, Architectural Association, 17, 211, 220, 237, 238
Derb Jdid housing project, Casablanca, 74–5, 76
Desai, Madhavi, 25n, 269n
Desai, Miki, 25n, 269n

"Desert of Modernity" exhibition (Berlin), 84n
Design Group Nigeria, 133
"Design Today in America and Europe" show (1959), 191, 195–200, *201*
Dessau, Bauhaus school, 113, 119
developed and underdeveloped countries, 216
Development Planning Unit, UCL, 239, 251
developmentalism: in Brazil, 42–3, 45; modernism as, 9–12
Di Carlo, Gian Carlo, 78
Dieste, Eladio, 51, 56n
Diner, Dan, 267n
Dirlik, Arif, 27n
Dominican Monastery, Ibadan, 133
Dorich, Luis, 86, 90, 91, 95, 97–101, *98*, 107n, 108n, 109n, 110n
Dostluk (Turkish newspaper), 168
double functioning of architecture, 184n
Drew, Jane, 17, 123, 124, 140n, 149, 211, 225, 230n, 238
Drewal, Margaret Thompson, 135n, 139n
Drexler, Arthur, 197, 208n
Driver, Felix, 234n, 253n
DSIR (Department of Science and Industrial Research), 214, 215, 223
Dubrovnik, CIAM congress held in, 71, 102
Dufton, A. F., 222
Dulles, John Foster, 191, 206n
Durell Stone, Edward, 149, 150
Dutt, Dinesh, 207n
Dutta, Arindam, 143, 155, 162n, 163n, 208n, 229, 235n

Eames, Charles, 110n, 170, 189, 201, 204, 209n
Eames, Ray, 170, 189, 209n
EAP (*El Arquitecto Peruano*), 90, 92, 103
Ecochard, Michel, 59–61, 67, 71, 73, 74, 76, 79, 81, 83n, 84n; dismissal of (1952), 65; influence of, 62–5; Service of Urbanism *see* Service of Urbanism, Morocco
Ecole des Beaux Arts *see* Beaux Arts School, Casablanca
Edrich, Carol Gray, 230n
Efrat, Zvi, 136n
Egbor, A. A., 118, 137n
EGBORAMI Company, 118
Eggener, Keith L., 28n, 234n
Eiffel Tower, 144
El Arquitecto Peruano, 94
El Comercio, 94
Eldem, Sedad Hakki, 165, 168, 175, 176, 185n
Elderfield, John, 207n
Eleb, Monique, 82n, 83n, 84n, 253n, 269n
Elleh, Nnamdi, 138n
Elliott, Simon, 106
Emmery, Pierre Andre, 59
ENI (*Escuela Nacional de Ingeniería*), Peru, 92
En-lai, Zhou, 258, 259, 268n
Ensminger, Dr., 196
episteme, 228
Erskine, Ralph, 71
Escobar, Arturo, 11, 27n, 231n, 232n
Espacio en el Tiempo (Quesada), 92, 93, 94
Estado Novo (New State), 42
Etchells, Frederick, 26n
ethnic groups: Morocco, 64, 65; Nigeria, 114, 135n

Eurocentrism, 14, 32
European modernism, 35; Morocco as "laboratory" for, 81, 84n
European modernization, 42–3
Evans, I. G., 213, 231n
Evolving Housing concept, Morocco, 76, 79, 81
exhibitions, 78, 84n, 90, 141–61, 144, 145, 156, 191; Ceylon 65, 150–1, *152*, 153, 154, 156, 159; *Gam Udawa* (Village Re-awakening) movement, 156–60, 161; India *see under* India
EXPO 1970, Osaka, 152
Expresión de Principios de la Agrupación Espacio, 94

Fabunmi, M. A., 129, 139n
Falola, Toyin, 139n
FAM (*Frente de Arquitectura Moderna*), 91
Faraoui, Morocco, 66, *67*, 72, 73, 78
Farias, Agnaldo, 53n
Fathy, Hasan, 1
Fei Xiaotong, 19
Fernandes, Florestan, 52n
Ferrari Hardoy, Jorge, 99
Ferraz, Geraldo, 33, 34, 53n, 54n
Ferraz, José Carlos de Figueiredo, 45, *46*
Ferraz, Marcelo, 48, 56n
Ferro, Sérgio, 51, 56n
Festival of Britain, Skylon reconstruction, 145
Festivals of India (1983-86), 155
Fiore, Renato, 35, 54n
First/Second World, 256
Fishman, Robert, 252
Fletcher, Banister, 24, 28n
Foláranmi, Stephen, 139n
Ford Foundation, in India, 7, 196–7, 207n
formalism/formalist architecture, 37–8, 68
Forty, Adrian, 25n, 54n
Forum magazine, 78
Foster, Hal, 28n
Foucault, Michel, 229
Foxlee, R. W., 231n
Foyle, Arthur, 232n
Frampton, Kenneth, 20–1, 28n, 33, 52n, 209n, 235n
Fraser, J. M., 231n
Fraser, Valerie, 25n, 54n, 55n, 267n, 269n
freedom, architecture of, 48
Frey, Albert, 182, 185n
frustration, 172, 184n
Fry, Maxwell, 17, 123, 124, 140n, 149, 211, 225, 230n, 238
Fuller, Buckminster, 110n, 195, 207n
Fuller, Mia, 26n

Gaba, Lester, 192
Gaitán, Jorge, 99
Gam Udawa (Village Re-awakening) movement, 156–60, 161
GAMMA Group, Morocco *see* Group GAMMA (Groupe d'Architectes Modernes Marocains), Morocco
Gandhi, Mahatma, 149, 200, 201, 203, 204
Ganguly, Sumit, 207n
Ganju, Ashish, 155
Garden City, 96
Gardner-Medwin, Robert, 213, 214, 231n

Garland, Carlos, 110n
Garrido Lecca, Jorge, 109n
Gatelumendi, Ernesto, 109n
Geist, A. L., 52n
Gellman, Irwin F., 87, 107n
Ghosh, D. P., 207n
Gibberd, Sir Frederick, 151
Giedion, Sigfried, 4, 26n, 60, 61, 90, 91, 99–101, 108n, 110n, 176; *Space, Time and Architecture*, 92
Gilardi, Mario, 109n
Gillespie, Richard, 232n
Girard, Alexander, 191–2, 201, 204
Gitler, Inbal Ben-Asher, 7, 15, 113–35
Givoni, B., 224
Glass House (Casa de Vidro), Brazil, 44
Gloag, John, 198, 208n
Global South, 260
globalism, modernism as, 4–9
globalization, 255, 268n
Glover, William J., 143, 162n
Godefroy, 84n
Godineau, Isabelle, 106
Goldhagen, Sarah, 19, 28n, 81
"Good Neighbor Policy," US government, 87
good sense, 168, 182–3
"Good-Life Modernism," 170, 171, 179, 180, 182
Goodwin, Philip, 34, 53n
Gordon, Leonard A., 207n
Graham, Bruce, 110n
Gramsci, Antonio, 167, 168, 177, 183n, 184n
Green Architecture, 241, 242, 252
Grier, Katherine, 208n
Gropius, Walter, 4, 26n, 35, 37, 60, 90, 94, 96, 98–9, 100, 101, 108n, 109n, 110n, 122, 189
Group GAMMA (Groupe d'Architectes Modernes Marocains), Morocco, 12, 57–8, 82n; *Architecture + Urbanism* (*A+U*), 58, 72, 73, 76, 78; *Architecture d'Aujourd'hui*, 58, 66, 69; and Candilis, 65–9; as CIAM Morocco, 60, 61; continuity of, as institution, 59, 71–3; development of anthropological approach, 73–8; development of vernacular interest, 78–81; disbanding of (1959), 58; genesis, 59–62; *habitat (housing) for the largest number*, 59, 62, 63, 64, 65, 66, *70*, 73, 77; and transition of Morocco after independence, 69–71; *see also* CIAM (*Congress International d'Architecture Moderne*); Morocco/Moroccan modernism
Group of Five, 259
Guggenheim, Michael, 232n
Guha, 207n, 208n
Guillén, Mauro, 52n
Gujarat, 189
Gunasekara, Valentine, 149, 152, 163n, 164n
Gunatileke, Sir Oliver, 162n
Gutiérrez, Ramón, 52n

Habermas, Jürgen, 25n, 52n
habitat, concept, 67
habitat for the largest number, Morocco, 63, 65, 66, *70*, 73
Hailey, Lord, 216
Haraway, Donna, 211, 230n
Harrison, John, 137n
Harrison, Wallace, 108n

Harvard University Graduate School of Design, 101
Hassard, John, 233n
Hausa-Fulani (ethnic group), 114, 135n
Havinden, Michael A., 231n, 232n
Havkin, Daniel, 137n
Hayden, Corinne P., 233n
Haynes, Douglas Melvin, 231n, 232n
Hebrew University, Jerusalem, 122, 124
Hecker, Zvi, 120
Henderson, W. A., 254n
Hennayake, Nalani, 157, 161, 163n, 164n
Hensens, Jean, 76
Hentsch, Jean, *58*
Hermassi, Elbaki, 25n
Hernandez, Felipe, 85–6, 106n
Hess, David J., 230n
Heynen, Hilde, 26n, 28n, 102, 110n, 135, 230n
Hibbert, J. G., 231n
high-rise buildings: Morocco, 74; Peru, 88; Singapore, 10
Hilton, Conrad, 11
Hilton Hotel, Istanbul, 16, 167, 175, 180
"Hiltonculuk," 16, 165, *166*, 167, 175, 176, 183
historian, role, 176–7
Histradrut (Israeli Federation of Trade Unions), 116, 117
Hitchcock, Henry-Russell, 26n, 108n, 110n, 167, 175, 183n, 184n
Hitler, Adolf, 239
Hobsbawm, E. J., 14, 27n, 268n
Hoddesdon, 8th CIAM congress, 60, 61, 82n
Hoffenberg, Peter H., 206n, 209n
Holford, William Graham, 213
Holm, Lonberg, 108n
Holston, James, 25n
Home, Robert K., 231n
Hopper, J. R., 184n
"Horizontal Property Law," Peru, 88
Horkheimer, Max, 20, 28n
Hosagrahar, Jyoti, 143
Housing Advisory Panel, 214
housing for the largest number see social housing (*housing for the largest number*), Group GAMMA
Howell, 60
Huarochiri expedition, 103
Hughes, Alice, 193
Hughes, Thomas Parke, 234n
Hulusi, Ihap, *173*
Hunstanton School, 236, 242
hybridization, Peruvian, 85–6, 92, 103, 104

Ibadan, University of, 114, 115, 124
ideal, Plato's notion of, 199
Idelson, Benjamin, 122
Ife Shrines (Fabunmi), 129
Ife University *see* Obafemi Awolowo University (OAU) Campus, Ile-Ife (Nigeria)
Imperial Agricultural Bureau, 215
Imperial Institute, 214
Império, Flavio, 51
India: American view of Indians, 191; ashram life, 200; bureaucracy in, 200; Central Building Research Station, 221; crafts tradition, 194; "Design Today in America and Europe" show

(1959), 191, 195–200, *201*; and Ford Foundation, 7, 196–7, 207n; "International Exhibition on Low Cost Housing (1954), 204; Koenigsberger in Mysore, 240–1; mass production and consumption, 196–7, 200; modernism and Third World, 260–5; postcolonial, and MoMA, 189–206; post-independence international trade, 193–4; relations with US, 191, 194; "Textiles and Ornamental Arts of India" show (1955), 191–3; *see also* Chandigarh
Indian architecture, 155
Indianness, 194
Indic architectural styles, 144
individualism, within common sense modernism, 177–8
Indonesia: Bandung Conference *see* Bandung Conference (Afro-Asian Conference), 1955; indigenous traditions, 156, 157
Ingersoll, T. G., 251
İnşaat ve Mimarlik Atölyesi (İMA), 166, 177
Instituto de Urbanismo, Peru, 88, 90, 101
"International Exhibition on Low Cost Housing (1954), 204
International Monetary Fund (IMF), 216
International Style architecture, 119, 155; in Turkey, 7, 167, 168, 175
International Style, The (Hitchcock and Johnson), 108n
Irbouh, Hamid, 84n
Irwin, John, 192
Isaac, Harold R., 191, 206n
Isenstadt, Sandy, 25n
Ismail, Sir Mirza, 239
Israel: Agricultural Cooperatives Headquarters, Tel Aviv, 126, 127; aid to developing countries, 116; declaration of State of (1948), 119; Hebrew University, Jerusalem, 122, 124; isolation of, 115; National Master Plan, 120; Productivity Institute, 118; progressiveness, 116; socialism, 116; Soroka Medical Center, Beer-Sheba, 120, 122; technical assistance programs, to Africa, 115–19; Technion Institute of Technology, Haifa, 120, 122, 124; and Third World, 140n; *see also* Sharon, Arieh; Sharon, Eldar
Izenour, Steven, 163n
Izmir: American Pavilion in, 168, *169*; co-op house plans, 179; International Fair (1957), 168, 174

Jacobs, Jane M., 27n
Jakarta, 156
Jarzombek, Mark, 170, 172, 179, 184n
Jaubert, Gaston, 71, 74
Jayakar, Pupul, 192, 195, 201
Jayatileke, Sumangala, 163n
Jeanneret, Pierre, 18, 149, 189, 190, 202, 203–4, 209n
Jeanneret-Griz, Charles-Édouard *see* Le Corbusier
Jeffries, Sir Charles Joseph, 232n
Jianfei, Zhu, 25n
Johnson, Philip, 26n, 108n, 170
Johnson, Randel, 52n
Johnstone, S. J., 231n
Josic, 66

JVP (*Janata Vimukthi Peramuna*), People's Liberation Front (Sri Lanka), 154, 158

Kaçel, Elâ, 16, 165–83, 184n
Kahatt, Sharif S., 12, 85–106
Kahn, Louis, 23, 129, 149, 243, 268n
Kalia, Ravi, 253n
Karamental Studio, 180
Karim, Farhan Sirajul, 18, 189–206
Kasbahs (Morocco), 66, 78
Kassner, Lily, 135
Kaufman, Edgar, Jr., 191–2, 198, 202, 208n
Kaul, T. N., 268n
Kauntze, W. H., 231n
Kenealy, Nancy, *193*
Kennedy, 84n
Kent, Kate P., 192, 206n, 209n
Kenyatta, Jomo, 116
kibbutzim, 116
Kim magazine, 176
King, Anthony D., 26n, 230n, 232n
Kingham, Norman, 231n
Kirkham, Pat, 209n
Kirsh, Karin, 26n, 209n
Kluska, Walter, 230n
knowledge: 4, 20, 23, 24, 25; local, 228, 230n; objective, 173; power-knowledge, postcolonial network of, 213, 227–9; relational, 177, 184n; situated, 211; technoscientific, 211–12, 216, 224, 226, 228; visual, 172, 184n
KocabaşoĞlu, U., 184n
Koch, Carl, 174
Kocher, A. Lawrence, 185n
Kocher Weekend House, 182
Koenigsberger, Otto H., 17, 18, 149, 211, 237–40, 242, 243, 245–9, 251, 253n; career/ achievements, 239–40; in Mysore, 240–1
Koenigsberger, Renate, 252
Kolsal, Ali, 185n
Koral, Füreya, 180
Kortan, Enis, 185n
Krämer, Kark, 136n
Krapf-Askari, Eva, 138n
Kreinin, Mordechai E., 136n, 137n
Krieger, Milton, 115, 135n, 136n, 139n
Krishna Murthy, K., 208n
Kruschev, Nikita, 144
Kuan, Seng, 25n
Kubitschek, Juscelino, 42, 48, 55n
Kulasinghe, A. N. S., 151
Kulasinghe, Jack, 159, 160, 164n
Kushner, Marilyn, 162n
Kusno, Abidin, 157, 163n
Kuwait Mat Project, 237, 244, 245–9

La Charte d'Athens (Le Corbusier), 108n
La Cité, 61
La Tourette Convent, nr Lyon (Le Corbusier), 127
Labor Party, Israel, 116
Lai Chee Kien, 27n
Laitin, David D., 135n
Lang, John T., 269n
Lang, Jon, 25n
Latin America: modernity in, 32, 33, 50, 85; *see also* Brazil; Peruvian Modern Project

Latour, Bruno, 212, 221, 222, 223, 228, 230n, 233n, 234n, 235n
Laufer, Leopold, 136n, 140n
Law, John, 233n, 234n
Le Corbusier, 4, 23, 26n, 35, 38, 40, 55n, 68, 69, 83n, 92, 94, 98, 99, 101, 102, 109n, 122, 149, 182, 189, 224, 268n; "Application of the Athens Charter" plenary session, 61; and Jeanneret, 203; *La Charte d'Athens*, 108n; La Tourette Convent, nr. Lyon, 127; and Warchavchik, 33, 37
Le Roux, Hannah, 133, 136n, 137n, 138n, 139n, 140n, 230n, 234n, 253n
Lea, Sir Frederick M., 218, 231n, 232n, 233n
Lecca, Gerardo, 109n
Lee, Leo O., 28n
Leeward Islands, 225
Lefaivre, Liane, 28n, 234n, 235n
Lefèvre, Rodrigo, 51
Legault, Réjean, 19, 28n
Lemos, Carlos, 33, 37, 40, 53n, 54n
Lerner, Daniel, 170–1, 172, 183n, 184n
Levin, Ayala, 135
Levin, Michael, 138n
Levin, R. I., 184n
Lévi-Strauss, Claude, 54n
Levitas, R., 27n
liberation movement, Morocco, 65
Lico, Gerard, 163n
Liernur, Jorge F., 90, 107n
Life, 174, 194
Lima, Zeuler, 48, 56n
Lima Housing Plan, 88, 91, 96, 105
Linder, Paul, 94, 101, 107n, 109n
lines, 37
Lippsmeier, Georg, 230n
Lira, José, 33, 35, 53n, 54n, 56n
Liu Yunhe, 28n
Liverpool School of Tropical Medicine, 214, 216
living zoning, Athens Charter four function, 61, 83n
Llosa, Manuel B., 108n
Lobo, Carlos Gonzalez, 51, 56n
Lods, Marcel, 61
Loeffler, Jane C., 27n, 140n, 150, 163n
London School of Tropical Medicine, 216
Lu, Duanfang, 1–25, 25n, 26n, 27n, 28n, 183, 206, 267
Ludena, Wiley, 97, 107n, 109n
Lughod, Abu, 64
Lundy, Victor, 150
Lutyens, Edwin, 144
Lutzowstrasse housing, Berlin, 250
Lyautey, Marshall, 238

Macchiavello, Carlos Morales, 90, *98*, 108n, 110n
Mackenzie, John M., 231n
Mackie, Jamie, 163n
MacLeod, Roy, 232n
Mahiyangana, *Gam Udawa* exhibition at, 158
Mahoney, Carl, 252
Maia, Prestes, *46*
de Maissonseult, Jean, 59
Malachowski B, Ricardo, 109n
Malaya, Design and Research Branch, 221
Malik, M. L., 209n
Al Mansour, Yacoub, 82n

Mannheim, Karl, 184n
Mansfeld, Alfred, 137n
Mansingh, Surjuit, 207n
Manson, Patrick, 216
Manual of Tropical Housing and Architecture,
    251
Mao Zedong, 259
Mar, José Matos, 102, 110n
Marcos, Imelda, 156
MARS (Dutch group), 63, 225
Marshall Plan, 7, 170
Martins, Carlos, 41, 53n, 54n
Martins, Livraria, 54n
Mas, Pierre, 61, 69, 73, 84n
Masey, Jack, 207n
Mason, Mike, 267n
MASP *see* Museum of Art, São Paulo (MASP)
mass media, 171
Masson, Alain, 75–6
Massu, Claude, 81, 84n
Mattie, Eric, 162n
Maurer, Louis, 109n
Mayekawa, Kunio, 110n
Mayhew, Alan, 251
Mazrui, Ali A., 135n
McCarthy, Kathleen D., 207n
McClintock, Ann, 135, 140n
McDonald, Gay, 206, 207n
McGowan, Abigail S., 206n, 209n
McLaren, Brian, 52n
McNeil, Donald, 28n
Meherally, Yusuf, 206n
Mehrotra, Rahul J., 163n
Mehta, Rustam J., 208n
Mello, Joana, 53n
Mendelsohn, Erich, 138n
Méndez, Oscar Vargas, 109n
Mercer, Kobena, 26n
Meredith, David, 231n, 232n
Merriam, Allen H., 25n
Metcalf, Thomas R., 144, 162n
"Metropolis and the Emergence of Modernism,
    The" (Williams), 50
*Metropolitan Future of a City with a Great
    Historical Heritage* (Lima conference), 91
Mexico, Tropical Architecture conference, 238
Meyer, Hannes, 119, 203
Meyer-Maril, Edina, 135
Mies van der Rohe, Ludwig, 35, 94, 108n, 189
Migdal, Joel S., 140n
Miller, Nicola, 32–3, 52n, 53
Mindlin, Henrique E., 34, 110n
Minhas, Salman S., 254n
minimalism, and modernism, 37
Ministry of Health and Education, Brazil, 36, 37,
    41, 42
Mitchell, Timothy, 143, 162n
Mitter, Partha, 265, 266, 269n
"Modern American house," 168–70, *169*
Modern Art Week (1922), 47, 53n
modern culture, 168
modernism: aesthetic vs. profitable commodity,
    202; ambiguous, in Brazil, 32, 33–42;
    ambivalent, in Brazil, 32, 43–50;
    Americanization of, 16, 43, 85, 167; artistic
    and literary, emergence, 50–1; as "closed
    system of discourse," 266; cosmopolitan

reading of, 255–67; as developmentalism,
    9–12; European, 35, 81; as globalism, 4–9;
    good sense, 182–3; as nationalism, 12–16; as
    postcolonialism, 16–19; as style of life, 183n;
    and Third World, 229, 256, 260–5; universal,
    22, 23
Modernist House (Casa Modernista), Brazil, 11,
    33, 34, 36–42, *39*, 51; ambiguous
    modernism, presenting, 32, 38; forms, 37,
    38; materials, 36, 37
modernity, modernization contrasted, 32–3
modernization: of Brazil, 42; European, 35, 42–3;
    modernity contrasted, 32–3
Moffett, Noel, 137n, 139n
Mohammad, S. Z., 138n
Mohammed V., 84n
MoMA (Museum of Modern Art), New York, 90;
    exhibition artefacts, 200; and postcolonial
    India, 189–206
Monléon, J. B., 52n
Montagne, Eugenio, *98*
von Moos, Stanislos, 269n
Morales M., Carlos, 91, 107n
Morey, Raul, 109n
Morgan, Conway Lloyd, 207n
Morocco/Moroccan modernism, 12, 57–81;
    civilizing mission, concept, 57, 65; courtyard,
    79–80, 81; ethnic groups, 64, 65; Evolving
    Housing concept, 76, 79, 81; Group Gamma
    see Group GAMMA (Groupe d'Architectes
    Modernes Marocains), Morocco; as
    "laboratory" for European modernism, 81,
    84n; nuance, 57, 69; pedestrian network
    typology, 62; shantytowns, 62, 63, 64, 65,
    71, 73, 74; transition after independence,
    69–71, 74, 79, 81; vertical housing schemes,
    64, 66; *see also* Agadir; Casablanca
Morris, William, 198
Morton, Patricia, 143, 144, 148, 162n
Moscow, American National exposition in, 145,
    194
moshav settlements, Israel, 116
"Mostra di Architettura Spontanea" (exhibition),
    78
Movimento Modernista (modernist movement),
    Brazil, 34, 35, 38
Movimiento Social Progresista political group,
    103
Mukherjee, Ananda Gopal, 207n
Mumford, Eric, 82n, 91, 108n, 110n
Mumford, Lewis, 269n
Mumtaz, K. K., 252
Museum of Art, São Paulo (MASP), 44–50, 52n;
    ambivalent modernism of, 32, 50; displays,
    46–7; gallery space, 46, 47; original layout,
    56n; restrictions, 45–6; and São Vicente
    museum, 48–9; site of *see* Avenida Paulista,
    Brazil; structure, 44–6
Muslims, Morocco, 64, 65
Muttiah, Subbiah, 163n
muxarabi, 41
Mysore, India, 240–1

Nadau, Thierry, 84n
Nadelman, Nathan E., 136n, 140n
nascent modernization, 35
Nasser, Abdel, 259

National Assembly, Dacca (Bangladesh), 129
National Building Research Institute, South
    Africa, 221
National Library, 244
National School of Design and Fashion, 196
nationalism, modernism as, 12–16
NATO (North Atlantic Treaty Organization), 2
Nehru, Jawaharlal, 149, 192, 200, 239, 258–9,
    260, 261–2, 268n, 269n
neighborhood units, 62, 86, 91, 95–7, *98*, 105
Neira, Eduardo, 86, 100, 102, 106
Nelson, George, 194
Nelson, Paul, 71, 189
neo-classicism, 262
Neo-Colonial movement, 34
neo-colonialism, 6, 117, 143, 144
network building, 217–24
Neumann, Alfred, 120
Neutra, Richard, 71, 86, 90, 91, 92, 94, 108n
Neves, Julio, 56n
New Culture Design Centre, Ibadan, 133
New Deal (Roosevelt), 260
New Dehli, 14, 262, 269n
New Talborj, Gaadir, 79
New Third World Modernism, 265–7
New York: Soviet exposition in, 145; World Fairs,
    41, 144–5
Nichols, P. Don, 163n
Nid d'Abeilles, architecture in, 66, 67, 77
Niemeyer, Oscar, 33, 40, 44, 45, 94, 99, 104,
    110n, 151, 224
Nigeria: Architects Co-Partnership, 220; ethnic
    groups, 114, 135n; independence, 114;
    interpretation of Modernism, 123–33; OAU
    Campus *see* Obafemi Awolowo University
    (OAU) Campus, Ile-Ife (Nigeria); post-colonial,
    and founding of OAU, 114–15
Nitzan-Shiftan, Alona, 138n
Nixon, Richard M., 144
Nkrumah, Kwame, 259
Noerr, Gunzelin Schmid, 28n
Non Aligned Movement (NAM), 259, 260, 265
Nowicki, Matthew, 269n
NSIC (National Small Industry Corporation), 194,
    195
Nsukka, University of, 115
nuance, Morocco, 57, 69
Nurse, R. W., 231n
Nwoko, Demas, 132, 133, 139n

Oakman, Daniel, 144–5, 162n
OAU Campus *see* Obafemi Awolowo University
    (OAU) Campus, Ile-Ife (Nigeria)
Obafemi Awolowo University (OAU) Campus,
    Ile-Ife (Nigeria), 7, 15, 113–35; Assembly Hall,
    118; courtyards, 122; founding of, and
    post-colonial Nigeria, 114–15; general plan of
    campus, 120–3; Humanities Faculty, 121,
    123, *124*, 127; Institute of Education, 126;
    Institute of Technology campus, 122; and
    Israeli technical assistance programs to
    Africa, 115–19; Planning Committee, 115,
    119; Sharon, commissioning as architect of,
    119–20; and Yoruba cultural self-definition,
    115
Obas (Yoruba town/tribal leaders), 118
Obeyesekere, R., 163n

objective knowledge, 173
Ockman, J., 183n
Odría, Manuel, 97
Odúduwà (mythic ancestor of crowned Yoruba
    kings), 120, 138n; Odúduwà Hall, 125, 127,
    129, 130, 133
O'Gorman, Juan, 130
Ojo, Olusola, 136n
Okeke, Uche, 132, 139n
Okeke-Agulu, Chika, 132, 139n
Okpara, Michael Iheonukara, 116
Oldenziel, R., 208n
Olgyay, Victor and Aladar, 241
de Oliveira, Olivia, 56n
Oliveira, Lucia Lippi, 55n
Oluorogbo Shrine, 129
Oluwasanmi, H. A., 138n
On Modern Architecture ("Acerca de Arquitetura
    Moderna") manifesto (Warchavchik), 35
Onabamiro, Sanya, 115
Önal, Maruf, 16, 165–6, 168, 177–82, 185n;
    criticism, 180–1; house of, 178–82
Ong, Aihwa, 230n
ONPU (*Oficina Nacional de Planeamiento
    Urbano*), Peru, 88–9, 95, 96, 105
Opa Oranmiyan (staff of Oranmiyan), 131–2
OPEC oil crisis, 154, 241
Order of Architects, Morocco, 73
ordinariness, 167, 175
Ortiz, Renato, 52n
Osborne, Michael A., 230n
Othman, Sidi, 66
Ouarzazate, housing blocks in, 68, 76
Overy, Paul, 26n

Packard, Randall M., 231n, 232n
Pahlavi master plan, 244
Pakistan, 261
Palansuriya, L. S., 164n
Palladian revival, in architecture, 144
Palladino, Paolo, 232n
Pallamin, Vera Maria, 48, 56n
Pampulha complex, Brazil, 36, 37, 41
Pan-American Congress of Architecture, 101
Papadaki, Stamo, 224
Paris, Expositions of 1867 and 1931, 144
Parnas, Ziva, 137n
Passive and Low Energy Architecture (PLEA),
    252
Pedregulho Residential Complex, Rio, 43, 55n
Pedret, Annie, 82n, 83n, 84n
People's Liberation Front, Sri Lanka (JVP), 154,
    158
Pepis, Betty, 192
Perera, Nihal, 155, 163n
perfect mediocrity, 167, 177
perfection, Aquinas' notion of, 199
Perriand, 189
Perry, Clarence, 109n
Peru, 12, 85–106; Agrupación Espacio *see*
    Agrupación Espacio; Chimbote project, 87–8,
    91, 97; CIAM *see* CIAM (*Congress
    International d'Architecture Moderne*);
    Housing Plan (1945), Lima, 96; hybridization,
    85–6, 92, 103, 104; *Instituto de Urbanismo*,
    88, 90, 101; modern architecture, 104–6;
    Peruvian Modern Project, 85, 87–9, 104,

105–6; *unidades vecinales see unidades vecinales* (neighborhood units)
Pevsner, Nikolaus, 4, 26n
Pheng Cheah, 163n
Philippines, indigenous traditions, 156, 157
Piacentini, Marcello, 34
Pieris, Anoma, 15–16, 27n
Pinch, T. J., 234n
Pinseau, Daniel, 81
Pinson, Daniel, 84n
Piolin Circus, 47
Piotrowski, Andrzej, 209n
Plan de Vivienda (Lima's Housing Plan), 88, 91, 96, 105
Plan Piloto (Lima), 95, 96
Poelzig, Hans, 239
Point Four Program (Truman), 208n, 216–17
"Popular Recreational Program," Peru, 89
Porteus, Colin, 253n
Portuguese colonial architecture, 34
postcolonialism: India, 189–206; modernism as, 16–19; power-knowledge, postcolonial network of, 213, 227–9
postwar political culture, 145–9
Pott, A. W., 231n
power-knowledge, postcolonial network of, 213, 227–9
Prado y Ugarteche, Manuel, 87, 104, 107n
Prakash, Aditya, *263*
Prakash, Gyan, 143
Prakāsh, Vikramāditya, 13–14, 18–19, 25n, 26n, 143, 162n, 206n, 232n, 255–67
Premadasa, Ranasinghe, 156, 158, 160, 161
Prost, Henri, 238
Provincializing Europe (Chakrabarty), 24
Public Works Department, Colombo, 149

Quesada, Luis Miró, 12, 86, 94, 101, 104, 107n, 108n, 109n, 110n; *Espacio en el Tiempo*, 92, 93, 94

Rabat-Salé, 60
Radhakrishnan, Rajagopalan, 28n
Radhakrishnan, S., 200
Rahmi, Bedri, 180
Ranger, Terence, 14, 27n
Ranjan, M. P., 189, *205*, 210n
Raphael (Raffaello Sanzio da Urbino), 47
red color, symbol of, 48, 49
reflexivity, 177
Regional Modernism, 265
Reidy, Affonso Eduardo, 40–1, 44
reinforced concrete, 36, 41, 45
relational knowledge, architectural knowledge as, 177, 184n
Renoir, Pierre Auguste, 47
"reversed pyramids," 123, 126
Ribeiro, José Augusto, 55n
Riesman, D., 184n
Rifkind, David, 135
Rio School (Escola Carioca), 40–1
de los Rios, Jorge, 109n
Rizvi, Kishwar, 25n
Road Research Laboratory, Tropical Unit, 223
Robbins, Bruce, 163n
Robinoff, Arthur, 207n
Robinson, D. C., 233n

Robinson, Jennifer, 28n
Robinson, Joyce Henry, 208n
Rodker, John, 26n
Rodrigo, Winston, 163n
Rogers, Ernesto N., 71, 81, 95, 97, 99, 100, 109n, 110n
Rome, Adam Ward, 253n
Roosevelt, Franklin D., 7, 87; New Deal, 260
Rosner, Victoria, 208n
Ross, Andrew, 230n
Roth, A., 185n
Roudolph, Paul, 110n
roughness, aesthetics of, 49, 51
Rowe, Peter G., 25n
Roy, Ananya, 15, 27n
Royer, Jean, 253n
Rua Itápolis, house on, 38
Rua Santa Cruz, House on *see* Modernist House (Casa Modernista)
Rubin, Don, 139n
Rubin, Harold, 119, 120, 128–9, 130–1, 138n, 139n
Rudolph, Paul, 224, 252n
Rudowsky, Bernard, 78

Saarinen, Eero, 23, 189
Sachs, Wolfgang, 232n
Said, Edward, 28n, 143, 162n
Sakr, José, 110n
Sánchez-Griñan, Fernando, 110n
Sandler, Daniela, 11–12, 31–52
São Paulo, Brazil, 35, 36, 43, 44, 54n
São Vicente, Museum of Art at, 48–9
Sauvy, Alfred, 2, 25n, 267n
savings banks/savings plans, 171, 172, *173*
Scheuch, Empresa Gráfica Teodoro, *97*, *98*, 109n
Scheuch, Hilde, 109n
Schultz, Norber, 60, 82n
Schumacher, E. F., 156, 163n
Schwartz, Jorge, 53n
science and technology, as social constructions, 211
Science Wars, 230n
Scobell, Andrew, 207n
Scott, James C., 10, 27n, 228, 235n
Scott Brown, Denise, 163n
Scriver, Peter, 26n, 143, 162n, 206n, 232n
Sears mail-order house, 171
SEATO (South East Asian Treaty Organization), 267n
Second Arts Building, Bath, 249–50
sector central (Lima), 95, 96
secularism, 261, 262, 269n
Segawa, Hugo, 55n
selective mode, 242
self-help, 103
Seminario T., Alberto, 109–10n
Semiramis, architecture in, 66
Seneviratne, Oliver, 163n
Seoane, Enrique, 94
Sert, José Louis, 71, 81, 86, *88*, 90, 91, 95–6, 97, 99, 100, 101, 104, 108n, 109n, 110n, 122; *Can Our Cities Survive?* 92
Service of Urbanism, Morocco, 69, 71, 74, 75, 79; renaming as CHU, 73, 84n
Seshadri-Crooks, Kalpana, 28n
Sevcenko, Nicolau, 54n

Shah, Manubhai, 200, 202
shantytowns, Morocco, 62, 63, 64, 65, 71, 73, 74; *see also* Carrières Centrales (Casablancan shantytown)
Sharma, C. V. J., 269n
Sharma, Ursula, 209n
Sharon, Arieh, 15, *112*, 113, 117–19, 121–34, *125*, *128*, *131*, 137n, 138n, 139n; commissioning as architect of OAU, 115, 119–20; emigration to Palestine (1920), 119
Sharon, Eldar, 15, *112*, 113, 118, 120, *121*, 124–5, *126*, 127, *128*, 133, 134
Shils, E., 184n
Shoup, Brian, 207n
Sidi Othman, housing scheme for, 66
Siedlung, 96
Silva Brito, Mário da, 53n
de Silva, Minette, 149, 154
Singapore, 10, 13
single-family house design, 172
Sinhalese language, Ceylon, 150
Sitguna preparatory meeting, Commission II, 61
situated knowledge, 211
Smithson, Alison and Peter, 18, 69, 78, 84n, 101, 236–8, 246–9, 252n, 253n, 254n; and Tropical Architecture, 242–5
Sobin, Harris J., 254n
social housing (*housing for the largest number*), Group GAMMA, 59, 62, 63, 64, 65, 66, *70*, 73, 75, 77
Söderström, Ola, 232n
solar architecture, 241
Solar Architecture, 250, 251
Solar Energy and Building (Szokolay), 251–2
Solel Boneh (construction company), 116, 134, 137n; A.M.I. sub-division, 117, 118
Soroka Medical Center, Beer-Sheba, 120, 122
Soulbury, Lord (former Governor General of Ceylon), 149
South Africa, National Building Research Institute, 221
Space, Time and Architecture (Giedion), 92
Space Needle exhibition (1962), 145
spaces of hope, 19
Sparkle, Penny, 198, 208n
Sri Lanka: Freedom Party, 153; socialism, effect on, 154; *see also* Ceylon
Stagno, Bruno, 28n, 235n
Stalder, Laurent, 82n
State Engineering Corporation (SEC), Ceylon 65 exhibition, 151
Stein, Clarence, 170, 184n
Stockdale, Frank, 213, 231n
Studer, Andre, *58*, 66, 67
Suharto, Mrs, 156
Suito, Renato, 110n
Sukarno, President, 257, 259
sun consciousness, 250
sun diagrams, and Kuwait Mat Project, 246, 247
surrealists, 65
Sustainable Architecture, 250, 251
Sustainable Development, 252
de Syllas, S. M., 231n
Szokolay, Steven, 251, 254n; *Solar Energy and Building*, 252–3

Tabb, Bruce, 106

Tagra, Vinod, 207n
Talking Architecture, Vanlı, 176
Tange, Kenzo, 110n
Tastemain, Henri, 61, 71, 79, 82n, 83n, 84n
Taut, Bruno, 239
Taylor, Walter A., 234n
Team 10, CIAM, 57, 69, 81, 101
Team Magazine (Shultz), 82n
Technion Institute of Technology, Haifa, 120, 122, 124
technocentrism, 32
technoscientific knowledge, 211–12, 216, 224, 226, 228
Teixeira, Anísio, 40
Tel Aviv, Agricultural Cooperatives Headquarters, 126, 127
Tennessee Valley Authority (TVA), and Peru, 87
Teriba, Adedoyin, 135
Tessenow, Heinrich, 239
"Textiles and Ornamental Arts of India" show (1955), 191–3
Thatcher, Margaret, 141
Third World, 2–3, 256–60; alternative, 257; and Israel, 140n; and modernism, 229, 255, 256, 260–7; South American universities, 115; terminology, 2; Western Modernism, example, 140n
Thomas, Darryl C., 268n
Thompson, E. P., 27n
Thompson, Mark, 208n
Tidy, Michael, 135n
Tito, Josef Broz, 259
Tizón F., Gabriel, 110n
traditional materials, use of, 36, 37, 79
Tropical Architecture, 17, 237–8, 251–2; afterlife, 242; and climatic design, 224; Conference (1953), 211; geopolitics, 227; and hygiene, 237–8; at Ibadan, 124; and Smithsons, 242–5
Tropical Building Division (TBD), Building Research Station, 17, 212, 213, 217–24, *223*, 228
Tropical Products Institute, 223
Tropical Programme (1954), 149
Tropical Unit, Road Research Laboratory, 223
tropics, climatic design in, 226
Truman, Harry, 90, 208n; doctrine of 1947, 150; Point Four Program, 208n, 216–17
TSA (*trame sanitaire ameliorée*), 74
Turkey (1950s), 165–83; common sense, learning from, 171–5; good sense modernism, 182–3; Hilton Hotel, Istanbul, 167, 175, 180; individualism within common sense, 177–8; International Style, 7, 167, 168, 175; modernization via good life, 168–71
Turner, John, 103
Tutuola, Amos, 139n
Twins Seven Seven, 129
Two Worlds theory, 257
two-dimensional works, 46
two-story units, evolving housing (Morocco), 76
Tyrwhitt, J., 109n
Tzonis, Alexander, 28n, 234n, 235n

Uduku, Ola, 138n, 139n
Umenne, S. IK., 138n

UNAM (Universidad Autónoma de México) campus buildings, 129–30
unidades vecinales (neighborhood units), 86, 91, 95–7, *98*, 105
Union Internationale des Architectes, 73
Unité d'Habitation, Marseilles, 61, 69, 83n
United National Party, Ceylon/Sri Lanka, 147, 153, 154, 161
United Nations (UN), 268n
United States: Americanization of modernism, 16, 43, 85, 167; Bio-Climatic Architecture, 241; furniture industry, 198; and International Style, 168; and modernism in Turkey, 170; National Exhibition in Moscow, 145, 194; Pan-American Congress of Architecture, 101; postwar American architecture, 167; relations with India *see under* MoMA (Museum of Modern Art), New York
universal modernism, 22, 23
University College London (UCL), Development Planning Unit at, 239, 251
Urbanism Department, reform of administrative system (Ecochard), 63
Urbanistic Legislation, 88
USIA (United States Information Agency), 194
USIS (United States Information Service), 168, 173
utopianism, 7
Utzon, John, 22

Vale, Lawrence J., 14, 27n
Valega, Manuel, *98*
Van Heyk, 78
Vanlı, Şevki, 16, 165, 166, 175–7, 183n, 185n
vão livre do MASP (free span of MASP), 47
Vásquez, Luis, 110n
Vaughan-Richards, Allan, 133, 139n
Velarde, Hector, 100, 110n
Venegas, Ramón, 110n
Venturi, Robert, 163n
Vera, Luis, 107n, 110n
Verlag, Karl Kramer, 83n
vernacular architecture (Group GAMMA), 78–81
vernacular furnishing, 209n
Vers une Architecture, 94
Vesentini, José William, 55n
Vignaud, Claude, 84n
Village India Complex, 155
visible politics, 229
visual knowledge, 172, 184n
Vlach, John Michael, 136n
Von Osten, Marion, 64

Wakeham, Roberto, 109n
Wallerstein, Immanuel M., 232n
Warchavchik, Gregori, 11, 32–41, *39*, 43–4, 53, 54n, 55n; criticism of, 33–4, 35, 37, 41;

immigration to Brazil, 34, 50, 51; as Ukrainian Jew, 56n
Warchavchik, Mina, 38
"Weather and the Building Industry" conference (1950), 224
Weerakoon, Jayathi, 152, 163n
Weese, Henry, 140n
Weisman, 108n
Weiss, Daniel, 82n, 106
Weissenhofsiedlung, 5
Werkbund, 5
West African Research Station, 215, 221
Westad, Odd Arne, 268n
Western Pacific, 225
Wharton, Annabel J., 10, 27n, 183n
Wheeler, Monroe, 193, 206n
Wiener, Paul Lester, 86, *88*, 90–1, 92, 95–6, 97, 107n, 108n, 109n
Williams, Carlos, 86, *104*, 107n, 110n
Williams, Patrick, 135n, 140n
Williams, Raymond, 50–1, 56n
Williams, Richard, 25n, 52n
Windsor-Liscombe, Rhodri, 230n
Winslow, Deborah, 163n
Wirth, L., 184n
Wisnik, Guilherme, 54n
Wolf, Eric R., 3, 25n
Wong, Lorenzo, 236–7, 252n, 254n
Wong Chong Thai, 28n
Woods, Bryce, 63, 66, 69, 84n, 87, 107n
Woost, Michael D., 163n
Worboys, Michael, 215, 231n, 232n
work, excessive emphasis on, 198
World Bank, 216
world system theory, 232n
Wright, Frank Lloyd, 176
Wright, Gwendolyn, 31, 64, 93, 94
Wu Huanjia, 23, 28n

Yeoh, Brenda S. A., 234n, 253n
Yom Kippur War (1973), 117
Yoruba art, 126, 129, 130, 132; and architecture, 133
Yoruba Palace, 122–3
Youssoufia quarter masterplan project, Morocco, *60*
Yuen, Belinda, 27n

Zachmann, K., 208n
Zalduendo, Ines, 106
Zapata, Eduardo, 107n
Zehrfuss, Bernard, 59
Zevaco, Jean-François, *58*, 62, 67, 68, 73, 75, 78, *80*, 82n, 83n, 84n
de Zevallos, Louis Ortiz, 90, 107n
Zevi, Bruno, 110n, 120, 176, 185n
Zoltan, Jerzy, 110n

Printed in Great Britain
by Amazon